Praise for

LINKing Authentic Assessment and Early Childhood Intervention
Second Edition

"The traditional focus of assessment is on identification of within-child deficits, dysfunctions, disorders, or disabilities. This practice of 'dising' children has led to much mismeasurement and to inappropriate assignment of children to non–evidence-based treatments or interventions that far too frequently have not worked. This book is a refreshing move away from such mismeasurement. It provides clear, coherent, practical, usable, and data-based best practices in matching early childhood assessments to instructional and behavioral interventions."

Jim Ysseldyke, Ph.D.
Birkmaier Professor of Educational Psychology
University of Minnesota; coauthor, *Assessment in Special and Inclusive Education, 11th Edition*

"A call to action to discard inappropriate and tired practices and rather, to use authentic assessment practices that give a truer and more useful representation of the child. . . . Professionals will be thrilled by the assessment reviews. . . . [The book] capture[s] what it takes for early childhood intervention teams to make more reasoned selections of assessment instruments for their programs and districts."

Susan R. Sandall, Ph.D.
Associate Professor, Special Education
University of Washington

"An essential and valuable resource for all of us who must make decisions at the local, state, or national level about selecting the best possible measures for assessing young children. . . . A 'must have' resource that will not sit on the shelf. The authors provide a solid foundation, a ringing endorsement, and also a road map for the use of authentic, appropriate, and useful assessment for young children."

Mary McLean, Ph.D.
Kellner Professor of Early Childhood Education
Department of Exceptional Education
University of Wisconsin–Milwaukee

"Maintains the authors' high standards for thoughtful and thorough analysis of assessment practices for young children . . . include[s] invaluable information on professional standards, evidence-based practices, authentic assessments, and summaries of critical information on available curriculum-based measures."

Jane Squires, Ph.D.
Professor, College of Education
Director, Center on Human Development
Director, Early Intervention Program
University of Oregon

"By linking authentic assessment and intervention, the authors convincingly present the best practice of identifying where the child is developmentally in the context of where he needs to go, steps to get there, and who is to help . . . an excellent reference standard!"

Glen P. Aylward, Ph.D., ABPP
Professor, Pediatrics & Psychiatry
Director, Division of Developmental-Behavioral Pediatrics/Psychology
Southern Illinois University School of Medicine

"The most comprehensive account available of how authentic assessment instruments can be used in early childhood intervention. It is a terrific resource and encourages the field to adopt more meaningful ways of evaluating childhood development."

Samuel J. Meisels, Ph.D.
President, Erikson Institute, Chicago

"The vision and standard set out by *LINKing Authentic Assessment and Early Childhood Intervention* will positively influence providers in their day-to-day practices and will also serve as a message to the field about the continuing need for research about existing assessment instruments and ongoing development of authentic, practical measures that help us evaluate and plan for the needs of all children."

Nan Vendegna
Director, Results Matter–Colorado

"A reliable and exhaustive source on the developmentally appropriate alternative to testing—the why, the how, and the who of authentic assessment."

Virginia Buysse, Ph.D.
Senior Scientist, FPG Child Development Institute
University of North Carolina at Chapel Hill

"Concrete guidelines combined with recommendations for specific tools make the information immediately useable. This book would be excellent for preservice training and for programs seeking to improve the linkage between assessment and intervention. I strongly recommend this book."

Mark S. Innocenti, Ph.D.
Associate Director
Early Intervention Research Institute
Center for Persons with Disabilities
Utah State University

"Early childhood professionals across disciplines will find this review and analysis of assessment tools highly useful in their practice."

Marci J. Hanson, Ph.D.
Professor, Department of Special Education
Director, SFSU Joint Doctoral Program in Special Education with UC Berkeley
San Francisco State University

LINKing Authentic Assessment and Early Childhood Intervention

LINKing Authentic Assessment and Early Childhood Intervention

Best Measures for Best Practices
Second Edition

by

Stephen J. Bagnato, Ed.D., NCSP
University of Pittsburgh Schools of Medicine and Education
Pittsburgh, Pennsylvania

John T. Neisworth, Ph.D.
The Pennsylvania State University
University Park, Pennsylvania

and

Kristie Pretti-Frontczak, Ph.D.
Kent State University
Kent, Ohio

·P·A·U·L·H·
BROOKES
PUBLISHING C?®

Baltimore • London • Sydney

Paul H. Brookes Publishing Co.
Post Office Box 10624
Baltimore, Maryland 21285-0624
USA

www.brookespublishing.com

Typeset by Integrated Publishing Solutions, Grand Rapids, Michigan.
Manufactured in the United States of America by
Sheridan Books, Inc., Chelsea, Michigan.

Individuals described in this book are composites or real people whose situations are masked and are based on the authors' experience. In all instances, names and identifying details have been changed to protect confidentiality.

The information in the At-a-Glances and Close Ups is provided for the convenience of the purchaser and is subject to change. Readers should contact the specific publishers of the assessments for the most up-to-date and accurate information.

Ages & Stages Questionnaires® and AEPS® are registered trademarks and ASQ-3™, Communication and Symbolic Behavior Scales™, CSBS™, CSBS Developmental Profile™, CSBS DP™, Easy-Score™, and Life Skills Progression™ are trademarks of Paul H. Brookes Publishing Co., Inc. ABLLS® is a registered trademark and service mark of Behavior Analysts, Inc. Behavior Rating Inventory of Executive Functioning® and BRIEF® are registered trademarks of Psychological Assessments Resources, Inc. BRIGANCE® is a registered trademark of Curriculum Associates, Inc. Creative Curriculum® is a registered trademark and service mark and Teaching Strategies GOLD™ is a trademark of Teaching Strategies, Inc. Early Learning Accomplishment Profile™ and E-LAP™ are trademarks of Kaplan Early Learning Company. HELP® and Hawaii Early Learning Profile® are registered trademarks of VORT Corporation. "Infant Toddler Social-Emotional Assessment" and "ITSEA" are trademarks of Yale University and University of Massachusetts. Inventory for Client and Agency Planning™, ICAP™, Scales of Independent Behavior–Revised™, and SIB–R™ are trademarks of Riverside Publishing, a subsidiary of Houghton Mifflin Harcourt. The Online Companion™ is a trademark of Cengage Learning. PEDI™ is a trademark of CRE Care. SCERTS® and The SCERTS Model® are registered trademarks and service marks of Barry M. Prizant, Amy M. Wetherby, Emily B. Rubin, and Amy C. Laurent. "SSIS," "Vineland," "The Work Sampling System," "BASC," "ASSIST," "Differential Ability Scales," "DAS," "Bayley Scales of Infant Development," and "BSID-II" are trademarks, in the U.S. and/or other countries, of Pearson Education, Inc. or its affiliate(s). Woodcock-Johnson® is a registered trademark of Houghton Mifflin Company.

Library of Congress Cataloging-in-Publication Data
Bagnato, Stephen J.
    LINKing authentic assessment and early childhood intervention : best measures for best practices. —
2nd ed. / by Stephen J. Bagnato, John T. Neisworth, and Kristie L. Pretti-Frontczak.
        p.   ; cm.
    Other title: Authentic assessment and early childhood intervention
    Rev. ed. of: Linking assessment and early intervention. c1997.
    Includes bibliographical references and indexes.
    ISBN-13: 978-1-59857-047-2 (pbk.)
    ISBN-10: 1-59857-047-1 (pbk.)
    1. Developmentally disabled children—Psychological testing.   2. Children with mental disabilities—Psychological testing.   3. Preschool children—Psychological testing.   4. Psychological tests for children.   5. Child development—Testing.   I. Neisworth, John T.   II. Pretti-Frontczak, Kristie.   III. Bagnato, Stephen J. Linking assessment and early intervention.   IV. Title.   V. Title: Authentic assessment and early childhood intervention.
    [DNLM: 1. Child Development.   2. Developmental Disabilities—diagnosis.   3. Early Intervention (Education)—trends.   4. Psychological Tests. WS 105.5.E8]
    RJ135.B342 2010
    618.92'8588—dc22   2010026017

British Library Cataloguing in Publication data are available from the British Library.

2021   2020   2019   2018   2017

10   9   8   7   6   5   4   3   2

Contents

About the Authors

Stephen J. Bagnato, Ed.D., NCSP, is a developmental school psychologist and professor of pediatrics and psychology at the University of Pittsburgh Schools of Medicine and Education. Dr. Bagnato holds joint appointments in psychology in education/applied developmental psychology and clinical/developmental psychology at the university. He is Director of the Early Childhood Partnerships Program at the university and Core Interdisciplinary Leadership Team Faculty Member for The University, Community, Leaders, and Individuals with Disabilities (UCLID) Center at the University of Pittsburgh.

In 1986, Dr. Bagnato received the Braintree Hospital National Brain Injury Research Award for his research on the impact of interdisciplinary intervention for young children with acquired and congenital brain injuries. In 2001, he was recipient of the University of Pittsburgh Chancellor's Distinguished Public Service Award for the innovation and community impact of his consultation and research programs in early childhood partnerships, and in 2008, Dr. Bagnato received The Pennsylvania State University Excellence in Education Alumni Award for his career of innovative national and international service and research in education and psychology. Dr. Bagnato was recently appointed to Governor Rendell's Pennsylvania Early Learning Council, a task force to influence early childhood intervention policy and practices through systems integration efforts among education, public welfare, and health.

Dr. Bagnato specializes in authentic curriculum-based assessment and applied program evaluation research for infants, toddlers, and preschoolers at developmental risk and with neurodevelopmental disabilities and neurobehavioral disorders and their families. He has published more than 120 applied research studies and professional articles in early childhood care and education, early intervention, early childhood special education, school psychology, neurodevelopmental disabilities, and developmental neuropsychology.

Dr. Bagnato is Director of Early Childhood Partnerships (ECP; http://www.earlychildhoodpartnerships.com), a community-based consultation, training, technical assistance, and research collaborative between Children's Hospital and The UCLID Center at the University of Pittsburgh with community partners. ECP consists of six core "partnership" programs: 1) *SPECS Program Evaluation Research Team* (Scaling Progress in Early Childhood Settings): authentic measurement of the efficacy and outcomes of high-quality early childhood intervention programs; 2) The *HealthyCHILD* School-Linked Developmental Healthcare Partnership: a field-validated Response to Intervention/Recognition and Response model using a mobile developmental health care team and a prevention–intervention continuum to meet the complex needs of preschoolers with acute and chronic medical conditions, developmental delays/disabilities, and challenging behaviors in-vivo in early childhood classrooms (e.g., Head Start, early intervention, early childhood education); 3) *TRACE* Center for Excellence in Early Childhood Assessment: research on the evidence base for promising early intervention assessment practices to guide policy changes for improved professional practices; 4) *COMET*—Center on Mentoring for Effective Teaching: research on the impact of mentoring to improve Head Start and early childhood intervention teacher practices; 5) Center to Investigate Violence and Injury in Communities (*CIVIC*): epidemiological research; and 6) *Early Childhood Research Systems*: innovative observational assessment procedures and database management of standards and assessment links.

For more than 10 years, Dr. Bagnato and his ECP program have been funded by the Heinz Endowments to conduct longitudinal research on the impact and outcomes of high-quality early childhood intervention programs on nearly 15,000 high-risk children in 30 school districts and regions across Pennsylvania (e.g., Early Childhood Initiative, Pre-K Counts).

Dr. Bagnato is a fellow of the American Psychological Association (APA) in Division 16 and past or current journal editorial board member for *Journal of School Psychology, School Psychology Review, School Psychology Quarterly, Journal of Psychoeducational Assessment, Journal of Early Intervention, Topics in Early Childhood Special Education, Infants and Young Children, Journal of Early Childhood and Infant Psychology, Child Assessment News,* and *Early Childhood Research Quarterly.*

Dr. Bagnato received the 1995 Best Research Article Award from Division 16 of APA (with John T. Neisworth) for his "national study on the social and treatment invalidity of intelligence testing in early childhood intervention." He is coauthor of the professional "best practice" policy statements and standards on early childhood assessment, evaluation, and early intervention for The National Association of School Psychologists and the Division for Early Childhood of the Council for Exceptional Children.

Dr. Bagnato is in demand to provide consultation on early childhood intervention "best practices," challenging and atypical behaviors, authentic assessment in early childhood, and authentic program outcomes evaluation research. In addition, he collaborates internationally with ATLANTIS, a joint United States–European Union grant on the design of a universal, web-based curriculum in early childhood intervention for preservice education of interdisciplinary professionals.

Dr. Bagnato's published books and instruments include the recently published assessment text *Authentic Assessment for Early Childhood Intervention: Best Practices* (Guilford Press, 2007) and the *Temperament and Atypical Behavior Scale (TABS): Early Childhood Indicators of Developmental Dysfunction* (Paul H. Brookes Publishing Co., 1999).

John T. Neisworth, Ph.D., is Professor Emeritus in Special Education at The Pennsylvania State (Penn State) University. Dr. Neisworth was Program Co-planner for the Pennsylvania Autism Conference & Institute, Academic Director of Penn State's Applied Behavior Analysis program, Consulting Co-director of the Penn State Autism Distance Program, Director of the Pennsylvania Early Intervention Institute, and Chair for Recommended Practices in Assessment for the Division for Early Childhood of the Council for Exceptional Children.

Dr. Neisworth has authored or coauthored numerous research articles and texts in special education, early intervention, and behavior analysis, including the *HICOMP Preschool Curriculum* (Bell & Howell Company, 1986), *Modifying Retarded Behavior* (Houghton Mifflin, 1973), and *Assessment for Early Intervention: Best Practices for Professionals* (with S.J. Bagnato; Guilford Press, 1991). His latest publication is *The Autism Encyclopedia* (with P.S. Wolfe; Paul H. Brookes Publishing Co., 2005).

He is Cofounding Editor of *Topics in Early Childhood Special Education* and an editorial board member of that journal as well as the *Journal of Early Intervention,*

Child and Family Behavior Therapy, and *Infants & Young Children*. He received the 1995 Best Research Article Award from the American Psychological Association (Division 16) for his 2002 article (with Stephen Bagnato) on the misuse of intelligence testing in early childhood.

Dr. Neisworth received the Lifetime Achievement Award from the Pennsylvania Association for Applied Behavior Analysis. He provides consultation and workshops for state and private early intervention agencies and is President of Behavior Technics Associates, a group devoted to application of behavioral strategies to educational and therapeutic efforts.

Kristie Pretti-Frontczak, Ph.D., is Professor in Early Childhood Intervention at Kent State University. She is also Director of the Center for Excellence in Early Childhood Research and Training. Dr. Pretti-Frontczak was recently nominated to the Division for Early Childhood (DEC)'s Executive Board, was past president of the Ohio Subdivision for DEC, and has received several awards for distinguished service to the field.

Dr. Pretti-Frontczak specializes in authentic assessment practices for accountability and programming, effective approaches to working with young children in inclusive settings (specifically regarding the implementation and evaluation of curriculum frameworks), and most recently on the application of response to intervention principles to early childhood settings. She served as a coauthor and chair of the curriculum committee for DEC's (2007) publication titled "Promoting Positive Outcomes for Children with Disabilities: Recommendations for Curriculum, Assessment, and Program Evaluation." She also serves on the editorial board for the *Journal of Early Intervention* and *Topics in Early Childhood Special Education*, where she served as Guest Coeditor on a special issue dedicated to using web-based technologies to improve early childhood special education professional development, research, and service delivery.

For 14 years, Dr. Pretti-Frontczak has directed the Early Childhood Intervention Specialist Program at Kent State University, where she is responsible for preparing preservice teachers to work with children with disabilities from birth to age 8. She has served as the principle investigator on several training grants, model demonstration grants, and research projects.

Dr. Pretti-Frontczak routinely provides consultation across the United States and abroad regarding recommended practices for working with young children and their families. In particular, she provides training and technical assistance to programs interested in the *Assessment, Evaluation, and Programming System for Infants and Children (AEPS®)*, Activity-Based Intervention (ABI), implementing and evaluating quality instructional models, and creating legally defensible and meaningful individualized education programs (IEPs).

Dr. Pretti-Frontczak's published books and instruments include *Assessing Young Children in Inclusive Settings: The Blended Practices Approach.* (with J.L. Grisham-Brown; Paul H. Brookes Publishing Co., in press); *Blended Practices for Teaching Young Children in Inclusive Settings* (with J.L. Grisham-Brown & M.L. Hemmeter; Paul H. Brookes Publishing Co., 2005); *An Activity-Based Approach to Early Intervention, Third Edition* (with D. Bricker; Paul H. Brookes Publishing Co., 2004); and *Assessment, Evaluation, and Programming System for Infants and Children (AEPS®), Second Edition: Volume 1. AEPS® Administration Guide* (with D. Bricker et al.; Paul H. Brookes Publishing Co., 2002).

Foreword

Professional volumes are plentiful in today's market, as are electronic materials whose purpose is to assist readers/users in adopting practices that will make professionals more effective in their work with young children. A few of these new books are substantive, offering valuable ideas that, if adopted, might significantly improve the quality of services offered to young children and their families. Forewords to these volumes can be instrumental in directing readers to those substantive books that contain ideas of merit. By *ideas of merit*, I mean content that professional consumers should take their valuable time to read, digest, and incorporate into their professional practice. That is the intent of this foreword—to urge potential readers to consider first reading *LINKing Authentic Assessment and Early Childhood Intervention, Second Edition*, and then consider adopting into their practice the use of authentic assessment and the linking of assessment to intervention.

As one contemplates the many uncertainties facing the nation's young children and those who work with them, the goals of valid assessment and effective intervention seem particularly crucial. The high stakes confronting young children in today's world require those of us who are educators and other service delivery personnel to carefully consider the choices we make about how to best assist children whose growth and development is compromised by economic conditions or disability. Federal, state, and local resources earmarked to assist these vulnerable children are limited; therefore, their allocation and use is of significant concern. From my perspective, our professional responsibility requires learning and using the most progressive, useful, and evidence-based ideas, principles, and practices available to the fields of early childhood and early childhood special education. Ideas of merit—even if they require significant change for individuals and the field—must be carefully examined, weighed, and tested against other practices. When better ideas are found, it is our obligation to institute them.

Since the 1980 edition of *LINKing*, Bagnato and Neisworth have been offering ideas of merit and now, with their coauthor Pretti-Frontczak, they have refined and expanded two extremely important themes: the use of authentic assessment and the linking of assessment to intervention.

As the authors note, this volume is "devoted to promoting early childhood assessment practices that are authentic, developmentally appropriate, and useful for planning and evaluating beneficial experiences for young children, especially those with special needs." The volume's second central theme is "linking assessment to intervention. By the concept of 'linking,' we mean that the content of what we assess about children is the same thing as the content of what we teach them to do. Put another way, what we intend to teach should be what we are assessing."

It is time that all professionals associated with the assessment and delivery of services to children who are at risk or have disabilities seriously consider the adoption of these two ideas of merit into their professional practice.

This volume is, in my judgment, one of the best resources for addressing the many challenges inherent in the accurate and reliable assessment of young children as they engage in the multitude of activities that bring meaning to their lives (i.e., authentic assessment) and for linking assessment and intervention activities.

The authors have assembled an array of potent and relevant information that reflects our most advanced thinking about authentic assessment/evaluation and the use of assessment results to guide intervention activities. In addition and importantly, the authors have devised a system for the objective evaluation of available measures. They then have employed this system to rate how well selected measures address the criteria that compose the system.

I believe that all professionals associated with the assessment and delivery of services to young children at risk and who have disabilities should first read this book and then place it on their desk for easy referral for several important reasons.

First, this is the fourth version of a work whose content has evolved over time as the fields of early childhood and early childhood special education have acquired superior understandings as well as evidence about assessment and intervention processes. This evolution of material since 1980 has helped lay the foundations for future growth in the assessment of young children and represents a maturing of the fields focused on young children. Second, this volume's content offers some of the very best thinking about how assessment of children should be conceptualized and conducted. An important theme is the adoption of assessment practices that meet current professional standards. Third, the book is an appropriate and useful combination of background and contextual offerings along with, I believe, the best effort at evaluating a range of assessment measures currently available to personnel working with young children. Finally, the content helps point us to future developments that should continue to improve our efforts at the challenging job of assessing young children's behavioral repertoires and delivering quality services.

This book has two sections. The initial section is devoted to carefully explaining why many current assessment/evaluation practices need to change. The authors make a powerful case for moving from conventional measurement to authentic measurement of young children that takes into account content, procedures, process, and evidence that leads to adopting different approaches to child assessment and evaluation. The authors further explain the need for assessment practices to meet standards for recommended practice that have been adopted by professional organizations. A particularly intriguing chapter is included on forecasting future directions that encompass computer-associated strategies, functional classification systems, performance probes associated with response to intervention, epidemiological measures of developmental status, and parameters of clinical judgment.

The second section of the book is devoted to providing a resource for professionals who are assessing or delivering services to young children to assist them in selecting a measure that best suits the child's and program's needs. To accomplish this goal, the authors developed a system to guide the selection of measures to be evaluated and an objective-based procedure to rate each of the selected measures. The ratings of each selected measure are presented in At-a-Glances, which provide a brief overview, and Close Ups, which provide more comprehensive information on the measure.

I am convinced that if adopted into practice, the material contained in this volume can move the fields of early childhood and early childhood special education toward improved assessment and intervention services for young children. Improved assessment and intervention will, in turn, assist children in becoming independent and contributing members to their families, schools, and the larger community. The purpose of this foreword has been to convince potential readers to expend the time necessary to not only read the important information contained in this volume but to also adopt much of the described practice into their daily dealings with young children.

Diane Bricker, Ph.D.
Professor Emerita
University of Oregon
Eugene, Oregon

Preface

Let's begin with a short story about a school psychology graduate student who wanted to specialize in preschool assessment. Roger had already done well in the required coursework in conventional assessment. He was now ready for a practicum in our preschool, which was a funded project within our special education program. Our approach to assessment was much different than the conventional approach taught in his prior courses.

Roger arrived at our office by 8:30 a.m., dressed in a suit and tie, looking very professional, and carrying several test kits. He stood at the doorway, smiling but evidently anxious; he was scheduled to assess Chris, a 4-year-old boy who was to be enrolled in our preschool. We needed to identify Chris's levels of capabilities so that we could design an initial instructional plan.

Roger put his kits on a table and said, "Good morning. The 'subject' [!] has already arrived and is in the preschool testing room with his mother. I studied the administration manuals for these three assessment materials. Which one do you recommend I should use?"

We told him, "Don't worry about those tests. Earlier this morning we set up the testing room to be a play area. There are a lot of toys and storybooks in the cabinet. Just get rid of the necktie and coat, get down on the floor, and play with him. After a while, estimate his status in the usual developmental areas—especially his social development." (Chris's mother was especially concerned with his preoccupation with solitary activities and apparent lack of social skills.)

Roger blanched, his mouth dropped open, and he seemed panicked. As a result of his prior training, Roger was "kit-dependent." Nevertheless, Roger and Chris got along just fine. Although not able to "do an assessment," Roger emerged from that session with firm determination to free himself from the constraints of test kits and to become knowledgeable about child development. Our goal, and his, was to use real situations and behaviors as a basis for authentic assessment: the epiphany we hoped for.

That semester, Roger had the opportunity to work with an interdisciplinary team in a practicum with a parent who had recently moved from another state. The mom was, to say the least, unhappy with the adversarial experience she had with the previous multidisciplinary team. She complained that each "team" member seemed to repeat the same or similar test demands; she exclaimed, "Why did the school psychologist, the speech-language pathologist, and the occupational therapist all require my daughter to stack those same damned wooden blocks?" (The multidisciplinary "team" did not really work together; team members used their specific materials . . . and all three required block-stacking!)

Before long, Roger was able to use curriculum-based assessment, real situations and materials, parent interviews and reports, and his new child development knowledge to profile children's attainments and needs. He is now an "enlightened" school psychologist who is "beyond" kits! (By the way, the mom was not only ecstatic with the new team, including Roger, but also became a vocal advocate for parent–professional cooperation.)

Over 25 years, in the previous editions of *LINKing* (1980 and 1987 by Aspen Publishers and 1997 by Paul H. Brookes Publishing Co.), we outlined the great changes happening in our profession. Measurement in early childhood was initially inherited from the conventional adult/school testing traditions, replete with standardized, norm-referenced tests. The major limitations of such testing became all too clear, causing us and many other professionals to demand a more sensible approach for program planning, monitoring performance and progress, and evaluating program impact. We advocated *curriculum-based assessment* (CBA) and other criterion-referenced materials as a far more accurate and helpful approach, especially when emphasizing an authentic approach.

This edition of *LINKing* extends the approach of criterion-referenced assessment but goes much further in asserting the primacy of the *authentic assessment imperative*. *LINKing* now provides 1) several chapters that explain the rationale and importance of realistic, authentic assessment linked to curricula; 2) a description and discussion of eight standards by which to choose and use assessment materials; 3) an innovative, Internet-based LINK consumer social validation process by which 1,083 national professionals identified the best measures for best practices based upon applying the 8 standards; and 4) "At-a-Glance" reviews of 54 assessment tools that meet the critical standards and "Close Ups" of 30 featured materials.

Over the years, we have always appreciated your acceptance of our views about assessment for early childhood intervention expressed in the long-term success of the previous editions of *LINKing*. These notions of authentic and curriculum-based assessment have obviously resonated with you and the field. We hope that you will find this new edition of *LINKing* even more compelling and usable. Appropriate and sensible measurement is a vital personal and even civil rights issue for all young children and families, but particularly for our most vulnerable ones. We send you off on this journey of exploring the *"best measures for best practices"* with our quotation as an admonition: "Misrepresenting children through mismeasuring them denies children their rights to beneficial expectations and opportunities" (Neisworth & Bagnato, 2004, p. 198).

Reference

Neisworth, J.T., & Bagnato, S.J. (2004). The mismeasure of young children: The authentic assessment alternative. *Infants and Young Children, 17*(3), 198–212.

Acknowledgments

We owe great appreciation to the dedicated work of our superb graduate students in applied developmental psychology, school psychology, and early intervention at the University of Pittsburgh, Duquesne University, and Kent State University. We highlight the collaborative work (arguably co-authorship!) of

- Teresa Brown, M.Ed.

- Nicole Garmen M.Ed.

- Sophia Hubbell, M.Ed.

- Cathryn Lehman, Ph.D.

- Ashley Lyons M.Ed.

- Eileen McKeating, Ph.D.

- Jennifer Salaway, Ph.D.

Also, we highlight the collaborative work of our colleague Marisa Macy, Ph.D., whose spirit, committed work, and collaboration on the TRACE Center assessment research syntheses and published research articles provided some of the important background studies for this book.

We owe much appreciation to the expert panel members (detailed in Section II) who provided superb analyses for the results of the LINK survey. Also, we are grateful to the many colleagues in the United States and internationally who work hard to serve the most vulnerable young children and families in everyday settings and routines and their commitment to use developmentally appropriate professional practices, often against administrative pressures. Their guidance, suggestions, and positive reactions to our drafts and our workshops helped to improve and promote this revision.

Our work has always been inspired by the experiences of the families and children with whom we work and of our own preschoolers: children, grandchildren, and cousins—the two Michaels, Mark, Samantha, Rachel, Isabella, and Gabriella—whose own preschool experiences and special friends have kept our work authentic. Thank you to Susan, whose own beliefs and commitment to the field and support of the work have helped make this book perhaps the best of the editions.

We want to express our thanks to the enduring support for our work and the legacy of this book from the folks at Paul H. Brookes Publishing Co. Special appreciation is extended to Melissa Behm, Heather Shrestha, and Johanna Cantler and the editorial committee for their hard work and creativity in producing what we believe is the best and the most appealing and engaging of the *LINKing* editions.

We express great affection and respect to our colleague—and mentor to one of us—Dr. Diane Bricker, who agreed heartily to contribute the inspiring foreword to this edition of *LINKing*. We and Dr. Bricker seem to have traveled the same road regarding assessment in our field. However, Dr. Bricker has always "walked the walk and talked the talk" about the appropriateness and evidence base for authentic and curriculum-based assessment. Her life's work "makes real" the story of linking authentic assessment for early childhood intervention.

To the memories of
Stephen J. Bagnato, Sr., and Anne Neisworth, cherished father and mother,
whose strong beliefs, self-reliance, and social consciences,
informed by "la via vecchia" and "Wahrheit, nicht Zahlen,"
nurtured each of our own personal beliefs and professional lives,
then, and even now

I

Authentic Assessment and Early Intervention in Context

1

Why Are Changes Needed in Early Childhood Measurement?

> *"Misrepresenting children through mismeasuring them denies children their rights to beneficial expectations and opportunities."*
> *(Neisworth & Bagnato, 2004, p. 198)*

Parents and professionals are and have been dissatisfied with how we measure what young children know and do. This dissatisfaction is particularly acute when we measure the capabilities of young children who appear slower or unusual in their development or challenging in their behavior. Assessment of young children is, indeed, a contentious issue with professionals and parents.

Measurement is not merely an administrative exercise. It must be practical, sensible, and representative and must benefit the child and family in tangible ways. When measurement does not show the child's everyday skills and uniqueness but merely highlights the child's limitations, it misrepresents the child. Ultimately, mismeasurement is a civil rights issue. It reinforces preconceived notions about the child, distorts the expectations of caregivers, and denies opportunities for development. Mismeasurement limits a child's potential before the child has a chance to learn and develop. It misrepresents—in insidious ways.

> We pass through this world but once. Few tragedies can be more extensive than the stunting of life, few injustices deeper than the denial of an opportunity to strive or ever hope, by a limit imposed from without, but falsely identified as lying within. (Gould, 1981, p. 28)

Rationale for Changes

As we discuss in the sections that follow, conventional tests and testing misrepresent young children. Moreover, conventional testing is at odds with the enlightened philosophy, purposes, and practices of the early childhood intervention (ECI) field. A rationale for needed changes in measurement for ECI must align with accepted values and practices in the field.

Misalignment with Early Childhood Intervention

The National Association for the Education of Young Children (NAEYC), the Division for Early Childhood (DEC) of the Council for Exceptional Children, and the Performance Standards of the National Head Start Association present a unified view on the perspectives and practices that are expected of professionals who work in the ECI field (see Chapter 3). These intersecting professional standards reflect the continuous maturing of the fields and also modifications to federal regulations.

Primary pillars of an enlightened, humanistic, and evidence-based approach to ECI include the following: developmentally appropriate practice, inclusion, natural environments, equity, and response to intervention (RTI). *Developmentally appropriate practice,* including measurement, presumes that professionals understand that young children learn best through play and through supports that match their stage of developmental and behavioral competence. *Inclusion* is the "contextual" centerpiece for intervention so that all children have opportunities to interact with peers in *natural everyday settings and routines,* at home, in school, and throughout the community. *Equity* means that both intervention and measurement must allow all children the opportunities and ways to show their best competencies. Universally designed assessments, curricula, and instructional methods allow all children to be evaluated, function, and learn despite their functional limitations. Federal regulations in the Individuals with Disabilities Education Act (IDEA) of 1990 (PL 101-476) and its amendments have mandated the concept and approach that all children need to have access to responsive help when the need is first noticed. RTI applied to ECI ensures that the status and progress of all children are regularly assessed without respect to traditional diagnoses, and tiered or graduated interventions are available to individualize instruction so that each child can learn and develop with tailored strategies. In fact, the National Academy of Sciences/National Research Council (NAS/NRC) (part of the task force of the President's Commission on Special Education) led the way to changes toward RTI when they recommended the "demise of IQ testing" for special education eligibility by asserting the following: "The committee regards the effort to assess students' decontextualized potential or ability as inappropriate and scientifically invalid" (Commission on Behavioral and Social Sciences and Education, 2002, p. 313). This groundbreaking statement declares the view of professionals in special education and early intervention that conventional testing practices are wasteful in time, effort, and usefulness and should be abandoned in favor of more sensible and useful approaches.

Limitations of Conventional Testing

Conventional testing in ECI can be defined as the administration of a highly structured array of testing tasks by an examiner in a contrived situation through the use of scripted examiner behaviors and scripted child behaviors in order to determine a normative score for purposes of diagnosis. The fundamental flaws of conventional tests and testing practices with young children in ECI have been detailed elsewhere (Bagnato, 2007; Bagnato, Neisworth, & Munson, 1997; Bagnato & Yeh Ho, 2006; Neisworth & Bagnato, 2004). There are four fundamental problems related to the following: 1) content, 2) procedures, 3) process, and 4) evidence.

Content

Conventional tests and testing emphasize nonfunctional content that has little relationship to children's competencies needed to meet the challenges of everyday situations and routines. Conventional tests and testing have no treatment validity or utility for intervention.

The major content issues of conventional testing include the following:

- Nonfunctional item content
- Insensitivity to developmental gains due to insufficient item content and skill sequences
- No treatment validity; these tests lack alignment with curricular content, standards, or expected intervention outcomes

Procedures

Conventional tests and testing attempt to create an "experiment" with each administration under the illogic that standardizing the materials and "scripting" the behaviors of both examiners and children will result in high internal validity and, thus, true results, or high external validity. This illogic has tragic consequences and only the illusion of truth for children with differences. The major procedural flaws of conventional testing include the following:

- Testing by unfamiliar "experts"
- Reliance on decontextualized and contrived test situations
- "Scripted" examiner behavior, materials, and procedures
- "Scripted" and restricted child behavior
- Expectations for developmentally inappropriate "test behavior"
- No universal design or accommodations for children with differences and disabilities

Process

Conventional tests and testing have been developed for professionals only and typically only for professionals working in isolation. The crucial role of parents and other familiar caregivers in providing assessment information is ignored or handled in a perfunctory manner. The scripted process reinforces administrative activities and is not responsive to the child. Conventional tests and testing reinforce negative expectations about the status, progress, and potential for children with disabilities. The major process issues of conventional testing include the following:

- Disrupts children's *play*—the natural mode of learning in early childhood
- Depends on independent and separate discipline-specific efforts rather than interdisciplinary teamwork
- Discourages real, integral parent partnership with professionals
- Diagnoses disabilities rather than capabilities

Evidence

Contrary to common presumption, conventional tests and testing have never been studied in their direct application to fulfill the central purposes of ECI, most notably eligibility determination, program planning, progress monitoring, and accountability. Major research predicaments with regard to conventional testing include the following:

- Development on and standardization for only typically developing children
- Lack of evidence of normative or field-validation research for use in ECI, especially for young children with disabilities

Justifiable Measurement Purposes for Early Childhood Intervention

The root of the word *assessment* is *assidere*, the meaning of which is to sit beside and get to know. It is sensible, then, to ask ourselves how often we are familiar with and knowledgeable about the young children that we test in ECI. And, more important than *our* ability to become familiar with the young children being tested is the *children's* need for this familiarity to become attached to significant adults, to become comfortable, to trust, and to do their best. Conventional testing is certainly not based on familiarity, knowledge, and bonding, despite admonishments and attempts to establish rapport.

Testing is a highly scripted event of administering an instrument to get a score that compares a child to peers who are presumably like the child on important dimensions for purposes of diagnosis of delay or disorder. Conversely, *assessment* is a flexible process of synthesizing qualitative and quantitative information about a child and his or her developmental context to identify strengths and needs, to plan individual programs, and to promote developmental progress. In ECI, measurement is not a test-centered process but, rather, a decision-making process: "Early childhood assessment is a flexible, collaborative decision-making process in which teams of parents and professionals repeatedly revise their judgments and reach consensus about the changing developmental, educational, medical, and behavioral healthcare needs of young children and their families" (Bagnato & Neisworth, 1991, p. xi).

The following assessment purposes are most justifiable for ECI:

1. Screening for and early detection of instructional or therapeutic needs
2. Detailing functional competencies
3. Planning individual curricular goals
4. Monitoring individual performance on goals
5. Detecting intraindividual progress
6. Documenting RTI (e.g., instruction, tutoring, therapy)
7. Evaluating program impact and outcomes aligned with standards and indicators

Screening for Early Detection of Needs

In early childhood, screening for early detection of developmental and behavioral needs should be a natural process during which parents, other caregivers, and familiar professionals offer descriptive examples of the child's actual functional skills in real-life settings. Authentic measures provide a menu of important landmark functional skills in various developmental domains so that parents and others can be attuned to whether the child is demonstrating these skills. Family-friendly authentic screening measures enable various caregivers to "cast a wide net" in order to highlight absent functional skills that may require a closer look. Screening is not diagnostic; it merely sets the stage for help by alerting everyone to the child's individual needs.

Detailing Functional Competencies to Plan Individual Curricular Goals

Authentic curriculum-based measures are particularly well suited for guiding parents and professionals in identifying a child's functional competencies (e.g., both strengths and needs) and the level of assistance needed as a basis for planning individual goals for instruction or therapy. The sequential goals and levels of assistance in the curriculum reflect teachable skills in daily routines through which the effectiveness of help is evaluated.

Monitoring Individual Performance on Goals to Detect Intraindividual Progress Via Response to Intervention

One of the most unique aspects of early intervention is that all practices are devoted to the individual rather than the group. The results of authentic assessment generate individual functional goals for each child in a hierarchy of simple to complex skills. *Monitoring changes in children's acquisition and performance of individual competencies related to their goals during ECI is the central purpose of authentic assessment.* The significance of these improvements in skill acquisition is based on the degree of change from each child's preintervention functional profile (i.e., single-subject designs and intraindividual progress). Early intervention is focused on benefiting individual children through customized instruction and therapy.

Evaluating Program Impact and Outcomes Aligned with Standards and Indicators

Authentic assessment is particularly well suited to enable researchers and policy-makers to evaluate the overall impact and outcomes of programs for individual children and to aggregate these data for group analysis purposes. The developmental and/or functional content of authentic assessment measures aligns well with the content of both state and federal early learning standards and outcome indicators. Within these justifiable purposes, the primary purpose of assessment in the field is to link assessment and intervention: to design individual plans for care, instruction, and therapy.

Foundations of Assessment for Early Childhood Intervention

The foundations for assessment in ECI are built on three sources: 1) professional values codified in recommended or "best practice" competencies by professional organizations, 2) position statements by national task forces, and 3) evidence from practice-based research studies. In this respect, early intervention offers an evidence-based standard for professional practice through its fusion of consensus values and applied developmental science.

Professional "Best Practice" Standards on Assessment in Early Childhood

Professional standards are a unique contribution of the ECI field. Chapter 5 provides a more in-depth overview of the "best practice" standards for assessment in early childhood. This section merely highlights some of the major sources for these standards and their implications for effective practice.

The NAEYC produced one of the earliest and best known manuals of professional practice standards for early childhood care and education. *Developmentally Appropriate Practice* (Bredekamp, 1987; Copple & Bredekamp, 1997, 2008) articulates the entire compendium of standards from curriculum, to parent involvement, to transition, to assessment. The official NAEYC (2003) professional statement on curriculum and assessment, *Early Childhood Curriculum, Assessment, and Program Evaluation,* was published as an expansion of the *Developmentally Appropriate Practice* manual in these areas.

The DEC publishes a professional practice standards manual, *DEC Recommended Practices,* which is devoted to young children with developmental delays and disabilities and is regularly revised and updated (Sandall, McClean, & Smith, 2005). In 2007, the DEC composed and published its own parallel expansion of the curriculum and assessment standards, *Promoting Positive Outcomes for Children with Disabilities.*

Overall, the NAEYC and DEC standards are aligned and offer a strong case for using authentic assessment procedures as best practice in early childhood care and education and early intervention. These standards have a strong humanistic appeal and demonstrate the values and concerns related to identifying and helping individual children to succeed under the care and instruction of committed teams of parents and professionals. These teams focus on building children's *strengths* as well as helping children to compensate for and overcome limitations through tailored instruction, therapy, and assistive technology in inclusive settings without the need for undue labeling. Although professional standards are values based, they encompass many practices that are evidence-based.

Task Force Position Statements on Assessment in Early Childhood

Since about 2000, several task forces convened by private organizations or government-associated bodies have produced position statements on assessment in ECI. They include the following:

- *Taking Stock* (Schultz & Kagan, 2007)

- *Community-Level School Readiness: Definitions, Assessments* (Zaslow, Calkins, Halle, Zaff, & Margie, 2000)

- *Recognizing and Responding to the Developmental and Learning Challenges of Young Children* (Horowitz, 2006)

- *Early Childhood Assessment* (Snow & Van Heme, 2008)

These professional statements have emphasized issues such as high-stakes testing or assessment to document accountability of ECI programs. Perhaps the most well known—and, arguably, controversial—of these statements are those of the PEW Foundation (*Taking Stock*) and the NAS/NRC (*Early Childhood Assessment*). Both of these efforts are long treatises on many aspects of testing or assessment of young children. *Early Childhood Assessment* perhaps provides the more balanced viewpoint of the two by acknowledging that authentic assessment has a purpose in the field and that more flexible and functional assessment procedures, rather than conventional testing, are necessary for young children with disabilities. Nevertheless, the conclusions of these statements seem to support high-stakes normative testing of infants and preschoolers for accountability purposes and are in opposition to the NAEYC and DEC practice standards. The statements do not include convincing research, especially concerning the value and validity of conventional practices for young children with disabilities.

Evidence-Based Research on Assessment for Early Childhood Intervention

Early interventionists, policy makers, and researchers alike recognize that traditional methods of detecting developmental delay fail to identify an untold number of young children who need early intervention services and supports. In this recognition, the U.S. Department of Education, Office of Special Education Programs, has funded institutes (e.g., Tracking, Referral, and Assessment Center for Excellence [TRACE]) to explore the evidence base for both conventional and alternative strategies for determining the eligibility of infants and toddlers for Part C early intervention services. The reported national incidence of delay/disability in this age group (3%–18%), and thus the need for services, is far higher than those currently receiving such services (Fujiura & Yamaki, 2000; Lewit & Baker, 1996).

The Pennsylvania satellite of TRACE has produced a research synthesis and associated practice guide on the evidence base and process for using clinical judgment (known in federal legislation as "informed clinical opinion") to determine eligibility for early intervention (Bagnato, Smith-Jones, Matesa, & McKeating-Esterle, 2006). The TRACE satellite in Pennsylvania also has produced research syntheses and selected practice guides on other methodologies for early intervention eligibility and associated measurement purposes: conventional tests and testing (Bagnato, Macey, Salaway, & Lehman, 2007b), authentic assessments (Bagnato, Macey, Salaway, & Lehman, 2007a), team assessment models (Bagnato & McKeating-Esterle, 2007), assessments of social and self-regulatory deficits (Yeh Ho & Bagnato, 2007), and presumptive eligibility (Fevola, Bagnato, Matesa, & Lehman, 2006). (To download research syntheses, go to http://www.earlychild hoodpartnerships.org; click on the TRACE section for downloads of our research syntheses.)

Contrary to popular professional belief, the general evidence base for measurement in ECI, especially for young children with disabilities, is weak and often nonexistent. Few studies have been conducted to define the validity of most measurement practices to accomplish any purpose in ECI (e.g., eligibility, planning, progress monitoring, and accountability). The TRACE research syntheses provide the details of this exploration. In brief summary, a thorough analysis of more than 1,800 studies and position papers identified fewer than 30 studies that provided even minimal support for the validity of current testing practices in the field and even fewer studies that conducted research in real-life settings to promote practice-based evidence for professionals. The following summary identifies the number of evidence-based studies that were identified to support the validity of the use of the various types of measurement or classification strategies in ECI to accomplish important purposes: conventional tests (0), authentic assessment (3), clinical judgment (0), presumptive eligibility (1), social-emotional indicators (0), and team models (0). The most promising practices were determined for authentic assessment, clinical judgment, and social-emotional strategies, if critical standards were implemented to structure the processes. Although still relatively small, the evidence base for authentic assessment is the only one that encompasses the critical purposes of eligibility determination, program planning, progress monitoring, and accountability in ECI.

This edition of *LINKing* is devoted to promoting early childhood assessment practices that are authentic, developmentally appropriate, and useful for planning and evaluating beneficial experiences for young children, especially those with special needs. We link professional standards and their evidence base and offer a system for evaluating the quality of the current testing and assessment measures with a focus on those measures that are the most authentic and that have advanced practice-based evidence.

In brief, in this edition of *LINKing* we advocate measurement that represents— *portrays*—young children. In Chapter 2, we promote the authentic assessment alternatives that advance the developmental progress of our most vulnerable young children rather than the unjustified conventional testing that misrepresents and thwarts crucial early development.

2

What Is Authentic Assessment?

> "Much of developmental psychology . . . is the science of the strange behavior of children, with strange adults, in strange settings for the briefest possible periods of time."
> *(Bronfenbrenner, 1979, p. 19)*

Few people have captured the inauthentic quality of conventional testing better than Urie Bronfenbrenner in his incisive criticism of laboratory research in developmental psychology. Regarding both testing and research in ECI, the overriding issue is *developmental appropriateness*—the extent to which our philosophy and practices match with the way young children actually grow and behave in their natural environments, especially during play.

Authentic assessment is the developmentally appropriate alternative to conventional testing. Authentic assessment is championed by the major national organizations in ECI. It has a current and expanding evidence base for "best professional practices" to accomplish the purposes within the ECI fields.

Authentic assessment refers to the systematic recording of developmental observations over time about the naturally occurring behaviors and functional competencies of young children in daily routines by familiar and knowledgeable caregivers in the child's life. (Bagnato & Yeh Ho, 2006, p. 16)

The definition above highlights three essential features of the authentic assessment alternative. First, authentic assessment encompasses a deliberate plan for investigating the natural behaviors of young children through natural tactics—observation, not *testing*. Next, it requires and relies upon natural "in situ" observations of children's capabilities in their typical settings (e.g., home, classroom, child care, community). These observations of children's typical functional competencies of real-life social communication and problem-solving skills are captured using direct observation, interviews, ratings, video and audio recordings, and/or probes of facilitated play. Finally, authentic observational assessments are completed and contributed by *familiar and knowledgeable caregivers in the child's life.*

In this chapter, we summarize authentic assessment and its elements through explanation and illustration. We focus particularly on the preeminent purpose for assessment in ECI—helping children. Next, we emphasize the importance of the developmental context of assessment. Finally, we link authentic assessment to recommended professional and evidence-based practices (discussed fully in Chapter 4).

The primary purpose of this book is to present authentic assessment materials and methods that represent the *best measures for best practices*. In this chapter, we summarize succinctly the most important features of authentic assessment as the alternative for ECI. Readers are referred to a much more complete analysis of authentic assessment in our companion self-instructional textbook, *Authentic Assessment for Early Childhood Intervention: Best Practices* (Bagnato, 2007).

Importance of Purpose in Assessment for Early Childhood Intervention

As detailed in Chapter 1, there are several purposes for assessment of young children, but the overarching purpose is the central theme of this book: linking assessment to intervention. By the concept of *linking,* we mean that the content of what we assess about children is the same thing as the content of what we teach them to do. Put another way, what we intend to teach should be what we are assessing.

We are all too familiar with the scenario in which teachers receive test results consisting of scores on this or that test; the question is, "How helpful are these test scores?" To what extent do the test scores link with what to teach—how do test scores inform instruction? It is no secret that test scores are not helpful; in fact, often they are detrimental by limiting teacher and parent expectations and, perhaps, foisting a negative label on the child.

It would be easy to ensure the similarity between what we assess and what we teach if we had a common road map—a hierarchy of important developmental skills essential for children's future functional competence. Fortunately, in ECI we have this road map—a curriculum. Developmental curricula enable professionals and parents to link observational assessment and instruction/intervention through the common developmental content. This updated edition of *LINKing* makes *linking* the primary criterion for inclusion of assessment measures in the book—*the best measures for best practices*, the planning of beneficial instruction.

Linking Assessment Through Curriculum Referencing

Imagine receiving, instead of test scores, assessment results that identify the things a child can and cannot do as well as the conditions under which the child can or cannot do those things. Such assessments provide teachable objectives for planned, developmentally appropriate teaching and a curriculum as well as content for assessing what has been learned.

A *curriculum* is an array of instructional objectives—what we want children to learn. In ECI, a curriculum consists of organized sets of objectives that are developmental expectations and that can be taught. Modern curricula in ECI emphasize content that is functional: objectives that have immediate utility for the child and for future success in predictable environments. Functional content in such curricula is organized in sequential hierarchies of skills and/or competencies that enable a more specific analysis of the child's current capabilities. We note, again, that functional content refers to curricular objectives that describe what the child *should* do and not specifically *how* to do it (e.g., an individual *communicates* what she wants rather than *says* what she wants).

The connection or linkage between assessment and instruction is made feasible, even easy, through the use of appropriate curriculum materials that lend themselves to direct assessment. There are two types of curriculum-based assessment methods:

- *Curriculum embedded:* Curriculum competencies (i.e., items) *are* the assessment content; assessment and instructional content are identical and integrated (e.g., *The Carolina Curriculum* and *Assessment Log* [Johnson-Martin, Attermeier, & Hacker, 2004a, 2004b; Johnson-Martin, Hacker, & Attermeier, 2004]).

- *Curriculum referenced:* Assessment content or items are compatible with items found in many different curricula and are therefore linkable (e.g., *Developmental Observation Checklist System* [Hresko, Miguel, Sherbenou, & Burton, 1994]).

Operational Dimensions for Authentic Assessment

In this section, we summarize attributes of assessment that make it authentic. We answer the *why, what, how, who, where,* and *when* of authentic assessment (see Table 2.1).

Why?

The overriding purpose of authentic assessment for ECI is to guide the planning of individualized goals for instruction or therapy. Authentic assessment provides profiles of the child's strengths and needs and generates functional goals that can guide intervention planning. Simply put, authentic assessment gives a truer picture of what the children really can and cannot do. Related purposes include mon-

Table 2.1.   Operational features of authentic assessment versus conventional testing

Dimension	Conventional testing	Authentic assessment
Where (places)	Decontextualized and contrived arrangements (e.g., clinic rooms)	Children's natural everyday settings, activities, and routines (e.g., preschool, child care, home, community)
What (content)	Standardized and contrived testing tasks that are neither functional nor of instructional value	Real-life competencies that are aligned with curricular objectives, have instructional value (treatment validity), and are functionally important for future success
How (method)	Single-session testing of narrow ranges of behavior	Natural observations of multiple samples of behavior over time in order to collect representative samples and to profile the strengths and needs of children
	Scripted examiner behavior and scripted child behavior through standardized procedures that do not allow alternate response modes or alternate stimuli to accommodate special needs	Flexibility and universal design allow children to demonstrate competencies in any way possible
Who (people)	Highly trained examiners such as psychologists who are unfamiliar to the child and not knowledgeable about the child's typical behaviors	Trained teachers, paraprofessionals, parents, and other informed caregivers who know and are familiar with the child and the child's typical behaviors
When (times)	Single, time-limited testing session	Repeated observations and probes over days, weeks, months, and even years
Why (purpose)	Determines a score to compare the child to typically developing same-age peers and to diagnose the severity of a disability, often erroneously	Identifies and designs individual instructional goals and strategies that can promote functional progress as the result of intervention
		Monitors progress periodically (2−3 times) throughout the year
Impact	Excludes children from beneficial educational opportunities and often prematurely labels children, which denies them their rights to positive expectations	Enables children to have appropriate and beneficial educational experiences and expectations

From Bagnato, S.J., & Yeh Ho, H. (2006). High-stakes testing with preschool children: Violation of professional standards for evidence-based practice in early childhood intervention. *KEDI Journal of Educational Policy, 3*(1), 30; reprinted by permission.

itoring individual progress during intervention as well as documenting the impact and outcomes of a program. In contrast, the purpose for conventional testing is solely to generate scores that are used to distinguish typical from atypical performance. These scores then are used to classify or diagnose the child. The advantage of authentic assessment is an emphasis on helping professionals to help the child through the design of special and effective interventions.

What?

Real behaviors relevant to the child's current daily functioning and to new situations are the content of authentic assessment. Authentic assessment captures *functional skills*—behaviors that are useful for meeting the challenges of daily life. The most important criterion is whether the child does a task or behavior, not how the child does it (e.g., initiates social interactions with peers vs. talks to peers to socialize). Sara may be able to initiate social interactions by gestures, notes, or other means that achieve the same function as talking to peers. Identification of the child's real behaviors in real situations allows professionals and parents to plan functional curricular goals for instruction that are critical for future success.

Authentic assessment measures contain sequences of functional skills; these sequences are the foundation of a curriculum to guide instruction. In this respect, authentic assessment has treatment validity—it directly links to intervention. The functional curricular content provides the blueprint—the *what*—for authentic observation. Unlike conventional testing, authentic observations are recorded in terms of these functional skills and are based on the extent to which children can demonstrate the behavior. Rather than merely pass/fail, authentic assessment allows graduated scoring of performance (e.g., does it most of the time; does it sometimes) or level of assistance needed (e.g., does it with some manual guidance; does it with verbal prompts) for the purpose of planning individualized and beneficial interventions.

How?

Authentic assessment relies on *observation* and record keeping of children's behavior. Authentic observation is a careful, deliberate, and systematic process of watching children work and play in real life. Observations include reports (e.g., remarks, statements, comments) based on seeing or hearing the child's actual behavior. Video and audio recording and the use of personal digital assistant (PDA) technology can capture the real behavior of children in their real environments and summarize the collected data, making authentic information gathering even more feasible.

It is often necessary to arrange circumstances and activities so that children will use social, language, and play skills that may not occur without such arrangements (i.e., referred to as *analog* settings). For example, we may want to see what Sara will do when one of her favorite toys is missing. We could wait for this to happen, but we cannot wait forever to observe a behavior that is unlikely to occur readily or consistently on its own. Professionals can "occasion" opportunities for a skill so that it can be more readily observed.

The process of authentic observational assessment is standardized by using structured protocols to record the *extent* to which a child displays expected behaviors. In most cases, a graduated rating format enables a professional or parent to observe and identify a child's skill levels through varying degrees of operationally defined competencies. Common graduated ratings include the following:

- *Always, sometimes, occasionally,* and *rarely*

- *Yes, no,* and *getting there*

- *Performance indicates mastery, performs most of the time, beginning to perform,* and *does not perform*

The competencies to be observed and recorded are arranged in age-referenced developmental sequences or hierarchies from easy to difficult or least mature to most mature, in which earlier competencies are prerequisites or precursors (i.e., building blocks) to later competencies. In many cases, what is standardized for observation is the terminal or expected behavior of the child, not how the child must respond to indicate competency. Therefore, a child who cannot walk can, nevertheless, display a skill such as getting across the room by crawling, using a wheelchair, using a walker, or rolling, which highlights the function of locomotion and not the limited physical topography of walking. Similarly, a child who is blind can show object permanence by tactilely searching around his or her body for a hidden toy. A child with no oral language can use signs or adaptive devices instead of vocal language or words to communicate needs.

Authentic assessment procedures enable observers or assessors to record naturally occurring behaviors or to probe and prompt the display of the behaviors through facilitated play activities. This procedure has the advantage of identifying the conditions under which the child displays a behavior—for example, with verbal or physical prompting—which, unlike conventional testing, guides directly the development of goals and instructional plans to help the child learn (Neisworth & Bagnato, 2004).

Who?

Optimal authentic assessment requires the observations and reports of familiar and knowledgeable caregivers in the child's life. Because young children form important attachments to adults and peers, familiarity and trust are important factors in their being able to demonstrate their true and full range of functional capabilities. Furthermore, regular caregivers (e.g., teachers, assistants, parents, other familiar adults) have the most intimate knowledge of the child's strengths and challenges based on their interactions with children in their daily caregiving. Authentic assessment, however, casts a wide net for gathering information. We do agree that individuals who are not necessarily familiar and knowledgeable with the child can, nevertheless, be prepared to collect and contribute authentic observations about children's behavior (e.g., counting the frequency of hitting, sharing toys, cooperating in play). The process of making decisions about children's capabilities pools all available information to form a more representative picture.

Where?

Using observations that occur in the natural context is arguably the distinguishing feature of authentic assessment. As opposed to conventional, decontextualized testing circumstances, authentic observations occur only in the children's natural everyday settings and routines (e.g., home, preschool, community). Early childhood professionals and even federal law (e.g., Individuals with Disabilities Education Improvement Act [IDEA] of 2004, PL 108-446) emphasize children's natural learning environments (NLE) as the basis for intervention. NLEs identify the ongoing, routine, typical circumstances and contexts of each child (i.e., home, preschool, community)—the child's natural *developmental ecology* that forms the environmental basis for real-life early learning and adaptation. Examples of such everyday contexts for both assessment and intervention include group circle time during preschool, games at the neighborhood playground, chore time at home, trips with mother to the grocery store, and reading with father at bedtime.

Analog contexts are a beneficial complement and sometimes alternative to full natural contexts. As mentioned previously, analog contexts are natural contexts in

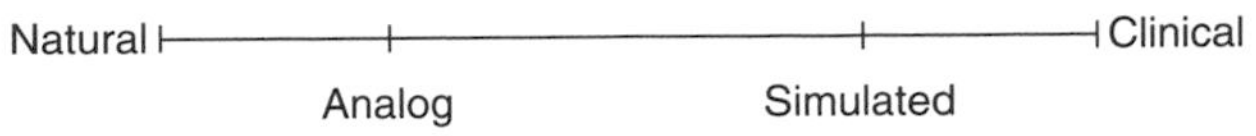

Natural ⊢————————┼————————————┼————————⊣Clinical

    Analog   Simulated

Figure 2.1. Schematic of the continuum of measurement contexts. (From Bagnato, S.J. [2007]. *Authentic assessment in early childhood intervention: Best practices* [p. 81]. New York: Guilford Press; reprinted by permission.)

which the activities, materials, toys, and even people are arranged, managed, and selected so as to occasion or prompt behaviors that may not be evidenced on a given day or that are inconsistent in the child's repertoire. In analog contexts, teachers, parents, and other professionals can choose toys and circumstances that will likely stimulate the child to act.

Figure 2.1 presents a continuum of measurement contexts from natural to contrived. This continuum can help professionals to distinguish their practices in terms of level of authenticity. (See also Table 2.2.)

When?

One-time observations, even in the natural context, are insufficient and often misleading. The validity of observations depends on a representative sample of children's behaviors. This can be obtained by pooling observations across various time points as well as across people and situations. Furthermore, children behave differently at different times of the day and demonstrate their skills under specific circumstances. Response to intervention and progress of children can be documented when observations are conducted regularly and in a serial manner. Authentic assessment requires repeated observations over time.

Summary

In summary, authentic assessment relies on natural observations of ongoing child behaviors in everyday settings and routines as compared with contrived arrangements such as tabletop tests and testing procedures. It relies on informed care-

Table 2.2. Comparative dimensions of measurement contexts

	Natural	Analog	Simulated	Clinical
Where?	Everyday routines	Everyday routines	Replica or set-up situations	Laboratory situations
What?	Spontaneous behaviors	Prompted natural behaviors	On-demand behaviors	Scripted examiner and child behaviors
How?	Observation	Observation	Structured tests and/or protocols	Psychometric tests
Who?	Informed caregivers	Informed caregivers	Trained professionals	Trained examiners
When?	Repeatedly	Repeatedly	Single session	Time-limited single session
Why?	Intervention	Intervention	Diagnosis	Diagnosis

From Bagnato, S.J. (2007). *Authentic assessment in early childhood intervention: Best practices* (p. 31). New York: Guilford Press; reprinted by permission.

givers to collect convergent and multisource information about children across various settings and to monitor gradual skill development. The content of the authentic measures links directly to the content of curricular goals in the curriculum packages used by most preschool programs. Many authentic measures are universally designed so that even children with special needs can demonstrate their skills and gains. Thus, authentic measures enable intra- and interindividual comparisons to facilitate more accurate estimates of capabilities. It is also important to note that authentic measures and assessment procedures align directly with the best practices standards of the major professional organizations in the ECI fields (i.e., NAEYC, DEC, Head Start) (Copple & Bredekamp, 1997; Head Start Bureau, 1992; Neisworth & Bagnato, 2004).

As our profession moves away from a preoccupation with conventional tests and testing and toward authentic assessment, we call on teachers and interdisciplinary professionals to embrace the professional standards of our major organizations with regard to these best practices. Chapter 3 offers details of these professional standards and, in particular, eight overarching standards for choosing and using authentic assessments. The standards provide the basis for evaluating the quality of assessment materials; these eight standards were used by professionals who rated the numerous assessment materials in Section II.

3

What Are the Professional Standards for Developmentally Appropriate Assessment in Early Childhood Intervention?

Standards are statements about essential criteria against which the quality of materials and practices are compared. We have all heard of the U.S. Bureau of Standards. There are, of course, standards in science, industry, and professions. For example, there are government standards for vehicular safety, children's toys, composition of prepared foods, and many other products and services. Professional organizations, such as the American Medical Association and the Behavior Analysis Certification Board, publish guidelines and standards for treatment to be followed by their members. Compliance with such standards provides a degree of uniformity in practice and assurance of treatment according to professional "best," recommended, or evidence-based practices. Standards are not written in stone; they can (and do) change as new evidence becomes available.

Standards for the developmental assessment of very young children require unique essential criteria that have been developed and officially sanctioned by interdisciplinary professional organizations whose members specialize in the development and early learning of children, birth to age 8. As we have observed, some influential professional organizations that represent only one interest group fall short in the value of their measurement standards, which are intended to be generic and apply to all professions.

In this chapter, we first summarize the unique professional practice standards in the fields of ECI regarding assessment of young children by referring to the professional practice manuals and position statements of the major organizations in the field. Then, we describe and illustrate the eight overarching standards derived from these professional standards and position statements that help professionals and parents to choose and use the best measures and practices. We describe each standard, list major aspects, and provide references to materials in this book that exemplify the standard. Table 3.1 offers a summary of the specific elements of the eight standards.

Professional Practice Standards for Developmentally Appropriate Assessment

Over a 25-year period, the major national professional organizations in ECI have produced, published, and updated collaborative documents on recommended practice standards for the fields that cover all aspects of the teaching and care of infants, toddlers, and preschool children. These practice standards serve as the foundation for preservice education of teachers and providers, for daily practice, and for certifying the quality of programs. Professional standards of practice in ECI are built on established values of the field and an emerging applied evidence base that supports ECI principles and practices.

Each of the professional organizations has produced specific cross-referenced practice standards about assessment, curriculum, and program evaluation for all young children. These standards drive our daily work with children and families and should, similarly, drive state and national policies and practices to document the progress of children and the impact of programs. Government policies and practices that ignore or run counter to these standards must be opposed and rejected by the field.

It is beyond the scope of this text to detail each of these standards, but below are selected examples of common recommended practice standards for assessment, curriculum, and progress and program evaluation, including accountability. These examples are taken from the following official standards and position statements: Bredekamp and Copple (2009); DEC, Council for Exceptional Children (2007); Head Start Bureau (1992); NAEYC and National Association of State Directors of Special Education (NAEYC, 2003); and Sandall, Hemmeter, Smith, and McLean (2005).

- Rely on developmental observations over time.

- Monitor performance during authentic, not contrived, activities.

- Integrate and link assessment and curriculum.

- Use past performances, not group norms, as the reference.

- Choose materials that accommodate the child's special functional needs.

- Use only measures that have high utility (treatment validity).

- Rely on curriculum-based assessments as the foundation, or mutual language, of team assessments.

Table 3.1.   Eight overarching standards for developmentally appropriate assessment materials and practices

Standards and quality indicators	Defined practice characteristics
Acceptability	Social validity; social worth or appropriateness of the scale's item content as reported by parents and other caregivers
Social competencies	Emphasizes socially valued and relevant content
Social detection	Yields socially noticeable changes in functioning within real-world settings
Social appropriateness	Uses assessment procedures acceptable to parents and other important caregivers
Authenticity	Extent to which the assessment content and methods sample naturally occurring behaviors in everyday situations
Functional content	Emphasizes competencies that are necessary for the child to participate effectively in daily life activities and routines
Observational methods	Relies only upon *in situ* observations and reports of familiar people to document child competencies
Natural situations	Captures information on child competencies in familiar classroom, home, and community settings and routines, including play
Collaboration	Parent–professional and interdisciplinary teamwork
Interdisciplinary procedures	Uses procedures that encourage different models of teamwork (e.g., interdisciplinary, transdisciplinary) and role sharing among parents and professionals
Family- and culture-centered practices	Enables the integral engagement of parents, family members, and friends via "friendly" jargon-free materials, procedures, and practices that respect and align with cultural values, among which the family and partners can voice a preference
Evidence	Has a clear evidence base for use in early childhood intervention; materials designed, developed, and field-validated for young children, particularly those with special needs
Professional standards	Adheres to the unique philosophy, standards, and practices established by the various professional organizations within the early childhood intervention field (e.g., Division for Early Childhood, Head Start, National Association for the Education of Young Children)
Diversity representation	Incorporates children from diverse cultural, linguistic, socioeconomic, and disability backgrounds in the standardization group, if norm-referenced, and in field validations
Disability specificity	Provides evidence of a pooled typical/atypical norm group or disability-specific standardization for field-validation samples
Early intervention validation	Shows field-validation studies to demonstrate efficacy to fulfill each identified or targeted early childhood intervention assessment purpose (e.g., eligibility, programming, outcomes evaluation, accountability)
Multifactors	Collection of data across multiple methods, sources, settings, and occasions
Multiple situations	Gathers and records information about children's competencies across diverse places (e.g., classroom, home, community), routines (e.g., group circle, playground, lunch), and time of day (e.g., morning, evening)
Multiple persons	Pools data from several familiar caregivers (e.g., parents, family, friends, professionals) who have attachments to the child and interact with the child during daily events and life activities and across different settings
Multiple methods	Gathers information through multiple methods (e.g., interview, direct probes, permanent products, observations)
Multiple time points	Incorporates evidence of children's preintervention competencies and performances over several assessment time points
Sensitivity	Sequential arrangement and density of items in the skill hierarchy and the graduated scoring of children's performance on those items
Functional hierarchy	Organizes assessment content in a sequence of developmental competencies (e.g., younger to older; easier to harder) and/or known instructional steps (e.g., simple to complex)

(continued)

Table 3.1. *continued*

Standards and quality indicators	Defined practice characteristics
Sufficient "item floors"	Contains a sufficient number of items in an assessment sequence to record even low functional levels and to detect the smallest increments of measurable changes in performance, both quantitative and qualitative
Graduated scoring	Uses multipoint ratings or classifications to record and document the extent and conditions under which competencies are demonstrated
Universality	Design and/or accommodations, which enable all children to demonstrate their underlying and often unrealized functional capabilities (i.e., identifies both strengths and needs)
Equitable design	Designs assessment items so that any child can demonstrate underlying competence; emphasizes functional rather than topographical content (form); and adheres to universal design concepts (i.e., designed for all children, including those with disabilities, without heavy reliance on adaptations or special design; promotes full integration; acknowledges differences as a part of everyday life; e.g., "gets across the room" versus "walks across the room")
Alternate materials	Allows the use of alternate and often multisensory materials to elicit an individual child's functional capabilities
Alternate responses	Allows alternate ways for individual children to show their competencies despite sensory, physical, behavioral, social-emotional, linguistic, and cultural differences or functional limitations
Utility	Treatment validity; usefulness of the scale and the assessment process to accomplish specific early childhood intervention purposes, especially planning and evaluating interventions
Curricular linkages	Encompasses assessment items whose functional content can match to curricular competencies as instructional objectives, specifically or generally
Intervention content	Identifies what to teach (i.e., assessment identifies which children need to learn which skills and/or concepts and where to begin instruction and/or intervention)
Intervention methods	Informs how to teach (i.e., assessment provides guidance on instructional strategies that facilitate the child's optimal functioning)
Performance monitoring	Detects changes in performance across skills and concepts during and/or after intervention

- Defer a diagnosis until evaluation of a child's response to a tailored set of interventions (RTI).

- Use scales with sufficient item density to detect even small increments of progress.

- Use scales that emphasize functional and universal items.

- Use scales that promote the inclusion of families in decision making and infuse cultural aspects in the process.

- Use scales that require data collection from multiple sources, settings, people, and occasions

- Use scales that have been specifically designed and/or field-validated for specific ECI purposes (i.e., accountability) and with specific target samples of children.

Eight Major Standards for Developmentally Appropriate Assessment

There are eight overarching standards for developmentally appropriate assessment: acceptability, authenticity, collaboration, evidence, multifactors, sensitivity, universality, and utility.

Acceptability

We emphasize three aspects of acceptability. First, assessment materials must have item content that is judged to be worthwhile; that is, the items should identify skills that parents as well as professionals judge to be important and appropriate. "Waits for his or her turn in a game," "finds own shoes," and "communicates a need" are examples of skills that everyone would agree are worthwhile for children to learn; these objectives are *socially valid*. Norm-referenced, standardized tests typically have items that are *not* seen as worthwhile to teach—for example, "strings beads," "stands on one foot for 10 seconds," and "stacks three blocks." The defense of such items is that they are, by psychometric inference, exemplars of an underlying psychological or developmental process of a larger pool of items that are useful. In truth, the utility and acceptability of such items are questionable, at best.

Second, not only must the assessment *content* be regarded as worthwhile, but the *administration* procedures also must be seen as acceptable. Many, if not most of us, can recount "war stories" of child assessment scenarios in which the procedures run counter to even common sense: demands of strangers in a strange environment to perform tasks and answer questions, quick pacing of items and time demands on the child, and references to things and experiences that may be culturally inappropriate. These are but a few of the issues related to "administering tests." In sharp contrast, authentic assessment is not "administered"; instead, child behavior in the child's familiar situations is observed and reported by familiar people. Sometimes, we can structure a setting (analog) in order to enable a behavior rather than waiting for the opportunity to occur. (These issues are discussed elsewhere, especially under *Authenticity*).

The third issue of acceptability concerns child progress. To be acceptable, improvements in child competence (or decreases in problematic behavior) should be *evident* to parents and professionals. *Social validity* is used to refer to changes that are apparent—changes that are noticeable by those who are familiar with the child. An improved score on a test may or may not correspond to improved performance as reported by those familiar with the child. Gaining 10 points on a communication scale may be claimed, but if parents or others familiar with the child do not detect any real improvement, then the point gain as reported by the test is not *socially valid*. What does a psychometric point gain matter if improvements in a child's functioning are not real or detectable in the real world? We strive to help children make progress that makes authentic differences in their lives, not merely in their scores.

The following should be considered when evaluating the *acceptability* of assessment content and materials:

1. Do the materials emphasize content that is considered (especially by the child's parents) to be socially valued and important?

2. Is progress as assessed by the content and materials matched by changes that are socially noticeable? Are changes registered by the materials matched by real-life changes in child skills; are they noticeable by people who are familiar with the child?

3. Do the materials use *procedures* that are acceptable to parents and other significant caregivers?

For an example of an assessment tool that consumers rate as exemplary in *acceptability*, see the At-a-Glance for the *Assessment, Evaluation, and Programming System for Infants and Children (AEPS®), Second Edition* (Bricker, 2002) on page 99).

Authenticity

We might refer to authentic assessment as "reality assessment"—the extent to which a child's naturally occurring behavior in real, everyday settings is sampled and assessed. We can all agree that it would be foolish to assess the behavior of "fish out of water." Furthermore, although putting fish in a laboratory aquarium would provide much more information, the aquarium is still not the natural habitat of fish; we would not be able to observe how a fish interacts with its natural environment or with other fish. Obviously, it would make sense to observe and assess fish in their natural environments. Although this may seem obvious, all too often children are removed from their familiar settings and are taken to a "testing room," where they are tested by a stranger.

> At the heart of Authentic Assessment is [again] the issue of sampling behavior. In Authentic Assessment, we observe and/or obtain reports about a child's performance in and across natural settings and occasions. Appraisal of the child's developmental skills *as practiced in the child's real environments* cannot be done through "testing" by a stranger at a table with flashcards, blocks, and beads. Clearly, such conventional testing ignores the crucial requirement for valid sampling of behavior in order to make inferences about the presence, absence, fluency, and utility of skills. Use of psychometrically selected items administered in decontextualized settings results in biased samples of the child's functioning. (Bagnato, 2007, p. 22)

To be "authentic," we observe and record the child functioning in typical and important settings. Note that we refer to *functional behavior*—the child's activities in real, familiar, typical environments. The *function* of a behavior refers to what the behavior *does*, or what gets accomplished. "Gets across the room" (rather than "walks across the room") and "communicates what she wants" (rather than "says what she wants") are examples of functional skills that do not require specific ways to respond.

There is a real advantage to focusing on the function of a behavior: It enables us to appraise the performance of children who may not have typical means of expression; do they get it done, one way or another? Furthermore, looking at the function of a behavior also directs attention to the environments of children and how such environments may facilitate or limit progress. Professionals recognize the importance of the physical and social environment in child development, but many ignore or diminish the importance of the environment when it comes to assessment by using decontextualized and nonfunctional testing procedures.

A second feature of authentic assessment is *how* the assessment is conducted. Authentic methods rely on observations and reports of child functioning in natural (*in situ*) settings; the assessment is not "administered." Rather, we value reports and observations of parents and others familiar with the child; this information can supplement or challenge professional observations, signaling the need for further inquiry. Checklists, rating scales, frequency counts, and anecdotal reports are employed to obtain genuine appraisals of children's competencies. In addition to direct observation (which is not always feasible), parents as well as professionals can use video and audio recording and texting to capture children's behavior when it occurs.

The following should be considered when evaluating the *authenticity* of assessment content and materials:

1. Does the content emphasize *competencies* that are expected in real-life circumstances?

2. Are *real life settings*, familiar to the child (e.g., home, preschool, community), used for collecting information?

3. Does the material rely on *reports* by parents, professionals, and others familiar with the child?

For an example of an assessment that consumers rate as exemplary in *authenticity*, see the At-a-Glance for *The Carolina Curriculum for Infants and Toddlers with Special Needs, Third Edition (CCITSN)* (Johnson-Martin, Attermeier, & Hacker, 2004b), and *The Carolina Curriculum for Preschoolers with Special Needs, Second Edition (CCPSN)* (Johnson-Martin, Hacker, & Attermeier, 2004), on page 123.

Collaboration

The concept of *teamwork* has been so overused in business and education that its importance often seems diminished. Despite the perceived overuse of this concept, it is important to recognize how essential working together and collaborating actually is. Assessment materials we use can be a significant resource for promoting collaboration. Professionals and publishers are recognizing the role of collaboration in our efforts to assess children authentically. Many of today's assessment materials include parent-friendly instructions and jargon-free, illustrated forms written at an appropriate language level. These materials also honor the importance of family- and culture-centered practices. Furthermore, many materials provide separate assessment protocols for related professionals (e.g., physical therapists, speech-language pathologists). These professionals can observe a child and record their assessments, which are then discussed within the team along with parents' comments.

Authentic assessment is based on observing and noting children's behavior in real circumstances. Indeed, authentic assessment is built on a foundation of cooperative information gathering. Because no one professional can observe children in all of their natural settings all day long, it is important to work together to obtain a comprehensive and representative sample of behavior. Certainly, we need to work with parents to learn how their children get along in the home setting, how they behave in the evening, and if there are sleep problems. Interdisciplinary professionals cooperate across settings and times to produce a fuller picture of children's actual skills and challenges. It should be noted, too, that collaborative assessment can be seen as a process that can promote enthusiasm among service providers and parents that can go beyond the assessment process itself.

The following should be considered when evaluating the quality of *collaboration* in assessment content and materials:

1. Do the materials promote the input of parents and other professionals (with collaborative materials or procedures)?

2. Is the content jargon free and the format "parent friendly" so that parental involvement is facilitated?

3. Are assessment procedures designed for parents to employ when assessing their children easy for them to use and record?

4. Are the materials and procedures consistent with the family's cultural values and practices?

For an example of an assessment tool that consumers rated as exemplary in *collaboration*, see the At-a-Glance for *Transdisciplinary Play-Based Assessment, Second Edition* (Linder, 2008), on page 238.

Evidence

Many assessment materials, including most of the widely used conventional tests, have little or no real published evidence of their appropriateness for young children with developmental challenges or, especially, their validity in accomplishing the major purposes for assessment in the ECI field (i.e., eligibility, program planning, progress monitoring, accountability). Conventional measures are typically standardized with and for children without special needs. *Standardization* itself is not a bad thing. To standardize procedures is simply to state how items should be presented, in what sequence, the time permitted, and so forth. These procedures were used with the standardization samples of children employed in the development of the materials. When materials and procedures are standardized, it is then possible to give the test the same way it was given in the development of the test materials. Following standardized procedures provides a level playing field so that differences in assessment results can be attributed to the child being tested and not to differences in how, when, or where the items were administered.

Standardized procedures can be "tight" or "loose." Some materials are developed that allow items to be given in any sequence, with no strict time requirements, and responded to in various ways; this allows expression by children with a range of verbal, auditory, and motor skills (loose standardization). *The important aspect is that the materials must be used in the same way they were used in the standardization process.* Most often, usual administration procedures are "tightly" standardized for use with samples of children with typical developmental skills. Most tests are not based on materials specifically for or field-validated with young children who have significant developmental challenges. Children may be asked to point to choices, say their answers, sit and listen carefully, and do other things that typically developing children can do. Standardization designed for "standard children," however, is not at all sensible for children who do not or cannot dutifully sit, listen, talk, and perform.

Some standardized assessment scales add a subsample of children with special needs so that there can be a claim that the materials are appropriate for these children. The performance of these children is supposed to be indicative of typical performance of children with the same special needs; however, the performance requirement is *still based on procedures designed for typically developing children.* Tacking on a subsample of children after the measure has been standardized for children with typical development is not the same as designing procedures from the outset that apply to a wide array of children, if not all children. To be acceptable, assessment measures must be developed for and based on samples of children with whom the measures will likely be used. Clearly, the issue of sampling is crucial.

Professionals who do research certainly recognize the critical role of sampling. We make inferences based on samples. Of course, we wish to make generalizations beyond the sample of the population represented by that sample. When we assess a child's developmental or behavioral status, we wish to make inferences about that child's functioning beyond the particular assessment items and situation. We may consider assessment as an attempt to obtain a fair sample of behaviors that permit us to make inferences concerning that child's actual behavior in real situations. Both the content of the sample and the sampling plan (how assessment items are selected) come into play for enabling valid inferences.

> Even if our conclusion concerns only one individual, the measurements we have taken are only a sample of all that might be made, and in assigning particular values to the measured magnitudes we are making an inference, based on that sample, of what other measurements would yield. (Kaplan, 1964, p. 41)

The following should be considered when evaluating the *evidence* for assessment content and materials:

1. Is information presented showing that the materials are consistent with relevant professional standards and practices (e.g., DEC, NAEYC)?

2. If the assessment is norm referenced, were children with disabilities included in the original standardization group used during development of the materials?

3. If the assessment is norm referenced, are there either disability-specific standardization samples (with separate norms) or norms based on pooled data from typical and disability samples?

4. Are there field-validation studies concerning the use of the materials for eligibility, program planning, outcomes evaluation, and/or accountability?

For an example of an assessment tool that consumers rate as exemplary in *evidence*, see the At-a-Glance for *Adaptive Behavior Assessment System–Second Edition* (*ABAS-II*; Harrison & Oakland, 2003) on page 93.

Multifactors

To capture a more accurate picture of a child's status, we need comprehensive information. The multifactor standard requires collection of information from several settings, assessors, occasions, and methods. The reason for the multifactor requirement is to provide a wide base of information on child functioning. All of us are aware that young children may behave differently in different situations, at different times, with different people, and when different methods (e.g., direct observation vs. parent report) are used.

It is recognized by parents as well as professionals that a child may not "perform" in an assessment situation the same as he or she would at home or at grandmother's house. Likewise, different occasions can generate different outcomes (e.g., circle time vs. playground vs. lunch time). Regarding time of day for assessment, certainly children may be "more cooperative" in the morning than during their usual nap time! We also must note that even developmental landmarks (e.g., walks around room) may be evident one day but not the next. New or emerging skills often are displayed intermittently, with return to a prior skill until the new skill is consolidated. This is called *developmental oscillation* (Ausubel, 1965). For example, on Monday, Jimmy walks around the kitchen for the first time, so Mom calls neighbors and grandparents to come see Jimmy perform his new skill. On Wednesday, however, Jimmy just crawls around the kitchen, especially when surrounded by new observers! After a few weeks, sometimes less, Jimmy will use his new competence with less and less use of the less advanced behavior.

The way in which information is collected (i.e., multiple methods) also can offer further insight into children's developmental status or progress. Several methods of assessment are available, and each can enhance the information basis for decision making. Assessment can include direct observation, parent interview, and children's permanent products (e.g., drawings, recorded speech, standardized testing). Assessment teams can use video and/or audio recording of a child's behavior to capture information in multiple environments and occasions. Recordings can be directly observed by several individuals when feasible. It should be pointed out that data gathered across situations and occasions may be complementary or at odds. As you might expect, we are more confident about multifactor assessment when information is consistent; conflicting information, however, may also be valuable and can alert us to look further to resolve or explain differences. Information provided by parents (e.g., through interviews and/or parent-reported observations of the child) that is different from that provided by professional observations can be cause for a closer look or may be seen as contributing a parent perspective that enriches the data pool (Suen, Logan, Neisworth, & Bagnato, 1995).

Conducting multifactor assessment involves more than one person; indeed, it is not feasible for one person to be in several places, on different occasions, and use multiple types of assessment methods! Even if a clinical psychologist in a clinical setting *could* collect multifactor information (which is not the reality!), the quality of information is enhanced by having multiple observers. We emphasize that parents be partners in assessment. Increasingly, materials are available that either include separate parent-friendly materials or include parents in the professional materials.

The following should be considered when evaluating the *multifactor* quality of assessment content and materials:

1. Can the materials be used to collect and record children's skills in different environments (e.g., preschool, home, community) and at different times (e.g., morning, evening)?

2. Can assessment information contributed by parents and professionals be combined so that information from parents is not merely supplemental?

3. Are multiple assessment methods employed (e.g., interviews and reports, direct observation, permanent products)?

4. Can the materials be used over time (i.e., repeatedly) to record progress (e.g., preintervention and at several other time points)?

For an example of an assessment tool that consumers rate as exemplary in *multifactors,* see the At-a-Glance for *Preschool and Kindergarten Behavior Scales—Second Edition* (*PKBS-2;* Merrell, 2003) on page 217.

Sensitivity

We use the term *sensitivity* to mean how well the sequential array of assessment items detect even slight differences in child functioning. (*Sensitivity* is defined differently with respect to screening tools.[1]) Children who have more profound disabilities require assessment and/or curricular materials that are sensitive enough to detect minimal functioning and changes (i.e., that have low enough *item floors*). Typically, materials that are sensitive have a greater item *density* (i.e., a greater number of items for a given skill). A sensitive scale may have 10 steps/items for assessing "washing own hands," whereas there may be only a few items for this skill in typical developmental tests. Teachers, physical therapists, and other specialists know how important it is to use materials that are responsive to small differences and changes when working with children with more serious disabilities. The changing competencies and recovery of children who have sustained serious head trauma, for example, can be assessed successfully with materials designed to detect minimal status and increments in progress. Parents as well as professionals absolutely require "fine grain," sensitive scales that can document a child's progress.

Graduated scoring is another major advantage of sensitive scales. Because there are a greater number of items for a given skill, scoring also can be sensitive. Some scales use task-analyzed subtasks so that scoring can indicate which steps are accomplished and which are not. For example, "eating with a spoon" may include anywhere between a few to 10 or more steps, and those steps can be used to show progress within a skill.

Some scales make possible a graduated scoring for each progressive level of assistance needed—from minimal to maximal support—for accomplishing a given skill. The range of assistance levels often includes *does it independently, needs minimal assistance, needs assistance in some steps,* and *needs full assistance.* Parents are grateful when they can see even small increments in skill development; graphic

---

[1]*Sensitivity* can be defined as the percentage of children (who may be at risk) who are correctly identified as requiring follow-up diagnostic assessment. If all children in a group are identified as being "at risk" and follow-up assessments confirm this, the sensitivity is 100%. Although 100% is seldom achieved, good screeners will have high "hit rates," often 80% or more.

displays or other recording of these small steps are valued by all who work with the child.

The following should be considered when evaluating the *sensitivity* of assessment materials:

1. Is content of the materials organized in progression of behaviors: developmental sequences, easier to harder, or steps in a task analysis?

2. Are there enough items within a skill sequence to detect even small increments of progress?

3. Is graduated scoring available so that level of assistance (e.g., *does task with full, some, partial assistance*) or degree of accomplishment (e.g., *partial, almost, complete*) can be identified?

For an example of an assessment tool that consumers rate as exemplary in *sensitivity*, see the At-a-Glance for *Vulpe Assessment Battery–Revised* (Vulpe, 1994) on page 250.

Universality

Efforts of advocates and disability organizations have resulted in many modifications of the environment that make life less burdensome for individuals with disabilities. In the last 50 years, we have seen numerous changes that we now take for granted. Doors that automatically open, curbs that are sloped, and international icons for restrooms and traffic signals are a few examples of "universal design."

By *universal*, we refer to structure and procedures that can be used by a wide array of individuals (typical or otherwise) with few or no modifications specifically for disabilities. The goal is to avoid stigmatizing features that call attention to disability. The idea behind *universality* is for environments and the things people use to be useful by *all* people, without disability-specific features that separate "normal" from "disabled" (separate is not equal). People with physical limitations, older adults, and people carrying packages all benefit from automatic doors. Note that automatic doors are not disability specific, nor do they stigmatize anyone who uses them. Likewise, sloped curbs are not just a modification for people in wheelchairs but are also appreciated by people riding a bicycle, pushing a stroller, or using a skateboard. Increasingly, voice recognition is an option for composing and writing emails instead of typing on a computer keyboard. A major concept of universal design is that design elements should be built in for a wide range of users rather then added on or supplemented after the fact.

The principles that guide universal design for the physical environment also apply to teaching, learning, and assessment. Applied to assessment, there are three aspects to consider. First, there should be multiple means of representation. Assessment items, questions, or instructions should provide various ways to communicate what is being assessed. Printed instructions, ready-made flash cards, or standard environmental arrangements do not serve a wide range of capabilities. Children with auditory, visual, language, motor, behavioral, or affective challenges might well be able to do what is being assessed but not understand, see, or hear the assessment item or instruction. For example, Billy might be quite capable of putting on his shoes but might not perform if he is not presented with stimuli that communicate to him. Billy might not clearly hear the instruction or Billy might not be able to put on the shoes provided because they are somewhat different from the shoes he has been wearing. Even with authentic assessment, the setting should be arranged to assure that the behavior to be assessed is clearly possible, given that the student has that competency. In brief, "passing" or "not passing" the assessment item should be a function of the student's competency (i.e., can he do it) rather than the instructions or circumstances.

The second aspect of universal design refers to multiple means of actions and expression. Alternatives must allow children to "show what they know" despite sensory, motor, social-emotional, language, or cultural differences. For example, Aaron may know the names of his friends but not be able to say their names; however, he may be able to identify them by pointing to pictures of them.

The final characteristic of universal design concerns motivation. Children may understand instructions and be provided with familiar objects but not perform because they are not at all motivated to perform. Or, a child may "have the concept of permanency" but not express or demonstrate it. For example, Rachel may not care about finding the little rabbit that the school psychologist hides under the plastic cup, even with repeated prompting; however, she will easily find a favorite toy at the bottom of her toy chest. Following the concept of universal design, it is important to try to assure that the child wants to perform and that motivation is not the issue.

The following should be considered when evaluating the *universality* of assessment materials:

1. Provide assessment items, objects, or arrangements that are certain to communicate what is expected.

2. Make available multiple means for a child to express a skill. The *function* of the behavior is what is important, not exactly how it is done.

3. Assure (not presume) that there is motivation to demonstrate a skill.

For an example of an assessment tool that consumers rate as exemplary in *universality,* see the At-a-Glance for *Desired Results Developmental Profile access* (Desired Results *access* Project, 2007) on page 138.

Utility

Usefulness and *helpfulness* are words roughly equivalent to *utility.* It seems obvious that assessments should be useful or helpful. *Treatment validity* frequently is used to refer to the utility of an intervention. Professionals in our field need to determine child developmental status and instructional objectives as well as track progress; useful assessment provides that information. In brief, assessment must inform intervention—it must have *utility.*

We have referred to this utility standard as the *LINKing* of assessment and intervention—perhaps the most important standard because all others depend on the degree to which the assessment tool provides useful and beneficial information to help the child to develop and progress. This is the primary purpose of ECI.

Frequently, however, the procedures and materials used in assessing infants and young children are not useful to parents, teachers, or therapists; they do not provide profiles of child strengths and needs, nor can they be used to assess progress. Standardized/norm-referenced materials used for "eligibility determination" typically have little or no utility for instruction. We refer to this kind of assessment that leads to nowhere as "dead-end" assessment. Intelligence tests and numerous developmental tests are designed to determine a child's developmental status compared with a norm group. These materials (as previously discussed) offer no real guidance for what or how to teach; they result in scores that do not inform us of a child's profile of strengths or needs. The time, money, resources, and unnatural circumstances involved with such testing are not justified (Bagnato & Neisworth, 1995).

Fortunately, well-designed authentic assessment materials are available that do offer great utility; they offer a scope and sequence of skills that can be employed for determining status, selecting objectives, tracking progress, and evaluating programs.

The following should be considered when evaluating the *utility* of assessment materials:

1. Do items describe child competencies that match curricular items and therefore serve as instructional objectives?

2. Does use of the materials identify *what* the child needs to learn and where to begin instruction and/or therapy?

3. Do the materials inform *how* to teach; that is, do they provide guidance on what instructional strategies to employ (e.g., pace of instruction, visual and/or auditory stimuli, kind and use of reinforcement)?

For an example of an assessment tool that consumers rate as exemplary in *utility*, see the At-a-Glance for *HELP*®—*the Hawaii Early Learning Profile*® (Holt, Gilles, Holt, & Davids, 2004; Parks, 2007) on page 172.

Summary

This chapter summarized the ECI professional practice standards for assessing young children. It described the eight overarching standards that professionals and parents can use to select the best assessments to use: acceptability, authenticity, collaboration, evidence, multifactors, sensitivity, universality, and utility. Chapter 4 explains how to apply authentic assessment to fulfill the purposes of ECI.

4

How Can Professionals Apply the Best Measures for Best Practices?

It is helpful to identify the array of high-quality authentic assessment measures and systems for use by professionals in ECI. With our LINK standards, consumers can appraise more clearly the qualities that distinguish the best measures to select and apply, thus ensuring the best practices in their programs. Yet, beyond identifying the strongest measures, few resources show professionals how to actually *apply* authentic assessment to fulfill the unique and essential purposes for ECI. (See Bagnato, 2007, for more detailed how-to descriptions of authentic assessment in action.)

This chapter offers a concise "how-to" primer on applying authentic assessment for ECI specific purposes: screening, eligibility, program planning and progress monitoring, program outcomes evaluation, and accountability. We define each purpose and discuss issues related to each for ECI practices. Then, for each purpose we apply the authentic assessment motif of *why, what, how, where, who,* and *when,* using a tabular format with bullets to summarize best practices (as introduced in Chapter 2). Finally, we suggest specific authentic assessment measures that are suited particularly well to fulfill each purpose. Let's get started!

Screening

One of the least understood yet most important purposes of ECI is screening to detect probable delays in development and, thus, risk status. Within ECI, *screening* can be defined as the process of briefly and efficiently sampling landmark developmental capabilities of individual young children or groups of children in a region for the purpose of detecting possible delays or differences in development as a basis for more comprehensive assessment to confirm or refute the screening results and to establish the basis for service eligibility.

As defined, screening is a process of "casting a wide net" within a sample or population of children to identify those children who are likely to have developmental delays. Screening can involve various modes, such as interviewing parents and child care providers and completing short screening measures. The results of a screening typically indicate whether a child's skill levels reach a criterion level or cut-off that distinguishes typical from atypical development. However, a critical point is that screening measures, even those that are authentic, are merely samples or probes of development involving a few landmark skills. Screening measures are short and general in nature; they are often insensitive and inaccurate. Recall the poor track record for the *Denver Developmental Screening Test* (Frankenburg & Dodds, 1969), which is able to identify severe developmental problems that are easily observed without testing but is essentially insensitive in detecting the most important and more widespread concern—mild developmental delays and at-risk status. The results of screening can justifiably be viewed as more an index of the level of concern that a parent or other caregiver has about a particular child. The point often missed by professionals is that screening measures provide results that must be confirmed or refuted through a follow-up process of more comprehensive and thorough authentic assessment. *Children cannot and should not be diagnosed with a developmental delay based on the results of screening measures.*

The concept of universal screening (screening all children) has gained new importance in its application to newborn hearing screening in statewide programs and, within education, the RTI movement. A common feature of various RTI models is the reliance on universal classroom screenings and probes of children's development, social behavior, and early literacy as the baseline for planning tiered interventions (e.g., instructional and behavioral) of graduated intensity.

Table 4.1 offers suggestions on applying authentic assessment for best practices in screening and also summarizes the essential features of authentic assessment for screening. Because screening always requires confirmation through detailed assessment, choose an available product that is a *comprehensive assessment system.* This will ensure continuity and similarity between the screening and full measures and among sampled and predicted behaviors. The *Ages & Stages Questionnaires®, Third Edition* (*ASQ-3™*; Squires & Bricker, 2009) and the *Temperament and Atypical Behavior Scale* (*TABS*; Bagnato, Neisworth, Salvia, & Hunt, 1999) are reliable, valid, sensitive, and evidence-based screeners.

It is noteworthy that the *TABS* was approved officially by the American Academy of Pediatrics as one of the few primary measures of social-behavioral characteristics that should be used by pediatricians due to its excellent psychometric qualities, ease of use, and its capacity to qualify infants and toddlers and preschoolers for early intervention services.

Table 4.1. Authentic assessment in action for best practices in screening

Authentic dimension	Authentic best practices in screening
Why?	To identify level of parent and caregiver concerns To identify probable developmental delays To detect likely at-risk status in a population of children in a region To target and plan for needed levels of intervention in a classroom
What?	General developmental competencies Social-behavioral and self-regulatory skills Early literacy skills
Who?	Parents Other caregivers
Where?	In the home In child care In classrooms In family support centers In community health centers and events In Head Start and Early Head Start programs
When?	At least four times per year in infancy Twice per year in preschool At the beginning of the year in preschool classrooms (Data should be synthesized across several times and occasions.)
How?	Recommended measures: *ASQ-3™, ASQ:SE, TABS, PKBS-2* Recommended practices: • Use the *ASQ-3™* regularly for Child Find and tracking in early intervention systems. • Use the *ASQ:SE* for monitoring children's social-emotional behavior. • Use the *TABS* screener to target regulatory difficulties and atypical temperamental characteristics and the *TABS* full measure to confirm a regulatory disorder and to gain quick eligibility for both early intervention and wraparound behavioral support services. • Use *PKBS-2* in Head Start and other early childhood programs to screen for probable behavioral support needs through response to intervention in classrooms and programs at entry.

Key: ASQ:SE, Ages & Stages Questionnaires®: Social-Emotional (Squires, Bricker, & Twombly, 2002); ASQ-3™, Ages & Stages Questionnaires®, Third Edition (Squires & Bricker, 2009); PKBS-2, Preschool and Kindergarten Behavior Scales—Second Edition (Merrell, 2003); TABS, Temperament and Atypical Behavior Scale (Bagnato, Neisworth, Salvia, & Hunt, 1999).

Choose screening measures that 1) enable parents and other knowledgeable and familiar caregivers to be the primary source for representative information about the child, and 2) are family friendly in their presentation and response format and jargon free in their language and required reading level. Screening for tracking must be planned and implemented so that the monitoring of status and progress can be regularly appraised and changes in developmental trajectory readily noted to trigger a professional response.

The *Preschool and Kindergarten Behavior Scales—Second Edition* (PKBS-2; Merrell, 2003) has been field-validated as an efficient, universal preschool RTI probe to serve as a sensitive programmatic measure. These probes can be used to set social-behavioral goals based on child needs; plan graduated interventions; and document the relationship among intensity of behavioral consultation to teachers, changes in teacher instructional and management behaviors, and increasing social skills and decreasing problem behaviors (Bagnato et al., 2004).

Eligibility

Can anyone think of a less humane approach for providing help to vulnerable children (and adolescents and adults, for that matter) than one in which they must be identified first with a serious and significant problem before help can be delivered? Even before help is provided and we get to know the child's response to intervention, we are required by regulation to apply a label of disability or psychopathology to them; the label is too often erroneous as well as biased by insurance provisions (i.e., payment approved only if a label such as autism is applied). The medical model still prevails in early intervention and special education after all these years, even though we know that labels based on personal impairments fail to inform intervention.

Think of how much more humane and effective would be a system and approach that required professionals and parents to estimate the extent of help that a particular child needs as the basis for eligibility determination—*service-based eligibility.* We know that—with more than 90% accuracy—professionals and parents can reach consensus in a reliable way and reach a valid conclusion when asked the following question: "Can this child succeed in a general education or community setting without support services? Yes or no." Note that the question focuses on the expected goal—successful inclusion—rather than on the personal defect of the child. In addition, it also includes the critical dimension of help needed. If we answer "yes," the child does not need services; if we answer "no," the child needs services. We then can spend our valuable time discussing the type and extent of help needed rather than debating whether a standard score of 75 or 81 meets the state cutoff for the definition of *developmental delay.*

Unfortunately, after our 40 years in the field, we hold out little hope that the eligibility system will change in the United States as long as services must be rationed; insurance reimbursements apply to education and behavioral support; and no universal system exists for ECI. As eternal optimists, however, we have hope that the great potential of the RTI movement is exploited and applied to change the system to one based on need rather than personal limitations.

In the meantime, we can do two positive things: 1) identify those authentic assessment measures that provide the truest appraisal of both strengths and intervention needs and 2) identify ways to "game" the system (you may need to use creative tactics) so that all who need help can be declared eligible. Within ECI, *eligibility* can be defined as an interdisciplinary process of assessing comprehensively the individual developmental and functional capabilities of young children in such a way as to generate a profile of normative scores; to compare the scores to state criteria for developmental delays; and to form the basis for entry into services.

Note that the operational feature for determining eligibility is a metric by which professionals can fulfill state definitions for developmental delay (e.g., 25% of chronological age, 1.5 standard deviations below the mean) to "diagnose" a child's degree of limitations and to officially determine eligibility for ECI services. Using this definition for eligibility, professionals can select and apply those authentic and curriculum-based assessments that can be scored via developmental age scores, IRT-derived cut-off levels, and traditional standard scores. Unlike conventional tests, some authentic assessment measures have been specifically field-validated for eligibility determination purposes.

Moreover, recall that professional standards for ECI require that all child assessments, irrespective of the purpose, must be authentic as well as useful for individualized program planning—they must have treatment utility and validity. This admonition applied to eligibility means that the selected measures must both document eligibility in authentic ways and also generate intervention goals and strategies. Also, authentic assessment for eligibility can uncover "hidden" strengths, using alternate response modes and materials.

Table 4.2 summarizes the essential features of authentic assessment and offers suggestions for best practices in eligibility determination. Within this summary, several features are noteworthy because of their direct impact on best practices. To actually apply authentic assessment for eligibility determination, professionals and their programs must make systemic changes in traditional routines and timelines to meet best practices. The following guidelines outline some of these steps:

- Choose an authentic scale *to unify* interdisciplinary and interagency teamwork—the team's assessment scale (rather than an individual professional's scale).

- Match the team assessment model to the needs and preferences of each child and family (interdisciplinary or transdisciplinary).

- Share assessment roles among parents, other caregivers, and interdisciplinary team members.

- Rely on parent observations and judgments for hard-to-observe competencies (e.g., eating, dressing, playing with siblings).

- Reframe your assessment role as "orchestrator" of authentic assessment.

- Spread team assessment activities over time (e.g., 15–30 days) rather than the traditional one-shot, 45-minute testing model.

- Sample skills only in natural or analog contexts, relying on several people.

- Use probes to sample expected skills in the proper context (e.g., math problems at a desk, social communication on the playground).

- Ensure samples over several situations and occasions.

- Employ materials that are easy to understand, jargon-free, and written in a language common to all team members.

- Use several metrics to portray curricular performance (e.g., developmental rate − developmental age / chronological age × 100; true standard scores; age scores).

- Use technology (e.g., personal digital assistant, videotapes, audiotapes, pictures) to collect ecological data for support and validation.

Table 4.2.   Authentic assessment in action for best practices in eligibility determination

Authentic dimension	Authentic best practices in eligibility determination
Why?	To document the extent to which a child's developmental scores align with state standards for entry into early intervention services by signifying a delay in development
	To generate data on the child's functional profile of strengths, limitations, and instructional support needs to initiate the process of individualized program planning
	To identify "hidden" strengths in functional capabilities via alternate and universal designs
What?	Profile of functional capabilities across six developmental domains and the interrelatedness/interdependence of the child's development
	Emphasis on social-behavioral and self-regulatory skills, early literacy skills, and social-communication skills
Who?	Parents
	Other familiar caregivers
	Interdisciplinary professionals who are familiar with and knowledgeable about the child, development, and appropriate interventions and/or services
Where?	In the home
	In child care
	In early childhood classrooms
	In school-based pre-K programs
	In family support centers
	In community centers: recreation centers, churches
	In Head Start and Early Head Start programs
When?	As soon as the screening test results are confirmed by full authentic assessments
	When the parent officially requests a multidisciplinary evaluation
	(Data should be synthesized across several representative times and occasions [e.g., days, weeks, months].)
How?	Recommended measures: *AEPS®, ABAS-II, DOCS, ICAP™, BDI-2* (with recommended modifications in the future)
	Recommended practices:
	• Use *AEPS®* as the best field-validated curriculum-embedded system to link eligibility and programming via response to intervention cut-off scores.
	• Use *ABAS–II* as the best field-validated curriculum-referenced measure to link eligibility and programming via national normative standard scores and combined parent and provider data.
	• Use the *DOCS* as one of the most authentic systems for both eligibility and initial goal planning via national normative standard scores; field-validated in longitudinal studies.
	• Use *ICAP™* as a nationally normed measure to also identify critical therapeutic services and service delivery arrangements for the child based on the assessments.
	• Petition the publisher of the *BDI-2* and its authors to enhance the authenticity, utility, and promise of the *BDI-2* in the following ways: 1) eliminate the test kit of fixed objects; 2) revise the item content of the cognitive and language subtests so that the behaviors are directly observable in natural settings; and 3) conduct national, in situ field-validation trials on the *BDI-2* so that it will have been truly validated for the specific purpose of eligibility determination.

Key: ABAS-II, Adaptive Behavior Assessment System–Second Edition (Harrison & Oakland, 2003); AEPS®, Assessment, Evaluation, and Programming System for Infants and Children, Second Edition (Bricker, 2002); BDI-2, Battelle Developmental Inventory, Second Edition (Newborg, 2004); DOCS, Developmental Observation Checklist System (Hresko, Miguel, Sherbenou, & Burton, 1994); ICAP™, Inventory for Client and Agency Planning™, (Bruininks, Hill, Weatherman, & Woodcock, 1986).

Individualized Programming and Performance Monitoring

"Every child is an individual" and "individualized education" are clichés we have all heard over and over. An examination of "individualized plans" for children, however, often reveals remarkable similarities despite the intent to individualize. It is not uncommon to see objectives and comments that appear to have been cut and pasted from one plan to another. There may be, and even *should be*, great similarities among objectives for children of the same age, but individualized plans for children with developmental needs should certainly include rather specific objectives. For example, one should be able to discriminate Billy's plan from Susan's plan (with their names removed). An individual plan must be tailored to the child. The child's plan should be clear and able to be shared with parents and professionals who help the child. But what information is supplied to teachers who will be responsible for the education of the students in their programs? The scores and syndrome labels provided are of little to no help in identifying the goals and specific objectives professionals need; such "information" has little *treatment validity*. In fact, a case can be made that the scores and labels associated with normative, psychometric testing are actually detrimental and produce distorted expectations and stigma.

Fortunately, curriculum-based assessment (CBA) is recognized as the most useful form of assessment for truly helping plan for children with special needs. An appropriate CBA can be used to identify starting points, plan the child's program, and track performance and progress over time. Furthermore, an appropriate CBA provides a common language that facilitates cooperation among professionals and parents. We provide the following definitions of *curriculum* and *CBA* to set the stage for this preeminent purpose for authentic assessment.

Curriculum refers to an organized framework in which the content of what children are to learn, the processes through which they achieve identified outcomes, and the changes in their performance over time are specified. A curriculum should guide 1) *what* to teach, 2) *how* to teach most effectively, 3) *where* to teach, and 4) *how* to know if instruction was successful.

We can think of a curriculum as a road map. First, we identify where we are (starting points). Second, we specify where we want to go (goals). Third, we plan the routes we can take to get to the destinations. We may encounter obstacles and detours, requiring revisions of the plan. At any time, we can share the itinerary, travel plans, progress, and challenges on the way with other professionals and parents. It also should be noted that curricula are available for children with varying types and levels of special needs. Sometimes, it is useful to select a specific curriculum that addresses the special needs of children with significant sensory, motor, affective, or cognitive differences. These curricula offer objectives and teaching suggestions suited to special challenges.

To select an appropriate curriculum, consider several factors (in addition to the eight standards for authentic assessment):

1. Sometimes, there is a great advantage to selecting a curriculum that encompasses a wide age range. This is especially helpful when a child is making the transition from an infant to a preschool program. A curriculum with a compre-

hensive age range greatly reduces many of the issues experienced in making the transition from one program to the next. An increasing number of curricular materials provide an inclusive array of objectives, providing seamless interagency planning.

2. Although a child may have disability-specific difficulties (e.g., gross motor), most professionals choose curricular materials that address all developmental/functional domains. Progress within all areas of development is our overall goal rather than preoccupation with special difficulties.

3. Curricular materials can offer real help for including parents in selecting initial objectives, planning goals, designing interventions, and verifying the child's progress (a social validity measure to confirm the teacher's evaluation of the child's status). Some curricula include parent-specific materials that enable parents to assess children's functioning at home and in the community and to help their children practice new skills in authentic settings.

4. Increasingly, children with special needs are part of programs that are inclusive or blended (i.e., encompass children with a spectrum of abilities and needs). Playing and learning alongside children of typical development has become a real priority, and curricula are available that promote participation among children. Cross-age activities, integrative projects, and unit plans are included in some curricular materials; these can be of great assistance in promoting inclusion. For further inclusion, a curriculum may recommend teaching strategies that proceed from disability-specific to more typical tactics (e.g., one-to-one sessions, to small group, to whole-class instruction). A curriculum that is applicable for all children being served further promotes the success of inclusive efforts.

5. The emphasis on documenting child performance gives even greater prominence to the curriculum as a tool for ongoing assessment. Measures such as intelligence tests and general developmental scales are practically useless for detecting child progress within a program; these measures are global and lack the specificity and sensitivity for detecting and displaying child performance and progress. An appropriate curriculum can be the major basis for documenting the great advances in skills that can be registered by the curriculum within a high-quality ECI program.

In summary, selecting and using the right curriculum—one that includes assessment—equips the professional with materials and practices for profiling a child's functional status (i.e., determining who needs to learn what), for planning a program to advance child skills, for meaningfully involving parents in planning and assessing progress, and for documenting program impact.

Table 4.3 offers suggestions on applying authentic assessment for best practices in individualized programming and performance monitoring. Within this summary, several features are noteworthy because of their direct impact on best practices. To actually apply authentic assessment for programming and performance monitoring, professionals and their programs must make systemic changes in the traditional routines and timelines to meet best practices. The following guidelines outline some of these steps:

Table 4.3. Authentic assessment in action for best practices in individualized programming and performance monitoring

Authentic dimension	Authentic best practices for individualized programming and monitoring
Why?	To determine children's current level of performance
	To match instruction to children's need, interests, and preferences as well as family priorities and concerns
	To document changes in children's performance over time
What?	Children's performance across all areas of development (e.g., motor, communication, social, adaptive) and content (e.g., literacy, math)
	Children's interests and preferences
	Family priorities and concerns
Who?	Parents
	Other familiar caregivers
	Interdisciplinary professionals who are familiar and knowledgeable about the child, development, and appropriate interventions and/or services
Where?	In the home
	In child care
	In early childhood classrooms
	In school-based pre-K programs
	In family support centers
	In community centers: recreation centers, churches
	In Head Start and Early Head Start programs
When?	At the start of services to set "baseline" performance and identify priorities
	Entire curriculum-based assessment (CBA) readministered for all children 2–4 times a year to track performance
	Select portions of the CBA readministered for select children who need supported practice on targeted areas (e.g., participation, play with objects, manipulation of objects)
	Daily and/or weekly data collected on select skills from CBA for individual children that are targeted as priority needs for intensive instruction
How?	Recommended measures: *AEPS®, CCITSN, CCPSN, HELP®, The OR Project, Every Move Counts*
	Recommended practices:
	• Use the *AEPS®, CCITSN, CCPSN,* or *HELP®* to plan objectives and strategies and evaluate performances for young children with special needs in inclusive programs.
	• Use the *The OR Project* or *Every Move Counts* to plan and promote for young children with significant sensory and functional limitations.

Key: AEPS®, Assessment, Evaluation, and Programming System for Infants and Children, Second Edition (Bricker, 2002); CCITSN, The Carolina Curriculum for Infants and Toddlers with Special Needs, Third Edition (Johnson-Martin, Attermeier, & Hacker, 2004b); CCPSN, The Carolina Curriculum for Preschoolers with Special Needs, Second Edition (Johnson-Martin, Hacker, & Attermeier, 2004); Every Move Counts, Every Move Counts: Sensory-Based Communication Techniques (Korsten, Dunn, Foss, & Francke, 1993); HELP®, HELP®–the Hawaii Early Learning Profile® (Holt, Gilles, Holt, & Davids, 2004; Parks, 2007); The OR Project, The Oregon Project for Preschool Children who are Blind or Visually Impaired, 6th edition (Anderson et al., 2007).

- Choose a CBA that is comprehensive (i.e., covers all developmental and content areas) and can be used with all children being served.

- Ensure that family members and other familiar caregivers have opportunities to discuss the child's performance across daily activities as well as resources, priorities, and concerns.

- Summarize assessment information and identify patterns in children's development that in turn assist teams in identifying individual—as well as groups of children's—needs for instruction.

- Use a tiered model of progress monitoring and performance reporting to ensure data-driven decision making and appropriate revisions to instructional efforts.

- Use a combination of summary methods (e.g., visual, numerical, narrative) to depict children's performance at a given point in time as well as their performance over time (i.e., how they are responding to instruction).

Program Outcomes Evaluation

Increasingly, ECI programs are required by funding agencies to collect ongoing information on improvements in their quality and their apparent effectiveness for children and families. Simply, human services agencies must justify their continued existence! Head Start has been under the most recent scrutiny regarding its capacity to promote early school success for young children who are at risk due to limitations in acquiring early literacy skills.

Family support programs must demonstrate that parents and families are satisfied with the services that they receive, and changes in family's coping skills, reduction in stress, and capacity to support their children must be documented. Early intervention programs for children with disabilities and challenges must document that the intensity of services promotes developmental progress, even for the most complex child issues.

Within ECI, *program outcomes evaluation* can be defined as an ongoing process of formative and summative analysis of the interrelationship among child, program, family, and programmatic factors that produce beneficial outcomes for young children and families. Program evaluation not only requires an evaluation research design but also specific measurement strategies (i.e., both qualitative and quantitative) that can capture ongoing progress of children and changes in program quality and be sensitive to improvements over time. Most program evaluators employed by ECI programs use a collaborative approach of "participatory action research" to engage stakeholders in designing and implementing their own research (Bagnato et al., 2004); this process increases buy-in and also fosters competence and confidence about conducting their own program evaluations. In terms of measurement requirements (as described previously), *formative evaluation* refers to assessment that is ongoing (e.g., daily, weekly, monthly) and that can be used to modify and improve ongoing program practices. *Summative evaluation* refers to measurement strategies to document overall program impact on child and family outcomes at the end of a specified time (typically end of the program year). Because of the developmental and functional approach common to most programs within ECI, the same measures often can serve both formative and summative purposes.

Table 4.4 summarizes and offers suggestions on applying the essential features of authentic assessment for program outcomes evaluation. Within this summary, several features are noteworthy because of their direct impact on best practices.

Table 4.4. Authentic assessment in action for best practices in program outcomes evaluation

Authentic dimension	Authentic best practices in program outcomes evaluation
Why?	To implement ongoing programmatic evaluation of child, family, and program factors to quickly modify and improve those practices for quality improvement purposes
	To document program quality, impact, and outcomes on child, family, and program elements to support estimates of "efficacy"
	To provide efficient and tangible conclusions about program quality and outcomes for funders, community stakeholders, and consumers
What?	Profiles of developmental status and progress of children during intervention
	Profiles of parent and/or family status and progress during intervention
	Profiles of program quality (e.g., including teaching practices, service delivery)
Who?	Parents
	Other caregivers
	Interdisciplinary professionals who are familiar and knowledgeable about the child
Where?	In the home
	In child care
	In early childhood classrooms
	In school-based pre-K programs
	In family support centers
	In community centers: recreation centers, churches
	In Head Start and Early Head Start programs
When?	At a minimum, over three time points to cover the intervention period (e.g., September, January, and May for a typical early childhood intervention [ECI] program)
How?	Recommended measures: *DOCS, BSSI-3, ICAP™, ABAS-II, WSS*
	Recommended practices:
	• Use the *DOCS* transactional measurement "system" (e.g., Developmental Checklist, Parental Stress and Support Checklist, Adjustment Behavior Checklist) as an integrated program evaluation framework using an integrated national norm group across the three measures; *DOCS* has been field-validated for this specific purpose over 10 years in longitudinal ECI research with typical and atypical groups in Pennsylvania (see Bagnato, 2002; Bagnato et al., 2004).
	• Use the *BSSI-3* as a simple and efficient, yet sensitive and powerful, authentic appraisal of children's early learning skills aligned with state standards; *BSSI-3* has been field-validated in ECI research in the Pre-K Counts in Pennsylvania initiative on at-risk children and 30 school district–community partnerships.
	• Use *ICAP™* as a nationally normed measure to identify critical therapeutic services and service delivery arrangements for a child based on assessments; the *ICAP™* can be used over time to document program impact and outcomes correlated with service intensity.
	• Use *ABAS-II* as the best field-validated system to synthesize parent and provider data for program evaluation purposes; this system has been field-validated for program outcomes evaluation purposes in Pennsylvania for children ages 0–3 and 3–5 in early intervention—The Pennsylvania Early Intervention Outcomes Study (Bagnato et al., 2006).
	• Use the *WSS* for ongoing appraisal of child performance within classroom settings; this system has been used in statewide program evaluation data collection efforts in Pennsylvania and Minnesota.

Key: ABAS-II, Adaptive Behavior Assessment System–Second Edition (Harrison & Oakland, 2003); *BSSI-3, Basic School Skills Inventory—Third Edition* (Hammill, Leigh, Pearson, & Maddox, 1998); *DOCS, Developmental Observation Checklist System* (Hresko, Miguel, Sherbenou, & Burton, 1994); *ICAP™, Inventory for Client and Agency Planning™* (Bruininks, Hill, Weatherman, & Woodcock, 1986); *WSS, The Work Sampling System®* (Meisels, Marsden, Jablon, Dorfman, & Dichtelmiller, 1998).

To actually apply authentic assessment for program outcomes evaluation purposes, professionals and their programs can follow these guidelines:

- Choose, optimally, an authentic measurement system that integrates several separate scales to measure child, family, and program variables.

- Select an integrated system that is simple to use yet sensitive in capturing evidence of change for all variables.

- Choose a system that has specific field-validation evidence to support its use in community-based program outcomes evaluation.

- Require and infuse the use of the system by all professionals in the ECI program as a normal part of their everyday work routines.

- Purchase or create an integrated computer database network (local area network, or LAN) that enables quick input of data and responsive reports to enable administrators to use the data for formative changes in program practices.

Accountability

Much controversy surrounds the testing of infants, toddlers, and preschoolers, particularly those with disabilities and delays, but no measurement purpose generates more controversy than accountability. *Accountability* within ECI can be defined as the state and federal government requirement of ECI programs to gather child status and progress data (i.e., entry and exit), using uniform instruments so as to determine children's attainment of predetermined objectives, to compare the quality of programs for unspecified but implied corrective actions.

Arguably, the most famous accountability effort is contained in the No Child Left Behind (NCLB) Act of 2001 (PL 107-110) legislation and regulations. The accountability movement associated with NCLB pressures ECI to employ a downward extension of a "tests and testing" school-age model. Advocates for young children, although proponents of accountability, are concerned that existing models are detrimental not only to children but also to their families and the programs and personnel who serve them (Harbin, Rous, & McLean, 2005).

Although the ECI field generally supports the need to monitor the progress of young children, little agreement exists on how desired information should be obtained; who should collect the information; and, perhaps most importantly, how the information should be summarized and interpreted. Moreover, there is a dearth of research on ECI accountability assessment practices. Many of the current efforts are driven by K–12 models or, worse yet, appear to parallel earlier national accountability mandates under the National Reporting System (NRS) initiated by the Head Start Bureau. The now defunct NRS was the first national effort to collect uniform outcomes data in Head Start programs; much justified controversy accompanied the NRS as an exemplar of what *not* to do (i.e., engage in conventional testing procedures, focus on limited areas of development, use measurements with no relationship to curricular goals) when assessing for accountability purposes.

Many regulations are being proposed and implemented without regard for professional best practices, without evidence on the usefulness and benefits of such regulations to children and families, and in the glaring absence of research. In particular, state and federal outcome indicators (e.g., Office of Special Education Programs) are being proposed to document accountability.

Although accountability methods and standards must meet professional standards, they must also be sensible and equitable. Policies must reflect the uniqueness and diversity of the ECI field (e.g., settings in which children spend time, education level of teachers) compared with school-age intervention and the individual needs of vulnerable young children and families. It is impossible to craft constructive policies without the integral participation of professionals and researchers who work daily in this field. We advocate for such sensible, equitable, and professionally sanctioned policies and practices.

In our view, there are three overriding requirements for accountability assessments in ECI:

1. The measure has been designed specifically for accountability purposes.

2. The measure has a clear evidence base, having been field-validated for accountability purposes in systemwide studies.

3. The measure adheres to the eight standards for developmentally appropriate and authentic assessment in this book and championed by the ECI professional organizations.

Table 4.5 summarizes and offers suggestions on applying the essential features of authentic assessment for accountability. As stated previously, it is important to recognize the current scarcity of evidence for professional practices regarding assessment for accountability. In the meantime, the following are some recommendations to guide your practice:

- No current conventional or authentic assessment system is adequate for use in accountability in terms of design, simplicity, utility, and evidence base.

- The *Early Development Instrument* (*EDI*; Offord Centre for Child Studies, 2007/ 2008) and perhaps the *The Work Sampling System*® (*WSS*; Meisels, Marsden, Jablon, Dorfman, & Dichtelmiller, 1998) have some of the essential characteristics for credible accountability purposes.

- Colorado, Kentucky, and Pennsylvania (and perhaps other states) have been in the forefront of developing statewide ECI assessment for accountability that links measures, content, standards, and computer databases; they can serve as helpful consultants to others in this formative and still ill-defined effort.

- Ensure that your accountability assessment systems give prominence to assessments of program and family status as well as child progress. Never report child outcome data in the absence of program and family data. Always conduct an analysis and interpretation of the impact of the program variables on child and family outcomes; in this way, program evaluation research and accountability purposes always coincide.

- Choose measurement methods for accountability that have a credible basis for use, chief of which is a clear evidence base to fulfill this ECI purpose.

Table 4.5.   Authentic assessment in action for best practices in accountability

Authentic dimension	Authentic best practices in accountability
Why?	To implement ongoing evaluation of child status and progress during participation in an early childhood intervention (ECI) program
	To align child status, performance, and progress data to uniform state and national outcome standards that recognize that patterns of progress are individual and that, for some children with severe disabilities, "maintaining developmental course" is a good outcome
	To collect complementary data on program and service characteristics
	To apply outcomes of accountability assessments to improve program practices rather than for sanctioning teachers or programs
What?	Profiles of developmental status and progress for children during intervention
	Profiles of parent and/or family status and progress during intervention
	Profiles of program quality (e.g., teaching practices, service delivery)
Who?	Parents
	Other caregivers
	Interdisciplinary professionals who are familiar and knowledgeable about the child
Where?	In the home
	In child care
	In early childhood classrooms
	In school-based pre-K programs
	In family support centers
	In community centers: recreation centers, churches
	In Head Start and Early Head Start programs
When?	At a minimum, over three time points to cover the intervention period (e.g., September, January, and May for a typical ECI program)
	(Using only entry and exit assessments represents a too limited sample for any meaningful interpretation.)
How?	Recommended measures: No conventional or authentic assessment system has been designed specifically for accountability purposes in ECI. Few can show an evidence base for such use. The current best bets, given both promising features and some evidence base, are *AEPS®, DOCS, BSSI-3, ABAS-II, WSS,* and *EDI.*
	Recommended practices:
	• Use the *AEPS®* as a uniform programwide measurement system to integrate the "linked" purposes of eligibility, program planning and progress monitoring, and accountability. Content has been aligned with many state early learning standards and has been sorted into the OSEP categories; states use the *AEPS®* for this purpose in their data systems.
	• Use the *DOCS* transactional measurement system (i.e., Developmental Checklist, Parental Stress and Support Checklist, Adjustment Behavior Checklist) as an integrated program evaluation framework using an integrated national norm group across the three measures; *DOCS* has been field-validated for this specific purpose over 10 years in longitudinal ECI research with typical and atypical groups in Pennsylvania (see Bagnato, 2002; Bagnato et al., 2004).
	• Use the *BSSI* as a simple and efficient, yet sensitive and powerful, authentic appraisal of children's early learning skills aligned with state standards; the *BSSI* has been field-validated in ECI research in the Pre-K Counts in Pennsylvania initiative on at-risk children and 30 school-district–community partnerships.
	• Use the *ABAS–II* as the best field-validated system for accountability purposes in Pennsylvania for children 0–3 and 3–5 in early intervention (Bagnato et al., 2006); *ABAS–II* content has been cross-walked to PA early learning standards and OSEP categories.
	• Use the *WSS* for ongoing appraisal of child performance within classroom settings. This system is required for use in statewide accountability efforts in Pennsylvania in all types of ECI programs; the content is cross-walked to PA early learning standards.
	• Review and consider the use of the *EDI* for accountability purposes given its development for "epidemiological" research in Australia and Canada. It is simple to use but effective.

Key: ABAS-II, Adaptive Behavior Assessment System–Second Edition (Harrison & Oakland, 2003); *AEPS®, Assessment, Evaluation, and Programming System for Infants and Children, Second Edition* (Bricker, 2002); *BSSI-3, Basic School Skills Inventory—Third Edition* (Hammill, Leigh, Pearson, & Maddox, 1998); *DOCS, Developmental Observation Checklist System* (Hresko, Miguel, Sherbenou, & Burton, 1994); *EDI, Early Development Instrument* (Offord Centre for Child Studies; 2007/2008); *WSS, The Work Sampling System®* (Meisels, Marsden, Jablon, Dorfman, & Dichtelmiller, 1998).

Summary

In this chapter, we have presented guidelines for authentic assessment in action to fulfill five specific ECI purposes: screening, eligibility, program planning and progress monitoring, program outcomes evaluation, and accountability. We believe that the overview of the issues under each purpose and the "action" tables that align recommended practices with the authentic assessment motif from Chapter 2 will generate debate and consensus discussion within your programs to enhance your actual use of authentic assessment.

In Chapter 5, the final chapter of Section I, we attempt to forecast trends in authentic assessment based on some unique model developments that have occurred since 2000. We hope that these profiles will spur interest and innovation in authentic assessment by the next generation of interdisciplinary researchers in ECI.

5

What Are "Forecasts" of Promising Practices in Authentic Assessment?

In Section II, we provide detailed reviews of the many commercially available authentic assessments that professionals can choose and use in their daily work with young children. There is a surprising array of innovative, useful, and validated authentic tools that are available to link assessment and intervention as an alternative to conventional testing. Nevertheless, our design and developmental research on appropriate assessments for young children, especially those with disabilities, is incomplete and insufficient. As asserted, conventional tests are generally inadequate in meeting all standards, but most authentic measures themselves are rated by consumers and experts to have weak design features with regard to universality, some aspects of utility, collaboration, and sensitivity.

We have been "holding our finger to the wind" to forecast new and creative developments in authentic assessment that represent next-step innovations to enable this option to be realized. In the following segments, we review some of best of these innovations under the following formats: portable and computer-assisted database; functional classification; performance probes; epidemiological assessment; and informed opinion.

Portable and Computer-Assisted Database Formats

Advancements in computer and microtechnology have the promise to transform traditional paper-and-pencil recording assessment formats. Computer technology uses responsive and integrated formats to make authentic assessment more portable, more immediate, and unobtrusive. Currently, some publishing companies sell assessment content on handheld personal digital assistants, which makes the assessment direct and immediate. Further advancements in this arena could transform authentic assessment, making portable and computer-assisted database formats the preferred approach for data collection in our field. Perhaps the ultimate format would be to have audio and video recordings that collect and score data automatically as children play with objects and interact with adults and peers. Obviously, some types of behavior are more amenable to this approach than others.

Perhaps the best current example of a computer-microtechnology format for assessment in natural environments is Language ENvironment Analysis (LENA) System. Research has shown that children who receive exemplary and quality early childhood care are likely to outperform their peers in cognitive and language abilities in the first 3 years of life (Burchinal & Roberts, 1996). Furthermore, high-quality early education has been associated with higher levels of cognitive and mathematics performance in the elementary school years (Campbell & Ramey, 1995). In the past, the quality of early childhood education often was defined by structural components (e.g., safety, adult–child ratios, schedule, physical environment). Today's research efforts concentrate on the actual processes and ever-changing interactions in the social environment. In 1995, Betty Hart and Todd Risley published groundbreaking research results demonstrating a strong correlation between adult spoken words and child language outcomes. This research was also the basis for a landmark book: *Meaningful Differences in the Everyday Experience of Young American Children* (Hart & Risley, 1995). The implications of Hart and Risley's exploration has led to a broad understanding that the quality of early childhood education is dependent less on structural components and more on the frequency and intensity of teacher–child and parent–child interactions.

It has been well documented that naturalistic communication strategies have great potential to improve teacher–child interactions and early language outcomes in both home and center-based settings (Warren, Yoder, & Leew, 2002; Wilcox & Shannon, 1998). Naturalistic communication strategies are interventions with a profound evidence base that are widely supported in the field of early childhood for their effectiveness and flexibility when embedded in the context of regular activities and routines. The strategies have been shown to improve the communication and language of children with diverse learning abilities, specifically those who are from disadvantaged backgrounds, have developmental disabilities, or are on the autism spectrum (Allen & Cowen, 2008). It is important to note, however, that even the most remarkable intervention will only be effective if implemented with fidelity.

Naturalistic communication strategies are easy to implement, but measuring the frequency and intensity of ongoing teacher–child interactions presents a seemingly impossible task. In fact, very little is actually known regarding the extent to which naturalistic communication interventions are presently being implemented in early childhood programs. Until recently, recording every utterance of a child and environmental circumstances would require substantial funding and an army of research assistants; however, the LENA System holds promise to make such information collection possible.

The LENA System is the world's first automatic natural language environment analysis system (LENA Foundation, 2008). The LENA System was developed by the LENA Foundation, a not-for-profit organization based in Boulder, Colorado. The system was inspired by Hart and Risley's research. The goal for the LENA System's automatic vocalization assessment is to provide researchers, parents, and other early childhood professionals with an automated tool that can be used to screen children for language delays and to generate an objective expressive language development estimate as part of an overall evaluation, diagnostic, and treatment process. In particular, the LENA System is intended to minimize the effects of confounds inherent to evaluation in a clinical setting by collecting language data in the natural environment in an authentic and unobtrusive manner.

The following features highlight the unique elements of the LENA System:

- Uses a digital microprocessor and automatic speech-recognition technology to capture every utterance between caregivers and child, estimating the number of adult words, conversational turns, and child vocalizations

- Records up to 16 hours of continuous speech data

- Supports diagnosis, intervention, and research on the delays, disorders, and development of language for children 2–48 months of age

- Analyzes the natural language environment, screens for language delays, and generates expressive language estimates

- Provides probability rating for at-risk behavior based on the acoustic features in the voice signal of the child from a single day-long recording (see the automatic autism screen element of the LENA System)

- Allows for automatic processing of up to 120 day-long audio files per month

- Generates statistical information about the child's expressive language development and the quality of adult–child interactions with technical adequacy comparable to conventional clinical measures

- Provides a measure of intervention fidelity

- Provides percentile rankings for adult word counts, conversational turns, and child vocalizations compared with a normative sample as well as output reports given in monthly, daily, hourly, and 5-minute increments

- Allows export of entire audio file into other software programs for transcription and detailed acoustic analysis

- Provides developmental age for expressive and receptive language based on a 52-item parent-completed questionnaire

- Provides an automatic assessment of the sound distribution in the child's vocalizations, generating standard score information about a child's expressive language output on a given day (see the automatic vocalization assessment element of the LENA System)

- Provides information about the amount of time a child is exposed to television and other electronic media throughout the day

- Includes field-validation data on more than 465 children comprising 5,550 12- to 16-hour recording sessions, including the following:

    4,880 hours from 300 recordings contributed by 31 families of children diagnosed with a language delay

    2,260 hours from 145 recordings contributed by 21 Spanish-speaking families

    4,250 hours from 260 recordings contributed by 34 families of children diagnosed with autism

For more extensive information, refer to the LENA Foundation's natural language corpus (http://www.lenafoundation.org/DataServices/Database.aspx).

The LENA System illustrates an approach for the future of authentic assessment; the tie to technology will enable professionals and parents to collaborate in unique ways to gain a truly representative picture of the child's capabilities and the impact of social and physical environmental factors on the child's competence. The most needed improvements are to 1) reduce the cost to make broad use possible by early childhood programs and 2) combine the LENA System with a video format for complete appraisal.

Functional Classification Systems

For years, researchers, policy makers, and practitioners alike have advocated for the development, design, and use of assessment and planning frameworks for individuals with disabilities that cross interdisciplinary fields—especially education and medicine. Almost 50 years ago, G.D. Stevens (1962) pioneered and advocated a special education taxonomy based on human functioning (e.g., communication, mobility), rather than topography or disease, that would reduce jargon and facilitate cross-professional use.

In 1980, the World Health Organization (WHO) published the first version of its classification system, the *International Classification of Impairments, Disability and Health*. Now called the *International Classification of Functioning, Disability and Health* (*ICF*; WHO, 2001), it continues to provide a unified and standard framework for the description of health and health-related states. The *ICF* systematically sorts and describes domains for a person with a particular health condition and functional capabilities, providing a uniform and standardized tool that can be used across disciplines worldwide.

The Institute of Medicine's report, *The Future of Disability in America*, made 18 recommendations, 3 of which regarded the advantages of using the *ICF* in the United States (Committee on Disability in America, Jette, & Field, 2007):

- *Recommendation 2.1*: Adoption of *ICF* by key agencies (Centers for Disease Control, Census Bureau, Bureau of Labor Statistics, Interagency Committee on Disability Research) as conceptual framework for disability monitoring and aligning disability measures with *ICF*

- *Recommendation 6.1*: Collaborative process to identify research priorities on *ICF* environmental factors

- *Recommendation 10.3*: Governmentwide inventory of disability research activities to facilitate cross-agency strategic planning and priority setting

The U.S. Department of Education has adopted the use of a selected *ICF* (*International Classification of Functioning, Disability and Health: Children and Youth Version,* or *ICF-CY*) in its *Early Intervention Databook* (Version 1.0). This is a good start in encouraging other agencies to take the same action (Simeonsson, 2006).

Description of the *ICF* Formats

The *ICF* and the *ICF-CY* (WHO, 2007a) represent innovative and landmark functional classification formats from the WHO that can be used by all countries and all professional disciplines for individuals with disabilities. The *ICF* formats consist of the dimensions sketched in Figure 5.1. Part 1 is functioning and disability, which includes body functions and structures, activities and participation, and contextual factors.

Body functions represent the physiological functions of body systems. The body functions include mental functions; sensory functions and pain; voice and speech functions; functions of the cardiovascular, hematological, immunological, and respiratory systems; functions of the digestive, metabolic, and endocrine systems; genitourinary and reproductive functions; neuromusculoskeletal and movement-related functions; and functions of the skin and related structures.

Body structures are anatomical parts of the body, such as organs of the body. There are structures of the nervous system; the eye, ear, and related structures; structures involved in voice and speech; structures of the cardiovascular, immunological, and respiratory systems; structures related to the digestive, metabolic, and endocrine systems; structures related to the genitourinary and reproductive system; structures related to movement; and skin and related structures. Significant problems, deviation, or loss of body function and structure is described as *impairment*.

Activity is the execution of a task or action by an individual. Activity limitation may arise when an individual has difficulty in executing activities. *Participation* is defined as involvement in a life situation. There could be participation restriction when an individual experiences problems in involvement in life situa-

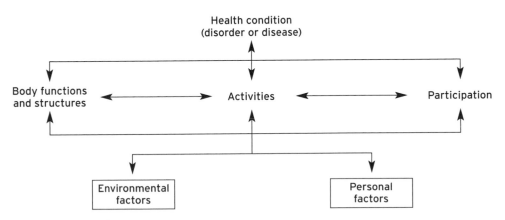

Figure 5.1.   Dimensions of the *International Classification of Functioning, Disability and Health* (World Health Organization [WHO], 2001) and the *International Classification of Functioning, Disability and Health: Children and Youth Version* (WHO, 2007a). (From WHO. [2001]. *International classification of functioning, disability and health: ICF-CY* [p. 18]. Geneva: Author; reprinted by permission.)

tions. Within this domain are learning and applying knowledge; general tasks and demands; communication; mobility; self-care; domestic life; interpersonal interactions and relationships; major life areas; and community, social, and civic life.

Environment factors include the physical, social, and attitudinal environments in which people live and conduct their lives. This domain includes products and technology; natural environment and human-made changes to environment; support and relationships; attitudes; and services, systems, and policies.

Personal factors are the internal influences that affect functioning and disability. The domain of personal factors include age, race, gender, food preferences, individual psychological assets, fitness, lifestyle, habits, upbringing, coping styles, education, social background, and other health conditions.

Development and Need for the Children and Youth Version

Professionals need to adopt a common set of developmentally appropriate standards for use with children, but educational and medical professionals often do not share a common perspective on diagnoses of young children or the efficacy of early childhood intervention. The *ICF-CY* is a unique version of the *ICF* geared specifically toward children and youth younger than 18 years old.

The need for a children and youth version of the *ICF* was due to the failure of the *ICF* to describe health conditions that occur early in the lifespan. A child is dynamic in nature, making the transition from childhood to adulthood; however, the *ICF* is not developmental in nature and could not provide the precursors to adult behaviors. Indicators of functional risks are important for disease prevention and early intervention. According to Lollar and Simeonsson (2005), the *ICF-CY* framework provides a developmental and behavioral approach for understanding functioning in children and youth that the *ICF* did not provide. The *ICF-CY* has been used in international research and practice to plan individualized education programs (IEPs) for children with developmental disabilities (Tokunaga, 2008). The *ICF-CY* is derived from and is compatible to the *ICF*; however, it reflects the developmental stages of a child and contains a more detailed taxonomy regarding body functions and structures, activities, participation, and environments specific to infants, toddlers, children, and adolescents.

The expansion of the *ICF* to the *ICF-CY* involved the expansion of description, the assignment of content to unused codes, the modification of inclusion and exclusion criteria, and the expansion of qualifiers. The major components of the *ICF-CY* are the same as the components of the *ICF* from which it is derived. The *ICF-CY* also complements the *International Statistical Classification of Diseases and Related Health Problems, Tenth Revision* (ICD-10; WHO, 2007b) and provides the framework and standard language for the description of health and health-related states in children and youth. The *ICF-CY* offers a conceptual framework: a common language and terminology for documenting problems involving functions of the body, activity limitations, participation restrictions, and environmental factors seen in infancy, childhood, and adolescence. The framework can be used across disciplines and is intended for use by educators, researchers, clinicians, policy makers, and family members (WHO, 2007a).

The *ICF-CY* was developed with a four-foundational rationale: 1) the *practical* rationale based on the need for a comprehensive classification of childhood disability that will be used across service systems; 2) the *philosophical* rationale for a

classification system sensitive to the physical, social, and psychological characteristics of children and adolescents in the spirit of the implementation of the United
Nations (1998) Convention on the Rights of the Child regarding access to health
care, education, social, and other services; 3) the *taxonomical* rationale based on the
fact that the *ICF-CY*, as derived from the *ICF*, describes codes that will be useful in
assessing more mature functioning; and 4) the rationale of the *public health need* of
preventing childhood disability in the population. The *ICF-CY* provides a common
terminology for description of the health status, activity level, and participation restriction of infants, toddlers, children, and adolescents and the impact the environment plays in their well-being. It is used broadly in Europe and other countries for
the following purposes:

- Collecting and recording statistical data for management information systems

- Measuring quality of life, environmental factors, and other outcome measures

- Conducting clinical needs assessment, vocational assessment, and rehabilitation and outcome evaluation

- Guiding the development of health and disability policies and their implementation

- Designing curricula and to raise awareness for social action, such as awareness
  on the United Nations Convention on the Rights of Persons with Disabilities.

   The major factors relating to children that constitute the main theme of the
content of the *ICF-CY* are as follows:

- The child is seen in the context of the family because of the dependency on family from infancy to adulthood. The physical, social, and psychological development of the child is greatly influenced by interactions in the family.

- With regard to developmental delay, children and adolescents differ in the development of body function, structures, and skills. Variations in development
  seen in children and adolescents are defined in terms of developmental delays
  and are good indicators to identify children at risk of disabilities. The concept
  of *delay* or *lag* in the *ICF-CY*—a concept not necessary in the *ICF*—is a very important qualifier that must be considered in documenting problems of body
  functions, body structures, and activities and participation.

- Participation and environment

   The *ICF-CY* has domains for *activities* and *participation* that indicate what the
child is able or not able to do. These domains have two qualifiers: 1) the *performance qualifier* is what the individual does in his current environment and 2) the *capacity qualifier* signifies the individual's involvement in life situations. Activities
and participation can be limited or restricted in childhood and adolescent stages in
the form of delays or lags in the expected levels of activities and participations
(WHO, 2007a).
   Improved participation in the community and in life activities for individuals
with disabilities is one of the major purposes for early intervention; therefore, evaluating and monitoring participation and restriction in participation is needed to
define the success of a rehabilitation outcome (Perenboom & Chorus, 2003). There
has been a shifting of focus away from improvement in children's body functions

to a priority for social activity and participation of children with disabilities in life situations. This has become increasingly necessary due to the new classification of disease and health by the WHO, which emphasizes the potential environmental factors that might influence activities and participation (Mihaylov, Jarvis, Clover, & Beresford, 2004). Activities and participation for children mostly take place in their homes and school environments (Fevola, Bagnato, & Kronk, 2009).

Table 5.1 shows an example of the intersection among the *ICF-CY* codes, IEP objectives, *The Carolina Curriculum* (Johnson-Martin, Attermeier, & Hacker, 2004b; Johnson-Martin, Hacker, & Attermeier, 2004) objectives, and the *Vineland Adaptive Behavior Scales, Second Edition (VABS-II*; Sparrow, Cicchetti, & Balla, 2005) assessed content for a 3-year-old child with Down syndrome.

The most needed improvements to the *ICF-CY* to realize promise are as follows:

1. Recognize that the *ICF-CY* is NOT an assessment instrument but rather a universal classification framework that must be used in concert with existing tools.

2. Intersect the content of the *ICF-CY* with existing authentic assessment measures such as the *VABS-II* and *ABAS-II* (Harrison & Oakland, 2003; Kronk, 2004; Fevola, Bagnato, & Kronk, 2010).

3. Develop new measures that are short and efficient and that enable teams to "enter" at an appropriate level of the *ICF-CY* taxonomy to begin individualized planning.

4. Develop new codes for the *ICF-CY* that provide taxonomies for tiered interventions or modifications in social and physical environments to guide program planning.

5. Develop new measures of "participation" to advance the further development of the *ICF-CY* model.

Table 5.1. *ICF-CY* codes intersected with early childhood intervention authentic assessments and individualized education program (IEP) objectives

IEP goal	CCITSN/CCPSN objective	VABS-II objective	ICF-CY code
Uses 4-word sentences in conversation	15f: Uses complete sentences with adjectives	Uses sentence of 4–6 words	D1333: Acquires syntax
Reads common signs in community	Reads and obeys common signs	Names buildings and signs	D1402: Understands words in community
Initiates social interactions with peers and adults	14f: Sustains social conversation for several turns	Tells favorite activities	D3500 & D3501: Starts and sustains conversation
Names 10 uppercase letters	10u: Recognizes 10 letters	Recognizes 10 printed letters	D1400: Recognizes printed symbols
Reads 10 words in books	14g: Reads books to others	Reads 10 words	D1401: Sounds out words

Key: CCITSN, *The Carolina Curriculum for Infants and Toddlers with Special Needs, Third Edition* (Johnson-Martin, Attermeier, & Hacker, 2004b); CCPSN, *The Carolina Curriculum for Preschoolers with Special Needs, Second Edition* (Johnson-Martin, Hacker, & Attermeier, 2004); ICF-CY, *International Classification of Functioning, Disability and Health: Children and Youth Version* (WHO, 2007a); VABS-II, *Vineland Adaptive Behavior Scales, Second Edition* (Sparrow, Cicchetti, & Balla, 2005).

Performance Probes for Response to Intervention

There is a pressing need by early interventionists for brief and efficient assessment strategies for multiple purposes, including screening, identifying general intervention goals, and monitoring performance. In particular, practitioners need efficient tools to conduct classroom-based and programwide screenings for Tier 1 supports as they implement RTI models. Too many of our most popular and conventional assessment tools are diagnostic in nature, have few direct links to intervention, and are simply too time consuming to use and too expensive to purchase. The cost–benefit ratio for their use can no longer be sustained, especially under the new federal and state RTI mandates.

Since 2000, researchers have adopted the curriculum-based measurement and general outcome measurement methodology developed for school-age children and modified its content and process so that it fits early childhood intervention needs (Deno, 2003; VanDerHeyden, 2005). These modified methods of intermediate assessment enable teams to implement the three-tiered RTI process much more responsively. Of particular promise is the *Individual Growth and Development Indicators* (*IGDI*; Greenwood, Carta, Walker, Hughes, & Weathers, 2006; McConnell, McEvoy, & Priest, 2002), developed to assess infant and toddler communication, social, movement, and problem-solving skills.

Advantages of using the *IGDI* include the following:

- Can be used frequently

- Easy to conduct

- Provides a standardized and continuous measure during the first 3 years of life

- Generates a growth and development trajectory over time

- Documents both level and rate of developmental growth during intervention compared with peers

Four *IGDI* probes have been developed with key skill areas sampled:

1. *Early Communication Indicator:* Gestures, vocalizations, single-word utterances, multiple word utterances

2. *Early Movement Indicator:* Transition to position, grounded locomotion, throw/roll, trap/catch

3. *Early Social Indicator:* Positive nonverbal behavior, positive verbal behavior, negative behavior

4. *Early Problem-solving Indicator:* Looks, explores, functions, solutions

Researchers of the *IGDI* have conducted promising studies on the use of tools to accomplish various ECI purposes, including the following: screening quarterly or more often to generate growth curves and to identify risk status; determining eligibility compared with local norms; monitoring progress within and across developmental domains; and guiding the planning and evaluation of the impact of individualized interventions. The *IGDI* does not result in the planning of specific goals and objectives for individualized family service plan or IEP development.

The most needed improvements for the *IGDI* to realize promise are as follows:

1. Develop a parallel version or integrated version of the *IGDI* that is universally designed to assess the "functional" capabilities of young children in communication, movement, social behavior, and problem-solving skills rather than the topography of their behaviors.

2. Infuse flexibility in the standardized procedures of the *IGDI* so that it can become more authentic and be used naturally within the daily settings and routines of the home or preschool and not require fixed "administration."

3. Develop a companion curriculum and strategies to link with *IGDI* item content.

Epidemiological Measures of Developmental Status for Descriptive and Accountability Purposes

Most measures are designed for individual purposes such as diagnosis. Few measures have been validated and used to collect data on *populations* of children. In this regard, many measures are too long and too technical to complete for intended purposes, let alone for epidemiological purposes. Although data are collected on individual children, it is aggregated for population-level purposes. Arguably, accountability fits this description.

One of the most unique measures currently available, the *Early Development Instrument* (*EDI*; Janus & Offord, 2000), was developed in Australia and modified in Canada for both countries' National Longitudinal Surveys of Children and Youth. The *EDI* has been implemented on more than 290,000 children from 1998 to 2004. It is a universal measure of child development competencies for children ages 4 and 5 before they enter first grade. A 104-item checklist, the *EDI* is completed by kindergarten teachers in the second half of a school year. The measure samples landmark developmental skills in the following five functional domains:

1. Physical health and well-being

2. Social competence

3. Emotional maturity

4. Language and cognitive development

5. Communication and general knowledge

In addition, the *EDI* collects information on child demographic variables and other variables such as students who are learning English as a second language, students who have special needs, and other preschool variables.

The *EDI* was designed for exclusive use with whole populations of children and cannot be interpreted at an individual level for a diagnostic purpose. The following uses of the *EDI* illustrate its validated purposes:

•   Help communities assess how well they are doing in supporting young children

- Monitor changes in developmental status

- Serve as a population-level measure for interpreting outcomes for groups of children

- Yield results that could be used by communities to identify weak and strong sectors

- Encourage communities to mobilize and make plans to improve children's outcomes

- Sample a community's diverse population

- Improve program practices within regional centers

In Australia, a 4-year pilot study was completed in 60 communities involving 37,000 children from more than 1,000 primary schools. Results demonstrated that the *EDI* could be used successfully and efficiently by teachers to document individual child competencies. The *EDI* can be used within all departments of government, especially health and education, and can connect community programs to provide a national baseline to compare communities and regions so as to target and improve early childhood development opportunities. The *EDI* proved to be the perfect tool to mobilize community efforts for local children before they entered school. The *EDI* was slated to be implemented nationally in Australia in 2009.

The most needed improvements for the *EDI* to realize promise are as follows:

1. Develop a universally designed version of the *EDI* to sample the "landmark" functional capabilities of young children with disabilities.

2. Intersect the content of the *EDI* with Canadian and Australian early learning standards in the Ministries of Education.

3. Work with state Departments of Education in the United States to jointly use the *EDI* to enhance collaboration on broad international efforts to improve early childhood education.

Informed Opinion (Clinical Judgment)

Early interventionists, policy makers, and researchers recognize that traditional methods of detecting developmental delays fail to capture sufficient numbers of young children who need early intervention services and supports. Reported national incidence of delay and/or disability, and thus the need for services, is far greater than those currently receiving such services.

Clinical judgment or *informed opinion* is the federally sanctioned alternative method to promote early intervention eligibility determination. However, although numerous states have regulations that support the use of clinical judgment, no state or the federal government has produced an operational definition or methodology to guide professionals in producing reliable and valid decisions using clinical judgment. Because clinical judgment is practiced extensively in early intervention, is supported by federal regulations, and its use is expanded in regulatory revisions, steps must be taken to ensure that valid, reliable, and useful information results from its application.

Informed opinion, clinical judgment, refers to

The knowledgeable perceptions of caregivers and professionals about the elusive capabilities and contexts of children that must be defined and quantified so that an individual and a team can reach an accurate decision about a child's eligibility for early intervention. (Bagnato, McKeating-Esterle, & Bartolomasi, 2007, p. 1)

This definition suggests some of the practice characteristics that are common in the research literature and applicable to early intervention: 1) multisource information from knowledgeable caregivers across situations; 2) definitions to guide ratings on subtle, elusive attributes of the child; and 3) accurate consensus decision making by both parents and professionals.

Determining the true extent of delay and/or functional disability for infants and toddlers is difficult due to many factors but, particularly, to the inadequacies of most conventional developmental measures that render them inappropriate for young children: lack of universal design features, scripted examiner and child behaviors, unrepresentative standardization samples, and absence of prospective disability-specific field validations (Bagnato, 2007; Benn, 1994; Macey, Bagnato, Lehman, & Salaway, 2007; Shonkoff & Meisels, 1991).

Part C of the IDEA Amendments of 1997 (PL 105-17, 20 U.S.C. § 1432[5], 1435 [a][1]), in response to these limitations, mandates that informed clinical opinion be included in eligibility determination. IDEA 2004 (PL 101-476, 20 U.S.C. § 303.300) states that the use of informed clinical opinion is particularly warranted "when standardized instruments are unavailable, unreliable or inappropriate for use in measuring developmental delay or evaluating a diagnosed condition such as autism spectrum disorder or pervasive developmental delay." Recent revisions to the legislation (§ 303.320[b][2]) would require that "the lead agency allow qualified personnel to use their informed clinical opinion to assess a child's present level of functioning in each of the developmental areas identified in the proposed § 303.21 (a)(1) and to establish eligibility, even when other instruments fail to establish eligibility." Moreover, the IDEA revisions state that a child's medical and educational records can be reviewed to establish eligibility based on clinical judgment and informed clinical opinion regarding current functional capabilities without assessing either the child or family directly.

In light of the fact that clinical judgment is practiced extensively in early intervention and underscored by federal regulations and that its use is instituted in regulatory revisions, steps must be taken to ensure that valid, reliable, and useful information results from its application. Bagnato and colleagues at the Pennsylvania satellite for the TRACE Center for Excellence in Early Childhood Assessment published a research synthesis on clinical judgment and determined that the method has merit but limited prospective research support (Bagnato, Smith-Jones, Matesa, & McKeating-Esterle, 2006).

Because of federal mandates for using clinical judgment as an early detection strategy and a lack of an evidence base specific to early intervention, we conducted as a first step a pilot study in Pennsylvania. The study investigated the concurrent validity of a measure that compared a structured approach for documenting informed clinical opinions to performance-based assessments to document the comparative validity and accuracy in determining early intervention eli-

Table 5.2. Early clinical judgment measures

Instrument	Age range	Domains	Sample	Technical adequacy
SPECS and *Infant Developmental Team Program* (Bagnato & Neisworth, 1990)	Birth to 24 months and 24–72 months	Communication, Sensorimotor, Physical, Self-regulation, Cognition, Self-social Developmental Support, Behavioral, Communication, Gross/Fine Motor Support, Vision, Hearing and Medical Support, Special, Transition Support and Teamwork	1,300 children, 31% typical and 69% with developmental delays	Acceptable reliability for decision making for all 19 dimensions (*r* = .73–.93) Test–retest reliability (*r* = .88) Content and construct validity Classification accuracy for 22 disability categories (*r* = .64–.99) Discriminant function (*r* = .83)
ABILITIES Index (Simeonsson & Bailey, 1991)	Birth–21 months	Audition, Behavior and Social Skills, Intellectual Function, Limbs, Intentional Communication, Tonicity, Integrity of Physical Health, Eyes, Structural Status	254 children, 213 parents, 133 teachers, and 135 interdisciplinary professionals	Interrater reliability: among interdisciplinary professionals (*r* = .73); among professionals and parents (*r* = .67) Test–retest reliability (*r* = .67) Concurrent validity (*r* = .65–.91) Discriminant function (*r* = .83)
Temperament and Atypical Behavior Scale (TABS; Bagnato, Neisworth, Salvia, & Hunt, 1999)	11–71 months	Detached, Hyper-Sensitive/Active, Underreactive, Dysregulated	621 typically developing children and 212 atypically developing children	Internal consistency Reliability: .95 in at-risk sample, .88 in not-at-risk sample Content and construct validity Superb sensitivity and specificity Recommended by the American Academy of Pediatrics
ASQ-3™ (Squires & Bricker, 2009)	1–66 months	Communication, Gross Motor, Fine Motor, Problem Solving, Personal-Social	15,138 children	Test–retest reliability Construct validity .86 specificity overall Concurrent validity .86 Sensitivity .86
ASQ:SE (Squires, Bricker, & Twombly, 2003)	3–66 months	Self-regulation, Compliance, Adaptive Functioning, Autonomy, Affect, Interaction with People	2,633 children	Internal consistency of .82 Test-retest reliability 94% Sensitivity 78.6% Specificity 98.2%

Key: ASQ:SE, Ages & Stages Questionnaires®: Social-Emotional; ASQ-3™, Ages and Stages Questionnaires®, Third Edition; SPECS, System to Plan Early Childhood Services.

gibility (Bagnato, McKeating-Esterle, Fevola, & Hawthorne, 2007). Results revealed that SPECS ratings relying on informed opinions based on existing health and developmental information in children's record files were found to be significantly correlated with results from the performance-based assessment of children's functioning in assessing children for early intervention. Regression analyses and multiple correlations produced significantly positive and moderate results within corresponding developmental domains, ranging from $r = .37$ to $r = .68$. All reported results were significant at the level $p < .01$. Results suggest that the use of an informed-opinion measure based on record review (average review time = 15 minutes) that structures and quantifies opinions and judgments provides comparable accuracy to a performance-based test (average assessment time = 30–60 minutes) regarding the functional capabilities of young children with delays or disabilities. Not only was the clinical judgment measure just as accurate as the performance measure, it was more economical in terms of professional time and effort.

Because of the latitude to use informed opinions for early intervention, basic and prospective research is needed to examine 1) the extent of use of informed opinion for eligibility determination nationally; 2) the most effective process and procedures used to facilitate informed opinions by parents and professionals; and 3) the reliability, validity, and utility of informed opinions for eligibility determination. Table 5.2 summarizes the characteristics of some of the most promising authentic measures of child capabilities and need based on informed opinions of parents and professionals. These measures include the *System to Plan Early Childhood Services (SPECS)*, the *ABILITIES Index* (Simeonsson & Bailey, 1991), the *TABS* (Bagnato, Neisworth, Salvia, & Hunt, 1999), the *ASQ-3*™ (Squires & Bricker, 2009), and *Ages & Stages Questionnaires®: Social-Emotional (ASQ:SE*; Squires, Bricker, & Twombly, 2002). The most needed improvements for informed opinion are 1) conduct national field studies to validate the use of the most promising informed opinion measures for eligibility determination and initial service delivery decisions and 2) revise federal and state regulations to support the need for services rather than the extent of developmental delay as the basis for eligibility.

Summary

This chapter provided forecasts of developments in authentic assessment formats. It reviewed innovations in portable and computer-assisted database, functional classification, performance probes, epidemiological assessment, and informed opinion formats and provided recommendations for how these formats can improve. Section II provides detailed reviews of commercially available authentic assessments.

II

Professional Standards and the LINK Social Validity Study

with Sophia Hubbell and Eileen McKeating

Over the years, professionals have asked us constantly, "What is the best test to use?" Of course, there is no answer to that question. The "best" measure depends on many factors. One of the most critical factors is the purpose for using the measure—to determine eligibility for services, to conduct population-based screenings, or for program accountability. As our research references allude, few measures have been truly field validated to accomplish these unique ECI purposes. Even those traditional measures that are advertised and promoted to be the *best* fail the "stress test." In addition to purpose, other important factors influence the decision to choose and use a particular measure, as indicated in Chapter 3. In general, decisions about choosing and using measures depend on whether the measure meets professionally sanctioned and often evidence-based standards for developmentally appropriate practice.

Since the earliest edition of *LINKing* (Bagnato & Neisworth, 1981), our intent has been to produce a useful resource for *interdisciplinary professionals* (i.e., practitioners, administrators, therapists, and researchers, as well as parents and caregivers) in ECI to make important decisions about choosing and using the type of assessment measure or system that would meet their programmatic needs. *LINKing* is intended to be a major resource guide in ECI that infuses professional and evidence-based standards into the decision-making process at the local, state, and national levels about choosing and using the best measures for best practices.

In this edition of *LINKing,* we use the concept of social validation through consumer satisfaction to analyze the extent to which measurement tools frequently promoted and used with young children (birth to 8 years) in ECI programs meet professional and evidence-based standards for best practice. Simply, to what extent do these tools have the necessary qualities that allow them to work equitably and effectively to accomplish important purposes for *all* young children in ECI programs?

To accomplish this, we have designed and implemented a LINK consumer social validation rubric and process that is systematic, web-based, and self-instructional. LINK allows consumers to systematically rate identified measures against recommended professional practice standards and to determine the extent to which they are met. LINK rating icons allow consumers to compare the qualities of various measures to guide their decision making.

The following section discusses and illustrates the LINK process. First, we review past and current procedures to rate the quality of assessment measures. Second, we present how measures were chosen for this analysis. Third, we discuss the LINK process using professional practice standards. Fourth and finally, we present the comparative analysis of results for the measures that distinguishes and documents those measures "good enough" to be reviewed in the book.

Past Consumer Validation Efforts

During the 1980s and 1990s, a series of focus groups and qualitative consumer satisfaction surveys were conducted with more than 4,000 parents and professionals. These consumers were asked to rate ECI assessment measures (i.e., those that are curriculum-embedded, curriculum-compatible, and norm-referenced) on a Likert scale across six standards. The resultant number was referred to as a *LINK index* (i.e., 3.0, *exemplary*; 2.5, *high*; 2.0, *acceptable*; 1.5, *low*; 1.0, *negligible*). Only measures receiving a 2.0 LINK index or higher were included in the 1997 edition of *LINKing* (Bagnato, Neisworth, & Munson, 1997). Specifically, snapshots were created for 52 measures that were deemed acceptable, and close-ups were created for 46 measures to indicate those measures with the highest developmentally appropriate qualities. Consumers' strong responses proved that the 1997 edition of *LINKing* served as an objective and valuable reference for those interested in selecting and implementing assessment measures that best met their program goals, population served, and recommended practice.

Selection of Assessment Measures for This Edition of *LINKing*

As noted in earlier chapters, this edition of *LINKing* provides a critical review of assessment measures for ECI whose content promotes a link to instruction and/or intervention for the benefit of young children. The process of identifying assessment measures began in the fall of 2007. We started with a list of measures reviewed in the 1997 edition and then systematically searched for other measures. The search included the following steps:

1. Review of publisher catalogs and web sites as well as conversations regarding forthcoming publications

2. Discussions with local and state early childhood personnel regarding the assessments they used

3. Search of the primary literature

4. Review of various assessment databases (e.g., NIEER assessment database), compendiums (e.g., Halle & Vick, 2007; Niemeyer & Scott-Little, 2002; Research Department, Florida Children's Forum, 2004), and surveys to determine the most frequently used and/or recommended measures for ECI by interdisciplinary professionals (e.g., Pretti-Frontczak & Brewer, 2005).

Selection criteria were that the measure 1) was intended for use in the early years (emphasis on birth to age 8); 2) was accessible to the U.S. public; and 3) had enough items that, even if not intended primarily for programming (i.e., for linking assessment and instruction/intervention), the scale had the capability to generate individual goals and perhaps identify intervention strategies. Measures designed solely for screening, diagnosis, evaluating environments, and curriculum-based probes were excluded from our review in this regard. The search process ultimately resulted in a total of 87 measures. See Appendix II.1 for an alphabetical listing of the measures identified for review.

LINK Consumer Social Validation Process of Assessment Measures

In an effort to generate usable ratings, consumers and experts were asked to participate in a review of 87 measures. The following sections provide a description of the actions taken to levy consumer and expert ratings across 8 standards for the 87 measures.

National Consumer Ratings

During this same time period, an electronic, web-based consumer social validity survey was designed by the authors based on the eight standards outlined in Chapter 3. As described in Chapter 3, the six standards used in the 1997 edition were expanded to eight for the current edition based on emerging revisions in the DEC Recommended Practice Standards. Therefore, survey items (beyond basic demographic information) were generated for each standard.

The LINK consumer survey consists of 26 items (2–4 questions per standard) and was originally rated on a 3-point Likert Scale. See Figure II.1 for a sample of the original survey items for the Authenticity standard. A pilot of the survey was distributed to 10 providers to determine how long the survey took to complete and whether survey questions were clear. Revisions were made, and the survey was reformatted and posted online in March 2008. See Appendix C for a complete copy of the online consumer survey. You can also visit us online at http://ehhs.kent .edu/link to serve as a consumer rater now!

Authenticity: Extent to which the assessment content and methods sample naturally occurring behaviors in everyday situations

How functional or important are the competencies described in the assessment items for participation in everyday activities?

- ☐ Neither functional nor important; item content is primarily composed of discrete behaviors that children normally would not need to demonstrate during daily routines and activities

- ☐ Some function or importance; item content is a mix of nonfunctional, discrete behaviors and more functional behaviors necessary for children's active participation during daily routines and activities

- ☐ Functional and important; most item content is necessary for children's active participation in daily routines and activities

Who conducts the assessment, and what procedures (how) do they use to collect the information?

- ☐ Unfamiliar people administer a test to the child through contrived procedures

- ☐ Either familiar or unfamiliar people use a combination of direct testing through contrived procedures and observational assessment of the child's actual behavior in natural environments

- ☐ Familiar people conduct the assessment primarily through observation in natural environments

Where is assessment information gathered?

- ☐ Mostly in contrived testing arrangements

- ☐ Through a combination of contrived testing and observations in natural environments

- ☐ Almost all information is gathered through observations of daily interactions within familiar classroom, home, and community routines

---

Figure II.1.   Original consumer social validity survey items for authenticity standard.

After the survey was posted online, broad efforts were made to recruit early childhood teachers, providers, therapists, and other ECI team members (i.e., users of the 87 assessment measures). Requests were made to state and national listservs (e.g., Part C/619 coordinator listservs, posted on NECTAC notes) and professional organizations (NAEYC, DEC, American Psychological Association/National Association of School Psychologists Early Childhood Interest Group, American Educational Research Association), and flyers were distributed at local, state, and national conferences.

In December 2008, the first round of data were exported for analysis. The survey was then revised so each item was rated on a 5-point Likert scale for more fine-grained analysis. See Figure II.2 for a sample of the revised survey items for the Authenticity standard. Efforts to obtain consumer social validity ratings continued through May 2009. Consumer social validity ratings from March 2008 through May 2009 were collected from 1,083 users and compiled for this edition of *LINKing*. The consumers primarily represented women (94%) of white non-Hispanic ethnicity (88%), whose primary roles were either as a therapist/specialist (24%), lead classroom teacher (21%) or administrator/supervisor (21%). Most of the consumers worked in preschool special education (39%), home-based early intervention (30%), public school preschool (22%), or center-based early intervention (21%). Consumers represented programs in suburban (38%), urban (36%), and rural (26%) settings.

Authenticity: Extent to which the assessment content and methods sample naturally occurring behaviors in everyday situations.

How functional or important are the competencies described in the assessment items for participation in everyday activities?

0. Neither functional nor important; item content is primarily composed of discrete behaviors that children normally would not need to demonstrate during daily routines and activities

1. Falls between Statements 0 and 2 in meeting the standard

2. Some function or importance; item content is a mix of non-\functional, discrete behaviors, and more functional behaviors necessary for children's active participation during daily routines and activities

3. Falls between Statements 2 and 4 in meeting the standard

4. Functional and important; most item content is necessary for children's active participation in daily routines and activities

Who conducts the assessment, and what procedures (how) do they use to collect the information?

0. Unfamiliar people administer a test to the child through contrived procedures

1. Falls between Statements 0 and 2 in meeting the standard

2. Either familiar or unfamiliar people use a combination of direct testing through contrived procedures and observational assessment of the child's actual behavior in natural environments

3. Falls between Statements 2 and 4 in meeting the standard

4. Familiar people conduct the assessment primarily through observation in natural environments

Where is assessment information gathered?

0. Mostly in contrived testing arrangements

1. Falls between Statements 0 and 2 in meeting the standard

2. Through a combination of contrived testing and observations in natural environments

3. Falls between Statements 2 and 4 in meeting the standard

4. Almost all information is gathered through observations of daily interactions within familiar classroom, home, and community routines

---

Figure II.2.   Revised consumer social validity survey items for authenticity standard.

Consumers tended to use the assessment measures frequently (i.e., 37% used the measures they rated 2–5 times a year, and 28% used the measures they rated 6–12 times a year). Consumers also used the assessment measures they rated on a variety of children including those who were typically developing (42%), those at risk (64%), and those with identified disabilities/delays (81%). Table II.1 provides a summary of the purposes for which consumers used various assessment measures and the extent to which they found the measure useful, appropriate, or meaningful for such a purpose. The top purpose an assessment measure was used for was monitoring children's progress. Across all purposes, however, consumers found the measures to be less useful, appropriate, or meaningful for the purpose for which they were using it. Most consumers learned to use the assessment measure they rated through a workshop (38%), followed by 24% who taught themselves. Table II.2 provides a summary of the primary reason consumers used a given assessment. The top reasons included that the assessment measure was re-

Table II.1. Purposes for which consumers used the various assessment measures rated and the extent to which they found the measures useful, appropriate, or meaningful

Purpose	Percentage who used measure	Percentage who rated as useful
Screening	41	32
Determining eligibility for special education	38	29
Writing or updating individualized family service plans and/or individualized education programs	45	34
Planning intervention and/or activities	51	40
Monitoring children's progress	59	47
Program evaluation	19	14
State accountability reporting	24	15
Federal accountability requirements	16	11

quired, provided useful information, and allowed for observations of children during daily activities such as play. These findings were similar to those Pretti-Frontczak and Brewer (2005) found, in that 30% of their sample indicated the top reason for using the measure was because it was required, followed by 15% who indicated use because it allowed for observations of children during play.

Table II.2. Ranked primary reasons consumers used assessment measure rated

Reason	Ranked percentage
Required	25.6
Provides useful information	16.7
Allows for observations of children during daily activities such as play	12.2
Already in place	10.5
It is valid and reliable	7.3
Includes the family or other professionals	5.6
Applicable for my children	5.4
Clear and easy to use	4.5
Broad scope and sequence	3.7
Matches my curriculum	2.8
Promotes teaming and collaboration	2.1
Comfortable with the instrument	1.5
Saves me time	1.5
Covers a wide age range	0.7

The LINK Expert Panel Consensus

For the second stage of the LINK process, we followed these steps:

1. Selected a national panel of assessment experts in ECI

2. Enabled the assessment experts to complete the LINK survey across certain measures as a "second pass" to guide the determination of which measures would be included in the book

3. Facilitated a conference call roundtable process by which the national experts reviewed collected data and reached consensus on the classification of the measures on the eight standards and their likely ratings in the book

4. Conducted a final consensus analysis by the book authors using a combination of the user surveys, expert ratings, and conference-call consensus to apply the final quality classifications on each measure

5. Applied LINK icons and nominal classification based on a 5-point scale (i.e., exemplary, notable, acceptable, marginal, and unacceptable) both to reach agreement on the final designations for each assessment measure and to determine the final group of measures to be included in the book

In February 2009, a group of seven national experts were invited to participate in the final determination process of the most authentic assessment measures. Experts were asked to rate the assessments with which they were most familiar. The role of the expert was to provide a second-level analysis of the quality of each assessment measure to confirm and buttress the consumer surveys.

Experts represented state leaders as well as higher education faculty and those responsible for providing state and/or national training and technical assistance on early childhood assessment. We are grateful for the work of the following experts in the LINK validation process: Jennifer Grisham-Brown, Louise Kaczmarek, Jim Lesko, Marisa Macy, Beth Rous, Lisa Schneider, and Nan Vendegna. Each expert was given a unique identifier and asked to access the survey online and rate a given assessment measure according to the eight standards using the revised 5-point scale.

Lastly, the three authors augmented the expert panel and rated assessment measures they were most familiar with—in particular, any assessment that was lesser known to the greater public, that was used for low-incidence disabilities and specialized purposes, or that had few ratings from consumers to ensure every measure was reviewed by consumers or experts. In all, ratings from 1,083 consumers, 7 experts, and 3 authors were used to derive a consensus LINK social validity index for 81 measures. Six measures were removed from the original list after closer review determined critical elements were missing and/or the measure was no longer in print and therefore not available to the public.

The consumer rating process used in *Consumer Reports* for analyzing the quality and usefulness of commercial products inspired the LINK social validation process. The *Consumer Reports* process examines consumer ratings of the use, durability, cost, reliability, and other qualities of common consumer products (e.g., cars, computers, refrigerators). The ratings are used to document and classify the comparative qualities of different products made by different companies as well as the level of confidence to be placed in each product. The LINK icons aim to serve a similar purpose in helping consumers make informed choices.

Results of the Consumer Social Validation Process of Assessment Measures

In an effort to serve as a consumer's guide, consumer social validity ratings, expert ratings, and author ratings were converted into icons (see Figure II.3). The ○ icon indicates the measure was unacceptable and did not meet quality standards for use in ECI. The ◓ icon indicates the measure marginally met the standard. The ◑ icon

	Unacceptable	Marginal	Acceptable	Notable	Exemplary
LINK icon	○	◔	◐	◑	●

Figure II.3. LINK icons for unacceptable, marginal, acceptable, notable, and exemplary ratings.

indicates the measure was acceptable in meeting the standard. The ◑ icon indicates the measure has notable features in meeting the standard. The ● icon indicates the measure has exemplary features in meeting the standard. Appendix II.2 provides LINK icons for the consensus ratings (i.e., consumer, expert, and author) across the eight standards and overall. The 81 assessment measures were classified as conventional (*n* = 19) or authentic/alternative (*n* = 62) using the definitions provided in Chapters 1 and 2. LINK indexes aggregated for consumers, experts, and authors by standard and overall were generated for both the conventional and authentic/alternative assessment measures. Figure II.4 provides the LINK icons graphically representing consensus ratings and a comparison of conventional and authentic/alternative assessment measures.

Summary of LINK Findings

A review of LINK indexes in Appendix II.2 indicates that the authentic/alternative measures did well across most standards (i.e., consistently received ◐ and ◑), fairing poorest on the *utility* standard and best on the *acceptability* standard. When ratings for the 19 conventional measures were reviewed and/or combined, they faired slightly better on the *acceptability*, *evidence*, and *sensitivity* standards than on *authenticity*, *collaboration*, *universality*, and *utility* standards.

All authentic/alternative measures received an overall LINK index of ◐ or higher with the exception of the *Developmental Programming for Infants and Young Children: Volumes 4 and 5. Preschool Assessment and Application* (D'Eugenio & Moersch, 1981), the *EDI* (Janus & Offord, 2000), and the *Learning Accomplishment Profile, Third Edition (LAP-3;* Stanford, Zelman, Harding, Peisner-Feinberg, 2004), which received an overall LINK index of ◔. All conventional measures received an overall LINK index of ◔ or lower with the exception of the *Autism Screening Instrument for Educational Planning—Third Edition* (Krug, Arick, & Almond, 2008), which received an overall LINK index of ◐.

Following a review of the consumer ratings (see Appendix II.2), the 81 assessment measures were sorted into three classifications: 1) those considered to have met the highest standards with an overall LINK index of ◑ and ●, thus warranting a Close Up presentation in the book regarding exemplary qualities; 2) those considered to have done an adequate job meeting the standards with an overall LINK index of ◐, warranting a shorter At-a-Glance treatment; and 3) those with an overall LINK index of ◔ or lower, indicating their failure to meet minimal qualities that align with early childhood professional assessment standards.

Standard	Aggregated LINK indexes for conventional measures	Aggregated LINK indexes for alternative measures
Acceptability	◑	◕
Authenticity	◔	◕
Collaboration	◔	◕
Evidence	◑	◕
Multifactors	◔	◕
Sensitivity	◑	◕
Universality	◔	◕
Utility	◔	◑
Overall	◔	◕

Figure II.4. Combined LINK indexes for consumer social validity survey ratings, expert panel ratings, and author ratings for conventional and alternative assessment measures.

What Are the Best Assessment Measures?

Although the previous section summarized LINK indexes for all 81 measures, the following section provides a more detailed report for certain measures. Specifically, At-a-Glance sheets and Close Up reviews are provided. This section contains 54 At-a-Glance sheets for measures that received an overall LINK index of ◑ or higher and 30 Close Up reviews for measures that received an overall LINK index of ◕ and ●. Measures with more than one age level (e.g., an infant/toddler level or version and a preschool level or version) were combined in the At-a-Glance and Close Up sheets and reviews.

The purpose of the 54 At-a-Glance sheets is to provide consumers with a quick reference regarding the basics of the measure (i.e., name, authors, publication date, cost). The sheet also provides a brief statement regarding the type of assessment, age ranges covered, domains and/or subtests, population targeted, technology features, and other languages in which the measure has been translated. In a number of instances, the assessment did not contain technology-related components and/or, to date, had not been translated. In these cases, we have written *none*. A key aspect of the At-a-Glance sheets includes a brief review of "other features" that make comparisons between measures possible (e.g., degree to which the measure covered all areas of development, whether the measure had or could be aligned to federal and state standards). Specifically, 11 other features were rated by the authors and their graduate students in terms of whether the measure had high, medium, or low evidence/ability related to the feature (see Appendix II.3 for a full description of the 11 features and scoring criteria). Several assessments reviewed consist of more than one age level (e.g., infant/toddler and preschool). In such instances, Other Feature ratings were provided for the assessment as a whole rather than providing ratings for each level. Lastly, the At-a-Glance sheets contain consumer social validity ratings in the form of LINK icons.

The purpose of the 30 Close Up reviews is to provide greater insight and illustrations of what makes the measure exemplary. Close Up reviews are divided into four sections. Each Close Up begins with a brief statement regarding qualities and unique attributes that distinguish the measure from others. Then, each measure is described according to three of the most critical LINK standards (i.e., *authenticity, collaboration,* and *utility*). Examples from the measures are also provided to illustrate for consumers how the measures address three critical LINK standards. A third section of each Close Up is a summary regarding the measure's evidence base. Although the term *evidence base* can be interpreted many different ways, we chose to look for evidence along a continuum where a measure may have promising evidence (i.e., anecdotal evidence and/or professional wisdom exists to support the measures practices and features), more "probable" evidence that is supported by existing theory or recommended practices, and "pure" evidence in terms of research focused on the measure's psychometric properties or validation of use. The final section of the Close Up reviews includes consideration and recommendations made by the authors.

Appendix II.I. Alphabetical listing of 87 assessment measures included in the initial review

ABLLS®-R: The Assessment of Basic Language and Learning Skills-Revised

Adaptive Behavior Assessment System-Second Edition (ABAS-II)

Ages & Stages Questionnaires®, Third Edition (ASQ-3™): A Parent-Completed Child Monitoring System

Ages & Stages Questionnaires®: Social-Emotional (ASQ:SE): A Parent-Completed, Child-Monitoring System for Social-Emotional Behaviors

Assessment, Evaluation, and Programming System for Infants and Children (AEPS®), Second Edition

Autism Screening Instrument for Educational Planning–Third Edition (ASIEP-3)

Basic School Skills Inventory–Third Edition (BSSI-3)

Battelle Developmental Inventory, Second Edition (BDI-2)

Bayley Scales of Infant Development®-Second Edition (BSID®-II)

Beautiful Beginnings

Behavior Assessment System for Children, Second Edition (BASC™-2)

Behavior Rating Inventory of Executive Function®-Preschool Version (BRIEF®-P)

Behavioral Characteristics Progression (BCP)

Birth to Three Assessment and Intervention System-Second Edition (BTAIS-2)

BRIGANCE® Inventory of Early Development-II (IED-II)

Callier-Azusa Scale G-Edition

The Carolina Curriculum for Infants and Toddlers with Special Needs, Third Edition (CCITSN)

The Carolina Curriculum for Preschoolers with Special Needs, Second Edition (CCPSN)

CAS-2: Cognitive Abilities Scale-Second Edition

Communication and Symbolic Behavior Scales™ (CSBS™), Normed Edition

The Creative Curriculum® Developmental Continuum for Infants, Toddlers & Twos

The Creative Curriculum® Developmental Continuum for Ages 3–5

Desired Results Developmental Profile access (DRDP access)

Desired Results Developmental Profile-Infant/Toddler Instrument (DRDP-R, IT)

Desired Results Developmental Profile-Preschool Instrument (DRDP-R, PS)

Developmental Assessment for Students with Severe Disabilities-Second Edition (DASH-2)

Developmental Assessment of Young Children (DAYC)

Developmental Observation Checklist System (DOCS)

Developmental Profile 3 (DP-3)

Developmental Programming for Infants and Young Children: Volume 2. Early Intervention Developmental Profile–Revised Edition

Developmental Programming for Infants and Young Children: Volumes 4 & 5. Preschool Assessment and Application

The Devereux Early Childhood Assessment (DECA)

Devereux Early Childhood Assessment for Infants and Toddlers (DECA-I/T)

Differential Ability Scales® (DAS®)

Early Development Instrument (EDI)

The Early Learning Accomplishment Profile™ (E-LAP™)

Early Screening Inventory–Revised™ (ESI-R™) 2008 Edition

Every Move Counts: Sensory-Based Communication Techniques

FACTER: Functional Assessment and Curriculum for Teaching Everyday Routines

Focused Portfolios: A Complete Assessment for the Young Child

The Functional Emotional Assessment Scale (FEAS) for Infancy and Early Childhood

The Galileo Pre-K Online System for the Electronic Management of Learning

HELP®–the Hawaii Early Learning Profile®

HighScope Child Observation Record (COR) for Infants and Toddlers

HighScope Preschool Child Observation Record (COR)

Humanics National Infant-Toddler Assessment

Humanics National Preschool Assessment

Individualized Assessment and Treatment for Autistic and Developmentally Disabled Children

Infant Toddler Social-Emotional Assessment™ (ITSEA™)

Infant-Toddler and Family Instrument (ITFI)

Infant-Toddler Developmental Assessment (IDA)

INSITE Developmental Checklist: Assessment of Developmental Skills for Young Multidisabled Sensory Impaired Children

Inventory for Client and Agency Planning™ (ICAP™)

Kaufman Assessment Battery for Children, Second Edition (KABC-II)

Kaufman Survey of Early Academic and Language Skills (K-SEALS)

Kent Inventory of Developmental Skills (KIDS)

Learning Accomplishment Profile–Diagnostic, Third Edition (LAP-D)

Learning Accomplishment Profile, Third Edition (LAP-3)

Life Skills Progression™ (LSP™): An Outcome and Intervention Planning Instrument for Use with Families at Risk

McCarthy Scales of Children's Abilities

Miller Assessment for Preschoolers (MAP™)

Mullen Scales of Early Learning (MSEL)

New Portage Guide Birth to Six

The Oregon Project for Preschool Children who are Blind or Visually Impaired, 6th edition (The OR Project)

The Ounce Scale

Partners in Play: Assessing Infants and Toddlers in Natural Contexts

The Pediatric Evaluation of Disability Inventory (PEDI™)

Preschool and Kindergarten Behavior Scales–Second Edition (PKBS-2)

Psychoeducational Profile: Third Edition (PEP-3)

Reynell-Zinkin Developmental Scales for Young Visually Handicapped Children (RZS)

Rosetti Infant-Toddler Language Scale

Scales of Early Communication Skills for Hearing-Impaired Children (SECS)

Scales of Independent Behavior–Revised™ (SIB–R™)

The SCERTS® Model: A Comprehensive Educational Approach for Children with Autism Spectrum Disorders

School Function Assessment (SFA)

SKI-HI Language Development Scale, 2nd Edition

Social Skills Improvement System Rating Scales (SSIS™ Rating Scales)

Stanford-Binet Intelligence Scales (SB5), Fifth Edition

Temperament and Atypical Behavior Scale (TABS): Early Childhood Indicators of Developmental Dysfunction

Transdisciplinary Play-Based Assessment, Second Edition (TPBA2)

Vineland Adaptive Behavior Scales, Second Edition (Vineland™-II)

Vineland Social Emotional Early Childhood Scales (Vineland™ SEEC)

Vulpe Assessment Battery-Revised: Developmental Assessment • Performance Analysis • Individualized Programming for the Atypical Child

Wechsler Preschool and Primary Scale of Intelligence™–Third Edition (WPPSI™-III)

Woodcock-Johnson® III NU Tests of Achievement

Woodcock-Johnson® III NU Tests of Cognitive Abilities

The Work Sampling System®

Appendix II.2
Combined LINK Indexes

The following is a matrix showing the combined LINK indexes for consumer social validity ratings, expert panel ratings, and author ratings for 81 assessment measures. As explained in Section II, the ○ icon indicates the measure was unacceptable and did not meet quality standards for use in ECI. The ◔ icon indicates the measure marginally met the standard. The ◑ icon indicates the measure was acceptable in meeting the standard. The ◕ icon indicates the measure has notable features in meeting the standard. The ● icon indicates the measure has exemplary features in meeting the standard.

Assessment measure	Acceptability	Authenticity	Collaboration	Evidence	Multifactors	Sensitivity	Universality	Utility	Overall
ABLLS®-R: The Assessment of Basic Language and Learning Skills–Revised	◑	◑	◑	◑	◑	◑	◑	◑	◑
Adaptive Behavior Assessment System–Second Edition (ABAS-II)	◑	◑	◑	◑	◑	◑	◑	◑	◑
Ages & Stages Questionnaires®, Third Edition (ASQ-3™): A Parent-Completed Child Monitoring System	◑	◑	◑	◑	◑	◑	◑	◑	◑
Ages & Stages Questionnaires®: Social-Emotional (ASQ:SE): A Parent-Completed, Child-Monitoring System for Social-Emotional Behaviors	◑	◑	◑	◑	◑	◑	◑	◑	◑
Assessment, Evaluation, and Programming System for Infants and Children (AEPS®), Second Edition	◑	◑	◑	◑	◑	◑	◑	◑	◑
Autism Screening Instrument for Educational Planning–Third Edition (ASIEP-3)	◑	◑	◑	◑	◑	◑	◑	◑	◑
Basic School Skills Inventory–Third Edition (BSSI-3)	◑	◑	◑	◑	◑	◑	◑	◑	◑
Battelle Developmental Inventory, Second Edition (BDI-2)	◑	◑	◑	◑	◑	◑	◑	◑	◑
Bayley Scales of Infant Development®-Second Edition (BSID-II®)	◑	◑	◑	◑	◑	◑	◑	◑	◑

Assessment								
Behavior Assessment System for Children, Second Edition (BASC™-2)	◑	◑	◑	◑	◑	◑	◑	◑
Behavior Rating Inventory of Executive Function®-Preschool Version (BRIEF®-P)	◑	◑	●	◑	◑	◑	◑	◑
Behavioral Characteristics Progression (BCP)	◑	◑	◑	◑	◑	◑	◑	◑
BRIGANCE® Inventory of Early Development-II (IED II)	◑	◑	◔	◑	◑	◑	◑	◑
Callier-Azusa Scale G-Edition	◑	◑	◑	◑	◑	◑	◑	◑
The Carolina Curriculum for Infants and Toddlers with Special Needs, Third Edition (CCITSN)	◑	◑	◑	◑	◑	◑	◑	◑
The Carolina Curriculum for Preschoolers with Special Needs, Second Edition (CCPSN)	◑	◑	◑	●	◑	◑	◑	◑
CAS-2: Cognitive Abilities Scale-Second Edition	◑	◑	◑	◑	◔	◑	◑	◔
Communication and Symbolic Behavior Scales™ (CSBS™), Normed Edition	◑	◑	◑	◑	◑	◑	◑	◑
The Creative Curriculum® Developmental Continuum for Infants, Toddlers & Twos	◑	◑	◑	◑	◑	◑	◑	◑
The Creative Curriculum® Developmental Continuum for Ages 3-5	◑	◑	◑	◑	◑	◑	◑	◑
Desired Results Developmental Profile access (DRDP access)	◑	◑	◑	◑	◑	◑	◑	◑

(continued)

Assessment measure	Acceptability	Authenticity	Collaboration	Evidence	Multifactors	Sensitivity	Universality	Utility	Overall
Desired Results Developmental Profile-Infant/Toddler Instrument (DRDP-R, IT)	◑	◑	◔	◑	◑	◑	◑	◑	◑
Desired Results Developmental Profile-Preschool Instrument (DRDP-R, PS)	◑	◑	◑	◑	◑	◑	◕	◑	◑
Developmental Assessment for Students with Severe Disabilities-Second Edition (DASH-2)	◑	◑	◑	◑	◑	◑	◑	◑	◑
Developmental Assessment of Young Children (DAYC)	◑	◑	◑	◑	◑	◔	◔	◔	◔
Developmental Observation Checklist System (DOCS)	◑	◑	◑	◕	◕	◑	◑	◔	◑
Developmental Profile 3 (DP-3)	◑	◑	◑	◑	◑	◑	◑	◔	◑
Developmental Programming for Infants and Young Children: Volume 2. Early Intervention Developmental Profile-Revised Edition	◑	◑	◑	◑	◑	◔	◑	◔	◑
Developmental Programming for Infants and Young Children: Volumes 4 & 5, Preschool Assessment and Application	◔	◑	◔	◔	◔	◑	◔	◔	◔
The Devereux Early Childhood Assessment (DECA)	◑	◑	◕	◑	◑	◑	◑	◑	◑
Devereux Early Childhood Assessment for Infants and Toddlers (DECA-I/T)	◑	◑	◕	◑	◕	◑	◑	◑	◑
Differential Ability Scales® (DAS®)	◔	○	○	◔	○	◔	○	○	○
Early Development Instrument (EDI)	◔	◔	◔	◑	◑	◑	◔	◑	◔

Instrument								
The Early Learning Accomplishment Profile™ (E-LAP™)	◑	◑	◑	◑	◑	◑	◑	◑
Early Screening Inventory–Revised™ (ESI-R™) 2008 Edition	◔	◔	◔	◔	◔	◔	◔	◔
Every Move Counts: Sensory-Based Communication Techniques	◕	◕	◕	◕	◕	◕	◕	◕
FACTER: Functional Assessment and Curriculum for Teaching Everyday Routines	●	●	●	◕	◕	◕	◕	◕
The Functional Emotional Assessment Scale (FEAS) for Infancy and Early Childhood	◑	◑	◑	◑	◑	◑	◑	◑
The Galileo Pre-K Online System for the Electronic Management of Learning	◕	◕	◕	◕	◕	◕	◕	◕
HELP®–the Hawaii Early Learning Profile®	◕	◕	◕	◕	◕	◕	◕	◕
HighScope Child Observation Record (COR) for Infants and Toddlers	◕	◕	◕	◕	◕	◕	◕	◕
HighScope Preschool Child Observation Record (COR)	◕	◕	◕	◕	◕	◕	◕	◕
Humanics National Infant-Toddler Assessment	◕	◑	◕	◑	◕	◕	◕	◑
Humanics National Preschool Assessment	◕	◕	◑	◕	◕	◕	◕	◑
Individualized Assessment and Treatment for Autistic and Developmentally Disabled Children	◔	◔	◔	◔	◔	◔	◔	◔
Infant Toddler Social Emotional Assessment™ (ITSEA™)	◑	●	◕	●	◕	◕	◕	◕
Infant-Toddler and Family Instrument (ITFI)	◑	◑	◑	◑	◑	◔	◔	◑

continued

Appendix II.2.   (continued)

Assessment measure	Acceptability	Authenticity	Collaboration	Evidence	Multifactors	Sensitivity	Universality	Utility	Overall
Infant-Toddler Developmental Assessment (IDA)	◑	◑	◑	◑	◑	◑	◑	◑	◑
INSITE Developmental Checklist: Assessment of Developmental Skills for Young Multidisabled Sensory Impaired Children	◑	◕	◔	◔	◑	◑	◑	◑	◑
Inventory for Client and Agency Planning™ (ICAP™)	●	●	●	●	●	◑	◑	◕	◕
Kaufman Assessment Battery for Children, Second Edition (KABC-II)	◕	◔	○	◔	○	◔	◔	○	◔
Kaufman Survey of Early Academic and Language Skills (K-SEALS)	◑	◔	○	◑	○	◔	◔	◔	◔
Kent Inventory of Developmental Skills (KIDS)	◑	◑	◑	◑	◑	◑	◔	◑	◑
Learning Accomplishment Profile–Diagnostic, Third Edition (LAP-D)	◑	◑	○	◕	◑	◕	◔	◑	◑
Learning Accomplishment Profile Third Edition (LAP-3)	◑	◑	○	◑	◑	◕	○	◔	◑
Life Skills Progression™ (LSP™): An Outcome and Intervention Planning Instrument for Use with Families at Risk	◕	◕	◑	◑	◕	◑	◑	◑	◑
McCarthy Scales of Children's Abilities	◑	○	○	◑	○	◔	◕	○	◑
Miller Assessment for Preschoolers (MAP™)	◔	◔	○	◑	◔	◔	◔	○	◔
Mullen Scales of Early Learning (MSEL)	◑	◔	○	◑	○	◔	◔	◑	◔
New Portage Guide Birth to Six	●	●	●	◕	◕	◕	◕	◕	◕

Assessment								
The Oregon Project for Preschool Children who are Blind or Visually Impaired, 6th edition (The OR Project)	◐	◐	◐	◐	◐	◐	◐	◐
The Ounce Scale	◐	◐	◐	◐	◐	◐	◐	◐
Partners in Play: Assessing Infants and Toddlers in Natural Contexts	◐	◐	◐	◐	◐	◐	◐	◐
The Pediatric Evaluation of Disability Inventory (PEDI™)	◐	◐	◐	◐	◐	◐	◐	◐
Preschool and Kindergarten Behavior Scales—Second Edition (PKBS-2)	◐	◐	◐	◐	◐	◐	◐	◐
Psychoeducational Profile: Third Edition (PEP-3)	◔	◔	◔	◔	◔	◔	◐	◐
Scales of Independent Behavior–Revised™ (SIB–R™)	◐	●	◐	◐	◐	◐	◐	◐
The SCERTS® Model: A Comprehensive Educational Approach for Children with Autism Spectrum Disorders	◐	◐	◐	◐	◐	●	◐	◐
School Function Assessment (SFA)	◐	◐	◐	◐	◐	◐	◐	◐
SKI-HI Language Development Scale, 2nd edition	◐	◐	◐	◐	◐	◐	◐	◐
Social Skills Improvement System Rating Scales (SSIS™ Rating Scales)	◐	◐	◐	◔	◔	◔	◐	◐
Stanford-Binet Intelligence Scale (SB5), Fifth Edition	◔	○	○	◐	◔	◐	○	◔
Temperament and Atypical Behavior Scale (TABS): Early Childhood Indicators of Developmental Dysfunction	◐	◐	◐	◐	◐	◐	◔	◐

continued

Assessment measure	Acceptability	Authenticity	Collaboration	Evidence	Multifactors	Sensitivity	Universality	Utility	Overall
Transdisciplinary Play-Based Assessment, Second Edition (TPBA2)	◕	◕	◕	◑	◕	◕	◕	◕	◕
Vineland Adaptive Behavior Scales, Second Edition (Vineland™-II)	◕	◑	◑	◕	◑	◑	◑	◑	◑
Vineland Social Emotional Early Childhood Scales (Vineland™ SEEC)	◕	◕	◕	◑	◑	◔	◑	◑	◔
Vulpe Assessment Battery–Revised: Developmental Assessment • Performance Analysis • Individualized Programming for the Atypical Child	◑	◑	◑	◕	◑	◑	◑	◑	◑
Wechsler Preschool and Primary Scale of Intelligence™–Third Edition (WPPSI™-III)	◕	◔	○	◔	○	◑	◔	◔	◔
Woodcock-Johnson® III NU Tests of Achievement	◕	○	○	◔	○	◔	◔	○	◔
Woodcock-Johnson® III NU Tests of Cognitive Abilities	◔	○	○	◔	○	◔	○	○	○
The Work Sampling System®	◕	●	◕	◕	◕	◕	◕	◕	◕

Appendix II.3
Other Features

As a general rule, we are looking for the assessment (in which there are items that are scored) to do a good job linking to instruction. Therefore, the benefit of the doubt is given to the assessment only when the "other feature" promotes the link to instruction versus to an ancillary purpose.

Validated Purposes

Defined as evidence (e.g., wisdom, recommended practice, research) that documents the validity for using the assessment for the intended purpose set out by the developers. Many assessments may morph or become revised over time. If the measure is advertised to address multiple purposes, then it needs evidence for each purpose; however, weight is given to evidence to support the direct and useful link between assessment and instruction.

- *High:* Considerable evidence exists to validate the tool for the purposes for which it was developed, designed, and/or intended, AND evidence exists that the assessment links well to instruction.

- *Medium*: At least some evidence exists to validate the tool for the purposes for which it was developed, designed, and/or intended, OR evidence exists that the assessment links well to instruction.

- *Low*: Little to no evidence exists to validate the tool for the purposes for which it was developed, designed, and/or intended, AND little to no evidence exists that the assessment links well to instruction.

Curricular Links

Defined as supports, strategies, and/or content related to promoting the direct link between assessment (could be assessment items and/or assessment summaries) and instruction and/or intervention. Provides a direct and useful link to guiding and revising instructional efforts (i.e., who needs to learn what, who is ready to learn what, who needs what level of instruction).

- *High*: Contains considerable and easily identifiable supports, strategies, and/or content to promote the link between assessment and instructional planning and revision.

- *Medium*: Contains some easily identifiable supports, strategies, and/or content (even those that may take a sophisticated user to identify) to promote the link between assessment and instructional planning and revision.

- *Low*: Contains few to no identifiable supports, strategies, and/or content to promote the link between assessment and instructional planning and revision.

Comprehensive Coverage

Defined as all-encompassing and views development holistically. Does not exclude developmental or academic subject areas.

- *High*: Items cover and/or span the major areas of development (i.e., motor, adaptive, cognitive, communication, social) AND major content areas (e.g., early math, reading) and may even cover areas such as technology and health.

- *Medium*: Items cover and/or span mostly traditional developmental areas OR content areas OR may be missing several developmental and/or content areas.

- *Low*: Items cover only developmental areas OR content areas, and even those are missing critical concepts and skills.

Graduated Scoring

Defined as having ratings (i.e., how a child's performance is documented) that provide variability and depth.

- *High*: Three or more "rating" options AND uses a combination of quantitative and qualitative methods.

- *Medium*: Three or more "rating" options, but reliance is on quantitative ratings OR qualitative methods only.

- *Low*: Ratings are dichotomous only (e.g., yes/no, ready/not ready, mastered/not mastered, +/−).

Progress Monitoring

Defined as the documentation of changes and/or performance over time for the purpose of revising instruction and interpreting impact of instructional efforts.

- *High*: Ratings (quantitative and qualitative) are helpful in differentiating children, revising instruction, AND allowing for changes and/or performance over time to be documented.

- *Medium*: Ratings (likely quantitative or qualitative) are somewhat helpful in differentiating children, revising instruction, or allowing for changes and/or performance over time to be documented.

- *Low*: Ratings do not help differentiate children, revise instruction, or allow for changes and/or performance over time to be documented.

Standards Alignment

Defined as a match between the written, taught, and tested curriculum. It is when two educational components are matched.

- *High*: Documented link between two components (e.g., set of outcome and assessment items), AND provides information or evidence regarding most of the following:

  The alignment process (steps taken)

  The consistency of content in both the outcomes and assessment

  Comparable span of knowledge between outcomes and assessment

  Extent to which assessment items are evenly distributed across outcomes

  Consistency between the cognitive demands of the outcome and the assessment

  Expert validation or other steps taken to validate alignment

  Takes into consideration varying abilities (children will not be penalized)

- *Medium*: Documented link between two components (e.g., set of outcome and assessment items), but information or evidence regarding that alignment process and/or product is not provided, OR while no alignment has been done, a conceptual alignment is possible (i.e., at a face validity level, the items on the assessment would not align with most early learning content standards or federal outcomes).

- *Low*: No documented link between two components (e.g., set of outcome and assessment items), OR little to no conceptual alignment is possible. Even at a face validity level, the items on the assessment would not align with most early learning content standards or federal outcomes.

Diversity Features

Defined as means of encouraging tolerance for people of different backgrounds and understanding the impact of culture, language, and individual differences on development. Weight is given when diversity is also considered across related instructional efforts.

- *High*: Assessment items and practices were developed with consideration for cultural, linguistic, and individual diversity. Children are not penalized for differences, family and community contexts are considered, and modifications to reduce bias are allowed.

- *Medium*: Some assessment items and practices were developed with consideration for cultural, linguistic, and individual diversity. Children are not typically penalized for differences, family and community contexts are sometimes considered, and modifications to reduce bias may be allowed.

- *Low*: Assessment items and practices were *not* developed with consideration for cultural, linguistic, and individual diversity. Children *are* penalized for differences, family and community contexts are *not* considered, and modifications to reduce bias are *not* allowed.

Family Engagement

Defined as supports, strategies, and/or content related to how family members (or other important caregivers) can play a variety or roles (passive to active).

- *High*: Specific supports, strategies, and/or content to help improve communication and partnerships with families are provided. Recognizes that families (and other important caregivers) are critical in the lives of young children. Families are viewed as equal team members and have a variety of options or ways of participating in assessment *and* instructional efforts.

- *Medium*: Some supports, strategies, and/or content to help improve communication and partnerships with families are provided; *however*, families tend to have little choice and their role is typically passive (i.e., as informants). Families also may play a role in assessment but *not* instruction (or vice versa).

- *Low*: No supports, strategies, and/or content to help improve communication and partnerships with families are provided. Families are *not* viewed as equal team members and *do not have* options or various ways to participate in assessment *or* instruction.

Teamwork

Defined as supports, strategies, and/or content related to how professionals and family members can work together (e.g., plan together, gather information together, summarize and interpret together, revise instruction together). Weight is given to teamwork efforts across assessment and instruction.

- *High*: Extensive evidence exists that teamwork is conceptualized within a transdisciplinary framework in which members value role release, role extension, role sharing, and open and frequent communication across assessment AND instructional efforts.

- *Medium*: Some evidence exists that teamwork is conceptualized within a transdisciplinary framework in which members value role release, role extension, role sharing, and open and frequent communication across assessment OR instructional efforts.

- *Low*: Little to no evidence exists that teamwork is conceptualized within a transdisciplinary framework in which members value role release, role extension, role sharing, and open and frequent communication across assessment OR instructional efforts. Team members tend to operate within traditional discipline boundaries.

Professional Development

Defined as supports, strategies, and/or content related to initial and ongoing professional development regarding use of the assessment and how to link findings to guide instruction.

- *High*: Considerable attention is given in the materials (e.g., manual, web site) to the need for training to ensure accuracy and fidelity, AND suggestions and/or procedures for training (e.g., additional downloads, tutorials, list of trainers, menu of training options, training videos, self-study materials, FAQ blogs) are systematically provided.

- *Medium*: Some of the materials (e.g., manual, web site) address either the need for training to ensure accuracy and fidelity of assessment, OR suggestions and/or procedures for training (e.g., additional downloads, tutorials, list of trainers, menu of training options, training videos, self-study materials, FAQ blogs) are provided.

- *Low*: Very little if anything in the materials (manual, web site, etc.) addresses the need for training and/or approaches to training.

Technology

Defined as any electronic and/or web-based features designed to support any aspect of the assessment (e.g., online tutorials, interactive web site or even a place to download additional materials, scoring assist, handheld data entry devises, online data management system and/or interface with state databases). Weight is given to technology supports that promote the link between assessment and instruction (i.e., to assist with summarizing, interpreting, planning, and revising).

- *High*: Multiple interactive (e.g., blog, discussion board, online data management system, handheld devices) and static technology-based supports (e.g., downloads, FAQs, tutorials) exist, including those to promote the link between assessment and instruction.

- *Medium*: A single interactive/dynamic technology-based support OR a combination of static options exists.

- *Low*: No technology-based supports OR only static options exist.

Close Up on next page

ABLLS®-R: The Assessment of Basic Language and Learning Skills-Revised

Author(s): James W. Partington

Publication date: 2006

Publisher: Behavior Analysts

Web site(s): http://www.behavioranalysts.com

Cost: $64.95 (includes manual and one protocol)
WebABLLS® first year $100.00 per student profile; renewal $60.00 per year per student profile

Assessment type: Curriculum-referenced assessment

Age range: 2–12 years of age

Domains/subtests: Basic language and learner skills, academic skills, self-help skills, and motor skills with a particular emphasis placed on language

Population targeted: Children who have language delays, autism, or other developmental disabilities

Technology features: WebABLLS® electronic scoring and customized report generation

Translations: Spanish

Other features	Rating		Standard	Rating
Validated purposes	Low		Acceptability	◗
Curricular links	High		Authenticity	◗
Comprehensive coverage	High		Collaboration	◖
Graduated scoring	High		Evidence	◗
Progress monitoring	High		Multifactors	◗
Standards alignment	Low		Sensitivity	◗
Diversity features	Low		Universality	◗
Family engagement	Medium		Utility	◗
Teamwork	Medium			
Professional development	Low		OVERALL	◗
Technology	Medium			

ABLLS®-R: The Assessment of Basic Language and Learning Skills-Revised

Author(s): James W. Partington

About the Measure

The *ABLLS®-R* is a curriculum-referenced, comprehensive system used to assess, track skills, and guide intervention for children with language delays, including children with autism and developmental delays.

It was developed to identify skill deficiencies and to implement and monitor intervention. This assessment is typically used for children from 2 to 12 years of age.

The *ABLLS®-R* provides a task analysis of skills and factors in the child's motivation to respond, ability to attend to environmental stimuli, and ability to generalize and spontaneously use skills.

Authenticity

The *ABLLS®-R* is used to document critical skills necessary to communicate effectively and to learn from everyday experiences. Based primarily on parent and/or educator observations of children in the natural environment, tasks reflect skills that are often challenging for children with developmental disabilities. The items are listed in approximate developmental sequence.

A parent, educator, behavior analyst, psychologist, speech-language therapist, other professional, or combination of individuals can complete the protocol. Information is gathered in three ways: from parents, from educators, and from individuals who regularly interact with the child. Information is obtained from direct observation of the child on different days and across settings and is also acquired through the formal presentation of tasks.

Many skills (e.g., *Takes a common object when offered*) can be observed in the natural environment. Other tasks (e.g., *The student will be able to arrange a set of picture cards in the appropriate sequence*) require a more formal presentation.

The focus of the *ABLLS®-R* is to inform intervention to help a child develop learning skills so that he or she will learn from daily activities without reliance on highly specialized instruction. Such information is invaluable for identifying individual outcomes for the child and family and for planning instruction and/or intervention.

Utility

The *ABLLS®-R* is designed to meet the challenges of assessing and planning interventions for children with language delays including children with autism and developmental delays. Many of the items are constructed to identify skills in different motivational conditions, with complex tasks, and in different contexts. The *ABLLS®-R* includes sections on Cooperation and Reinforcement Effectiveness and Spontaneous Vocalizations, which are not covered in many other assessments but are considered important when assessing children with autism and related developmental delays.

The detailed presentation of items in the *ABLLS®-R* contributes to its clarity and therefore its utility. Each item lists the task name, task objective, question, examples, criteria, and notes. Describing the task in each of these categories leaves no question as to how to interpret any given task. The protocol also contains skill-tracking grids for each student that provide documentation and a visual reference of the child's progress across domains (see Figure 1).

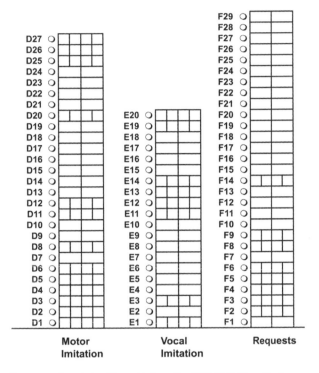

Figure 1. Sample tracking grids from the *ABLLS®-R*. (From Partington, J.W. [2006]. *ABLLS®-R: The Assessment of Basic Language and Learning Skills-Revised*. Walnut Creek, CA: Behavior Analysts; reprinted by permission.)

The level of item detail further assists the assessor in deciphering where the breakdown in skill acquisition has occurred and planning intervention accordingly. Above all, the usefulness of the *ABLLS®-R* lies in the direct linking of assessment tasks to instruction, intervention planning, and individualized education program development. The *ABLLS®-R* attempts to assess generalized learning skills on which other skills can be built and skills that help the child to learn from everyday experiences.

Collaboration

ABLLS®-R is to be completed by parents, educators, and other individuals who interact with the child on a regular basis. The accompanying guide discusses the importance of collecting information from several individuals in this capacity to get the clearest or most comprehensive picture of the child's abilities. The authors recommend gathering input from several individuals to fully understand the child's skill level. It is necessary to determine not only whether the child has the skill but also how he uses the skill (e.g., spontaneously, intermittently) and whether the skill is used consistently across contexts and settings.

Collaboration is enhanced through the *Notes* section on the score form, where information can be recorded regarding the child's performance on a particular item. For instance, one assessor might note under what conditions a child demonstrates a skill or the specifics of how the skill is performed. If a child demonstrates a skill unevenly in different environments, the discrepancy can be investigated and interventions or instructional strategies can be introduced to address generalization.

Evidence Base

Although the *ABLLS®-R* is used extensively by practitioners and researchers, validation studies are not available for the instrument. The publishers report that multiple studies attest that it is a "useful, descriptive measure used by the professional community." For example, Schwartz, Boulware, McBride, and Sandall (2001) and Aman and colleagues (2004) recommend the *ABLLS®-R* for assessing children with autism.

Considerations and Recommendations

- The protocol may be overwhelming to first-time users of the system; however, one of the many strengths of the *ABLLS®-R* is the comprehensive listing of tasks.

- Research on the *ABLLS®-R* is needed regarding evidence of the extent to which scores provide dependable information that is relevant to the desired score-based inferences.

Close Up on next page

A B C

Adaptive Behavior Assessment System– Second Edition (ABAS-II)

Author(s): Patti Harrison and Thomas Oakland

Publication date: 2003

Publisher: Western Psychological Services

Web site(s): http://www.portal.wpspublish.com

Cost: $199.00

Assessment type: Curriculum-referenced assessment with norms

Age range: Birth to 89; divided into five forms: *Parent/Caregiver Form, Birth–5; Parent Form, 5–21; Teacher/Day Care Form, 2–5; Teacher Form, 5–21;* and *Adult Form, 16–89*

Domains/subtests: Assesses adaptive functioning in skill areas specified in the *Diagnostic and Statistical Manual of Mental Disorders, Fourth Edition* and by the American Academy of Intellectual and Developmental Disorders, including Communication, Community Use, Functional Academics, Home Living, Health & Safety, Leisure, Self-Care, Self-Direction, and Social

Population targeted: Individuals who may be experiencing difficulties with the daily adaptive skills necessary for functioning in their environments (e.g., individuals with intellectual disability, learning difficulties, attention deficit disorder, or other impairments); $n \geq 2{,}500$ in national norms for preschool ages

Technology features: *Scoring Assistant Windows CD-ROM* produces technical report with composite scores, provides analyses of skill area strengths and weaknesses and composite score discrepancies, and plots skill area/composite score profiles.

Translations: *Parent Form, Birth–5; Parent Form, 5–21;* and *Teacher-Day Care Form, 2–5* are available in Spanish

Other features	Rating	Standard	Rating
Validated purposes	Medium	Acceptability	◕
Curricular links	Medium	Authenticity	◑
Comprehensive coverage	High	Collaboration	◕
Graduated scoring	Medium	Evidence	◕
Progress monitoring	Medium	Multifactors	◑
Standards alignment	Low	Sensitivity	◔
Diversity features	Medium	Universality	◔
Family engagement	High	Utility	◔
Teamwork	High		
Professional development	High	OVERALL	◕
Technology	Medium		

CLOSE UP

Adaptive Behavior Assessment System-Second Edition (ABAS-II)

Author(s): Patti Harrison and Thomas Oakland

About the Measure

The *ABAS-II* is a premier curriculum-referenced authentic assessment system. Its combination of collaborative features, focus on individual functioning in daily routines, and strong disability-specific normative structure and research evidence base in real-life community settings justify its wide and confident use by interdisciplinary professionals.

Although it is not a curriculum, the *ABAS-II* emphasizes core functional competencies that are teachable, linkable to objectives in most developmental curricula, and critical to promote individual progress.

The *ABAS-II* has the capacity and features to fulfill the major purposes for assessment in early childhood intervention.

Authenticity

The *ABAS-II* in form and use exemplifies authenticity in the assessment process. First, it focuses on adaptive skills as broad, functional competencies that underlie the capability of the child to affect their environment; its functional domains (e.g., Communication, Community Use, Functional Academics, Home Living, Health and Safety, Leisure, Self-Care, Social) capture daily functioning in real-life settings. Second, the *ABAS-II* relies on the observations of significant caregivers in the child's life that know the child well rather than presumed "experts." Third, the *ABAS-II* data derived from various caregivers can be triangulated to create a more representative portrait of the child's true functional capabilities across settings.

Utility

The *ABAS-II* has both the research base and the technical adequacy to support its use to fulfill the major purposes for assessment in early childhood intervention, including functional classification (i.e., diagnosis), general individualized goal planning for intervention, performance monitoring, and even program accountability.

The scoring of the *ABAS-II* recognizes that determination of capabilities is a complex and organic decision-making process rather than a contrived testing process. Thus, scoring supports collaborative decision making as the child's capabilities are classified via a graduated scoring system that is sensitive to individual variations in functioning (e.g., *Is Not Able, Never or Almost Never When Needed, Sometimes When Needed,* or *Always or Almost Always When Needed,* and *Check If You Guessed*). See Figure 1 for a sample of the rating scale. The *Check If You Guessed* option recognizes that all assessment involves some judgment that must be infused into the decision-making process.

ABAS-II items are functional and teachable as important competencies to be promoted in individual intervention and therapy and generalized to natural settings to foster future functional competence (see Figure 2 for sample items). The *ABAS-II* encompasses 457 competencies over

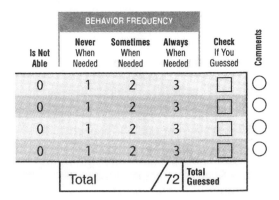

Figure 1. The rating scale used in the *ABAS-II*. (Material from the *ABAS-II* copyright © 2000, 2003, 2008 by Western Psychological Services. Normative Data copyright © 2000, 2003 by Western Psychological Services. Reprinted by permission of the publisher, Western Psychological Services, 12031 Wilshire Boulevard, Los Angeles, California, 90025, U.S.A. (www.wpspublish.com) Not to be reprinted in whole or in part for any additional purpose without the expressed, written permission of the publisher. All rights reserved.)

both the parent (*n* = 216) and professional (*n* = 241) forms, demonstrating both its comprehensiveness and situational breadth.

The variety of scores available on the *ABAS-II* support detection of developmental delay and even cautious diagnosis aligned with the *Diagnostic and Statistical Manual of Mental Disorders, Fourth Edition* and by the American Academy of Intellectual and Developmental Disorders categories to justify eligibility for various services in the human services system.

A unique aspect of the *ABAS-II* is that its item content has undergone initial cross-walking with the functional classification codes of the World Health Organization's *International Classification of Functioning, Disability and Health: Children and Youth Version* (ICF-CY). International professionals can now use the *ABAS-II* as an operational device for interdisciplinary teams to classify disability through functional analysis of activity and social participation (Fevola, Bagnato, & Kronk, 2010; Kronk, 2004).

		Behavior Frequency				
Health and Safety *continued*	Is Not Able	Never When Needed	Sometimes When Needed	Always When Needed	Check If You Guessed	Comments
21. Follows safety rules for fire or weather alarms at home.	0	1	2	3	☐	○
22. Carries hot containers safely and carefully.	0	1	2	3	☐	○
23. Uses electrical outlets or sockets safely.	0	1	2	3	☐	○
24. Cares for his/her minor injuries, for example, paper cuts, knee scrapes, or nosebleeds.	0	1	2	3	☐	○
			Total	/72	Total Guessed	

Leisure

1. Plays with a single toy or game for at least one minute.	0	1	2	3	☐	○
2. Plays alone with toys, games, or other fun activities.	0	1	2	3	☐	○
3. Looks at pictures in books or magazines with an adult.	0	1	2	3	☐	○
4. Watches for a few minutes as people play with toys or games.	0	1	2	3	☐	○
5. Plays simple games like "peek-a-boo" or rolls a ball to others.	0	1	2	3	☐	○

Self-Care

1. Swallows liquids with no difficulty.	0	1	2	3	☐	○
2. Nurses, drinks, or eats willingly, with little encouragement.	0	1	2	3	☐	○
3. Swallows soft, strained, or mashed food such as baby food or applesauce.	0	1	2	3	☐	○
4. Sleeps through most of the night, waking no more than one or two times.	0	1	2	3	☐	○
5. Opens mouth when offered food on a spoon.	0	1	2	3	☐	○

Figure 2. Sample items from three domains. (Material from the *ABAS-II* copyright © 2000, 2003, 2008 by Western Psychological Services. Normative Data copyright © 2000, 2003 by Western Psychological Services. Reprinted by permission of the publisher, Western Psychological Services, 12031 Wilshire Boulevard, Los Angeles, California, 90025, U.S.A. (www.wpspublish.com) Not to be reprinted in whole or in part for any additional purpose without the expressed, written permission of the publisher. All rights reserved.)

Collaboration

Parents, family members, and professionals (e.g., child care providers, teachers, therapists) provide the critical observations for collaborative decision making about a child's capabilities and needs. The *ABAS-II* format enables family members as well as professionals to contribute observations and judgment with ease via natural forms of assessment including direct observation, report, and interview.

Because it includes separate forms for parents, teachers/providers, and other professionals, the *ABAS-II* is particularly well suited for interdisciplinary team assessments using various team formats. Also, the *ABAS-II* has been used effectively and studied qualitatively with the ICF-CY in a clinical setting with teams of allied health professionals and parents for children with disabilities under the Maternal and Child Health Bureau, Leadership Education in Neurodevelopmental Disabilities (LEND) program at the University of Pittsburgh.

Evidence Base

Bagnato, S.J., Fevola, A., Suen, H., Hawthorne, C., & McKeating-Esterle, E. (2006). *The Pennsylvania Early Intervention Outcomes Study (PEIOS): An authentic assessment and program evaluation outcomes and research initiative—Program outcomes research report.* Pittsburgh: Children's Hospital of Pittsburgh, Early Childhood Partnerships.

Pennsylvania research study on the *ABAS-II* for early intervention eligibility, progress monitoring (entry-exit), and accountability through alignment with OSEP child outcome indicators and PA Early Learning Standards.

Harrison, P.L., & Oakland, T. (2003). *Adaptive Behavior Assessment System manual* (2nd ed.). Los Angeles: Western Psychological Services.

The *ABAS-II* manual provides data regarding clinical and matched control group studies in field-validated settings for various disability categories and, most importantly, for developmental delay. Its normative sample for infants, toddlers, preschoolers, and early childhood (through Grade 3) exceeds 2,500. Reliability and validity data also are provided.

Youhua, W., Oakland, T., & Algina, J. (2008). Multigroup Confirmatory Factor Analysis for the Adaptive Behavior Assessment System-II Parent Form, Ages 5–21. *American Journal on Mental Retardation, 113*(3), 178–186.

Examines the content and structure of the *ABAS-II* through a multigroup factor analysis of its skill areas.

Considerations and Recommendations

- For multidimensional assessment in early childhood, the *ABAS-II* is a strong choice for teams in the eligibility determination process and to guide initial goal planning with curricular formats for IFSP and IEP development.

- Use of the *ABAS-II* can drive the movement for enabling "functional assessment and classification" to one day, finally, overturn the predominance of the medical diagnostic model in the disability fields.

Ages & Stages Questionnaires®, Third Edition (ASQ-3™)
A Parent-Completed Child Monitoring System

Author(s): Jane Squires & Diane Bricker
with assistance from Elizabeth Twombly
Robert Nickel, Jantina Clifford, Kimberly Murphy, Robert Hoselton,
LaWanda Potter, Linda Mounts, and Jane Farrell

Publication date: 2009

Publisher: Paul H. Brookes Publishing Co.

Web site(s): http://www.brookespublishing.com

Cost: $249.95 for starter kit; $199.95 for Questionnaires

Assessment type: Curriculum-referenced assessment*

Age range: 1–66 months, divided into 21 age intervals with a separate questionnaire for each

Domains/subtests: Communication, Gross Motor, Fine Motor, Problem Solving, and Personal-Social

Population targeted: Infants and young children at risk; norm group: 15,138 children

Technology features: Questionnaires on CD-ROM; *ASQ-3™ Scoring and Referral DVD*; online management systems, including *ASQ Pro, ASQ Enterprise,* and *ASQ Family Access*

Translations: Questionnaires available in Spanish; second edition available in French and Korean

Other features	Rating	Standard	Rating
Validated purposes	High	Acceptability	◑
Curricular links	Medium	Authenticity	◑
Comprehensive coverage	Medium	Collaboration	◑
Graduated scoring	Medium	Evidence	◕
Progress monitoring	Medium	Multifactors	◐
Standards alignment	Medium	Sensitivity	◐
Diversity features	Medium	Universality	◐
Family engagement	High	Utility	◕
Teamwork	Low		
Professional development	High	OVERALL	◑
Technology	High		

Note: This tool is intended for developmental screening and monitoring, not assessment.

Ages & Stages Questionnaires®: Social-Emotional (ASQ:SE)

A Parent-Completed, Child-Monitoring System for Social-Emotional Behaviors

Author(s): Jane Squires, Diane Bricker, & Elizabeth Twombly, with assistance from Suzanne Yockelson, Maura Schoen Davis, and Younghee Kim

Publication date: 2003

Publisher: Paul H. Brookes Publishing Co.

Web site(s): http://www.brookespublishing.com
http://www.agesandstages.com

Cost: $194.95 for starter kit

Assessment type: Curriculum-referenced assessment*

Age range: 3–66 months, divided into eight age intervals with a separate questionnaire for each

Domains/subtests: Self-Regulation, Compliance, Communication, Adaptive, Autonomy, Affect, and Interaction with People

Population targeted: Infants and young children at risk who may need further assessment; norm group: >3,000 children

Technology features: Questionnaires on CD-ROM, *ASQ-SE in Practice DVD*; online management systems, including *ASQ Pro, ASQ Enterprise,* and *ASQ Family Access*

Translations: Questionnaires available in Spanish

Other features	Rating	Standard	Rating
Validated purposes	High	Acceptability	◕
Curricular links	Low	Authenticity	◕
Comprehensive coverage	Low	Collaboration	◕
Graduated scoring	Medium	Evidence	◕
Progress monitoring	Medium	Multifactors	◑
Standards alignment	Low	Sensitivity	◑
Diversity features	Medium	Universality	◑
Family engagement	High	Utility	◔
Teamwork	Low		
Professional development	High	OVERALL	◑
Technology	High		

*Note: This tool is intended for social-emotional screening and monitoring, not assessment.

Close Up on next page

A B C

Assessment, Evaluation, and Programming System for Infants and Children (AEPS®), Second Edition

AEPS
Assessment, Evaluation, and Programming System for Infants and Children
SECOND EDITION

VOLUME 2 Test
Birth to Three Years & Three to Six Years

DIANE BRICKER

Author(s): Series edited by Diane Bricker

Publication date: 2002

Publisher: Paul H. Brookes Publishing Co.

Web site(s): http://www.brookespublishing.com
http://aepslinkedsystem.com
http://www.aepsinteractive.com

Cost: *Complete AEPS®, Second Edition (Vols. 1–4)* $239.00
Volumes and forms also sold separately

Assessment type: Curriculum-embedded assessment

Age range: Divided into two levels: Birth to 36 months (0–3 years) and 36–72 months (3–6 years); curricula are packaged in separate volumes, while both test levels are contained within an individual volume

Domains/subtests: Fine Motor, Gross Motor, Adaptive, Cognitive, Social-Communication, and Social; domains subdivided into groups of related behaviors; test addresses skills from across content areas (e.g., reading, math, science, social studies)

Population targeted: Children who are at risk or who have a disability; also appropriate for identifying and monitoring development of children who are developing typically

Technology features: Web-based data management and electronic scoring available with *AEPSinteractive (AEPSi)*

Translations: Assessment available in Spanish

Other features	Rating	Standard	Rating
Validated purposes	High	Acceptability	◑
Curricular links	High	Authenticity	◑
Comprehensive coverage	High	Collaboration	◑
Graduated scoring	High	Evidence	◑
Progress monitoring	High	Multifactors	◑
Standards alignment	High	Sensitivity	◑
Diversity features	High	Universality	◑
Family engagement	High	Utility	◑
Teamwork	High		
Professional development	High	OVERALL	◑
Technology	High		

A B C

Assessment, Evaluation, and Programming System for Infants and Children (AEPS®), Second Edition

Author(s): Series edited by Diane Bricker

About the Measure

The *AEPS®* is the most comprehensive linked system that embraces the importance of working in collaboration with families and a transdisciplinary team.

The *AEPS®* continues to evolve and includes strategies and support for use during the eligibility process, for meeting OSEP accountability mandates, and for online collaboration.

The *AEPS®* test has an extremely strong research base to validate its use for specific and varied purposes in early childhood intervention.

Authenticity

The *AEPS®* is designed to measure children's competency on functional skills that are necessary to ensure their participation in daily routines and activities. For example, items such as *Opens front-opening garments using any functional means, Quiets to a familiar voice, Responds to communication from peers*, and *Indicates need to use toilet* illustrate an emphasis on function versus form.

The system relies primarily on observation of children conducted by familiar caregivers in the natural environment and, at times, during semi-structured play activities.

The Family Report (see Figure 1) in particular, allows teams to consider the child's competence and role during daily family and community activities and to examine the success or challenge

---

Family Report I

SECTION 1

Eating

1. Where, when, and with whom does your child usually eat breakfast, lunch, and dinner?

2. What kinds of food does your child eat?

3. Meals are usually enjoyable because

4. Meals can be difficult because

Date reviewed: _____   Noted changes: _____

Figure 1. Sample portion of *AEPS®* Family Report. (From Bricker, D. [Series Ed.]. [2002]. *Assessment, Evaluation, and Programming System for Infants and Children (AEPS®), Second Edition.* Baltimore: Paul H. Brookes Publishing Co.; reprinted by permission.)

each routine presents. Such information is invaluable for identifying individual outcomes for the child and family and for planning instruction and/or intervention.

Utility

The assessment is linked to a general curriculum guide that includes activity-based teaching suggestions, tips for environmental arrangements, instructional sequences, and other important considerations for each goal. The curriculum guides (Birth to Three Years and Three to Six Years) begin with several chapters pertaining to the correct use of the curriculum and how to most successfully implement the ideas contained therein. The *AEPS®* curriculum guides identify what should be taught and where to begin instruction and intervention and provide structured guidance for professionals on how to teach in a manner that facilitates children's optimal functioning. Furthermore, the composition of the *AEPS®* Child Observation Data Recording Form (CODRF) is such that continual observation of children's performance over time is encouraged; in this way, teams are able to monitor the changes that occur in a child's performance as various instructional techniques and intervention strategies are employed. Lastly, the fact that modifications are allowed and encouraged ensures the *AEPS®* test is culturally, linguistically, and individually nonbiased. See http://aepsblog.blogspot.com for more detailed information on how to make modifications to *AEPS®* test items.

Collaboration

The *AEPS®* is designed to be approached in a truly transdisciplinary manner, with families playing an integral role in the assessment and subsequent instructional efforts. Role sharing among all team members is viewed as critical to the success of the child. Thus, it is understood that each member of the team has expertise to provide during all aspects of the process (e.g., the teacher knows how to arrange the environment and elicit responses, the parent knows what the child likes and is likely to do, the speech therapist knows how the child enunciates a word and may consequently be able to decipher the meaning of utterances better than others). The *AEPS®* encourages caregivers to go above and beyond merely sharing information and instead asks that they work closely as team members during each step of the assessment and instructional process.

Evidence Base

The Early Intervention Management and Research Group provides an annotated bibliography of the research on the 1st and 2nd editions of the *AEPS®* on its web site: http://aepslinkedsystem.com/annotatedbio.html. Below is a summary of the annotated bibliography.

- The results of eight studies described the reliability of the measure, including test–retest and interrater reliability (Bailey & Bricker, 1986; Bricker, Bailey, & Slentz, 1990; Grisham-Brown, Hallam, & Pretti-Frontczak, 2008; Hsia, 1993; Macy, Bricker, & Squires, 2005; Noh, 2005; Sher, 1999; Slentz, 1986).

- Two studies documented the internal consistency of the measure (Bricker et al., 1990; Slentz, 1986).

- One study examined the effects of a training program on the fidelity of the *AEPS®* (Grisham-Brown, Hallam, & Pretti-Frontczak, 2008).

- Researchers in three studies analyzed the validity of the *AEPS®* for determining eligibility for special education services (Bricker et al., 2008; Bricker, Yovanoff, Capt, & Allen, 2003; Kim, 1997).

- Eight studies further examined the validity of the *AEPS®* including congruent, social, concurrent, construct, and treatment validity (Bricker et al., 1990; Bricker & Pretti-Frontczak, 1997; Cripe, 1990; Gao, 2008; Macy, Bricker, & Squires, 2005; Noh, 2005; Sher, 1999; Slentz, 1986).

- Researchers across seven studies identified the utility of the *AEPS®* for writing quality goals and objectives (Cripe, 1990; Hamilton, 1995; Hsia, 1993; Notari & Bricker, 1990; Notari & Drinkwater, 1991; Pretti-Frontczak & Bricker, 2000; Straka, 1994).

Considerations and Recommendations

- The heart and strength of the system remains firmly in linking authentic assessment information with developmentally appropriate instruction and/or intervention.

- Given the comprehensive nature of the system, it can be overwhelming, particularly to those without a strong background in child development. Users are encouraged to access publisher and author training and technical assistance supports. The following web sites include information about *AEPS®* training opportunities:

  http://brookespublishing.com/onlocation/topics/AEPS.htm

  http://aepslinkedsystem.com/trainings.html

  http://www.aepsinteractive.com/training.htm

- The *AEPS®* has one of the strongest evidence bases of assessments reviewed.

Autism Screening Instrument for Educational Planning— Third Edition (ASIEP-3)

Author(s): David A. Krug, Joel R. Arick, and Patricia J. Almond

Publication date: 2008

Publisher: PRO-ED

Web site(s): http://www.proedinc.com

Cost: $265.00 for the kit (manual, audio CD, set of toys/manipulatives; 25 of each record form)

Assessment type: Curriculum-referenced assessment with norms

Age range: 2 years, 0 months to 13 years, 11 months

Domains/subtests: Components are *Autism Behavior Checklist of Behavioral Characteristics, Sample of Vocal Behavior, Educational Assessment* (In-Seat Behavior, Receptive Language, Expressive Language, Body Concept, and Speech Imitation), and *Prognosis of Learning Rate*

Population targeted: Designed to help parents and professionals identify individuals with autism, facilitate placement, and guide educational program planning and progress monitoring; norm group: 1,049 individuals, ages 18 months to 35 years, 172 of whom were previously diagnosed with autism; 62 individuals, ages 3 years to 23 years, all of whom were previously diagnosed with autism; and 953 adults, 95% with mental retardation diagnosis

Technology features: Audio CD used for *Interaction Assessment* to signal observation intervals

Translations: None

Other features	Rating	Standard	Rating
Validated purposes	Medium	Acceptability	◕
Curricular links	Medium	Authenticity	◕
Comprehensive coverage	Medium	Collaboration	◑
Graduated scoring	Medium	Evidence	◕
Progress monitoring	High	Multifactors	◕
Standards alignment	Low	Sensitivity	◐
Diversity features	High	Universality	◑
Family engagement	Medium	Utility	◕
Teamwork	High		
Professional development	Medium	OVERALL	◑
Technology	Medium		

Cover image from Krug, D.A., Arick, J.R., & Almond, P.J. (2008). *Autism Screening Instrument for Education Planning—Third Edition* (ASIEP-3). Austin, TX: PRO-ED; used with permission.

Basic School Skills Inventory— Third Edition (BSSI-3)

Author(s): Donald D. Hammill, James E. Leigh, Nils A. Pearson, and Taddy Maddox

Publication date: 1998

Publisher: PRO-ED

Web site(s): http://www.proedinc.com

Cost: $118.00 per kit (manual and 25 forms); $67.00 for manual; $57.00 for 25 forms

Assessment type: Curriculum-referenced assessment with norms

Age range: 4–8 years

Domains/subtests: Samples basic early learning competencies considered essential for school success from the areas of Spoken Language, Reading, Writing, Mathematics, Classroom Behavior, Daily Living Skills, and Overall Skill Level

Population targeted: Children who are at high risk for school failure, who need more in-depth assessment, and who should be referred for additional study; norm group: $n = 757$

Technology features: None

Translations: None

Other features	Rating	Standard	Rating
Validated purposes	Medium	Acceptability	◗
Curricular links	Medium	Authenticity	◗
Comprehensive coverage	Medium	Collaboration	◔
Graduated scoring	Medium	Evidence	◐
Progress monitoring	Medium	Multifactors	◗
Standards alignment	Medium	Sensitivity	◐
Diversity features	Medium	Universality	◔
Family engagement	Low	Utility	◖
Teamwork	Low		
Professional development	Medium	OVERALL	◐
Technology	Low		

Cover image from Hammill, D.D., Leigh, J.E., Pearson, N.A., & Maddox, T. (1998). *Basic School Skills Inventory—Third Edition* (BSSI-3). Austin, TX: PRO-ED; used with permission.

Close Up on next page

A B C

Behavior Assessment System for Children, Second Edition (BASC™-2)

Author(s): Cecil R. Reynolds and Randy W. Kamphaus

Publication date: 2004

Publisher: NCS Pearson

Web site(s): http://psychcorp.pearsonassessments.com

Cost: $485.00 for the Hand Scored Starter Kit

Assessment type: Curriculum-referenced assessment with norms

Age range: 2–25 years; the *Teacher Rating Scales* and *Parent Rating Scales* each have three levels: preschool (2–5 years), child (6–11 years), and adolescent (12–21 years); the *Self-Report of Personality* has three levels: child (8–11 years), adolescent (12–18 years), and college (18–25 years)

Domains/subtests: Activities of Daily Living, Adaptability, Functional Communication, Leadership, Social Skills, and Study Skills

Population targeted: Children in educational or clinical settings who are diagnosed with or suspected of having emotional and/or behavior issues; multiple norms are available for each scale including norm groups of the general population, all clinical conditions, learning disabilities, attention-deficit/hyperactivity disorder, male only, female only, and clinical 19–21 years still in high school; preschool norm group sizes range from 125 to 1,200

Technology features: *BASC™-2 ASSIST* and *BASC™ ASSIST PLUS,* which are scoring and reporting software; *BASC™ POP,* which is a portable observation program that can be loaded onto desktop computers, laptops, and personal digital assistants

Translations: Spanish

Other features	Rating	Standard	Rating
Validated purposes	High	Acceptability	◗
Curricular links	Medium	Authenticity	◗
Comprehensive coverage	Medium	Collaboration	◗
Graduated scoring	High	Evidence	◗
Progress monitoring	Medium	Multifactors	◗
Standards alignment	Low	Sensitivity	◗
Diversity features	Medium	Universality	◗
Family engagement	High	Utility	◗
Teamwork	Low		
Professional development	Medium	OVERALL	◗
Technology	Medium		

Behavior Assessment System for Children, Second Edition (BASC™-2)

Author(s): Cecil R. Reynolds and Randy W. Kamphaus

About the Measure

The *BASC™-2* is a well researched, multimethod, multidimensional authentic assessment used for diagnosis and educational classification of emotional and behavioral disorders.

The second edition includes expansive normative data on a wide demographic pool from both clinical and educational settings.

The assessment's subdomains elicit information that provides a clear picture of how a child's behavior influences adaptation to daily routines. The *BASC™-2* should be used by teachers, parents, and other professionals who know the child's typical behavior best. The various instruments within the *BASC™-2* system support this collaborative approach, with psychologists aiding in the interpretation of results.

Authenticity

There are five components of the *BASC™-2* assessment. They can be used individually or collectively depending on the intended use of the resulting data.

The Teacher Rating Scale (TRS) and Parent Rating Scale (PRS) consist of behaviors that could occur during a child's typical daily activities. For example, *Congratulates others when good things happen to them* and *Cannot wait to take turn* are included in both the preschool TRS and the PRS.

The Structured Developmental History (SDH) prompts the administrator to gather primarily medical information, achievement dates of key developmental milestones, and social history from parents either as part of an interview or as a parent-completed questionnaire. Here are some sample items from the SDH:

- Is this child closer to one parent than the other (yes/no)? If yes, which?

- Has this child ever had psychological counseling or therapy?

- Prefers playing with younger children (yes/no)

- What activities does this child enjoy?

The Student Observation System (SOS) is a structured method of collecting information about a child's typical functioning in a classroom setting. The authors note that completing a few observation sessions across days and activities on a child will increase the reliability of the data. Each observation session lasts 15 minutes. The items on the SOS data collection form (see Figure 1) are examples of specific behaviors that could be observed in any classroom setting. The focus of the SOS is clearly on gathering detailed information on a child's functioning in his or her usual classroom setting with no interference or contrived situations produced by the observer. The fifth component is the Self Report of Personality (SRP), which can only be used with children who are 8 years old or older and have at least third grade reading level.

Part A–Behavior Key and Checklist

Directions: Use the following list of behaviors as a reference during the 15-minute observation period of Part B. At the end of the period, mark the frequency of each behavior. If the behavior occurred, indicate if it was disruptive.

Check one:
NO = Not Observed
SO = Sometimes Observed
FO = Frequently Observed
If behavior is Disruptive, check **Dis.**

1. Response to Teacher/Lesson
Listening to teacher/classmate or following directions
Interacting with teacher in class/group
Working with teacher one-on-one
Standing at teacher's desk
Other

2. Peer Interaction
Playing/working with other student(s)
Talking with other student(s)
Touching another student appropriately
Other

3. Work on School Subjects
Doing seat work
Working at blackboard or computer
Other

4. Transition Movement
Putting on/taking off coat
Moving around room (appropriately)
Preparing materials for beginning/end of lesson
Being out of the room
Other

5. Inappropriate Movement
Fidgeting in seat
Walking around classroom
Playing at blackboard inappropriately
Being removed from the classroom
Using work materials inappropriately
Passing notes
Copying answers
Jumping out of seat
Running around classroom
Sitting/standing beside desk (on floor)
Sitting/standing on desk
Clinging to teacher
Other

6. Inattention
Staring blankly/daydreaming
Doodling
Looking around
Looking at hands
Fiddling with object(s)/fingers
Other

7. Inappropriate Vocalization
Laughing inappropriately
Tattling
Teasing
Making disruptive noises
Arguing/talking back to teacher
Arguing with student
Talking out
Crying
Other

8. Somatization
Sleeping/head down
Complaining of not feeling well
Other

9. Repetitive Motor Movements
Finger/pencil tapping
Foot tapping/swinging
Spinning an object
Rocking
Hand flapping/waving
Pacing
Talking/humming/singing to self
Other self-stimulatory behavior

10. Aggression
Kicking others
Hitting others with hand
Throwing object(s) at others
Destroying property
Pushing others
Steal
Oth

11. S
ad-bang
ye-gouging
Biting or chewing nonfood items (pica)
Other self-mutilation

12. Inappropriate Sexual Behavior
Engaging in sexual or imitative sexual behavior with a partner
Engaging in sexual or imitative sexual behavior without a partner
Touching others inappropriately
Masturbating
Other

13. Bowel/Bladder Problems
Enuresis
Encopresis
Other

14. Other

Part B–Time Sampling of Behavior

Directions: At the end of each 30-second interval, observe the child's behavior for approximately 3 seconds (for example, when the stopwatch reads 0:30–0:33). Then place a check mark (✓) in the time column next to each category of behavior that occurred during that interval.

Adaptive Behaviors
Response to Teacher/Lesson
Peer Interaction
Work on School Subjects
Transition Movement

Problem Behaviors
Inappropriate Movement
Inattention
appropriate ocalizat
Repetitive Motor Movements
Aggression
Self-Injurious Behavior
Inappropriate Sexual Behavior
Bowel/Bladder Problems

Comments:

Figure 1. Student Observation System data collection form. (*Behavior Assessment System for Children, Second Edition (BASC™-2)*. Copyright © 2004 NCS Pearson, Inc. Reproduced with permission. All rights reserved.)

Utility

The *BASC™-2* has been validated for a number of different uses including as a diagnostic tool for certain behavioral disorders, as a screener for adaptive behavior issues, and as a tool for identifying appropriate intervention goals.

In preschool-age children, the *BASC™-2* can detect the following clinically significant maladaptive behaviors: aggression, anxiety, attention, attention-deficit/hyperactivity disorder (including subtypes combined, primarily inattentive, and primarily hyperactive/impulsive), generalized anxiety disorder, posttraumatic stress disorder, separation anxiety disorder, overanxious disorder, and avoidant disorder.

When used as a screening tool at the preschool level, the *BASC™-2* assesses adaptive behavior in the subcategories of Activities of Daily Living, Adaptability, Functional Communication, Leadership, and Social Skills.

All of the measures include items worded as positive and negative statements. For example, in the SOS, *Touching another student appropriately* is a positively stated item, whereas *Kicking others* is a negatively stated item. Reynolds and Kamphaus (the authors) recommended using test items with extremes scores (positive or negative, depending on the wording of the item) as target behaviors for intervention. For example, if on the TRS a child receives a rating of *Always* for the behavior *Refuses to join group activities*, the psychologist may plan or help the teacher to plan an intervention focused on increasing the child's participation in group activities. In another example, if on the PRS a child receives a rating of *Never* for the behavior *Makes friends easily*, the psychologist may plan or help the teacher to plan an intervention for home and school focused on teaching the child skills for making friends.

Collaboration

Depending on which measure the test administrator chooses to use, he or she will collaborate with the child's parents and/or the child's teacher to gather information. The SDH component includes numerous open-ended questions that can elicit significant input from the child's parents if the parents are willing to provide detailed information. The PRS and TRS consist of close-ended questions and therefore do not allow for as much input. Using the results of the assessment, parents and teachers also can participate in the selection of intervention goals.

Evidence Base

Pearson Education, Inc. (2009). *BASC™ and BASC™-2 research bibliography*. Retrieved on July 31, 2009, from http://pearsonassess.com/NR/rdonlyres/45A61151-4AAC-412F-BB91-8CAE5F6FA7E6/0/BASC_BASC2_bib.pdf

The bibliography lists 137 publications from 1992 to 2005 related to the *BASC™* and *BASC™-2*. Fourteen of the publications are reviews of the *BASC™* or *BASC™-2*. Over half of the articles listed are reports from empirical studies including numerous studies documenting the psychometric properties (e.g., convergent validity, discriminate validity, treatment validity) of the *BASC™* and *BASC™-2*. Validation studies for Spanish language versions are also listed. The remaining items in the bibliography consist of research studies that utilize the *BASC™* or *BASC™-2*, descriptions of diagnostic criteria, and theoretical works.

Reynolds, C.R., & Kamphaus, R.W. (2002). *The clinician's guide to the behavior assessment system for children.* New York: The Guilford Press.

Describes numerous published research studies that support the reliability and validity of the first edition of the *BASC™*. The following studies are a brief indication of what research is included in the book:

- At least eight studies address the utility of the *BASC™* (Doyle, Ostrander, Skare, Crosby, & August, 1997; Hutchinson 1999; Johnson-Cramer, 1998; Nelson, Martin, Hodge, Havill, & Kemphaus, 1999; Ostrander, Weinfurt, Yarnhold, & August, 1998; Reynolds & Kamphaus, 1992; Shelby, Nagle, Barnett-Queen, Quattlebaum, & Wuori, 1998; Vaugh, Riccio, Hynd, & Hall 1997).

- At least four studies support the reliability of the *BASC™* (Kamphaus et al., 2000; Lett & Kamphaus, 1997; Murphy, 2000; Reynolds & Kamphaus, 1992).

- At least two studies describe the predictive validity of the *BASC™* (Thorpe, Kamphaus, Rowe, & Fleckenstein, 2000; Verhulst, Koot, & Van der Ende, 1994).

Considerations and Recommendations

- Various rating scales and the student observation system make this assessment a strong choice for identifying children's behavioral needs and planning appropriate interventions.

- The *BASC™-2* system should be implemented and interpreted by an individual with training in psychology that includes specific training in the use of psychological assessments.

- Despite its popularity, the *BASC™-2* should be used in early intervention with caution since its psychopathologic approach to diagnosis runs counter to the noncategorical (e.g., delay) foundation to service delivery in early childhood intervention.

Close Up on next page

Behavior Rating Inventory of Executive Function®-Preschool Version (BRIEF®-P)

Author(s): Gerard A. Gioia, Kimberly Andrews Espy, and Peter K. Isquith

Publication date: 2003

Publisher: Psychological Assessment Resources

Web site(s): http://www.parinc.com

Cost: $145.00 for the introductory kit (includes *BRIEF®-P Professional Manual*, 25 *Rating Forms*, and 25 *Scoring Summary/Profile Forms*)

Assessment type: Curriculum-referenced assessment with norms

Age range: 2 years, 0 months to 5 years, 11 months

Domains/subtests: Assesses executive function behaviors and self-regulatory attributes and difficulties using five clinical scales including: Inhibit, Shift, Emotional Control, Working Memory, and Plan/Organize; two validity scales, Inconsistency and Negativity, designed to measure inconsistent and/or excessively negative responses; clinical scales form three broad indexes: Inhibitory Self-Control Index, Flexibility Index, and Emergent Metacognition Index and a Global Executive Composite score

Population targeted: Preschool children including those with attention disorders, emergent learning disabilities, language disorders, pervasive developmental disorders, traumatic brain injuries, lead exposure, and other potential developmental, neurological, medical and psychiatric conditions; standardization sample: *n* = 460 (parents) and *n* = 302 (teachers), demographics representative of 1999 census; clinical samples consisted of children with a variety of disorders

Technology features: *Behavior Rating Inventory of Executive Function® Software Portfolio–Preschool Module (BRIEF®-P SP)*

Translations: Contact publisher for details

Other features	Rating	Standard	Rating
Validated purposes	Medium	Acceptability	◑
Curricular links	Low	Authenticity	◔
Comprehensive coverage	Low	Collaboration	●
Graduated scoring	Medium	Evidence	◔
Progress monitoring	Medium	Multifactors	◔
Standards alignment	Medium	Sensitivity	◔
Diversity features	Low	Universality	◑
Family engagement	High	Utility	◑
Teamwork	Medium		
Professional development	Low	OVERALL	◑
Technology	Medium		

Behavior Rating Inventory of Executive Function®-Preschool Version (BRIEF®-P)

Author(s): Gerard A. Gioia, Kimberly Andrews Espy, and Peter K. Isquith

About the Measure

The *BRIEF®-P* is a psychometrically sound, authentic, curriculum-referenced assessment of executive function in young children.

Its user-friendly organization assists in administration and gaining input from families and other familiar caregivers.

The theoretical basis and development of the tool are clearly articulated.

Authenticity

The *BRIEF®-P* utilizes parent and teacher input in assessing the behavior of young children ages 2 years to 5 years, 11 months across home and preschool environments. The rating form is to be completed by individuals who have extended contact with the child. Rating by both parents (if applicable) is desirable, and if more than one teacher interacts with the child regularly, it is beneficial to obtain ratings from those teachers or child care providers to get a complete picture of how the child responds in different environments. The raters are asked to report not only how frequently a child exhibits a behavior but also how often the behavior is problematic relative to other children of the same age. See Figure 1 for sample items from the *BRIEF®-P*. It is within routines in these everyday settings that executive functions such as planning, inhibition, working memory, and problem solving can be observed, providing an ecologically valid assessment.

During the past 6 months, how often has each of the following behaviors been a *problem*?
(Never, Sometimes, or Often)

1. Overreacts to small problems
6. Has explosive, angry outbursts
8. Does not stop laughing at funny things or events when others stop

---

Figure 1. Sample items from the *BRIEF®-P*. (Reproduced by special permission of the Publisher, Psychological Assessment Resources, Inc., 16204 North Florida Avenue, Lutz, Florida 33549, from the Behavior Rating Inventory of Executive Function-Preschool Version by Gerard A. Gioia, PhD, Kimberly Andrews Espy, PhD, Peter K. Isquith, PhD, Copyright 1996, 1998, 2000, 2001, 2003 by PAR, Inc. Further reproduction is prohibited without permission from PAR, Inc.)

Utility

The purpose of the *BRIEF®-P* is to detect early problems in self-regulation and aid in intervention and educational planning. Assessing executive functions is particularly important for young children because self-regulatory capacity emerges during the infant and preschool years. It is also challenging to assess executive functioning in young children due to the variability and inconsistency in young children's behavior.

In practical terms, the *BRIEF®-P* is easy to use and can be administered in approximately 10–15 minutes. As the Scoring Summary is completed, the results are transferred to a graph (see Figure 2). The plotting of scores assists in interpretation and provides a visual representation of the child's scores relative to the normative sample. The manual provides a script explaining the rating process to parents and teachers.

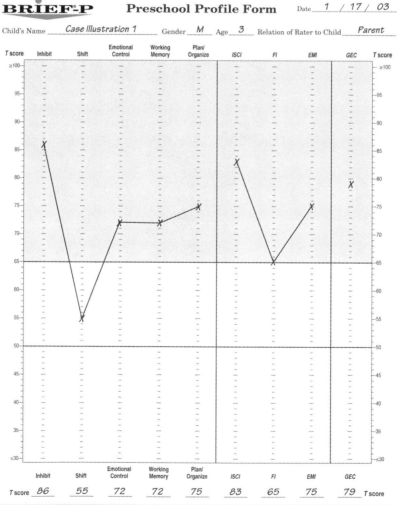

Figure 2. Sample of the preschool profile form with graphed scores. (Reproduced by special permission of the Publisher, Psychological Assessment Resources, Inc., 16204 North Florida Avenue, Lutz, Florida 33549, from the Behavior Rating Inventory of Executive Function–Preschool Version by Gerard A. Gioia, PhD, Kimberly Andrews Espy, PhD, Peter K. Isquith, PhD, Copyright 1996, 1998, 2000, 2001, 2003 by PAR, Inc. Further reproduction is prohibited without permission from PAR, Inc.)

Collaboration

The authors of the *BRIEF®-P* acknowledge the wealth of information that parents and caregivers have available to them regarding the behaviors of young children in their care. The manual stresses the importance of establishing rapport with the caregiver or teacher completing the form. The manual also provides two separate scripts for the professional to use as a guide when explaining the form to caregivers and teachers. Both guides are written in respectful language, requesting help to rate the child's behaviors. Both guides are sensitive to the task of the prospective raters, and the caregiver guide reflects family centeredness.

Evidence Base

Cwik, M., & Espy, K. (2003). External validity of the *BRIEF®-P* in normally developing preschoolers. *Journal of the International Neuropsychological Society, 9,* 297.

   An investigation of the convergent and discriminant validity of the *BRIEF®-P.*

Gioia, G.A., Espy, K., & Isquith, P.K. (2003). *BRIEF®-P: Behavior Rating Inventory of Executive Function–Preschool Version: Professional manual.* Lutz, FL: Psychological Assessment Resources.

   Standardization procedures and evidence of the reliability and validity of the *BRIEF®-P* are provided in addition to thorough descriptions of the development and conceptual basis of the *BRIEF®-P.*

Gioia, G.A., Isquith, P.K., & Espy, K. (2003). Construct validity of the Behavior Rating Inventory of Executive Function–Preschool Version. *Journal of the International Neuropsychological Society, 9,* 297.

   An examination of the *BRIEF®-P* construct validity using factor analysis.

Isquith, P.K., Crawford, J.S., Espy, K.A., & Gioia G.A. (2005). Assessment of executive function in preschool-aged children. *Mental Retardation and Developmental Disabilities Research Reviews, 11,* 209–215.

   Disciminant validity between attention-deficit/hyperactivity disorder (ADHD) subtypes was examined in this study.

Mahone, E.M., & Hoffman, J. (2007). Behavior ratings of executive function among preschoolers with ADHD. *The Clinical Neuropsychologist, 21,* 569–586.

   This study investigated convergent and discriminant validity of the *BRIEF®-P.*

Considerations and Recommendations

* As with most parent- and teacher-completed rating scales, the accuracy is dependent on the examiner's knowledge of the child and ability to answer the items; the use of multiple observers in a "triangulation" model enables the most representative information to be collected.

* Items are stated as negative responses (e.g., *Overreacts; Has explosive, angry outbursts*) and may present a challenge to the team in using a strength-based approach and/or identifying positive and prosocial replacement behaviors.

Close Up
on next
page

Behavioral Characteristics Progression (BCP)

Author(s): VORT Corporation, Joanne Gilles, Jim Mooney, and Patricia Teaford, et al.

Publication date: 1997

Publisher: VORT Corporation

Web site(s): http://www.vort.com

Cost: *BCP Instructional Activities* $59.95
   Assessment Record Booklets $6.00 each for 1-9, $5.50 each for 10-99, and $5.00 each for 100 or more

Assessment type: Curriculum-embedded assessment

Age range: Developmental age of 1-14 years; emphasis is on categories of behavior rather than age level

Domains/subtests: Dense and sequenced hierarchy of behavioral characteristics that have been grouped into strands from the areas of Cognition, Language, Gross Motor, Fine Motor, Social, Self-Help and Vocational

Population targeted: Children and adults with physical and intellectual delays and disabilities

Technology features: None

Translations: Spanish

Other features	Rating	Standard	Rating
Validated purposes	Low	Acceptability	◗
Curricular links	High	Authenticity	◗
Comprehensive coverage	High	Collaboration	◖
Graduated scoring	Medium	Evidence	◯
Progress monitoring	Medium	Multifactors	◗
Standards alignment	Medium	Sensitivity	◗
Diversity features	Low	Universality	◗
Family engagement	Low	Utility	◗
Teamwork	Medium		
Professional development	Low	OVERALL	◗
Technology	Medium		

Behavioral Characteristics Progression (BCP)

Author(s): VORT Corporation, Joanne Gilles, Jim Mooney, and Patricia Teaford, et al.

About the Measure

The *BCP* is a comprehensive, authentic, curriculum-embedded system for assessing and intervening for individuals with intellectual and behavioral exceptionalities.

Originally created by VORT and the Santa Cruz County Office of Education, this criterion-referenced assessment aims to directly link assessment to IEP development to instructional planning.

The system includes an assessment record booklet and instructional activities manual that contains thousands of lesson plans to assist in teaching self-help, motor, communication, social, and academic skills.

Authenticity

The *BCP* contains 2,300 observable characteristics that are grouped into strands (e.g., Sign Language, Honesty, Hygiene, Task Completion). Age is deemphasized through the functional hierarchies of the behavioral strands; however, the strands generally start at 1 year of age and proceed in developmental sequence to about 14 years of age, or what age is considered acceptable for the characteristic according to societal norms. An example of a sequence of skills in the attention strand under the cognitive domain is provided in Figure 1.

Information to score the *BCP* can be collected in various ways including through direct observation in natural settings, structured play, and caregiver interview. The protocol includes a list of all assessment items listed by domain, called the *index*. The team is instructed to review the index and determine which strands might be pertinent to the particular child and/or student. The rater then chooses the domain and strands to assess.

A B C

COGNITIVE	BCP Assessment Record	© 1997 VORT Corporation. May not be copied in any form. All rights reserved.

01
Attends to
easy/ familiar task from 0 to 5 seconds when supervised

Strand 01.
Attention Span

- Remains at task only when distractions are not present
- Ignores teaching-oriented classroom stimuli
- Attends to task only with continual direction/assistance
- Displays bored behavior during classroom activities
- Attends to others activities rather than own tasks
- Substitutes another activity for assigned task

02 Attends to easy/familiar task without supervision from 0 to 5	**03** Attends to easy/familiar task from 5 to 10 seconds when supervised	**04** Attends to easy/familiar task without supervision from 5 to 10	**05** Attends to easy/familiar task from 10 to 15 seconds when super-	**06** Attends to easy/familiar task without supervision from 10 to 15	**07** Attends to easy/familiar task from 15 to 30 seconds when super-	**08** Attends to easy/familiar task without supervision from 15 to 30
09 Attends to easy/familiar task from 30 to 45 seconds when super-	**10** Attends to easy/familiar task without supervision from 30 to 45	**11** Attends to easy/familiar task from 45 seconds to 1 minute when	**12** Attends to easy/familiar task without supervision from 45 seconds	**13** Attends to easy/familiar task from 1 minute to 5 min- utes when	**14** Attends to easy/familiar task without supervision from 1 minute to	**15** Attends to easy/familiar task from 5 min- utes to 10 min- utes when
16 Attends to easy/familiar task without supervision from 5 minutes	**17** Attends to easy/familiar task from 10 minutes to 25 minutes when	**18** Attends to difficult/novel task for 30 seconds to 1 minute when	**19** Attends to difficult/novel task for 30 seconds to 1 minute without	**20** Attends to difficult/novel task for 1 to 5 minutes when supervised	**21** Attends to difficult/novel task for 1 to 5 minutes without supervision	**22** Attends to easy/familiar task without supervision for 10 to 25 minutes
23 Attends to difficult/novel task for 5 to 10 minutes when supervised	**24** Attends to difficult/novel task for 5 to 10 minutes without supervision	**25** Attends to difficult/novel task for 10 to 25 minutes when supervised	**26** Attends to difficult/novel task for 10 to 25 minutes without supervision	**27** Works in small group for 0 to 5 minutes	**28** Works in small group for 5 to 10 minutes	**29** Attends to task(s) for full class period when supervised
30 Works in small group for 10 to 25 minutes	**31** Attends to task(s) without supervision for one full class period	**32** Works in small group for full class period or assigned time	**33** Remains at task 0 to 5 min- utes when dis- tractions are present	**34** Remains at task 5 to 10 min- utes when dis- tractions are present	**35** Remains at task 10 to 25 minutes when distractions are present	**36** Remains at task 25 to 45 minutes when distractions are present

Figure 1. Sample from the Assessment Record, Cognitive Area, Attention Span strand. (From the BCP by VORT Corporation, et al. © 1997. Published by VORT Corporation, PO Box 60132, Palo Alto, CA 94306.)

Utility

Because of the explicit instruction provided for many skills, the *BCP* is a valuable instructional tool for professionals new to the field or who may not have a repertoire of how to teach students using a variety of adaptive skills and skill sequences (see Figure 2).

The *BCP* is useful also as a curriculum-referencing sequence to supplement other developmental curricula that do not have its comprehensive item density. The 2,300 functional capabilities give the *BCP* exceptional sensitivity and usefulness for detailed goal-planning; however, the practicality of using the *BCP* as a core instrument for children is diminished given the number of items.

The materials procedure for children with disabilities can be adapted to respect and permit cultural values. The instructional activities manual provides a few suggestions for making adaptations.

01.01 Atends to easy/familiar task from 0 to 5 seconds when supervised

Abilities Required: vision, hearing, use of hands

Interest Level: preschool, primary

Matierials: puppet

1. Select any kind of hand puppet.
2. Place puppet on your hand and ask the pupil to keep his eyes on the puppet at all times.
3. Talk to the pupil through the puppet.
4. Say, "Hello, I'm Mr. Socky. I want to get to know you."
5. Give the puppet to the pupil to respond back.
6. Begin with only one or two questions and gradually increase as the pupil's attention and interest increases.

Figure 2.   Sample instructional activity. (From the BCP by VORT Corporation, et al. © 1997. Published by VORT Corporation, PO Box 60132, Palo Alto, CA 94306.)

Collaboration

Multidisciplinary team involvement is encouraged, as individuals with delays and disabilities, for whom this assessment was developed, often have complex needs. The *BCP* user's manual stresses parent involvement and a team approach to assessment and instructional planning, suggesting that the team chart progress and use the assessment to plan appropriate instruction. The authors suggest that the *BCP* adds the benefit of increasing communication between professionals and parents. Professionals are instructed to encourage families to make decisions regarding their level of participation and involvement in all aspects of assessment and planning (i.e., identifying realistic and priority goals).

Evidence Base

Smith, R.L. (1978). *A study of the interrater reliability of the Behavioral Characteristics Progression* (Doctoral dissertation). Retrieved December 4, 2009, from Dissertations & Theses: A&I (Pub. No. AAT 7911092)

This study examines the interrater reliability of the *BCP*.

Considerations and Recommendations

- The *BCP* should be considered primarily as a curricular "resource" of dense, functional skills that can supplement less extensive curricula for individuals with significant disabilities.

- Despite the many strengths of the *BCP,* research is needed regarding the technical adequacy (reliability, validity, bias) of the instrument as well as examinations of its use with intended populations.

A B C

BRIGANCE® Inventory of Early Development-II (IED-II)

Author(s): Albert H. Brigance and Frances P. Glascoe

Publication date: 2010

Publisher: Curriculum Associates

Web site(s): http://www.curriculumassociates.com

Cost: $189.00; additional items available separately

Assessment type: Curriculum-referenced assessment with norms

Age range: Birth to developmental age 7

Domains/subtests: Comprised of developmental skills and behaviors and curricular objectives across a number of areas including Preambulatory Motor Skills and Behaviors, Gross-Motor Skills and Behaviors, Fine-Motor Skills and Behaviors, Self-Help Skills, Speech and Language Skills, General Knowledge and Comprehension, Social and Emotional Development, Readiness, Basic Reading Skills, Manuscript Writing, and Basic Math

Population targeted: All children in early childhood settings, particularly center-based settings, including children with disabilities; nationally representative standardized sample: $n = 1{,}171$

Technology features: *BRIGANCE® IED-II Management System* keeps track of students' development and progress online; provides data for compliance with Head Start, IDEA 2004 (PL 108-446), Early Reading First, Reading First, and Office of Special Education Programs early childhood outcomes; electronic scoring also available

Translations: Ancillary materials, such as *BRIGANCE®* Screens, available in Spanish.

Other features	Rating	Standard	Rating
Validated purposes	Medium	Acceptability	◑
Curricular links	Medium	Authenticity	◐
Comprehensive coverage	High	Collaboration	◕
Graduated scoring	Low	Evidence	●
Progress monitoring	High	Multifactors	◐
Standards alignment	Medium	Sensitivity	◑
Diversity features	High	Universality	◐
Family engagement	Low	Utility	◑
Teamwork	Low		
Professional development	Medium	OVERALL	◐
Technology	Medium		

Callier-Azusa Scale G-Edition

Author(s): Robert D. Stillman

Publication date: 1978

Publisher: Callier Center for Communication Disorders

Web site(s): http://www.utdallas.edu/calliercenter

Cost: $20.00 per copy

Assessment type: Curriculum-referenced assessment

Age range: Birth to 8 years

Domains/subtests: Motor Development, Perceptual Development, Daily Living, Language, and Socialization

Population targeted: Infants and young children with sensory impairments, particularly children who are deafblind; initial field test: *n* = 100

Technology features: None

Translations: None

Other features	Rating	Standard	Rating
Validated purposes	High	Acceptability	◗
Curricular links	Medium	Authenticity	◗
Comprehensive coverage	High	Collaboration	◗
Graduated scoring	High	Evidence	◗
Progress monitoring	High	Multifactors	◗
Standards alignment	Low	Sensitivity	◗
Diversity features	Low	Universality	◗
Family engagement	High	Utility	◗
Teamwork	Medium		
Professional development	Medium	OVERALL	◗
Technology	Low		

A B C

Callier-Azusa Scale
G-Edition

Author(s): Robert D. Stillman

About the Measure

Few measures are available to guide the assessment of young children with multiple functional impairments, especially children with dual sensory disabilities.

The *Callier-Azusa Scale (CAS)* has a long and distinguished history of being the premier measure for the assessment of infants and preschoolers who are deafblind.

When originally designed in 1974, the *CAS* marked the first time that authentic assessment was emphasized as the most useful and equitable method to assess young children with significant disabilities.

Authenticity

Stillman (1974) described a *CAS* strategy of "observation of spontaneous behavior in structured and unstructured settings" (p. 2), conducted by a teacher or other caregiver over time in a flexible manner. Prefacing item content and demand with "may" enables professionals to observe functioning but only when the child's intact sensory and neuromotor systems set the stage for such capability. In addition, language competence in nonlanguage subscales is minimized; this enables the observer to document underlying capabilities.

The *CAS* focuses on functional domains that can highlight intact functional capabilities and attributes for children who are deafblind, including the development of self-concept and expressive communication through nonverbal means. Such examples include the following:

- Smiles, coos, babbles, or gives indication of recognition when a familiar person comes into the environment

- May initiate an activity that the teacher and child carry out often

- Anticipates that an object or person will provide stimulation

- Uses trial and error methods to remove annoying stimuli

- Moves in appropriate direction to show preferences

- Shows trust and mistrust of people

Utility

The *CAS* is well suited for documenting the current functional capabilities of the child who is deafblind and for providing a "functional" basis for program planning. The *CAS* also allows for tracking individual functional progress. The authors stress that teachers should use their creativity and knowledge of a child's interests and/or abilities rather than the *CAS* items literally to set goals and learning strategies. The utility of this tool is evidenced by the comprehensive listing of skills at earlier developmental levels, allowing the assessment of incremental changes or progress of children with multiple impairments. Another useful feature is the column of examples corresponding to specific items, which assists in skill interpretation. (See Figure 1.)

SOCIAL DEVELOPMENT 72

ITEM	EXAMPLE	COMMENTS
A. Interactions with Adults		
0. Shows no awareness of presence of an adult.	– Does not respond when picked up – Does not respond to adult's touch or voice	
1. Responds to person-to-person contact.	– Body adjusts to being held – Body reacts to being touched (may be marked by either withdrawing from or groping toward the source of stimulation) – Stops crying when picked up – Starts crying when laid down – Differentiates being held and not held	
2. (A) Studies or attends to adult visually or tactilely.	– Stares at adult – Stops crying at sight of adult – Feels adult's hand, body, cheek, etc. with own hand	
*(B) May attend to adult's voice.	– Attempts to localize sound of voice – Quiets to voice	
3. Responds with at least a single behavior to an adult's attempt to interact.	– Smiles or vocalizes in response to an adult's social act – Accepts a toy offered by an adult – Touches an adult's hand as the adult touches his/her body	
4. Differentiates familiar and unfamiliar adults.	– Quiets to stranger's voice – Stiffens when held by stranger – Smiles to familiar adult's face, voice, or touch – Sobers to unfamiliar adult's voice or face	

Figure 1. Sample items from the CAS protocol. (From Stillman, R.D. [1978]. *Callier-Azusa Scale G-Edition*. Dallas, TX: Callier Center for Communication Disorders; reprinted by permission.)

Collaboration

Teachers and parents can effectively use the *CAS* item guide to collaborate in home- and center-based assessment of children and to communicate in the process about next steps for planning sensible intervention strategies. The *CAS* must be given by individuals with extensive familiarity with the child's behavior and opportunities to observe the child for at least 2 weeks prior to completing the measure. The author states that scores are most valid when consensus-derived decisions are made by individuals who regularly interact with the child, such as teachers, parents, aides, and specialists.

Evidence Base

Day, P. (1974). *Validity of the ordinality of items in four subscales of the Callier-Azusa Scale (Edition E).* Unpublished manuscript, University of Texas at Dallas.

A study to determine whether the items (modified based on observed behaviors of deaf-blind children) in the *CAS* represent an ordinal scale.

Day, P., & Stillman, R. (1974). *Interobserver reliability of the Callier-Azusa Scale.* Unpublished manuscript, University of Texas at Dallas.

Interobserver reliability of 95 teachers, aides, and parents to investigate whether the *CAS* is more reliable when used by individuals or teams and in day school versus residential programs.

Rowland, C. (Ed.). (2009). *Assessing communication and learning in young children who are deafblind or who have multiple disabilities.* Portland: Oregon Health & Science University.

The scales featured and reviewed in this booklet reinforce the content validity of the *CAS* and other associated measures used to assess individuals with multiple disabilities.

Stillman, R. (1973). *Measuring progress in deaf-blind children: Use of the "Azusa Scale".* Dallas, TX: Callier Center for Communication Disorders. (ERIC Document Reproduction Service No. ED084729)

This study (*n* = 140 deafblind children) investigated the scale's usefulness for evaluation of behavior change, instructional planning, and program evaluation. Scores were collected at baseline and postintervention and compared with norms for typically developing children.

Considerations and Recommendations

- The *CAS* can be combined effectively with other curricular scales and formats and such systems as the *Vulpe Assessment Battery-Revised,* the *Developmental Assessment for Students with Severe Disabilities-Second Edition (DASH-2),* and *The Oregon Project for Preschool Children who are Blind or Visually Impaired, 6th edition,* to link assessment and intervention efforts.

- Research is needed regarding the effectiveness of interventions linked to the *CAS* content and to perhaps modify its content based on the outcomes of these studies.

Close Up on next page

A B C

The Carolina Curriculum for Infants and Toddlers with Special Needs, Third Edition (CCITSN), *and* The Carolina Curriculum for Preschoolers with Special Needs, Second Edition (CCPSN)

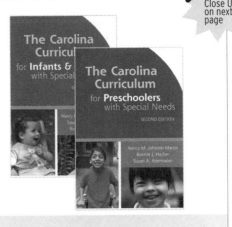

Author(s) for CCITSN: Nancy M. Johnson-Martin, Susan M. Attermeier, and Bonnie J. Hacker
Author(s) for CCPSN: Nancy M. Johnson-Martin, Bonnie J. Hacker, and Susan M. Attermeier
Publication date: 2004
Publisher: Paul H. Brookes Publishing Co.
Web site(s): http://www.brookespublishing.com
Cost: $48.95 for *CCITSN*; $48.95 for *CCPSN*

Assessment type: Curriculum-embedded assessment
Age range: Two levels based on developmental age: *CCITSN* for birth to 24 months; *CCPSN* for 24–60 months
Domains/subtests: Personal-Social, Cognition, Communication, Fine Motor, and Gross Motor
Population targeted: Children from birth to age 5 with moderate to severe disabilities
Technology features: Assessment logs and developmental progress charts available on CD-ROM or online in PDF format
Translations: *CCITSN* is available in Portuguese, Russian, Korean, Chinese, Spanish, and Italian; *CCPSN* is also available in Korean

Other features	Rating	Standard	Rating (*CCITSN*)	Rating (*CCPSN*)
Validated purposes	Low	Acceptability	◑	◑
Curricular links	High	Authenticity	◕	◑
Comprehensive coverage	High	Collaboration	○	○
Graduated scoring	High	Evidence	◕	◑
Progress monitoring	High	Multifactors	◕	●
Standards alignment	Medium	Sensitivity	◕	◕
Diversity features	Medium	Universality	◕	◕
Family engagement	Low	Utility	◕	◕
Teamwork	Medium			
Professional development	Medium	OVERALL (*CCITSN*)		◕
Technology	Low	OVERALL (*CCPSN*)		◕

CLOSE UP

The Carolina Curriculum for Infants and Toddlers with Special Needs, Third Edition (CCITSN), *and* The Carolina Curriculum for Preschoolers with Special Needs, Second Edition (CCPSN)

Author(s) for CCITSN: Nancy M. Johnson-Martin, Susan M. Attermeier, and Bonnie J. Hacker

Author(s) for CCPSN: Nancy M. Johnson-Martin, Bonnie J. Hacker, and Susan M. Attermeier

About the Measure

The authors of the *Carolina Curriculum* succeeded in their efforts to create a system that directly links assessment items to curricular activities for children with special needs.

The latest revision of the *Carolina Curriculum* made assessment items and related interventions continuous from birth to age 5 to meet the needs of preschool children developmentally functioning below 36 months in one or more domains.

The *Carolina Curriculum* provides special attention for children with atypical developmental pathways and serious impairments, making it a highly regarded and valuable system.

Authenticity

The authenticity of the *CCITSN* and *CCPSN* can be described in relation to the assessment process, assessment items, and the curricula.

The *CCITSN* and *CCPSN* assessments each consist of two components: a naturalistic observation of the child and a direct assessment. Both components can occur in any familiar setting such as a home or child care center. The observation component should last for about an hour, during which time the child's demonstrated skills are noted on the assessment log. Missing items can be assessed following the observation by interviewing the caregiver and/or directly testing the child.

The *CCITSN* and *CCPSN* assessment items focus on everyday experiences and functional skills for daily living. Examples of authentic assessment items from the *CCITSN* include *Entertains self with toys for short periods of time, Responds with correct gestures to "up" and "bye-bye,"* and *Pulls self to standing position*. Examples of authentic assessment items from the *CCPSN* include *Requests permission, Tears toilet tissue and flushes toilet after use,* and *Describes events that happened in the past*.

The focus of the *CCITSN* and *CCPSN* curricula is on developing children's functional skills. Intervention activities are designed to be included in typical daily routines and play activities. Further, intervention activities should lead to an increase in, or improvement of, functional skills that are useful to the child across many settings.

Utility

The *CCITSN* and the *CCPSN* include a detailed process, illustrated in Figure 1, for moving from assessment to individualized family service plan or individualized education program goals and objectives.

To facilitate movement between the *CCITSN* and *CCPSN*, the assessment items and corresponding curricular items are categorized under identical titles from one volume to the next, and there are a few overlapping items in each subdomain. For example, the subdomain Problem Solving/Reasoning under the domain Cognition occurs in both volumes. Further, the last five items in the *CCITSN* Problem Solving/Reasoning section are the same as the first five items in the *CCPSN* Problem Solving/Reasoning section.

Assessment items are highly adaptable, allowing children with significant impairments to demonstrate skills with modifications.

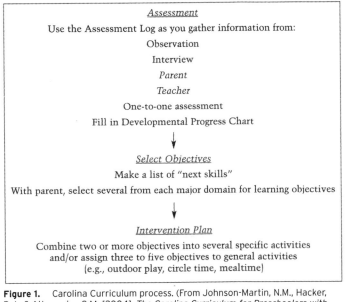

Figure 1. Carolina Curriculum process. (From Johnson-Martin, N.M., Hacker, B.J., & Attermeier, S.M. [2004]. *The Carolina Curriculum for Preschoolers with Special Needs, Second Edition* [CCPSN]. Baltimore: Paul H. Brookes Publishing Co.; reprinted by permission.)

Collaboration

The assessment can be completed by one or more professionals but should always include a parent and teacher or caregiver. As illustrated in Figure 1, parents are not only involved in the assessment but are also essential to the process of determining intervention goals. The authors purposefully limited the use of professional jargon throughout both the *CCITSN* and the *CCPSN* so that the tools are accessible to a variety of users. The manuals include suggestions as to when teachers or interventionists may want to seek guidance and support from specialists (e.g., speech therapist, occupational therapist, physical therapist).

Evidence Base

Del Giudice, E., Titomanlio, L., Brogna, G., Bonaccorso, A., Romano, A., Mansi, G., et al. (2006). Early intervention for children with Down syndrome in southern Italy: The role of parent-implemented developmental training. *Infants & Young Children, 19*(1), 50–58.

Examined the efficacy of parent-implemented intervention using the *CCITSN* compared with therapist-implemented intervention using Italy's National Health Service model.

Considerations and Recommendations

- The *Carolina Curriculum* is one of the oldest integrated assessment-curriculum systems.

- The *Carolina Curriculum* is ideal for children with moderate to severe disabilities.

- Research is needed to demonstrate the reliability, validity, and utility of scores and inferences made from the *CCITSN* and the *CCPSN*.

Close Up on next page

A B C

Communication and Symbolic Behavior Scales™ (CSBS™), Normed Edition

CSBS
Manual
Communication and Symbolic Behavior Scales
Normed Edition

Amy M. Wetherby
Barry M. Prizant

Author(s): Amy M. Wetherby and Barry M. Prizant

Publication date: 2003

Publisher: Paul H. Brookes Publishing Co.

Web site(s): http://www.brookespublishing.com

Cost: *Complete CSBS™ Kit* $599.00 (Manual, Toy Kit, 2 Outline Cards, 25 Caregiver Questionnaires, 25 Record Forms, sampling video, scoring video)
CSBS™ Kit without Toy Kit $275.00

Assessment type: Curriculum-referenced assessment with norms

Age range: 6–24 months for children with typical speech development or up to 6 years if developmental level of functioning is less than 24 months

Domains/subtests: Twenty-two rating scales organized into seven group clusters: Communicative Functions, Gestural Communicative Means, Vocal Communicative Means, Verbal Communicative Means, Reciprocity, Social-Affective Signaling, and Symbolic Behavior

Population targeted: Assessment for infants, toddlers, and preschoolers who have communication impairments or are at risk; norm sample *n* = 278

Technology features: Instructional videos for the Behavior Sample

Translations: None

Other features	Rating		Standard	Rating
Validated purposes	Medium		Acceptability	◐
Curricular links	Medium		Authenticity	◕
Comprehensive coverage	Low		Collaboration	◕
Graduated scoring	Medium		Evidence	◕
Progress monitoring	High		Multifactors	◑
Standards alignment	Medium		Sensitivity	◕
Diversity features	Medium		Universality	◕
Family engagement	Medium		Utility	◖
Teamwork	Low			
Professional development	Medium		OVERALL	◕
Technology	Low			

A B C

Communication and Symbolic Behavior Scales™ (CSBS™), Normed Edition

Author(s): Amy M. Wetherby and Barry M. Prizant

About the Measure

The *CSBS™* system is designed for the early identification of children with or at risk for communication delays as well as for documenting children's present communication skills and monitoring changes in those skills over time.

A strength of the *CSBS™* is that it allows teams to gather both qualitative and quantitative data about a child from familiar caregivers and professionals.

Given the need for a briefer instrument that could be used to screen for communicative competence (i.e., use of eye gaze, gestures, sounds, words, understanding, and play), the authors developed the *CSBS Developmental Profile™ (CSBS DP™)*.

Authenticity

The *CSBS™* uses a standardized format but does allow for some flexibility during administration. For example, the child can sit on a caregiver's lap if they are uncomfortable or become upset while being tested at the table. Data are collected by sampling children's behavior during structured activities. Activities used to elicit and obtain a behavior sample include the following:

1. *Communicative temptations:* The evaluator sets up a series of communicative temptations such as wind-up toys, bubbles, and toys in a bag. The evaluator waits to see if the child will perform the desired response (e.g., make a request, follow a direction, respond to a social game) and then prompts if necessary.

2. *Book sharing:* The child chooses a book and examines it and is then given another book. The parent is instructed to not guide the child but to respond to the child's lead by noticing or labeling pictures the child directs attention to.

3. *Symbolic play probes:* The child is given two different sets of toys, and the parent is directed to follow the child's lead while playing.

4. *Language comprehension probes:* The child is asked to identify body parts, agents, and possessors.

5. *Constructive play probes:* The child is given a set of materials (i.e., five blocks, five stacking rings, or six nesting cups) and encouraged to play with the materials.

Materials and sampling procedures are included in the *CSBS™* kit for each of the five activities listed above. Caregivers are asked to complete a *CSBS™ Behavior Sample: Caregiver Perception Rating Form* to indicate how typical the child's behavior was during the sample. The caregiver is present during the entire assessment and is instructed to react naturally but avoid directing the child. The assessment procedure takes 45 minutes to 1 hour to complete.

Utility

The *CSBS™* provides a profile of a child's strengths and needs in the areas of communication (e.g., joint attention, coordination of gestures and vocalizations), social affect (e.g., gaze shifts, shared positive affect), and symbolic abilities (e.g., language comprehension, constructive play). The information gathered regarding the child's behavior is used for prioritizing goals for intervention.

The manual provides general examples of interventions appropriate for children with deficits or delays in the areas of communication, social affect, and symbolic abilities. Examples include the following:

• *Expand the range of communicative functions:* "During mealtime or snack time, provide opportunities for child to request desired food, to request help opening a container, and/or protest undesired food."

• *Expand the use of social-affective signals:* "Provide opportunities for social referencing through proximity in positioning and presentation of materials (i.e., near and far away from face)."

• *Enhance symbolic level:* "Provide opportunities to engage child in appropriate use of objects and to model play at appropriate level for child during a variety of symbolic and constructive play experiences."

Collaboration

The *CSBS™* is to be administered by a certified speech-language pathologist, early interventionist, or other professional trained to assess young children. The caregiver is involved in the assessment process by being a participant during the behavior sample, by validating the results by completing the *CSBS™ Behavior Sample: Caregiver Perception Rating Form,* and as a reporter by completing the *CSBS™ Caregiver Questionnaire* (see Figure 1).

The *CSBS™ Caregiver Questionnaire* is designed to elicit information about the child's communication and symbolic abilities. The questionnaire can be given to the caregiver before the child is brought in for assessment. The evaluator can ask any questions for clarification regarding the questionnaire during the warm-up phase of the evaluation.

CSBS™   **Caregiver Questionnaire**

Child's name: _____   Date filled out: _____

Filled out by: _____   Relationship to child: _____

Please answer the following questions about how your child communicates. The questions will have to do with how your child expresses himself/herself. Feel free to give examples.

1. How does your child usually communicate? (check all that apply)

    _____ pointing   _____ gestures   _____ short phrases

    _____ sounds   _____ single words   _____ other (describe)

2. How has your child's communication changed over the past few months?

    _____

    _____

    _____

3. What does your child do when he/she needs help (e.g., opening a container, getting a toy to work?)

    _____

    _____

4. How does your child let you know that he/she wants an object that is out of reach?

    _____

    _____

Figure 1.   Sample items from the *CSBS™ Caregiver Questionnaire*. (From Wetherby, A.M., & Prizant, B.M. [2003]. *CSBS™ Caregiver Questionnaire*. Baltimore: Paul H. Brookes Publishing Co; reprinted by permission.)

Evidence Base

McCathren, R.B. (2000). Testing predictive validity of the communication composite of the Communication and Symbolic Behavior Scales. *Journal of Early Intervention, 23*(1), 36–46.

Report of the predictive validity of the communication composite of the *CSBS™* as a predictor of expressive vocabulary. The sample included 58 children 17–34 months of age who were functioning at the prelinguistic stage of language development. All participants had mild to moderate developmental delays as determined by the *Bayley Mental Development Indices*. Results indicated that the communication composite was a predictor of later expressive language.

Additional studies were conducted regarding aspects of the *CSBS DP™*, including validity, reliability, and standardization.

Considerations and Recommendations

- The *CSBS™* is an exemplary system to document children's pragmatic communication in everyday settings and routines; it uses observation and various analog strategies to elicit modes and samples of communication, making the *CSBS™* perhaps the best language assessment system for young children with special needs.

- To be truly useful as a linked system, more information is needed on how assessment information can be used to plan and revise interventions and monitor performance over time.

- Even though the *CSBS™* can be used for children who are 24–60 months chronological age and functioning between 8 and 24 months, the content related to the *CSBS™* would need to be more clearly linked to instruction to be useful for planning for the 24- to 60-month age group.

A B C

A B C

Close Up on next page

The Creative Curriculum® Developmental Continuum for Infants, Toddlers & Twos *and* The Creative Curriculum® Developmental Continuum for Ages 3-5

Author(s) for *Infants, Toddlers & Twos*: Teaching Strategies, Inc.

Author(s) for *Ages 3-5*: Diane Trister Dodge, Laura J. Colker, and Cate Heroman

Publication date for *Infants, Toddlers & Twos*: 2006

Publication date for *Ages 3-5*: 2002

Publisher: Teaching Strategies, Inc.

Web site(s): http://www.teachingstrategies.com

Cost: *The Creative Curriculum® for Infants, Toddlers & Twos Developmental Continuum Assessment Toolkit* $139.95
The Creative Curriculum® Developmental Continuum Assessment Toolkit $114.95

Assessment type: Curriculum-embedded assessment

Age range: Birth through 3 years and 3-5 years

Domains/subtests: Social/Emotional, Physical, Cognitive, and Language; *Infants, Toddlers & Twos* contains 21 objectives; *Ages 3-5* has 50 objectives

Population targeted: Designed for all young children

Technology features: Data management system

Translations: Spanish

Other features	Rating	Standard	Rating (Infants, Toddlers & Twos)	Rating (Ages 3-5)
Validated purposes	Medium	Acceptability	◕	◕
Curricular links	High	Authenticity	◕	◕
Comprehensive coverage	High	Collaboration	◑	◑
Graduated scoring	Medium	Evidence	◕	◕
Progress monitoring	Medium	Multifactors	◕	◕
Standards alignment	High	Sensitivity	◔	◔
Diversity features	Low	Universality	◕	◕
Family engagement	High	Utility	◕	◕
Teamwork	High			
Professional development	High	OVERALL (*Infants, Toddlers & Twos*)	◕	
Technology	High	OVERALL (*Ages 3-5*)		◕

Note: The above ratings are based on *The Creative Curriculum® Developmental Continuum*, the system available at the time of this writing. The new assessment, *Teaching Strategies GOLD™*, replaces both assessment Toolkits. See www.teachingstrategies.com for more information.

The Creative Curriculum® Developmental Continuum for Infants, Toddlers & Twos *and* The Creative Curriculum® Developmental Continuum for Ages 3–5

Author(s) for *Infants, Toddlers & Twos*: Teaching Strategies, Inc.

Author(s) for *Ages 3–5*: Diane Trister Dodge, Laura J. Colker, and Cate Heroman

About the Measure

A major strength of *The Creative Curriculum®* lies in the "curricular" resources and/or materials that provide a base for teachers in creating and supporting developmentally appropriate learning opportunities.

Curricular materials also support planning lessons and building upon children's interests with an emphasis on the importance of play.

The Creative Curriculum® began as a preschool resource and gradually added the infant and toddler components and the *Developmental Continuum*. The assessment component of *The Creative Curriculum®*, called the *Developmental Continuum* has been replaced by *Teaching Strategies GOLD™* (Heroman, Burts, Berke, & Bickart, 2010), an assessment system for children birth through kindergarten.

Authenticity

The Creative Curriculum® Developmental Continuum for Infants, Toddlers & Twos and *The Creative Curriculum® Developmental Continuum for Ages 3–5* have the same organizational structure and are designed to assess children's functioning in familiar environments with familiar toys and materials. *A Teacher's Guide to Using the Developmental Continuum Assessment System* outlines the process of ongoing assessment, including collecting, analyzing, and evaluating children's progress.

Each objective within *The Creative Curriculum® Developmental Continuum* consists of five steps for *Infants, Toddlers & Twos* and three steps for *Preschoolers* (see Figure 1 for a sample of steps from the *Infants, Toddlers & Twos Developmental Continuum*).

FROM *The Creative Curriculum® Developmental Continuum for Infants, Toddlers & Twos*

Objective 20 Shows an awareness of pictures and print

Step 1	Step 2	Step 3	Step 4	Step 5
Notices pictures • Gazes at pictures of faces on mobile • Looks and coos at photo on wall • Glances at pictures in board book	**Recognizes and shows a beginning understanding of pictures** • Touches pictures in book with various textures • Vocalizes when pointing to a picture • Points to picture of baby when you ask, "Where is the baby?"	**Recognizes that pictures have a meaning and can tell a story** • Points to picture and asks, "Dat?" • Says, "Cat'pillar," when she sees cover of *The Very Hungry Caterpillar.* • Turns pages of book to find favorite pictures	**Demonstrates an interest in print** • Chooses book from shelf and says, "Read, p'ease." • Watches teacher write name on painting and asks, "What dat?" • Point to "Itsy-Bitsy Spider" fingerplay chart on wall and says, "Bitsy spider."	**Shows beginning understanding that print is useful** • Recognizes some popular logos • Scribbles, folds paper, and announces, "Happy birthday!" • Points to letter on book cover and says. "That's my letter."

Figure 1. Example of five steps for Objective 20 of *The Creative Curriculum® Developmental Continuum for Infants, Toddlers & Twos*. From *The Creative Curriculum® Developmental Continuum for Infants, Toddlers & Twos*, by Teaching Strategies, Inc., 2006, Washington, D.C.: Author. Copyright 2006 by Teaching Strategies, Inc. Reprinted with permission.

Both levels of the *Developmental Continuum* provide information on children's performance that can be used as a way of identifying those who are or are not yet at the beginning level expected for a given age. The preschool continuum includes forerunner skills for each objective. Forerunner skills are examples of possible skills and behaviors on which you can build when planning for children before they reach Step 1. For example, the forerunner skills for the objective of *Demonstrates understanding of print concepts* (see Figure 2) are *Notices and responds to pictures, Finds own possessions when labeled with photo and name, Recognizes logos and pictures,* and *Points to print on a page and says, "Read this."*

The new assessment tool, *Teaching Strategies GOLD™* has 38 objectives (some of which have additional dimensions) organized on a developmental progression from birth through kindergarten. Dimensions are designed to delineate what teachers should consider related to a particular objective. For example, Objective 19 *Demonstrates emergent writing skills* is further delineated into two dimensions of *writes name* and *writes to convey meaning.* Each objective or associated dimensions are rated using a 10 point scale. See Figure 3 for an illustration of one objective.

FROM *Expanded Forerunners of The Creative Curriculum® Developmental Continuum for Ages 3–5*

Objective 45 Demonstrates understanding of print concepts

Forerunner 1	Forerunner 2	Forerunner 3
Notices and responds to pictures • Recognizes familiar book by its cover • Looks at picture in book when object in picture is named by an adult	**Finds own possessions when labeled with photo and name** • Child finds cubby that is labeled with her picture and name	**Recognizes logos and pictures** • Identifies McDonald's logo • Sees picture label of beads on shelf and says, "Beads go here."

FROM *The Creative Curriculum® Developmental Continuum for Ages 3–5*

Objective 45 Demonstrates understanding of print concepts

Forerunners	Step I	Step II	Step III
Points to print on a page and says, "Read this." **Recognizes logos** • Identifies McDonald's logo **Recognizes book by cover**	**Knows that print carries the message** • Points to printed label on shelf and says, "Cars go here." • Looking at the name the teacher has written on another child's drawing, says, "Whose is this?"	**Shows general knowledge of how print works** • Runs finger over text left to right, top to bottom as he pretends to read • Knows that names begin with a big letter	**Knows each spoken word can be written down and read** • Touches a written word for every spoken word in a story • Looking at a menu, asks, "Which word says pancakes?"

Figure 2. Example of Forerunners and Expanded Forerunners of *The Creative Curriculum® Developmental Continuum for Ages 3-5* Objective 45. Top image from *Expanded Forerunners of The Creative Curriculum® Developmental Continuum for Ages 3-5* (p. 22), by Teaching Strategies, Inc., 2005, Washington, DC: Author. Copyright 2005 by Teaching Strategies, Inc. Reprinted with permission. Bottom image from *The Creative Curriculum® Developmental Continuum for Ages 3-5* (p. 16), by Teaching Strategies, Inc., 2002, Washington, DC: Author. Copyright 2002 by Teaching Strategies, Inc. Reprinted with permission.

FROM *Teaching Strategies™ GOLD Objectives for Development & Learning: Birth Through Kindergarten*

Objective 17 Demonstrates knowledge of print and its uses

Dimension a. Uses and appreciates books

Not Yet	1	2	3	4	5	6	7	8	9
		Shows interest in books • Gazes at the pages of a book • Brings book to adult to read		**Orients book correctly; turns pages from the front of the book to the back; recognizes familiar books by their covers** • Hands teacher book and says, "Let's read *Corduroy!*"		**Knows some features of a book (title, author, illustrator); connects specific books to authors** • Says, "I want to read this Dr. Seuss book today." • Says, "Eric Carle wrote this book. He is the author."		**Uses various types of books for their intended purposes** • Selects the book about insects to identify the butterfly seen on the playground	

Dimension b. Uses print concepts

Not Yet	1	2	3	4	5	6	7	8	9
		Shows understanding that text is meaningful and can be read • Points to the words on the sign by the fish bowl and says. "Just one pinch!"		**Indicates where to start reading and the direction to follow** • Points to beginning of text on the page when pretending to read and moves finger left to right as she continues down the page		**Shows awareness of various features of print: letters, words, spaces, upper- and lowercase letters, some punctuation** • Points to the word *hippopotamus* and says, "That's a long word." • Says, "That means stop reading," as he points to a period at the end of a sentence.		**Matches a written word with a spoken word, but it may not be the actual written word; tracks print from the end of a line of text to the beginning of the next line** • Touches each word on the page while reciting the words from *Brown Bear, Brown Bear, What Do You See?* • Picks up finger and returns it to the beginning of the next line when pretend reading	

Figure 3. Example of Objective and a 10-point scale from *Teaching Strategies GOLD™*. From *Teaching Strategies GOLD™ Objectives for Development & Learning: Birth Through Kindergarten* (p. 92), by C. Heromen, D.C. Burts, K. Berke, & T.S. Bickart, (2010), Washington, DC: Teaching Strategies, Inc. Copyright 2010 by Teaching Strategies, Inc. Reprinted with permission.

Utility

The Creative Curriculum® Developmental Continuum Assessment Toolkits (available for both levels) include several reporting forms that are useful for interpreting assessment results. For example, the *Preschool Class Summary Worksheet* allows users to track progress for all of the students in a class across 50 objectives. Completing and reviewing the worksheet over time provides teachers with a basic picture of children's interests, strengths, and needs. The information also can be used for planning activities and instruction in an effort to help a group of children progress through the developmental continuum.

The Creative Curriculum® Developmental Continuum Assessment Toolkits also include forms that are useful for gathering and analyzing information about individual children. For example, the preschool *Child Progress and Planning Report* can be used to summarize an individual child's progress, gain input from a child's family, and plan individualized interventions or activities.

Collaboration

The Creative Curriculum® encourages programs to have a strong partnership with families. The *Preschool* and *Infants, Toddlers & Twos curricula* each contain a chapter about partnering with families. Topics addressed in the chapters include *getting to know families, making families feel welcome, communicating with families, partnering with families on children's learning,* and *responding to challenging situations.*

In addition, each chapter ends with a letter to families (see Figure 4) about how to support children's learning at school and at home in the areas that were discussed. The letters are

Figure 4. Example family letter from *The Creative Curriculum® for Preschool: A Letter to Families About Dramatic Play*. From *The Creative Curriculum® for Preschool, Volume 2: Interest Areas* (5th ed.) (p. 287), by D. T. Dodge, C. Heroman, L. Colker, & T. S. Bickart, 2010, Washington, DC: Teaching Strategies, Inc. Copyright 2010 by Teaching Strategies, Inc. Reprinted with permission.

available in English and Spanish and can be adapted to meet the specific needs of the program and family.

Evidence Base

A number of studies have been conducted to examine the reliability and validity of *The Creative Curriculum® Developmental Continuum* assessment systems. Summaries of the research studies can be retrieved from http://www.creativecurriculum.net/research_studies.cfm

The results of the study describe the reliability and validity of *The Creative Curriculum® Developmental Continuum for Infants, Toddlers & Twos* (Lambert & Capizzano, 2007).

The results of the study describe the reliability and validity of *The Creative Curriculum® Developmental Continuum for Ages 3-5* (Lambert, n.d.).

Four independent studies examined the validity or effectiveness of *The Creative Curriculum® for Preschool*, in classrooms where both the assessment and the curriculum were used (Abbott-Shim, 2000; Hartford Foundation, 2004; Lambert & Capizzano, 2005; Louisiana Department of Education, 2001).

Considerations and Recommendations

- The *Creative Curriculum®* can be used by a wide range of early childhood professionals, particularly those without a strong foundation in development and/or developmentally appropriate practices.

- Limited evidence and/or research is readily available to support the use of *The Creative Curriculum® Developmental Continuum for Infants, Toddlers & Twos* or *The Creative Curriculum® Developmental Continuum for Ages 3-5* for specific early childhood intervention purposes including program planning, documenting child progress, and reporting Office of Special Education Programs outcomes, especially for children with disabilities.

- The inaccessibility of such disability-specific research evidence coupled with the generalized character of the developmental objectives without accommodations may make *The Creative Curriculum® Developmental Continuum for Infants, Toddlers & Twos* and *The Creative Curriculum® Developmental Continuum for Ages 3-5* less appropriate for use with young children having special needs.

- As previously noted, *Teaching Strategies GOLD*™ has replaced the original consumer-rated *The Creative Curriculum® Developmental Continuum* and has undergone an extensive national field-validation in 2010 on 2,500 children (see http://teachingstrategies .com for up-to-date reports on research related to *Teaching Strategies GOLD*™). The results of the field validation suggest that *Teaching Strategies GOLD*™ holds strong potential for overcoming major limitations of the older system and may fulfill specific early childhood intervention purposes. As with new or even existing measures, however, research in professional journals and the wide use by diverse consumers serves as the deciding factor as to whether there is an evidence base to meet recommended practice standards and fulfill ECI assessment purposes.

AT-A-GLANCE

Close Up on next page

Desired Results Developmental Profile *access* (DRDP *access*)

DRDP *access*
Desired Results Developmental Profile *access*
Manual

Author(s): Desired Results *access* Project, California Department of Education, Special Education Division

Publication date: 2007

Publisher: California Department of Education, Special Education Division

Web site: http://draccess.org

Cost: Free downloads

Assessment type: Criterion-referenced assessment

Age range: Birth to 5 years

Domains/subtests: Self-Concept, Social and Interpersonal Skills, Self-Regulation, Language, Learning, Cognitive Competence, Math, Literacy, Motor Skills, and Safety and Health

Population targeted: Young children with disabilities

Technology Features: Web-based data collection system, online training modules, trainer materials, and resources

Translations: Materials for families available in Spanish, Mandarin, Tagalog, Vietnamese, and Hmong

Other features	Rating	Standard	Rating
Validated purposes	Medium	Acceptability	◑
Curricular links	Medium	Authenticity	◑
Comprehensive coverage	High	Collaboration	◑
Graduated scoring	High	Evidence	◑
Progress monitoring	Medium	Multifactors	◑
Standards alignment	High	Sensitivity	◑
Diversity features	High	Universality	◑
Family engagement	Medium	Utility	◐
Teamwork	Low		
Professional development	High	OVERALL	◑
Technology	Medium		

Desired Results Developmental Profile *access* (DRDP *access*)

Author(s): Desired Results *access* Project

About the Measure

The *DRDP access* was created to ensure inclusion of preschool age children with identified delays/disabilities in statewide assessments and to report progress on state and federal outcomes. It is an observation-based tool that describes children's development from birth to 5 years of age.

The measure is truly an authentic, universal, and evidence-based system, designed specifically to document in a representative manner the status and progress of young children with developmental disabilities.

The *DRDP access* has been validated for accountability purposes. Progress and status reports are also available for district administrators and teachers.

Authenticity

The *DRDP access* system includes 48 measures that are linked to the 4 desired results (DRs), which are 1) children are personally and socially competent (DR1), 2) children are effective learners (DR2), 3) children show physical and motor competence (DR3), and 4) children are safe and healthy (DR4). Within each desired result, the assessment measures a variety of functional skills. For example, DR1 Measure 15 contains an item related to turn taking (i.e., *Child develops increased understanding of taking turns and begins to purpose strategies for taking turns*).

The *DRDP access* employs universal design features and allows for individual adaptations so that the assessment more accurately reflects a child's abilities rather than the impact of the disability. Adaptations include the use of an augmentative or alternative communication system, use of an alternative mode for written language, visual support, assistive equipment or devices, functional positioning, sensory support, and alternative response mode.

Utility

The *DRDP access* is directly linked to the California Infant/Toddler Learning and Development Foundations and the California Preschool Learning Foundations, which are the state's standards. The assessment is administered twice a year and is useful for overall curriculum planning and for planning intervention for individual children.

Each assessment item included in the *DRDP access* is broken down on a developmental hierarchy rubric. The assessor chooses the level in the hierarchy that best describes the child's current level of functioning. Each level on the rubric gives examples of behaviors that could be observed at that level. For example, in Measure 4: Expressions of Empathy, a child who hugs another child who is sad would receive a score at Level 4. The action of hugging a child who is sad demonstrates the child's ability to "offer comfort to someone showing distress" (see Figure 1).

Measure 4

SOC 1 of 7

DR 1: Children are personally and socially competent
↓ Indicator: SOC—Children demonstrate effective social and interpersonal skills

↓ **Measure 4: Expressions of Empathy—**
Child shows awareness of other's feelings and responds to expressions of feelings by others in ways that are increasingly appropriate to the other person's needs

Mark the highest developmental level the child has mastered.

Descriptors	Examples
☐7 Shows concern for the future welfare of others	▸ Shows concern for what will happen to animals and characters in a story or movie.
☐6 Uses words or actions to demonstrate concern for what others are feeling	▸ Asks child, "Why are you crying?" When told he misses his mommy, says, "Don't worry, your mommy will be back soon." ▸ Puts arm around a child who is standing alone or signs, "Want to play with me?" ▸ Goes to a child whose tower fell down and helps to build the tower again. ▸ Brings a marker to a child who is looking for something to draw with.
☐5 Accurately labels own feelings, as well as those of others	▸ Draws picture representing child who is upset and makes a sad face herself. ▸ "Maria is laughing-she is happy today." ▸ Points out picture in book of someone who looks "mad."
☐4 Offers to comfort someone showing distress	▸ Goes to and hugs child who is sad. ▸ Offers special toy or object to child or adult who is showing distress. ▸ Calls or gets adult to help a child who is showing distress.
☐3 Shows concern when others are unhappy or upset	▸ Looks worried and waits to see if adult will come to help a child who is upset. ▸ Points to band-aid on someone's elbow and says "ouch" or "booboo." ▸ Moves next to a child who is showing distress.
☐2 Responds based on others' expressions of emotions	▸ Laughs when adult giggles. ▸ Stops playing or watches another child intently if that child is hurt or sad. ▸ Shows a fearful face if another child is sad or hurt. ▸ Claps hands when another child or adult claps hands. ▸ Looks at another child who is upset, but doesn't stop playing.
☐1 Shows awareness of others	▸ Cries when other children cry. ▸ Notices people. ▸ Smiles at other people.

☐	Emerging to the next level
☐	In the rare circumstance that you are unable to rate this measure, indicate the reason (circle one): absence other

Figure 1. Excerpt of DRDP *access* DR 1: Measure 4: Expressions of Empathy. (From Desired Results *access* Project. [2010]. *DRDP access Manual*. California Department of Education, Special Education Division, reprinted by permission.)

Collaboration

Each child's primary IEP service provider generally completes the *DRDP access*. The primary IEP service provider is encouraged to document progress across settings and over time. It is recommended that observations from parents and other providers be gathered to inform the rating of the instrument. A document explaining the importance of family observations is available at http://www.draccess.org/assessors/RoleOfFamilyObsv.html. Parents can also choose to be part of determining the adaptations or accommodations that will be used during their child's assessment. All children enrolled in state-funded preschool programs in California are required to complete some form of the *DRDP* assessment. When children are receiving IEP services and are also enrolled in a state-funded preschool program, the primary IEP service provider and the general education preschool teacher should collaborate to complete the *DRDP access*.

Evidence Base

California Department of Education, Special Education Division. (2008) *Reliability and validity of the Desired Results Developmental Profile access (DRDP access): Results of the 2005–2006 Calibration Study.* Retrieved on August 17, 2009, from http://www.draccess .org/assessors/ReliabilityAndValidity.html

The report describes a calibration study of the *DRDP access* utilizing a modern testing framework. It provides evidence of high reliability including reports of internal consistency, person separation, and test–retest reliability. In addition, it describes a detailed analysis supporting the content validity, discriminative validity, construct validity, sensitivity, and utility of the assessment. The sample for the study included an ethnically diverse group of 1,644 preschool-age children in California, including 887 children with disabilities.

Considerations and Recommendations

- The measures of the *DRDP access* can be mapped directly onto the three Office of Special Education Programs Child Outcomes for reporting purposes. The instrument has been aligned with the Head Start Standards and is being studied for alignment with the California Infant/Toddler Learning and Development Foundations and the California Preschool Learning Foundations, which are currently under development.

- The *DRDP access* includes a detailed description of how individual measures within a set of 10 indicators are sequenced and guidance for how to rate a child's performance along with full citations that support the order and inclusion of various items.

- The *DRDP access* is one of the exemplary methods to design, develop, and field-validate instruments for children with disabilities and should provide a roadmap for the development of future functional, authentic, and evidence-based systems.

D E F

Desired Results Developmental Profile-Infant/Toddler Instrument (DRDP-R, IT) *and* Desired Results Developmental Profile-Preschool Instrument (DRDP-R, PS)

Author: California Department of Education, Child Development Division

Publication date: 2006

Publisher: Child Development Division

Web site: http://www.cde.ca.gov/sp/cd/ci/DRDPforms.asp
  http://www.wested.org/desiredresults/training/index.htm

Cost: Free downloads

Assessment type: Criterion-referenced assessment

Age range for DRDP-R, IT: Birth through 35 months

Age range for DRDP-R, PS: 36 months to kindergarten

Age range for DRDP-R, SA (not reviewed): Kindergarten through 12 years

Domains/subtests: *DRDP-R, IT* includes Self-Concept, Social Interpersonal Skills, Self-Regulation, Language, Cognitive, Math, Literacy, Motor Skills, and Safety and Health. *DRDP-R, PS* includes Self-Concept, Social Interpersonal Skills, Self-Regulation, Language, Learning, Cognitive Competence, Math, Literacy, Motor Skills, and Safety and Health.

Population targeted: Children enrolled in publicly funded California preschools and child development centers and family child care home networks

Technology features: *DRDPtech* is the California Department of Education's (CDE) web-based computer support system for the *DRDP* assessment; it is provided by CDE at no cost to CDE-funded local agencies and is managed independently by those agencies; CDE also makes available online training, professional development, and assessment-system utilization support resources

Translations: Spanish versions of the *DRDP-R* and *DRDP© (2010)* instruments

Other Features	Rating (DRDP-R)	Rating (DRDP© 2010*)	Standard	Rating (DRDP-R, IT)	Rating (DRDP-R, PS)
Validated purposes	Medium	High	Acceptability	◑	◕
Curricular links	Low	Medium	Authenticity	●	◕
Comprehensive coverage	High	High	Collaboration	◔	◑
Graduated scoring	High	High	Evidence	◑	◑
Progress monitoring	High	High	Multifactors	◑	◑
Standards alignment	Medium	High	Sensitivity	◑	◑
Diversity features	High	High	Universality	◑	◕
Family engagement	Medium	Medium	Utility	◑	◑
Teamwork	Low	Low			
Professional development	High	High	OVERALL (DRDP-R, IT)		◑
Technology	High	High	OVERALL (DRDP-R, PS)		◑

Note: The recently implemented *DRDP© (2010)* instruments have now replaced the *DRDP-R* instruments in all programs funded by the California Department of Education. The *DRDP© (2010)* instruments are aligned to the California learning foundations for children from birth to kindergarten entry, as well as to the California standards for early elementary education. The *DRDP© (2010)* instruments have been extensively tested and studied, using multiple successive statewide samples, to establish the reliability and validity of the scales of measurement for each domain of development. *DRDPtech*, a computer application for the *DRDP© (2010)* instruments, will be released by January 2011.

  *Other Feature ratings for the *DRDP© (2010)* are based on extensive discussions with the developers and are not based on consumer survey feedback, expert panel opinion, or author ratings.

Developmental Assessment for Students with Severe Disabilities–Second Edition (DASH-2)

Author(s): Mary Kay Dykes and Jane N. Erin

Publication date: 1999

Publisher: PRO-ED

Web site(s): http://www.proedinc.com

Cost: $235.00 per kit (includes Examiner's Manual, 5 each of 5 Pinpoint Scales, 25 Priority Intervention Worksheets, 25 Comprehensive Program Record Forms, and 25 Cumulative Summary Sheets)

Assessment type: Curriculum-referenced assessment

Age range: Birth to 7 years of age

Domains/subtests: Social-Emotional, Language, Sensory-Motor, Activities of Daily Living, and Basic Academics skills

Population targeted: Individuals of all ages who function developmentally under 7 years of age or people with multiple disabilities

Technology features: None

Translations: None

Other features	Rating	Standard	Rating
Validated purposes	Low	Acceptability	◑
Curricular links	Medium	Authenticity	◑
Comprehensive coverage	High	Collaboration	◑
Graduated scoring	High	Evidence	◑
Progress monitoring	High	Multifactors	◑
Standards alignment	Medium	Sensitivity	◑
Diversity features	Low	Universality	◑
Family engagement	Low	Utility	◑
Teamwork	Medium		
Professional development	Low	OVERALL	◑
Technology	Low		

Note: The DASH-3 will be available from the publisher in 2011. Cover image from Dykes, M.K., & Erin, J.N. (1999). *Developmental Assessment for Students with Severe Disabilities-Second Edition (DASH-2)*. Austin, TX: PRO-ED; used with permission.

Developmental Observation Checklist System (DOCS)

Close Up on next page

Author(s): W.P. Hresko, Shirley Miguel, Rita Sherbenou, and Steve Burton

Publication date: 1994

Publisher: PRO-ED

Web site(s): http://www.proedinc.com

Cost: $186.00 per kit (*Examiner's Manual, 25 Cumulative Profile/Record Forms, 25 DC Profile/Record Forms, 25 ABC Profile/Record Forms, and 25 PSSC Profile/Record Forms*)

Assessment type: Curriculum-referenced assessment with norms

Age range: Birth to 6 years

Domains/subtests: Assesses General Development (DC), Adjustment Behavior (ABC), and Parent Stress and Support (PSSC); the DC is divided into four domains: Language, Social, Motor, and Cognition; measured areas include language, social ability, parental stress, parental support, fine and gross motor skills, child adaptability, cognitive, overall development, play skills, parent–child interaction, and environmental impact

Population targeted: Infants and young children who reside in the United States and whose dominant language is English; norm group: $n = 1,094$

Technology features: None

Translations: None

Other features	Rating	Standard	Rating
Validated purposes	High	Acceptability	◐
Curricular links	High	Authenticity	◐
Comprehensive coverage	High	Collaboration	◕
Graduated scoring	Low	Evidence	◕
Progress monitoring	High	Multifactors	◕
Standards alignment	High	Sensitivity	◑
Diversity features	Medium	Universality	◕
Family engagement	High	Utility	◔
Teamwork	High		
Professional development	Low	OVERALL	◕
Technology	Low		

Cover image from Hresko, W.P., Miguel, S., Sherbenou, R., & Burton, S. (1994). *Developmental Observation Checklist System (DOCS) Complete Kit*. Austin, TX: PRO-ED; used with permission.

Developmental Observation Checklist System (DOCS)

Author(s): W.P. Hresko, Shirley Miguel, Rita Sherbenou, and Steve Burton

About the Measure

The *DOCS* is one of the first and best of the curriculum-referenced, authentic developmental assessment measures with national norms.

Although it was originally designed as a screening tool (with 475 items!) for young children 0–6 years of age, the *DOCS* also (and with research evidence) serves as a sophisticated and comprehensive assessment system to 1) observe and record functional skills in natural settings and 2) examine and profile the transactional relationships among the child's development and behavior and the coping ability and stress within the family.

Authenticity

The *DOCS* emphasizes real-life tasks observed in everyday settings by people who know the child best—parents, teachers, and other familiar caregivers. For example, the DOCS emphasizes embedded skills within daily routines such as *expects an activity before it happens, repeats own behavior when has an effect, talks in own language,* and *sits and listens to stories.*

Utility

The *DOCS* is an assessment system based loosely on the Sameroff and Chandler (1975) transactional model, which attempts to quantify the complex interrelationships among child and family attributes without trivializing this complexity. The information can be used by interdisciplinary professionals and parents for intervention planning purposes that emphasize the child's needs within the family.

Within this transactional framework, professionals also can use the authentic and functional content of the *DOCS* to identify "next-step" skills as goals for individualized family service plan and individualized education program development.

Finally, the *DOCS* is one of few measures that recognizes the integrated quality of development. The *DOCS* emphasizes the overlap in developmental competencies by ensuring a cross-domain scoring of children's competencies in interrelated functional domains. For example, in Figure 1, which illustrates cross-domain scoring, if a child makes noises other than crying, the parent would check yes for Item 1. When reviewing the parent's responses, the assessor would then give the child a score of 1 in both the language and cognition lines for Item 1.

			Motor	Social	Language	Cognition

Yes   No

____ ____ 1. Makes noises other than crying.

____ ____ 2. Has recognizable cries for hunger, anger, and pain.

____ ____ 3. Quits fussing by him- or herself.

____ ____ 4. Lifts his or her head while being held under arms by an adult.

____ ____ 5. Quiets when he or she sees parent's face.

____ ____ 6. Quits fussing when he or she hears parent's voice.

____ ____ 7. Looks at a person close to him or her for a few seconds.

____ ____ 8. Raises his or her head and chest while lying on stomach.

____ ____ 9. Cries to get attention.

____ ____ 10. Stops activity when he or she hears voices.

____ ____ 11. Looks at an object such as a rattle for at least 10 seconds.

____ ____ 12. Turns his or her body partly to one side (beginning to roll).

____ ____ 13. Smiles when talked to or played with.

____ ____ 14. Expects activity before it happens (sucks before feeding; kicks feet and moves arms before being picked up).

____ ____ 15. Plays with his or her hands.

____ ____ 16. Smiles or laughs while being bounced, tossed, or engaged in other forms of physical play.

____ ____ 17. Holds a toy without dropping it.

____ ____ 18. Moves to see something better.

____ ____ 19. Steadily holds up his or her head for 5 seconds when held under arms by an adult.

Total for page 2

Figure 1.   Cross-domain scoring for *DOCS*. (From Hresko, W.P., Miguel, S., Sherbenou, R,, & Burton, S. [1994]. *Developmental Observation Checklist System [DOCS] Part 1 DC Profile-Record Form* [p. 2]. Austin, TX: PRO-ED; used with permission.)

Collaboration

The *DOCS* is to be completed through parent–professional collaboration, placing parents in a central role for describing and monitoring their children's developmental progress. Moreover, the three components of the *DOCS—the Developmental Checklist (DC), the Adjustment Behavior Checklist (ABC),* and the *Parent Stress and Support Checklist (PSSC)S*—all use a parent- and/or family-friendly report format.

The DC and the ABC are both 1-page documents that include 25 items. Parents rate the items using a four-point Likert scale: *very much like, somewhat like, not much like, or not at all like.* An example item is *refuses to eat at appropriate meal time.* The PSSC is also a brief, one-page document. As with the DC and ABC, the PSSC uses simple, jargon-free language. The PSSC encourages parent participation in the process by reassuring parents that all children experience times of difficult behavior. An example item from the PSSC is *has temper tantrums.*

Evidence Base

A series of published studies and monographs (i.e., Bagnato, 2002; Bagnato et al., 2002) report the use of the *DOCS* in a large 3-year longitudinal early childhood intervention study in Pennsylvania to fulfill multiple Early Childhood Initiative purposes: detection of delays, individualized goal-planning, progress monitoring and accountability, and sensitivity of research purposes.

Bagnato, S.J., Suen, H., Brickley, D., Jones, J., & Dettore, E. (2002). Child developmental impact of Pittsburgh's Early Childhood Initiative (ECI) in high-risk communities: First-phase authentic evaluation research. *Early Childhood Research Quarterly, 17*(4), 559–589.

This study examined the generalizability of the *DOCS* assessment items (G coefficient) on a sample of 90 at-risk, preschool-age children.

Gilbert, S.L. (1997). *Parent and teacher congruency on variations of a screening assessment: An examination (Report No. H023B50009).* Auburn, AL: Auburn University. Retrieved November 27, 2009, from http://www.eric.ed.gov/ERICDocs/data/ericdocs2sql/content_storage_01/0000019b/80/15/0e/46.pdf

This study examined differences in interrater reliability between parents and teachers on the *DOCS* checklist when presented with two variations of the checklist.

Morgan, F.T. (2005). Development of a measure to screen for reactive attachment disorder in children 0–5 years. Doctoral dissertation, Alliant International University, Fresno, CA. *Proquest Dissertations , 81,* AAT 3173576.

This study supported the predictive validity of the *DOCS-2* in detecting reactive attachment disorder in a randomized sample.

Considerations and Recommendations

*   The *DOCS* assessment competencies are compatible with most preschool curricula; the *DOCS* system also has the advantage of combining both curricula and normative elements to fulfill multiple early childhood intervention purposes.

*   The *DOCS* is useful for assessing a child's development in the context of the family. Moreover, the tool is valuable for identifying young children who may be at risk due to developmental delays, family stressors, or a combination of the two factors. It allows assessors to examine the bidirectional nature of child and parenting attributes.

*   The 1994 version of the *DOCS* needs to be redesigned and renormed. Reorganization by age ranges will make the long scale "friendlier" to complete. Communication with the author and publisher indicates that such revision is underway (expected by 2013).

Developmental Profile 3 (DP-3)

Author(s): Gerald D. Alpern

Publication date: 2007

Publisher: Western Psychological Services

Web site(s): http://portal.wpspublish.com

Cost: $348.00 for kit (Manual, 25 Interview Forms, 25 Checklists, and CD-ROM)
$199.00 for kit without CD-ROM

Assessment type: Curriculum-referenced assessment with norms

Age range: Birth through age 12

Domains/subtests: Physical, Adaptive Behavior, Social-Emotional, Cognitive, and Communication

Population targeted: Typically developing children or children at risk for developmental delays; much field-validation for children with autism; norm group: n = 2,216

Technology features: Unlimited use scoring and interpretation CD-ROM for use with PC with Windows 98, 2000, ME, XP, or Vista

Translations: None

Other features	Rating	Standard	Rating
Validated purposes	High	Acceptability	◖
Curricular links	High	Authenticity	◖
Comprehensive coverage	High	Collaboration	●
Graduated scoring	Low	Evidence	◐
Progress monitoring	Medium	Multifactors	◐
Standards alignment	Low	Sensitivity	◕
Diversity features	High	Universality	◐
Family engagement	High	Utility	◕
Teamwork	Medium		
Professional development	Medium	OVERALL	◐
Technology	Medium		

Developmental Programming for Infants and Young Children: Volume 2. Early Intervention Developmental Profile–Revised Edition

Editor(s): Sally J. Rogers, Carol M. Donovan, Diane B. D'Eugenio, Sara L. Brown, Eleanor Whiteside Lynch, Martha S. Moersch, and D. Sue Schafer

Publication date: 1981

Publisher: University of Michigan Press

Web site(s): http://www.press.umich.edu/esl

Cost: $2.50 per booklet (minimum order of 5 copies required)

Assessment type: Curriculum-referenced assessment

Age range: Birth to 36 months developmental age

Domains/subtests: Perceptual/Fine Motor, Cognition, Language, Social-Emotional, Self-Care, and Gross Motor

Population targeted: Children functioning developmentally within the 0- to 36-month age range; much field validation involving interdisciplinary team assessments for young children with autism and also with children experiencing acquired and congenital brain injuries

Technology features: None

Translations: None

Other features	Rating	Standard	Rating
Validated purposes	Medium	Acceptability	◑
Curricular links	High	Authenticity	◐
Comprehensive coverage	Medium	Collaboration	◑
Graduated scoring	Medium	Evidence	◐
Progress monitoring	High	Multifactors	◑
Standards alignment	Low	Sensitivity	◕
Diversity features	Low	Universality	◑
Family engagement	High	Utility	◕
Teamwork	High		
Professional development	Low	OVERALL	◑
Technology	Low		

Close Up on next page

DEF

Devereux Early Childhood Assessment for Infants and Toddlers (DECA-I/T) *and* The Devereux Early Childhood Assessment (DECA)

Author(s) for *DECA-I/T*: Mary Mackrain, Paul LeBuffe, and Gregg Powell

Author(s) for *DECA*: Paul LeBuffe and Jack Naglieri

Publication date for *DECA-I/T*: 2007

Publication date for *DECA*: 1999

Publisher: Kaplan Early Learning Co.

Web site(s): http://www.kaplanco.com

Cost: $199.95 per kit

Assessment type: Curriculum-referenced assessment with norms

Age range: Across forms age range is 1 month through 5 years; *DECA Infant* form is 1–18 months; *DECA Toddler* form is 18–36 months; *DECA* form is 2 years through 5 years

Domains/subtests: *DECA Infant* form includes Initiative and Attachment/Relationships scales and has 33 items; *DECA Toddler* form includes Attachment/Relationships, Initiative, and Self-Regulation scales and has 36 items; *DECA* includes Initiative, Self-Control, Attachment, and Behavioral Concerns scales and has 37 items

Population targeted: Typically developing children and children at risk for social-emotional problems; for *DECA-I/T*, *n* = 2,183; for *DECA*, *n* = 2,000

Technology features: Scoring Assistant CDs; web-based assessment and scoring system eDECA 2.0

Translations: Spanish

Other features	Rating	Standard	Rating (*DECA-I/T*)	Rating (*DECA*)
Validated purposes	Medium	Acceptability	◑	◑
Curricular links	Medium	Authenticity	◑	◑
Comprehensive coverage	Medium	Collaboration	◑	◑
Graduated scoring	High	Evidence	◖	◑
Progress monitoring	Medium	Multifactors	◑	◑
Standards alignment	High	Sensitivity	◖	●
Diversity features	Medium	Universality	○	●
Family engagement	Medium	Utility	◑	◑
Teamwork	Low			
Professional development	High	OVERALL	◖	◑
Technology	High			

The Devereux Early Childhood Assessment (DECA)

Author(s): Paul LeBuffe and Jack Naglieri

About the Measure

The *DECA* is a strength-based, social-emotional assessment and intervention system.

The *DECA* was designed to identify and develop characteristics of resilience, called *protective factors*, in young children. The protective factors include attachment, self-control, and initiative.

The *DECA* uses a tiered model of intervention to address the needs of children at all levels of social-emotional development.

Authenticity

The individual who rates a child using the *DECA* (called a *Rater*) must have known the child for at least 4 weeks and have observed the child regularly, including immediately preceding the assessment. Raters use observational accounts of child behavior over the 4-week period to complete the assessment items.

Raters are individuals who know the child well and who interact with the child on a regular basis, such as parents, teachers, and other familiar caregivers. Because the assessment relies on observations over an extended period of time, it takes into account a child's functioning in a variety of activities and settings.

The items on the *DECA Record Form* are behaviors that can be observed in any setting, during any activity, and do not require modifications to the child's normal routines. For each item, the Rater indicates the frequency with which the child demonstrated the behavior during the observation period (i.e., during at least the past 4 weeks) using a scale of *Never, Rarely, Occasionally, Frequently,* or *Very Frequently*. The following items are examples of child behaviors from the *DECA Record Form* that would be rated.

During the past 4 weeks, how often did the child:

- *Do things for himself/herself*

- *Have temper tantrums*

- *Share with other children*

- *Show affection for familiar adults*

Utility

The brevity of the *DECA* makes it quick to complete, though it does require prior knowledge of the child. The items are written using simple, jargon-free language that can be easily understood by parents. The *User Guide* in combination with the *DECA Classroom Strategies Guide* and *DECA Observation Journal* present detailed information about what interventions to provide to which children based on assessment results. Classroom and individual profile forms are included to help teachers and caregivers plan for both individual and group instruction. Profile forms can also be used to monitor individual and group progress over time (see Figure 1).

The *DECA Observation Journal* includes several additional forms to facilitate data collection, analysis, and planning for individual children and groups of children. A table helps users identify the appropriate form for specific situations (see Figure 2).

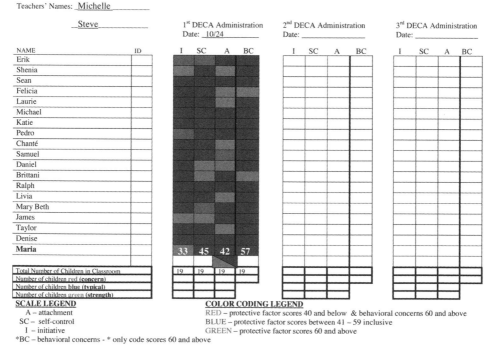

Figure 1. *DECA* Classroom Profile Form. (From LeBuffe, P., & Naglieri, J. [1999]. *The Devereux Early Childhood Assessment [DECA]* [p. 18]. Lewisville, NC: Kaplan Early Learning Company; reprinted by permission.)

Summary of DECA Planning Forms for Individual Children			
	Step(s)	**Form**	**Purpose**
All Children	**1-A: Get to Know Each Child** **4: Develop and Implement Plans** **5: Evaluate Progress**	*Observation Form* (Page 49)	Used for **all children** to conduct observations (initial, in response to DECA results, and ongoing).
	3: Summarize Results	*DECA Individual Profile* **Essential** (separate pad)	Used for **all children** to record *T*-Scores and Percentiles for parent and teacher ratings and to provide a key for interpreting *T*-scores.
	3: Summarize Results	*Individualized Planning Summary: Classroom at a Glance* (Page 56)	Used for **all children**. Used with *DECA Classroom Profile* to note next steps for each child, responsibilities of teachers and families, and time frames.
Protective Factors	**4: Develop and Implement Plans**	*Protective Factors Observations Summary* (Page 57)	Used for children with one or more **Protective Factors** *T*-scores of 40 and below, and, as needed, for children with one or more **Protective Factors** *T*-scores between 41 and 59 inclusive. Used with *Observation Forms* to summarize a child's use of skills and behaviors related to one or more protective factors.
	4: Develop and Implement Plans **5: Evaluate Progress**	*Individualized Protective Factors Plan* (Pages 58–59)	Used for children with one or more **Protective Factors** *T*-scores of 40 and below, and, as needed, for children with one or more **Protective Factors** *T*-scores between 41 and 59 inclusive. Used with *Protective Factors Observation Summary* to plan home and classroom strategies for supporting one or more protective factors.
Behavioral Concerns	**4: Develop and Implement Plans**	*Behavioral Concerns Observation Summary* (Page 60)	Used, as needed, for children who exhibit **challenging behaviors**. Used with *Observation Forms* to summarize information about a child's challenging behavior.
	4: Develop and Implement Plans	*Behavioral Concerns Observations: Review and Analysis* (Page 61)	Used, as needed, for children who exhibit **challenging behaviors**. Used with the *Behavioral Concerns Observation Summary* to summarize and discuss the behavior.
	4: Develop and Implement Plans **5: Evaluate Progress**	*Individualized Positive Guidance Plan* (Pages 62–63)	Used, as needed, for children who exhibit **challenging behaviors**. Used with *Behavioral Concerns Observations: Review and Analysis* to plan strategies to address the behavior.

46

Observation Journal: A Planning Resource for The Comprehensive DECA Program

Figure 2. Summary of *DECA* planning forms for individual children. (From Vacca, M. M., & Koralek, D. [1999]. *The Devereux Early Childhood Assessment [DECA] Observation Journal* [p. 46]. Lewisville, NC: Kaplan Early Learning Company; reprinted by permission.]

Collaboration

The *DECA* highlights the importance of family and teacher collaboration during assessment and intervention. The *DECA Manual* recommends having multiple Raters independently assess each child to provide information about how the child functions in different settings. The *Reflective Checklist for Partnerships with Families* (see Figure 3) is one example of how the DECA promotes parent-teacher collaboration.

Reflective Checklist for Partnerships with Families

Class
Color—Green

Teacher(s): _____   Date: _____

	Yes	Not Yet
1. Learn about each child's family, culture, and community.		
2. Use children's home languages at the program.		
3. Establish an ongoing system for exchanging information about each child with his or her family.		
4. Give families information about typical developmental skills and behaviors of young children.		
5. Use a variety of communication strategies to keep families informed about the program.		
6. Incorporate family involvement in the program design.		
7. Reduce and/or avoid adding to a family's stress.		
8. Support each child's relationship and connection with all nurturing family members, as legally appropriate.		

Figure 3.   Reflective Checklist for Partnerships with Families. (From LeBuffe, P., & Naglieri, J. [1999]. *The Devereux Early Childhood Assessment [DECA]* [p. 54]. Lewisville, NC: Kaplan Early Learning Company; reprinted by permission.]

The *DECA* also includes a family guide, called *For Now and Forever. For Now and Forever* is a 24-page booklet that can be given to families to help them understand social and emotional development in young children. The guide contains specific examples of strategies parents can use to support positive social and emotional development in their children including an annotated list of children's books grouped by protective factors. In addition, *For Now and Forever* encourages parents to communicate with their children's teachers on a regular basis.

Evidence Base

Blair, J.D. (2003). *Factor structure of the Devereux Early Childhood Assessment (DECA): Differences by age, race, gender, and rater.* Doctoral dissertation, University of South Florida.

Exploratory factor analysis of *DECA* using the standardization sample of 2,000 children.

Jaberg, P.E., Dixon, D.J., & Weis, G.M. (2009). Replication evidence in support of the psychometric properties of the Devereux Early Childhood Assessment. *Canadian Journal of School Psychology, 24*(2), 158–166.

Examination of the internal consistency, interrater reliability, and factor structure of the *DECA* with a sample of 780 kindergarten-age children.

Jones, S.C. (2003). *Childhood depression and resiliency: An evaluation of the Devereux Early Childhood Assessment Program.* Doctoral dissertation, University of Northern Iowa, Cedar Falls.

Examination of the effectiveness of the Devereux *Early Childhood Assessment Program* over a 3-month intervention period in two Head Start classes.

DEF

Layburn, K.A. (2004). *An evaluation of an early childhood assessment program and its effect on preschool children* (Doctoral dissertation). Available from ProQuest Dissertations and Thesis database. (UMI 3159391)

A study of the effectiveness of the *DECA* assessment and intervention program on a sample of 93 children.

LeBuffe, P., & Naglieri, J. (1999). *Devereux Early Childhood Assessment: Technical manual.* Lewisville, NC: Kaplan Early Learning Company.

The technical manual describes development and standardization of the DECA. It also presents several smaller studies used to analyze the internal consistency, test-retest reliability, interrater reliability, content validity, criterion validity, and construct validity.

Lien, M.T., & Carlson, J. (2009). Psychometric properties of the Devereux Early Childhood Assessment in a Head Start sample. *Journal of Psychoeducational Assessment, 27*(5), 386-396.

Examines the internal consistency of the *DECA* in a study of 1,208 children enrolled in Head Start.

LoMurray, M. (2007). *The fidelity of DECA program implementation by the BECEP Head Start Program.* Master's thesis, Minot State University, Bismarck, ND.

Examines the fidelity with which Head Start teachers in a public school-based program were able to implement the *DECA*.

Lowther, T.L. (2004). *The impact of a social skills intervention of the development of resiliency in preschool children* (Master's thesis). Available from ProQuest Dissertations and Thesis database. (UMI 1424930)

A study of the effectiveness of the *DECA* assessment and intervention program on a sample of 21 children.

Van Leeuwen, S. (2007). *Validity of the Devereux Early Childhood Assessment instrument.* Dissertation, University of British Columbia, Victoria.

Examines the reliability and internal validity of the *DECA* on a sample of 69 kindergarten children.

Considerations and Recommendations

- The *DECA* is unique in its assessment of protective factors and focus on promoting resiliency in young children.

- The *DECA* could be improved by adding specific instructions for assessing dual or multi-language learners, and including modifications for children with sensory, physical, and/or multiple disabilities.

The Early Learning Accomplishment Profile™ (E-LAP™)

Author(s): M. Elayne Glover, Jodi L. Preminger, and Anne R. Sanford

Publication date: 2002

Publisher: Kaplan Early Learning Co.

Web site(s): http://www.kaplanco.com

Cost: $17.95 for manual; $22.95 for scoring booklet; $349.95 for kit

Assessment type: Curriculum-referenced assessment

Age range: Birth to 36 months

Domains/subtests: Gross Motor, Fine Motor, Cognitive, Language, Self-Help, and Social-Emotional

Population targeted: Infants and toddlers with and without disabilities

Technology features: Software for analyzing data, electronic scoring protocol

Translations: Spanish

Other features	Rating	Standard	Rating
Validated purposes	Medium	Acceptability	◑
Curricular links	Medium	Authenticity	◑
Comprehensive coverage	Medium	Collaboration	◑
Graduated scoring	Low	Evidence	◑
Progress monitoring	Medium	Multifactors	◑
Standards alignment	Medium	Sensitivity	◑
Diversity features	Medium	Universality	◑
Family engagement	Low	Utility	◑
Teamwork	Low		
Professional development	Low	OVERALL	◑
Technology	Medium		

Close Up on next page

Every Move Counts

Sensory-Based Communication Techniques

Author(s): Jane Edgar Korsten Dixie K. Dunn, Teresa Vernon Foss, and Mary Kay Francke

Publication date: 1993

Publisher: PRO-ED

Web site: http://www.proedinc.com

Cost: $107.00 (videotape and manual)

Assessment type: Curriculum-embedded assessment

Age range: Infant through adult with communication functioning between birth and 18 months developmentally

Domains/subtests: Functional appraisal of intersecting sensory-communication capabilities

Population targeted: Children with severe disabilities, developmental delays, and/or autism or individuals who are unable or are perceived as being unable to communicate

Technology features: 10-minute video available showing *Every Move Counts* in action; supplemented by pictogram illustrations of positioning techniques

Translations: None

Other features	Rating	Standard	Rating
Validated purposes	High	Acceptability	◕
Curricular links	High	Authenticity	◑
Comprehensive coverage	High	Collaboration	◑
Graduated scoring	High	Evidence	◕
Progress monitoring	High	Multifactors	◑
Standards alignment	Medium	Sensitivity	◑
Diversity features	Low	Universality	◕
Family engagement	Medium	Utility	◕
Teamwork	High		
Professional development	High	OVERALL	◕
Technology	Medium		

Cover of *Every Move Counts: Sensory-Based Communication Techniques* by J.E. Karsten, D.K. Dunn, T.V. Foss, & M.K. Franke, 1993, Austin, TX: PRO-ED. Copyright 1993 by Responsive Management. Reprinted with permission.

Every Move Counts

Sensory-Based Communication Techniques

Author(s): Jane Edgar Korsten, Dixie K. Dunn, Teresa Vernon Foss, and Mary Kay Francke

About the Measure

Every Move Counts (EMC) is a unique curriculum-embedded assessment-intervention framework that is behaviorally based and fuses assessment and intervention into a singular and integrated process.

EMC is a unique departure from developmental curricular approaches that sequence typical age-related skills in a sequence. Rather, *EMC* relies on a functional-behavioral hierarchy that underlies an ongoing observational assessment of the interrelationship among the child's physical-sensory capability level and the child's social-communication capability level.

EMC is a specialized assessment-intervention system for individuals with diverse neuro-developmental disabilities who function within the birth to 18-month age range.

Authenticity

EMC operationalizes a unique assessment matrix that interrelates appraisal of sensorimotor capabilities with communicative functions. In the matrix illustrated in Figure 1, the physical levels, lettered *A, B, C,* and *D* pertain to the individual's motor abilities. The letters represent progression from *A*, the absence of gross motor movement to *D*, independent movement in the environment. The Roman numerals *(I, II, III, IV)* represent communicative levels, depicting the individual's ability to respond to environmental stimuli. This number progression proceeds from left to right, showing increasing capacity to respond or to cause events to occur. Each cell of the matrix corresponds to interventions in the instruction section of the manual. Behavioral characteristics, criteria for moving to each level, and suggested goals and objectives are provided in the instruction section of the manual as well.

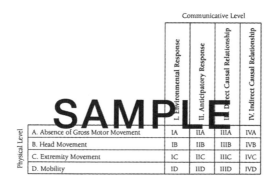

Figure 1. Communicative and Physical Skills Matrix. (*Note.* From *Every Move Counts: Sensory-Based Communication Techniques*, (p. 18) by J.E. Korsten, D.K. Dunn, T.V. Foss, & M.K. Franke, 1993, Austin, TX: PRO-ED. Copyright 1993 by Responsive Management. Reprinted with permission.)

The matrix illustrated in Figure 1 enables therapists to identify and interpret physical limitations in reference to their influence on social and communicative functions. *EMC* is conducted in a social setting where typical daily capabilities as well as, perhaps, enhanced capabilities—when modifications are made (e.g., proper positioning, prompts)—are observed.

The *EMC* system presents sensory-based activities in a behavioral reinforcement and prompt structure that encourages communication. The Sensory-Response Assessment identifies sensory experiences that an individual enjoys and identifies how that enjoyment can be communicated. The child's natural response then becomes a means to request these preferred activities or experiences. As the child moves through four levels of the program, this basic response is defined, refined, and expanded into a more functional and generalized communication system.

Utility

Once the integrated assessment is completed, the *Program Manual* and *Implementation Guide* identify field-validated strategies for intervening to develop social-communication skills. An accompanying videotape/DVD shows the *EMC* process "in action" and is supplemented by the pictograms in the manual.

The Stimulation Protocol (see Figure 2) is used to plan intervention efforts based on the integrated assessment information and provides an integration guide for interventionists and therapists to follow. The protocol/plan combines positioning techniques with communication stimulation strategies to develop more functional competencies for the child through natural routines. Various forms for recording the effectiveness of each therapy "trial" and for conducting environmental observations makes the *EMC* a perfect system for "single-subject" studies of intervention efficacy.

Activity	Presentation/ Withdrawal Intervals	Symbolic Representations				
		Object	Picture	Symbol	Gesture	Sign
Sock massage— rub client's hands and forearms firmly using a hand inside a tennis sock	5 sec./5 sec.	Tennis sock	Photo of object	Drawing of object, rebus symbol, or Blissymbol, or a two-dimensional representation of same color and shape as equipment	Reaching for stimulus; holding out arm to be rubbed	Sign for "rub"
Massage with rubber vegetable scrubber	5 sec./5 sec.	A slender cylinder of same color as handle of scrubber				Sign for "rub"
Hand/ball massage—rub client's palms firmly with a tennis ball	5 sec./5 sec.	Tennis ball or smaller ball				Sign for "rub"
Swinging in swing or sheet	5 sec./5 sec.	Something that represents swing or sheet			Movement pattern that represents the motion	Sign for "swing"
Wagon ride	20 yards or to a predetermined destination/ 5 sec./resume ride	Toy wagon or block with wheels added	Photo of object	Drawing of object, rebus symbol, or Blissymbol	Pointing to object	Sign for "ride" or "go"
Toy play	3 min./5 sec.	Similar toy				Sign for "play"
Switch activation	Naturally occurring interval/5 sec.	Object representing whatever is being activated			Point to item to be activated	Sign for the item to be activated
Participation in group snack	Naturally occurring turn/ 5 sec.	Cup and/or spoon			Point to item or bring hand to mouth	Signs for "eat," "drink," "cookie"...
Participation in group play	Naturally occurring turn/ 5 sec.	Object associated with play; carpet swatch for floor activity			Joining group	Sign for "play"

Figure 2.   Portion of Stimulation Protocol (*Note.* From *Every Move Counts: Sensory-Based Communication Techniques*, (p. 40) by J.E. Korsten, D.K. Dunn, T.V. Foss, & M.K. Franke, 1993, Austin, TX: PRO-ED. Copyright 1993 by Responsive Management. Reprinted with permission.)

Collaboration

Like the *Pediatric Evaluation of Disability Inventory (PEDI), EMC* was developed (under federal funding) by a team of interdisciplinary professionals as a common language and process to link authentic assessment and intervention for children with severe disabilities. *EMC* is a team assessment and intervention system that involves parents, family members, and therapists in the entire process, particularly the intervention process. The *Parent Guide* ensures the family's critical role in creating and carrying out effective activities with and for the child. *EMC* encourages a transdisciplinary approach.

Evidence Base

Although *EMC* was field validated under a federal Office of Special Education and Rehabilitative Services (OSERS) model development and research grant for children with severe disabilities, the report is not available, so the findings cannot be evaluated.

Considerations and Recommendations

- Even after nearly 20 years, *EMC* is an exemplar of a functional behavioral system applied in a creative way to promote the social-communication skills of children with severe disabilities.

- *EMC's* reliance on everyday activities, routines, and experiences makes it a strong authentic assessment framework whose overarching purpose is assessment to guide effective intervention planning and implementation.

- More research is needed to validate and update the system.

Close Up
on next
page

DEF

FACTER: Functional Assessment and Curriculum for Teaching Everyday Routines

Author(s): Joel R. Arick, Gary Nave, Tera Hoffman, and David A. Krug

Publication date: 2004

Publisher: PRO-ED

Web site(s): http://www.proedinc.com

Cost: $74.00 for the FACTER Elementary Kit (*Manual* and 5 *Student Booklets*)

Assessment type: Curriculum-referenced assessment

Age range: Early primary grade students (Grades 1–6); however, the functional nature of routines and skills also makes it appropriate for children in kindergarten

Domains/subtests: Living Skills, Transition, Academics, Leisure, Community, and Career, with related areas in Expressive Communication, Receptive Communication, Problem Solving, Teamwork/Social Skills, Motor Skills, and Functional Academics

Population targeted: Children with moderate to severe developmental disabilities

Technology features: Overview training DVD can be purchased separately

Translations: None

Other features	Rating	Standard	Rating
Validated purposes	Medium	Acceptability	●
Curricular links	High	Authenticity	●
Comprehensive coverage	High	Collaboration	●
Graduated scoring	High	Evidence	●
Progress monitoring	High	Multifactors	●
Standards alignment	Low	Sensitivity	◖
Diversity features	Low	Universality	◖
Family engagement	Low	Utility	◔
Teamwork	Medium		
Professional development	Medium	OVERALL	◔
Technology	Medium		

Note: Cover image from FACTER: Functional Assessment and Curriculum for Teaching Everyday Routines, by J.R. Arick, G. Nave, T. Hoffman, and D.A. Krug, 2004, Austin, TX: PRO-ED. Copyright © 2004 by PRO-ED, Inc. Reprinted with permission.

FACTER: Functional Assessment and Curriculum for Teaching Everyday Routines

Author(s): Joel R. Arick, Gary Nave, Tera Hoffman, and David A. Krug

About the Measure

Routines serve as the basic unit for assessment and instruction in *FACTER*. Children's functional everyday abilities and needs are examined through routines that are task-analyzed into core steps. Related skills that correspond to those identified routines also are selected for instruction to enhance the child's independence.

In the *FACTER* assessment phase, the child is rated on his or her independence level on 29 routines within six domains. In the *FACTER* instruction phase, various strategies are used to target the identified steps and routines to help the child gain independence in the areas of need.

Authenticity

The *FACTER* is completed by observing children in the context of home, school, and community settings during typical activities and routines. Children are not penalized if they require assistive technology or supports to perform routine tasks; the scale accounts for modifications and accommodations. For example, if a child can complete a routine using a wheelchair, picture schedule, or augmentative communication device without assistance from another person, he or she will be scored as independent for the tasks.

Utility

By focusing on routines, team members can gauge the child's level of independence and need for assistance. Information from the assessment is used to identify areas of instruction to help the child acquire important and functional skills (see Figure 1 for an example of functional skills related to removing outdoor clothing).

The combination of cognitive, communication, motor, social, and adaptive skills needed to enable the child to perform and/or participate during daily routines is the focus of the assessment. Not only are routine activities examined in the *FACTER*, but related skills are assessed, targeted for instruction, and individualized to meet each child's needs.

The *FACTER* manual provides specific set-up procedures and instructional strategies for each routine, which are then broken down or task-analyzed into steps. Figure 2 provides a sample activity from the chapter titled Transitioning within Classroom.

The assessment and intervention or teaching cycle is repeated on an ongoing basis to document student progress over time and to identify new areas for IEP planning and instruction.

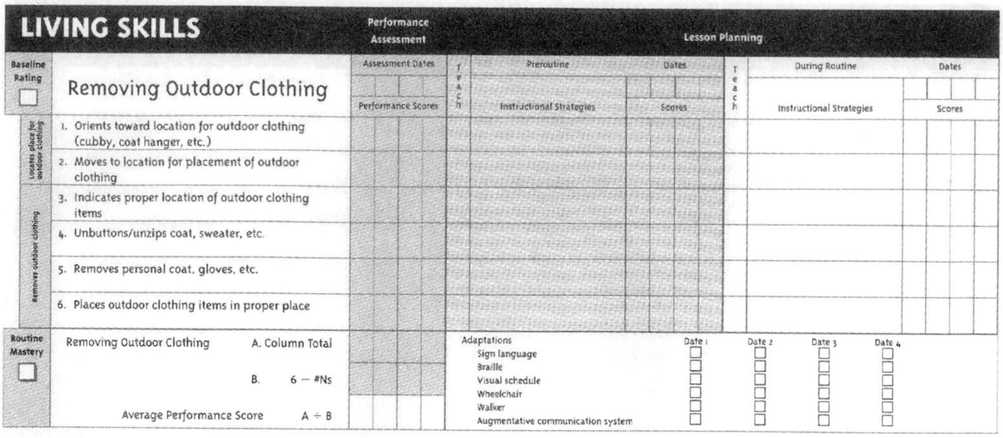

LIVING SKILLS — Performance Assessment — Lesson Planning

Baseline Rating ☐	Removing Outdoor Clothing	Assessment Dates / Performance Scores	Teach	Preroutine Instructional Strategies	Dates / Scores	Teach	During Routine Instructional Strategies	Dates / Scores
Locates place for outdoor clothing	1. Orients toward location for outdoor clothing (cubby, coat hanger, etc.)							
	2. Moves to location for placement of outdoor clothing							
Removes outdoor clothing	3. Indicates proper location of outdoor clothing items							
	4. Unbuttons/unzips coat, sweater, etc.							
	5. Removes personal coat, gloves, etc.							
	6. Places outdoor clothing items in proper place							

Routine Mastery ☐ — Removing Outdoor Clothing — A. Column Total; B. 6 − #Ns; Average Performance Score A ÷ B

Adaptations	Date 1	Date 2	Date 3	Date 4
Sign language	☐	☐	☐	☐
Braille	☐	☐	☐	☐
Visual schedule	☐	☐	☐	☐
Wheelchair	☐	☐	☐	☐
Walker	☐	☐	☐	☐
Augmentative communication system	☐	☐	☐	☐

Figure 1. Example of a Living Skills routine and associated items. (From Living Skills: Dressing for the Outdoors Assessment and Planning Form. In *FACTER: Functional Assessment and Curriculum for Teaching Everyday Routines–Elementary Student Booklet* [p. 8], by J.R. Arick, G. Nave, T. Hoffman, and D.A. Krug, 2004, Austin, TX: PRO-ED. Copyright © 2004 by PRO-ED, Inc. Reprinted with permission.)

Instructional Suggestions

Steps	Preroutine	During Routine
Completes activity		
1. Attends to cue that activity has been completed	• Create cue for "finished." • Practice using this symbol with student during other routines.	• When it is time to cease activity, hand the symbol to student.
2. Terminates activity in appropriate manner	• Create storybook with pictures of terminating activities in an appropriate manner. • Read the story aloud and have student identify the different behaviors.	• Before giving the "finished" cue, review the pictures if needed. • Remind student of the appropriate behaviors as needed.
Puts away materials		
3. Identifies materials to put away	• Create material lists for activities. • Practice listing tools and materials taken out at the beginning of activity and relisting same at the end of activity.	• Practice relisting materials used at the end of activity.

Figure 2. Instructional suggestions for transitioning within classroom. (From *FACTER: Functional Assessment and Curriculum for Teaching Everyday Routines*, by J.R. Arick, G. Nave, T. Hoffman, and D.A. Krug, 2004, Austin, TX: PRO-ED. Copyright © 2004 by PRO-ED, Inc. Reprinted with permission.)

Collaboration

Given the emphasis on assessing a child's performance within the natural environment, the *FACTER* is prime for collaborating with families and other familiar caregivers regarding children's ability to perform typical everyday "routines" and "related skills" for living.

Evidence Base

Appendix E in the *FACTER* provides a summary of reliability and validity studies of the *FACTER*, including the following:

- One study examined the *FACTER's* reliability (interrater and test–retest) and concurrent validity was conducted on 478 students with moderate to severe disabilities (Arick, Nave, & Hoffman, 2000).

- Two studies examined the instructional phase/component (i.e., the success or effectiveness when teaching was delivered within routines or through preteaching substeps of the routine) of the *FACTER* (Morgan, Shinn, Shea, & Sholes, 2002; Thompson, Combs, Shroeder, Morgan, & Feinstein, 2002).

Considerations and Recommendations

- One of the few measures for children with moderate to severe disabilities in the primary, middle, and high school grades that is both functional and normative.

- Compares favorably with the *School Function Assessment* in its focus on context and service needs.

The Functional Emotional Assessment Scale (FEAS) for Infancy and Early Childhood

DEF

Author(s): Stanley Greenspan, Georgia DeGangi, and Serena Wieder

Publication date: 2001

Publisher: The Interdisciplinary Council on Developmental and Learning Disorders

Web site(s): http://www.icdl.com

Cost: $39.50, includes manual and one protocol booklet

Assessment type: Curriculum-referenced assessment

Age range: Six versions: 7–9 months; 10–12 months; 13–18 months; 19–24 months; 25–35 months; and 3–4 years; each form has a caregiver and a child section

Domains/subtests: Measures emotional and social functioning in children and the capacity of caregivers to support their child's emotional development; areas include Regulation and Interest in the World, Forming Relationships (Attachment), Intentional Two-Way Communications, Development of a Complex Sense of Self, Representational Capacity and Elaboration or Symbolic Thinking, and Emotional Thinking or Development and Expression of Thematic Play

Population targeted: Infants and young children and their caregivers who are at risk or have difficulty with social engagement, attachment, play interactions, and emotional functioning

Technology features: Distance learning opportunities provided at http://www.icdl.com that include online video lectures, an e-library, and web radio show recordings.

Translations: None

Other features	Rating	Standard	Rating
Validated purposes	Low	Acceptability	◑
Curricular links	Medium	Authenticity	◐
Comprehensive coverage	Low	Collaboration	◑
Graduated scoring	Medium	Evidence	◑
Progress monitoring	Medium	Multifactors	◑
Standards alignment	Medium	Sensitivity	◑
Diversity features	Low	Universality	◐
Family engagement	High	Utility	◐
Teamwork	High		
Professional development	Medium	OVERALL	◑
Technology	Medium		

Close Up on next page

The Galileo Pre-K Online System for the Electronic Management of Learning

Galileo. Pre-K Online

Author(s): John R. Bergan

Publication date: Copyright 2002–2009

Publisher: Assessment Technology, Inc. (ATI)

Web site(s): http://www.ati-online.com

Cost: Annual subscription fee of $260 per class of 20–25 students
$200 fee for first-time users

Assessment type: Curriculum-embedded assessment with norms

Age range: 3–5 years; assessment scales for birth through 3 years also available but not reviewed

Domains/subtests: Social and Emotional Development, Language and Literacy, Early Math, Creative Arts, Approaches to Learning, Fine and Gross Motor Development, Nature and Science, and Physical Health Practices

Population targeted: All children in early childhood settings; norm sample is continuously up-dated with user data; historical norm data are available (e.g., N = 3,092 for the 2001 *Preschool Assessment*)

Technology features: Available online as well as offline with online data entry (i.e., paper-based option exists for recording observations and then entering them into Galileo); includes web-based applications for assessment, learning, management, and training

Translations: Spanish

Other features	Rating	Standard	Rating
Validated purposes	High	Acceptability	◑
Curricular links	High	Authenticity	◑
Comprehensive coverage	High	Collaboration	◔
Graduated scoring	High	Evidence	◔
Progress monitoring	High	Multifactors	◑
Standards alignment	High	Sensitivity	◔
Diversity features	High	Universality	◕
Family engagement	Medium	Utility	◑
Teamwork	Medium		
Professional development	High	OVERALL	◑
Technology	High		

GHI

The Galileo Pre-K Online System for the Electronic Management of Learning

Author(s): John R. Bergan

About the Measure

Galileo Pre-K Online is a unique, authentic curriculum-embedded system that has the capacity to analyze information about a child and then generate a comprehensive picture of the child's developmental status.

Galileo Pre-K Online can also generate a list of sample activities designed to match a child's given developmental level.

Authenticity

Galileo Pre-K Online includes research-based assessment scales to measure cognitive, social, and physical development. It allows for professionals to record ongoing observations in the child's natural environment multiple times per year. The system is able to generate multiple reports to document changes in a child's learning at various times across the year. *Galileo Pre-K Online* also includes the Galileo Scale Builder function, which allows programs to add or delete assessment indicators, create new scales, modify scales for children with special needs, or translate any of the scales into a different language.

Galileo Pre-K Online uses an electronic management system to organize assessment data from multiple sources such as teacher observations, parent input, and classroom projects into an integrated developmental profile. The developmental profiles can be used to help teachers record and monitor learning throughout the year. For example, in Figure 1, a teacher's observation and subsequent recording of a child's performance on the *Galileo v2 Language and Literacy Assessment* indicates that on 06/17/10 the child, Jeremiah Stone in the Butterflies Full-Day class, had demonstrated the ability to follow a one-step direction. As the child acquires more skills in the Language and Literacy area, the teacher can update the assessment.

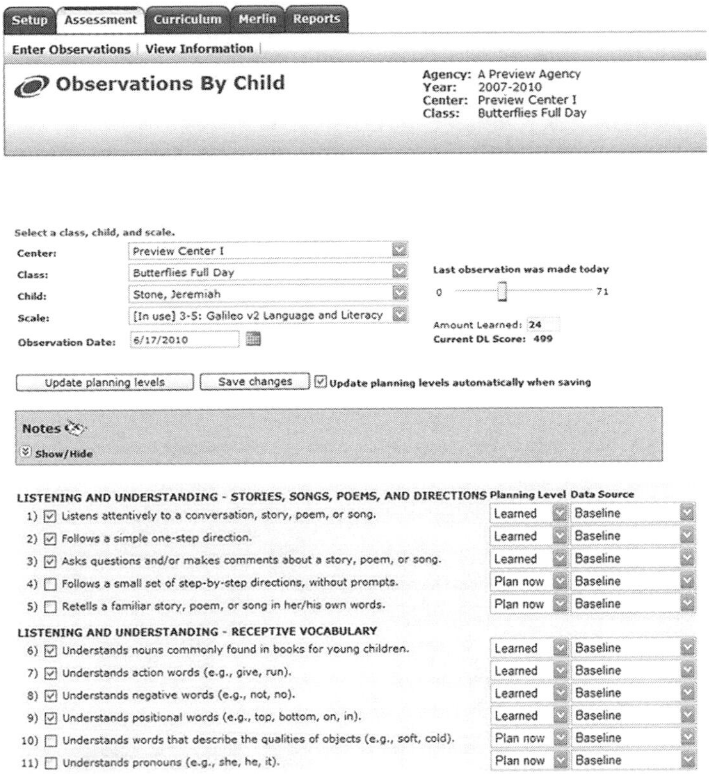

Figure 1. Illustration of the *Galileo Pre-K Online*'s electronic management system Assessment Component. (Reprinted by permission from Assessment Technology, Inc.)

Utility

Galileo Pre-K Online uses item response theory (IRT) to analyze a child's skills and predict the skills that are likely to emerge next. The information generated can be used to plan instruction at the individual or class level. Instruction can be planned based on the needs of a specific child, the readiness level of the class, or what is next in the curriculum sequence. For example, in Figure 2, two students have previously learned to listen attentively to a conversation, story, poem, or song; four children are ready to begin working on this skill; and activities are provided to promote learning.

Within *Galileo Pre-K Online,* educators can access an extensive library of activities and lesson plans. The lesson plans are filed electronically, which allows users to search for activities that work on specific skills identified through the assessment process. Lesson plans are aligned to the eight Head Start outcomes and provide suggestions for individual and group learning.

Galileo Pre-K Online includes an area for anecdotal note taking to help educators further document student performance. The system then organizes the notes in chronological order and by content area.

Individualization Plan

Title:	Language Skills
Date:	6/17/2010 - 6/17/2010
Class:	Butterflies Full Day

3-5: Galileo v2 Language and Literacy

Goal: 01) Listens attentively to a conversation, story, poem, or song.

Notes: Students will be given opportunity to view storybook pictures. We will think of familiar songs.

Name	Readiness Level
● Alcala, Gesselle	Ready Now
● Asberry, Raven	Learned
● Brown, Robert	Learned
● Doe, Jane	Ready Now
● James, Tiffany	Ready Now
● Roberts, Christina	Ready Now

Activities

- ● Poem: Five Little Leaves
- ● Self-portrait
- ● Song: Autumn Leaves
- ● Story: I Feel Orange Today

3-5: Galileo v2 Language and Literacy

Goal: 07) Understands action words (e.g., give, run).

Notes: Teacher will ask children to "Stand up," and look for all children to stand.

Name	Readiness Level
● Alcala, Gesselle	Ready Now
● Asberry, Raven	Ready Now
● Brown, Robert	Ready Now
● Doe, Jane	Ready Now
● James, Tiffany	Ready Now
● Roberts, Christina	Ready Now

Activities

- ● I Can Move

Figure 2. Planning instruction based on *Galileo Pre-K Online*. (Reprinted by permission from Assessment Technology, Inc.)

Collaboration

The *Galileo Parent Center* is a secure area in *Galileo Pre-K Online* where parents can log in and access current information about their child's learning and classroom experiences. Parents are able to generate a report in the Parent Center to gain information about their child's progress. Parents also are able to view a teacher's lesson plans. Within the Parent Center, parents are able to access the Times for Learning Library, which outlines activities that can be used in the home. Through the Parent Center, parents can be involved in assessing children's progress by observing and reporting evidence of skills included in the assessment. Teachers can also use the Parent Center to communicate with parents (e.g., reminders of upcoming events, progress updates). See Figure 3 for a screenshot of the Parent Center home page and parent-generated report.

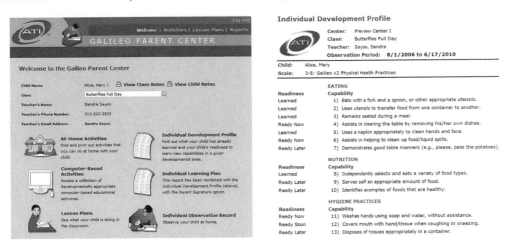

Figure 3. Screenshot of Parent Center home page and parent-generated report. (Reprinted by permission from Assessment Technology, Inc.)

Evidence Base

Bergan, J.R., Burnham, C.G., Feld, J.K., & Bergan, J.R. (2009). *The Galileo Pre-K Online System for the Electronic Management of Learning.* Retrieved on October 14, 2009, from the Assessment Technology, Inc., web site http://www.ati-online.com/pdfs/researchPreschool/GalileoTechManual.pdf

This report provides evidence of reliability, including internal consistency and interrater reliability. Validity of the developmental sequences and assessment-planning link is also discussed.

Bergan, J.R., Bergan, J.R., Rattee, M., Field, J.K., Smith, K., Cunningham, K., et al. (2003). *The Galileo System for the Electronic Management of Learning.* Retrieved on October 14, 2009, from the Assessment Technology, Inc. web site http://www.ati-online.com/galileoPreschool/PreWelcomeTechManual.html

This report provides evidence of reliability, including internal consistency and interrater reliability. In addition, it demonstrates measures of validity including content, construct, treatment, and social validity. The report also provides analysis of annual data for the years 1994 and 1998–2001; however, the psychometric properties of *Galileo Pre-K Online* are continuously updated using data from programs that use Galileo.

Considerations and Recommendations

- *Galileo Pre-K Online's* comprehensive online features provide teachers with the ability to easily and quickly analyze individual and group developmental performance based on authentic assessment procedures.

- As with any system that is online, there may be a learning curve for some users; however, hard copies of assessments can be printed out and used to record observations and then entered into *Galileo Pre-K Online* so that IRT analysis, individual, group, class, center, and program-level reports can be produced.

Close Up
on next
page

HELP®–the Hawaii Early Learning Profile®

Author(s) for *HELP® (0-3)*: Stephanie Parks

Author(s) for *HELP® for Preschoolers*: VORT Corporation et al.

Publication date for *HELP® (0-3)*: 2007

Publication date for *HELP® for Preschoolers*: 2004

Publisher: VORT Corporation

Web site(s): http://www.vort.com
https://osep.vort.com

Cost: *Inside HELP® Administration and Reference Guide (0-3)* $59.95
HELP® Strands (0-3) $3.25
HELP® for Preschoolers Assessment and Curriculum Guide $64.95
HELP® for Preschoolers Assessment Strands $3.25

Assessment type: Curriculum-embedded assessment

Age range: Birth through 3 years and 3-6 years

Domains/subtests: Cognitive, Language, Gross Motor, Fine Motor, Social, and Self-Help; domains further separated into 60 developmentally sequenced strands

Population targeted: Typically developing children and children with developmental delays

Technology features: *HELP® Online* with Office of Special Education Programs reporting system; automatically calculates scores for the Early Childhood Outcomes Summary Form

Translations: *HELP® Checklist (0-3), HELP® for Preschoolers Assessment Strands,* and additional materials are available in Spanish. The VORT Corporation web site reports that the *HELP®* has been translated into eight languages.

Other features	Rating		Standard	Rating
Validated purposes	Low		Acceptability	◑
Curricular links	Medium		Authenticity	◑
Comprehensive coverage	High		Collaboration	◑
Graduated scoring	Medium		Evidence	◐
Progress monitoring	Medium		Multifactors	◑
Standards alignment	Medium		Sensitivity	◑
Diversity features	Medium		Universality	◑
Family engagement	High		Utility	◑
Teamwork	Medium			
Professional development	Medium		OVERALL	◑
Technology	Medium			

GHI

HELP®—the Hawaii Early Learning Profile®

Author(s) for *HELP® (0-3)*: Stephanie Parks

Author(s) for *HELP® for Preschoolers*: VORT Corporation et al.

About the Measure

Given the inclusion of age indices and/or estimates, the *HELP®* is prime for supporting teams in establishing a child's expected developmental performance and planning individualized goals for intervention.

The *HELP®* was originally designed for children ages birth to 3 years. Later revisions added a preschool level (3-6 years) and further restructured the system to create a seamless birth to 6 continuum, including complementary support materials for children of all ages.

In line with its priority to encourage parental involvement, the *HELP®* is organized along a developmental continuum to facilitate communication with parents about their children's functioning.

Authenticity

The *HELP®* 0-3 covers 685 skills that are grouped into 58 strands. The *HELP® for Preschoolers* covers 622 skills that are grouped into 44 strands. Some of the same strands (e.g., communicating with others, walking/running, prewriting, social interactions, play) are included in both the 0-3 and preschool levels. The skills included in both levels follow a developmental hierarchy and are applicable to all children. Further, the *HELP® for Preschoolers* contains four strands that assess skills that would be appropriate only for children with specific disabilities; these strands are sign language, speech reading, swimming, and wheelchair skills. When assessing a child who is deaf, the sign language and speech reading strands can be used in addition to the other language strands used for all children. Assessment information is collected by direct observation of the child during daily activities and play, structured activities to elicit behaviors, and parent interview.

Utility

Inside HELP®: Administration and Reference Manual for HELP® 0-3, provides clear definitions, flexible assessment procedures, and descriptive credit criteria for each of the *HELP®* 0-3 skills (see Figure 1). In addition, family friendly definitions, assessment adaptations, and meaningful and culturally relevant assessment materials are included with each Strand, as well as guidelines for assessing parent-child interactions, supportive environments, and information to help understand why a child may be having difficulty in certain areas of development. Similar information is provided for ages 3-6 years in the *HELP® 0-3 for Preschoolers Assessment and Curriculum Guide*.

For both *HELP® 0-3* and *HELP® 3-6*, each skill has a unique ID number for easy cross-reference and linking between the assessment, curriculum, and intervention materials. Figures 1 and 2 show how the *HELP® 0-3* assessment links with the curriculum.

HELP® includes basic suggestions for administering the assessment under specific conditions and for children with different disabilities. For example, a suggestion for a child with a speech disorder would be, "Before you give the assessment, consult the child's speech therapist for specific suggestions and assistance."

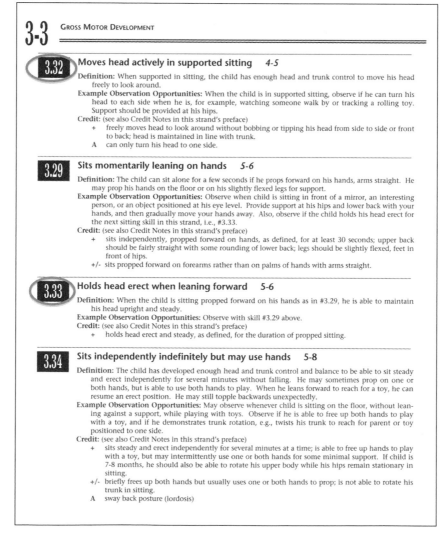

Figure 1. Skills 3.32 and 3.33 from *Inside HELP®*, p. 164. (From *Inside HELP®: Administration and Reference Manual for HELP®* 0-3, by VORT Corporation, et al. © 1996-2006. Published by VORT Corporation, PO Box 60132, Palo Alto, CA 94306.)

Collaboration

HELP® at Home (0-3) and *HELP® for Preschoolers Activities at Home (3-6)* both provide suggestions and activities for parents to use at home. There is at least one suggestion or activity for each skill in the 0-3 and 3-6 assessments. Suggestions are written from the child's point of view and include an introduction, materials, and activities that can be easily administered by parents or child care providers. For example, if a child is working on *Skill 3.32: Moves head actively in supported sitting*, the therapist/teacher could send home the corresponding activity form for this skill. See *HELP® at Home* in Figure 2.

Developing Good Head Control in Sitting

At this stage...

I am developing enough head and trunk control to move my head freely when I am sitting with some support. This control lets me look around as well as hold my head upright and steady when I am sitting propped on my hands or with support at my trunk.

Ideas to HELP:

1. Make sure I have enough trunk support when I am sitting. Let me practice sitting in the corner of a sofa, in my infant seat, car seat, high chair, or supported on your lap.

2. Adjust my infant seat, car seat, and high chair to more upright positions when I am able to sit without bobbing my head or flopping forward. This well let me move my head more freely to take a look around and, will encourage continued head and trunk control.

3. Sometimes when you are holding me in a sitting position, try this simple exercise to encourage increased head control. Tilt me slowly an inch or two toward my side. Wait for me to raise my head back up. Then repeat toward my other side. Try this to the tune of my favorite nursery rhyme.

4. Add "stuffing" to the sides of my seats, if my seats are too big, or to help steady my trunk. Stuffing can be small towel rolls or little pillows. Place my seat's safety belt around my hips where my legs bend. Support for my feet such as a footrest or the floor provides added support to help me work on head and trunk control.

5. Provide interesting things for me to look at or play with when I am sitting with support, e.g., place a suction cup toy on my high chair; let me sit in front of a mirror; or let me watch family members carrying out their daily activities.

6. Be sure to change my position after I have been sitting in a seat for 10-15 minutes, or sooner if I get bored or I start slumping forward.

! Important:

Even though I am learning to sit, I still need plenty of supervised opportunities to play on my tummy.

/!\ Safety Check:

Be sure the areas around me are soft and safe where I am sitting in case I plop over. Clear the area in front, back, and to the sides of me from any sharp edges, or hard objects and toys that could hurt me if I fall on or into them.

Notes:

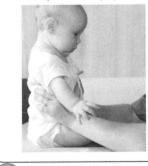

3.32 Moves head actively in supported sitting (4-5)
3.33 Holds head erect when leaning forward (5-6)
Also see: Appendix F-5 Positioning in sitting

HELP at Home © 1988, 2006 VORT Corporation. Be sure to read important terms and Instructions on pages ii-viii.   227

Figure 2. Skills 3.32 and 3.33 from *HELP® at Home*, p. 227. (From *HELP® at Home*, by Stephanie Parks Warshaw et al. © 1988-2006. Published by VORT Corporation, PO Box 60132, Palo Alto, CA 94306.)

Evidence Base

Bagnato S.J., & Murphy, J.P. (1989). Validity of curriculum-based scales with young neuro-developmentally disabled children: Implications for team assessment. *Early Education and Development, 1*(1), 50–63.

The concurrent validity of two norm-referenced and six curriculum-based assessments (CBAs), including the *HELP®*, were examined. Participants in the study were 50 infant and preschool children with diverse developmental delays. Results supported the concurrent validity of the CBAs. Findings also showed that when compared to the five other CBAs, the *HELP®* showed the most moderate and representative results and provided an exact match with the Gesell Developmental Schedules (norm referenced assessment) criterion.

Considerations and Recommendations

- The *HELP®* is particularly useful for working with children who are typically developing and children with mild delays and their families.

- The *HELP®* system includes innovative, useful, and important materials for helping teachers, children, and parents including *HELP® at Home* and *HELP® When the Parent Has Disabilities*.

- Research is needed on the *HELP®* even though it is considered an assessment process. In other words, whenever information from a test or other measurement procedure (e.g., the *HELP®* assessment process) is used to aid decision making (e.g., identify intervention targets, determine extent of a delay), evidence of the extent to which scores provide dependable information that is relevant to the desired score-based inferences must be gathered and evaluated.

Close Up on next page

HighScope
Child Observation Record (COR)

Author(s): HighScope Educational Research Foundation

Publication date: 2002, 2003

Publisher: HighScope Press

Web site(s): http://www.highscope.org
http://www.onlinecor.net

Cost: *Child Observation Record for Infants and Toddlers Administrator's Kit* $174.95
Preschool Child Observation Record Kit $174.95

Assessment type: Curriculum-embedded assessment

Age range: *COR for Infants and Toddlers* 6 weeks to 3 years; *Preschool COR* 2.5–6 years; materials also available for elementary and youth

Domains/subtests: *Infant-Toddler COR* includes Sense of Self, Social Relations, Creative Representation, Movement, Communication and Language, Exploration and Early Logic; *Preschool COR* includes Initiative, Social Relations, Creative Representation, Movement and Music, Language and Literacy, Mathematics and Science

Population targeted: Can be used for all children including those with special needs

Technology features: Online data management system (*Online COR*) can be used independent of the *HighScope Curriculum*; CD-ROM including *COR* forms

Translations: *COR for Infants and Toddlers* available in Spanish; *Preschool COR* available in Korean

Other features	Rating		Standard	Rating (*Infants/Toddlers*)	Rating (*Preschool*)
Validated purposes	High		Acceptability	◕	◕
Curricular links	High		Authenticity	◑	◑
Comprehensive coverage	High		Collaboration	◔	◔
Graduated scoring	High		Evidence	◕	◕
Progress monitoring	High		Multifactors	◑	◑
Standards alignment	High		Sensitivity	◕	◕
Diversity features	High		Universality	◕	◕
Family engagement	Medium		Utility	◕	◑
Teamwork	Medium				
Professional development	High		OVERALL (*Infants/Toddlers*)		◕
Technology	High		OVERALL (*Preschool*)		◕

G H I

HighScope
Child Observation Record (COR)

Author(s): HighScope Educational Research Foundation

About the Measure

The *COR* is a truly authentic assessment that can be linked with the associated curriculum or used as a stand-alone measure.

Originally designed only for use with the *HighScope Curriculum*, the *COR* has been promoted and used by a wide range of early childhood programs since 1992.

The *COR* looks broadly at all key areas of development using a strengths-based approach rather than looking at deficits or narrow skill acquisition.

Authenticity

The *Preschool COR* and *COR for Infants and Toddlers* allow for the systematic documentation of children's development through multiple observations while children are engaged in every-day activities. Information is collected at group care or school settings and through the collection of work samples. The *Preschool COR* consists of 32 scored items that are easily observable in natural settings, such as *Child uses a number word* and *Child identifies a problem with materials and asks for help*. Similarly, the *COR for Infants and Toddlers* includes 28 easily observable items such as *Child imitates the sound, facial expression, or gesture of another person* and *Child rolls from side to back*.

Utility

By linking the assessment items to the Key Developmental Indicators (KDIs), also called Key Experiences (the primary elements of the *HighScope Curriculum*), the authors facilitate the process of using assessment results to plan curriculum and intervention activities for children. For both the *COR for Infants and Toddlers* and the *Preschool COR*, some items link directly to High-Scope KDIs while other items relate generally to them. Figures 1 and 2 illustrate the direct and indirect links between the *COR* and KDIs. For example, the item *Listening and responding* is included on the *COR for Infants and Toddlers* under the strand Communication and Language and is listed as a KDI in the strand Communication and Language; whereas the item *Exploring categories*, which appears on the *COR for Infants and Toddlers* under the strand Exploration and Early Logic, does not appear explicitly on the Infant and Toddler KDI list. Instead, *Exploring categories* relates to several Infant and Toddler KDIs in strands ranging from Social Relations to Exploring Objects.

Lastly, according to HighScope Educational Research Foundation, state and local standards, federal child outcomes, professional organization standards, and Head Start Outcomes are compatible (i.e., can be aligned) with HighScope curriculum components including the *High-Scope COR*. See http://www.highscope.org/Content.asp?ContentId=250 for more information on alignment activities.

V Communication and Language

R. Listening and responding
S. Communicating interest nonverbally
T. Participating in give-and-take communication
U. Speaking
V. Exploring picture books
W. Showing interest in stories, rhymes, and songs

VI Exploration and Early Logic

X. Exploring objects
Y. Exploring categories
Z. Developing number understanding
AA. Exploring space
BB. Exploring time

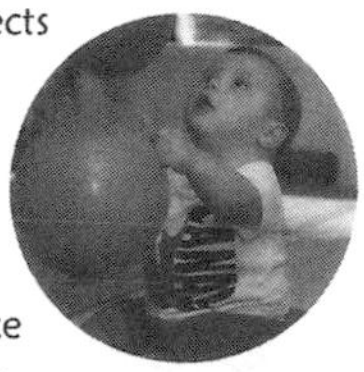

Figure 1. Infant and Toddler COR items. (From *HighScope Educational Research Foundation*. [2002]. *Infant-Toddler Child Observation Record [COR]*. Ypsilanti, MI: HighScope Press; reprinted by permission.)

Music
- Listening to music
- Responding to music
- Exploring and imitating sound
- Exploring vocal pitch sounds

Communication and Language
- Listening and responding
- Communicating nonverbally
- Participating in two-way communication
- Speaking
- Exploring picture books and magazines
- Enjoying stories, rhymes, and songs

Exploring Objects
- Exploring objects with one's hands, feet, mouth, eyes, ears, and nose
- Discovering object permanence
- Exploring and noticing how things are the same or different

Early Quantity and Number
- Experiencing "more"
- Experiencing one-to-one correspondence
- Experiencing the number of things

Figure 2. Infant and Toddler Key Developmental Indicators. (From *HighScope Educational Research Foundation*. [2002]. *Infant-Toddler Child Observation Record [COR]*. Ypsilanti, MI: HighScope Press; reprinted by permission.)

Collaboration

One or more teachers or child care providers can work together or separately to complete the *COR*. Parents are encouraged to participate in the assessment process, though they are not required to do so. The *Parent Guide* recommends parents offer written anecdotes of their children's activities or behaviors to their children's teacher or child care provider. The teacher or child care provider can then include the parents' anecdotal records in the children's *CORs* for a more complete picture of the child's functioning across settings. In addition, a *Family Report* is available to inform parents of their children's performance on the *COR*.

Evidence Base

HighScope Educational Research Foundation. (2003). Preschool COR development and validation. In *User guide: Preschool Child Observation Record* (pp. 29–35). Ypsilanti, MI: HighScope Press.

The appendix to the assessment tool describes a reliability and validity study as well as field testing of the *Preschool COR*. The field test resulted in modifications to the original assessment tool prior to the reliability and validity study. The sample for the reliability and validity study included 230 children—ages 3 years, 0 months to 5 years, 5 months— enrolled in Head Start. The report does not specify whether children with disabilities were included in the study. Findings regarding internal consistency, interrater reliability, internal validity, and external validity are provided.

HighScope Educational Research Foundation. (2002). Development and validation. In *User guide: Child Observation Record for Infants and Toddlers* (pp. 31–36). Ypsilanti, MI: High-Scope Press.

Parallel to the *Preschool COR*, the appendix to the *COR for Infants and Toddlers* describes a reliability and validity study as well as field testing. The field test resulted in modifications to the original assessment tool prior to the reliability and validity study. The sample for the reliability and validity study included 20 caregivers from eight different programs and their assessments of 50 children between 4 and 36 months of age. Children with disabilities were not included in this study. Findings regarding internal consistency, interrater reliability, and concurrent validity are provided.

Schweinhart, L., & McNair, S. (1993). Observing young children in action to assess their development: The High/Scope Child Observation Record study. *Educational & Psychological Measurement, 53*(2), 445–455.

Describes a study of the psychometric properties of the *High/Scope COR, First Edition*. The total sample included students of 64 Head Start teaching teams in southeastern Michigan. Although analysis clearly included use of multiple demographic statistics (e.g., age, parents' level of education, parents' employment), only ethnicity was specified. The results described internal consistency, interrater reliability, and concurrent validity of the measure.

Considerations and Recommendations

- Users will need a strong foundation in child development and the ability to document children's performance using narrative methods.

- Further research must be conducted to validate the *COR* for use in Office of Special Education Programs (OSEP) reporting.

- Users might find that the *COR* is not sensitive enough to detect small increments of change in development.

Humanics National Infant-Toddler Assessment *and* Humanics National Preschool Assessment

Author(s): Marsha Kaufman and T. Thomas McMurrain

Publication date for the 0-3 form: 2002

Publication date for the 3-6 form: 2000

Publisher: Humanics Ltd Partners

Web site(s): http://www.humanicspub.com

Cost: $24.95 for each manual; $37.95 for assessment forms (pack of 25)

Assessment type: Curriculum-referenced assessment

Age range: Birth to 3 years and 3-6 years

Domains/subtests: Social-Emotional, Language, Cognitive, Gross Motor, and Fine Motor; Hygiene and Self-Help are only on the 3-6 year assessment

Population targeted: Typically developing children, children with suspected disabilities, and children with identified disabilities

Technology features: None

Translations: None

Other features	Rating	Standard	Rating (*Infant-Toddler*)	Rating (*Preschool*)
Validated purposes	Low	Acceptability	◕	◕
Curricular links	Medium	Authenticity	◕	◕
Comprehensive coverage	Low	Collaboration	◕	◕
Graduated scoring	Low	Evidence	◔	◔
Progress monitoring	Medium	Multifactors	◕	◕
Standards alignment	Medium	Sensitivity	◑	◑
Diversity features	Low	Universality	◑	◑
Family engagement	Medium	Utility	◑	◑
Teamwork	Low			
Professional development	Low	OVERALL (*Infant-Toddler*)		◑
Technology	Low	OVERALL (*Preschool*)		◑

Infant Toddler Social-Emotional Assessment™ (ITSEA™)

Author(s): Alice S. Carter and Margaret J. Briggs-Gowan

Publication date: 2006

Publisher: NCS Pearson

Web site(s): http://psychcorp.pearsonassessment.com

Cost: $245.00 (includes all pieces required for both full and brief assessments)

Assessment type: Curriculum-referenced assessment with norms

Age range: 12–36 months

Domains/subtests: Measures Social Relatedness, Atypical Behaviors, and Maladaptive Behaviors; four domains: Externalizing, Internalizing, Dysregulation, and Competence; identifies key indicators of autism and pervasive developmental disorders

Population targeted: Young children who may be at risk for social-emotional disorders; $n = 600$; norm sample included children with diagnosed disorders

Technology features: CD-ROM for scoring

Translations: Spanish

Other features	Rating	Standard	Rating
Validated purposes	Medium	Acceptability	◑
Curricular links	Low	Authenticity	●
Comprehensive coverage	Medium	Collaboration	◕
Graduated scoring	Medium	Evidence	●
Progress monitoring	Medium	Multifactors	◐
Standards alignment	Low	Sensitivity	○
Diversity features	Low	Universality	○
Family engagement	Low	Utility	◖
Teamwork	Low		
Professional development	Low	OVERALL	◐
Technology	High		

G H I

Infant-Toddler and Family Instrument (ITFI)

Author(s): Nancy H. Apfel and Sally Provence

Publication date: 2001

Publisher: Paul H. Brookes Publishing Co.

Web site(s): http://www.brookespublishing.com

Cost: $25.00 for manual; $25.00 for package of forms

Assessment type: Curriculum-referenced assessment

Age range: 6 months to 3 years

Domains/subtests: Survey of family and child functioning using a Developmental Map, which includes Gross and Fine Motor Development, Social and Emotional Development, Language Development, Coping, and Self-Help Development

Population targeted: Infants and toddlers and their families

Technology features: None

Translations: None

Other features	Rating	Standard	Rating
Validated purposes	Low	Acceptability	◑
Curricular links	Medium	Authenticity	◑
Comprehensive coverage	Medium	Collaboration	◑
Graduated scoring	Medium	Evidence	◑
Progress monitoring	Low	Multifactors	◑
Standards alignment	Medium	Sensitivity	◑
Diversity features	Medium	Universality	◑
Family engagement	High	Utility	◖
Teamwork	Medium		
Professional development	Low	OVERALL	◑
Technology	Low		

Infant-Toddler Developmental Assessment (IDA)

Author(s): Sally Provence, Joanna Erikson, Susan Vater, and Saro Palmeri

Publication date: 1995

Publisher: PRO-ED

Web site(s): http://www.proedinc.com

Cost: $676.00 for complete kit

Assessment type: Curriculum-referenced assessment

Age range: Birth to 36 months

Domains/subtests: Addresses the health and development of children across the following areas: Gross Motor, Fine Motor, Relationship to Inanimate Objects (Cognitive), Language/Communication, Self-Help, Relationship to Persons, Emotions and Feeling States (Affects), and Coping Behavior

Population targeted: Children who are developmentally at risk

Technology features: Online training available through the IDA Institute

Translations: Parent Form available in Spanish

Other features	Rating	Standard	Rating
Validated purposes	Low	Acceptability	◐
Curricular links	High	Authenticity	◐
Comprehensive coverage	High	Collaboration	◐
Graduated scoring	High	Evidence	◐
Progress monitoring	Medium	Multifactors	◐
Standards alignment	Medium	Sensitivity	◐
Diversity features	Low	Universality	◐
Family engagement	High	Utility	◐
Teamwork	High		
Professional development	High	OVERALL	◐
Technology	Medium		

Cover image from Provence, S., Erikson, J., Vater, S., & Palmeri, S. (1995). *Infant-Toddler Developmental Assessment (IDA) complete kit with manipulatives and carrying case.* Austin, TX: PRO-ED; used with permission.

INSITE
Developmental Checklist
Assessment of Developmental Skills for Young Multidisabled Sensory Impaired Children

Author(s): Elizabeth Morgan

Publication date: 1989

Publisher: HOPE

Web site(s): http://www.hopepubl.com
http://www.skihi.org/INSITE.html

Cost: *Developmental Checklist Instructional Manual* $10.00
The INSITE Model Curriculum $90.00

Assessment type: Curriculum-referenced assessment

Age range: Birth through 6 years; short version birth through 2 years

Domains/subtests: Divided into nine developmental areas: Communication, Audition, Vision, Cognition, Gross Motor, Fine Motor, Self-Help, Social-Emotional Development, and Taction; developmental areas are further subdivided by skill categories and small steps within age ranges

Population targeted: Young children with sensory impairments and/or multiple disabilities

Technology features: None

Translations: None

Other features	Rating		Standard	Rating
Validated purposes	Medium		Acceptability	◑
Curricular links	High		Authenticity	◐
Comprehensive coverage	High		Collaboration	◔
Graduated scoring	Medium		Evidence	◔
Progress monitoring	Medium		Multifactors	◑
Standards alignment	Medium		Sensitivity	◑
Diversity features	Medium		Universality	◑
Family engagement	High		Utility	◐
Teamwork	Low			
Professional development	Medium		OVERALL	◑
Technology	Low			

Close Up on next page

Inventory for Client and Agency Planning™ (ICAP™)

Author(s): Robert H. Bruininks, Bradley K. Hill,
Richard F. Weatherman, and Richard W. Woodcock

Publication date: 1986

Publisher: Riverside Publishing

Web site(s): http://www.riversidepublishing.com

Cost: *Complete program* $196.00
25 Response Booklets $76.00
ICAP Compuscore CD-ROM $334.00

Assessment type: Curriculum-referenced assessment with norms

Age range: Infant to adult

Domains/subtests: Motor Skills, Personal Living Skills, Community Living Skills, Social and Communication Skills, and Broad Independence as well as eight categories of maladaptive behavior

Population targeted: Individuals with disabilities of all ages; norm group: n = 593 children ages 0–4 years; n = 647 children ages 5–11 years

Technology features: Computer scoring program for Windows

Translations: Spanish language forms

Other features	Rating	Standard	Rating
Validated purposes	Medium	Acceptability	●
Curricular links	Medium	Authenticity	●
Comprehensive coverage	High	Collaboration	●
Graduated scoring	High	Evidence	●
Progress monitoring	High	Multifactors	●
Standards alignment	Low	Sensitivity	◐
Diversity features	High	Universality	◐
Family engagement	Medium	Utility	◕
Teamwork	High		
Professional development	Medium	OVERALL	◕
Technology	Medium		

GHI

Inventory for Client and Agency Planning™ (ICAP™)

Author(s): Robert H. Bruininks, Bradley K. Hill, Richard F. Weatherman, and Richard W. Woodcock

About the Measure

The *ICAP™* is a comprehensive, authentic assessment system designed to document capabilities and service needs across the age range from early childhood to adulthood.

Perhaps the *ICAP™*'s most unique feature is a Rasch scaling process that buttresses its technical properties and lends credence to its link between adaptive behaviors, social behavior problems, and the system's service-level components.

The *ICAP™* was designed and field validated specifically for children with moderate to severe disabilities and complex medical, behavioral, and developmental service needs.

Authenticity

The *ICAP™* effectively triangulates data from interviews of caregivers and professionals, reviews of records, observation, and reports to create a representative functional portrait of the child's capabilities and needs. A unique feature of the *ICAP™* is a concise appraisal and rating on a scale of functional limitations and needed assistance to supplement the Adaptive Behavior analysis. The Adaptive Behavior analysis focuses on landmark functional capabilities and maladaptive behavioral concerns that can be observed in natural, everyday settings and that are teachable competencies that foster future independent functioning. See Figure 1 for sample items.

----

2. SOCIAL AND COMMUNICATION SKILLS

Does (or could do) task completely without help or supervision:

0. NEVER OR RARELY—even if asked

      1. DOES, BUT NOT WELL—or ¼ of the time—may need to be asked

            2. DOES FAIRLY WELL—or ¾ of the time—may need to be asked

                  3. DOES VERY WELL—always or almost always—without being asked

0	1	2	3	
○	○	○	○	1. Makes sounds or gestures to get attention.
○	○	○	○	2. Reaches for a person whom he or she wants.
○	○	○	○	3. Turns head toward speaker when name is called.
○	○	○	○	4. Imitates actions when asked, such as waving or clapping hands.
○	○	○	○	5. Hands toys or other objects to another person.
○	○	○	○	6. Shakes head or otherwise indicates "yes" or "no" in response to a simple question such as "Do you want some milk?"
○	○	○	○	7. Points to familiar pictures in a book on request.
○	○	○	○	8. Says at least ten words that can be understood by someone who knows him or her.
○	○	○	○	9. Asks simple questions (for example, "What's that?").
○	○	○	○	10. Speaks in three-or four-word sentences.
○	○	○	○	11. Waits at least two minutes for turn in a group activity (for example, taking turns at batting a ball or getting a drink of water).
○	○	○	○	12. Offers help to other people (for example, holds a door open for one whose arms are full or picks up an object dropped by someone else.)
○	○	○	○	13. Acts appropriately without drawing negative attention while in public places with friends (for example, a movie theater or library).
○	○	○	○	14. Responds appropriately to most common signs, printed words, or symbols (for example, STOP, MEN, WOMEN, DANGER).
○	○	○	○	15. Summarizes and tells a story so that it is understood by someone else (for example, a TV program or a movie).
○	○	○	○	16. Locates or remembers telephone numbers and calls friends on the telephone.
○	○	○	○	17. Writes, prints, or types understandable and legible notes or letters for mailing.
○	○	○	○	18. Locates needed information in the telephone yellow pages or the want ads.
○	○	○	○	19. Calls a repair service or the caretaker if something major such as the furnace or the refrigerator breaks down in the home.

Figure 1. Sample communication skills rating sequence and items from the *ICAP™* protocol. (Copyright © 1986 by The Riverside Publishing Company. *Inventory for Client and Agency Planning™ [ICAP™]* reproduced with permission of the publisher. All rights reserved.)

Utility

ICAP™ data can be used to accomplish major early childhood intervention assessment purposes from eligibility determination to performance monitoring. It is intuitive, easy to use, and effective in both content and process. The most innovative aspect of the *ICAP™* is its systematic, but concise, service delivery elements that are included in the national norms. These "service delivery levels" include Placements, Daytime Programs, Support Services, and Social and Leisure Activities. See Figure 2 for a sample of the Support Services and Social Leisure Activities form.

In addition, the Program Goals and Service Goals section of the *ICAP™* enables the team to identify individualized areas for intervention using the *Maladaptive Behavior Index* (rating of seriousness of problem to impede progress) as a focus for behavior management strategies. On the Adaptive Behavior scale, the 4-point rating format (e.g., 0 = *Never* to 3 = *Does very well— always or almost always—without being asked*) enables a sensitive monitoring of status and progress by incorporating prompts, and it also provides support in the appraisal of functioning.

The *ICAP™* is widely used for the purpose of determining competence and intensity of support needs for individuals with disabilities. The Centers for Medicaid & Medicare Services requires individual needs assessment–based practice but allows states to determine which tool(s) they use in rate setting.

H. Support Services

1. PRESENTLY BEING USED
(Mark all that apply)

2. NOT USED NOW, BUT EVALUATION NEEDED
(Mark all that apply)

1. None
2. Case management: _____
3. Home-based support service: _____
4. Specialized dental care: _____
5. Specialized medical care: _____
6. Specialized nursing care: _____
7. Specialized mental health services: _____
8. Specialized nutritional or dietary services: _____
9. Therapies—occupational, physical or speech: _____
10. Respite care (to aid caretaker or parent): _____
11. Specialized transportation services: _____
12. Vocational evaluation: _____
13. Other: _____

Comments:

G H I

Figure 2. Sample of the Support Services and Social Leisure Activities form from protocol. (Copyright © 1986 by The Riverside Publishing Company. *Inventory for Client and Agency Planning™ [ICAP™]* reproduced with permission of the publisher. All rights reserved.)

Collaboration

The *ICAP™* epitomizes teamwork among professionals and parents/caregivers. All sections of the system require multisource input from individuals who know the child's typical functioning and attributes well. The service delivery and maladaptive behavior sections drive a focused discussion and consensus about the child's individual programmatic needs. One can imagine the use of a nominal group technique or Delphi process supported by the protocol to guide the team's decision about service delivery components.

Evidence Base

Bruininks, R.H., Hill, B.K., Weatherman, R.F., & Woodcock, R.W. (1986). *Examiner's manual: ICAP™, Inventory of Client and Agency Planning™*. Allen, TX: DLM Teaching Resources.

Provides a summary of the developmental research on the *ICAP™* to establish reliability and validity, and highlights use of Rasch analyses to support the validity of the service-level components of the system. The normative sample included young children.

In addition, there are two studies that examine the validity of the *ICAP™* for older children (12+ years) and adults (Mcgrew, Bruininks, & Thurlow, 1992; Sturmey, 2001).

Considerations and Recommendations

- The *ICAP™* is generally unknown by early childhood professionals and is mostly used with adolescent/adult populations of individuals with mental retardation and other related disabilities. However, its early childhood elements are well chosen and can be a unique support for some programs that rely on conventional scales for eligibility and planning but that have no specific curriculum in place.

- The *ICAP™* highlights the value of a functional, authentic, and developmentally appropriate model for identifying needs rather than psychopathological categories, which have no treatment validity in early childhood

- The *ICAP™*, like the *Adaptive Behavior Assessment System-Second Edition (ABAS-II)*, *Pediatric Evaluation of Disability Inventory (PEDI)*, *School Function Assessment (SFA)*, and *Vineland Adaptive Behavior Scales, Second Edition*, has content that can be easily cross-walked with the *International Classification of Functioning, Disability and Health: Children and Youth Version (ICF-CY)* codes, especially the Environmental Codes for services and supports, and can be used to promote the wider use of a functional classification framework in the United States (and internationally) and to counter the prevailing, but faulty, medical model.

Kent Inventory of Developmental Skills (KIDS)

Author(s): Jeanette Reuter, Lewis Katoff, and Chris Gruber

Publication date: 2000

Publisher: Western Psychological Services

Web site(s): http://portal.wpspublish.com

Cost: $120.00 (includes all materials required for assessment)

Assessment type: Curriculum-referenced assessment with norms

Age range: Birth to 15 months (also for children up to 6 years of age whose developmental age is between 0 and 15 months)

Domains/subtests: Cognitive, Motor, Communication, Self-Help, and Social

Population targeted: Designed to evaluate developmental status of young children, regardless of whether they are considered at risk for developmental delays; $n = 706$ for typical norm group; $n = 613$ for children with disabilities norm group

Technology features: *KIDS CD* for recording, scoring, and creating reports

Translations: Translated into several different languages and used internationally given additional normative data (e.g., used in the Netherlands, Spain, Russia, and Hungary)

Other features	Rating	Standard	Rating
Validated purposes	Medium	Acceptability	◑
Curricular links	Low	Authenticity	◑
Comprehensive coverage	Medium	Collaboration	◑
Graduated scoring	Medium	Evidence	◑
Progress monitoring	Medium	Multifactors	◑
Standards alignment	Medium	Sensitivity	◑
Diversity features	Medium	Universality	◐
Family engagement	Medium	Utility	◑
Teamwork	Low		
Professional development	Low	OVERALL	◑
Technology	Medium		

J K L

Life Skills Progression™ (LSP™)

An Outcome and Intervention Planning Instrument for Use with Families at Risk

Author(s): Linda Wollesen and Karen Peifer

Publication date: 2005

Publisher: Paul H. Brookes Publishing Co.

Web site(s): http://www.brookespublishing.com

Cost: $44.95 for manual and CD-ROM

Assessment type: Curriculum-referenced assessment

Age range: Families of children from birth to 3 years of age

Domains/subtests: *Parent Scales* includes Relationships with Families and Friends, Relationships with Children, Education and Employment, Health and Medical Care, Mental Health, and Basic Essentials; *Infant Scales* includes Child Development

Population targeted: At-risk and high-risk parents and their children prenatally to age 3 years who are living in poverty

Technology features: CD-ROM contains instructions for using and scoring the *LSP™* and printable versions of PDF files

Translations: None

Other features	Rating	Standard	Rating
Validated purposes	Low	Acceptability	◑
Curricular links	Low	Authenticity	◑
Comprehensive coverage	High	Collaboration	◔
Graduated scoring	Medium	Evidence	◔
Progress monitoring	High	Multifactors	◑
Standards alignment	Low	Sensitivity	◔
Diversity features	High	Universality	◔
Family engagement	High	Utility	◔
Teamwork	High		
Professional development	Medium	OVERALL	◑
Technology	Medium		

Close Up on next page

New Portage Guide Birth to Six

Author(s): Nola Larson, Julia Herwig, Karen Wollenburg, Elizabeth Olsen, Wendy Bowe, Ruth Chvojicek, and Annette Copa

Publication date: 2003

Publisher: Cooperative Educational Service Agency 5, Portage Project

Web site(s): http://www.portageproject.org

Cost: *New Portage Guide Infant/Toddler* $149.95
New Portage Guide Preschooler $149.95

Assessment type: Curriculum-embedded assessment

Age range: Infant (birth to 9 months), Mobile Infant (9–18 months), Toddler (19–36 months), Preschooler (3–4 years), Preschooler (4–5 years), and Preschooler (5–6 years); can be used for children who are developmentally ahead of or behind their chronological age

Domains/subtests: Communication/Language/Literacy, Social-Emotional Development, Exploration/Approaches to Learning, Purposeful Motor Activity, and Sensory Organization; each domain is divided into subtests of related skills and behaviors; system as a whole includes skills that cover all content areas

Population targeted: Children with or without disabilities in home-based or center-based programs

Technology features: Online version in development

Translations: Spanish; previous edition has more than 30 translations

Other features	Rating	Standard	Rating
Validated purposes	High	Acceptability	●
Curricular links	High	Authenticity	●
Comprehensive coverage	High	Collaboration	●
Graduated scoring	High	Evidence	◑
Progress monitoring	High	Multifactors	◑
Standards alignment	High	Sensitivity	◑
Diversity features	High	Universality	◑
Family engagement	High	Utility	◑
Teamwork	Low		
Professional development	High	OVERALL	◑
Technology	Medium		

MNO

New Portage Guide Birth to Six

Author(s): Nola Larson, Julia Herwig, Karen Wollenburg, Elizabeth Olsen, Wendy Bowe, Ruth Chvojicek, and Annette Copa

About the Measure

New Portage Guide Birth to Six (NPG) materials are organized to allow the user to move easily from assessment information for an individual child or groups of children to planning activities.

Originally designed as a home-based intervention program, the *NPG* is now a comprehensive, curriculum-embedded assessment and intervention system that can be implemented in home-based and early childhood centers serving children with or without disabilities.

All of the materials included are color coded to match the corresponding age range, allowing users to quickly locate appropriate materials for a specific child or group of children.

Authenticity

The *Portage Guide Tool for Observation and Planning (TOP)* is a system for collecting and analyzing children's actions, behaviors, and language during everyday activities. Most of the items in the *TOP* are activities that naturally occur in children's daily lives. For example, *Explores objects with mouth* is an item from the Infant Birth to 9 Months Sensory Organization domain under the Senses strand. *Tries out different behaviors to test caregiver's responses and limits* is an item from the Toddler 18–36 Months Social Emotional Development domain under the Relationships strand. *Dresses and undresses self with some assistance* is an example from the 3–4 years Purposeful Motor Activity domain under the Independence/Self-Care strand. Finally, *Verbally shares experiences or possessions with peers* is an item from the Communication/Language/Literacy domain under the Communication strand that further exemplifies how items in the *TOP* are primarily naturally occurring behaviors for young children.

Utility

The *NPG* is well organized, and each element of the system is clearly explained, making it easy to use in a variety of settings. The *NPG* includes a *Group Summary Form* that facilitates planning in group care settings by providing a visual representation of the learning needs of all children. Because of its simplicity, the *NPG* would be especially useful for teachers with minimal training in early childhood development and education. All assessment items and activities are free from professional jargon.

The curriculum and assessment items are organized by age, developmental domains, and strands. Each age range is associated with a specific color (e.g., Infant Birth to 9 Months is purple, Toddler 18–36 Months is blue, and 3–4 Years is green). Each item on the *TOP* correlates specifically to an *Activity/Interaction Card*. The cards describe the importance of a specific skill and practical suggestions for promoting skill development in the daily routine and/or typical play activities.

Figure 1 illustrates the direct link between assessment items and curriculum items.

M N O

Exploration/Approaches to Learning

Developmental Strand: Science

27 DESCRIBES OR SHOWS WHAT THINGS DO

Why Is This Important?

Children begin to make scientific observations but their comments are confined to things they can actually see and touch.

Interactive Activities:

Gathering Information: Observe me in play at the center or around the house. Do I catch on to how things work, by watching and imitating? Can I tell someone where to put the video in the VCR or show you how to put the video in the rewind machine? Can I tell you, when asked, how to care for the hamster in the classroom? Use this information when planning activities that are appropriate for my level of understanding.

Daily Routine Activities:

Playtime: When given an opportunity to play in the grocery store dramatic area, I'll be able explain to others how we are to use the cash register, put things on the shelves and pack the grocery bags.

Continued on back

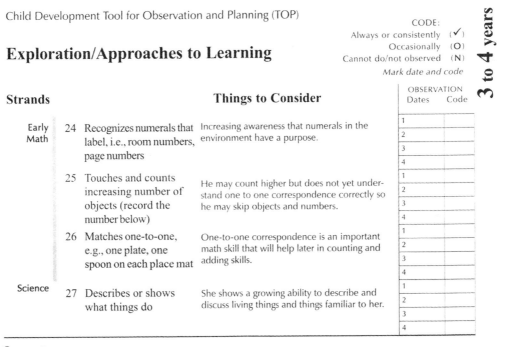

Child Development Tool for Observation and Planning (TOP)

Exploration/Approaches to Learning

CODE:
Always or consistently (✓)
Occasionally (O)
Cannot do/not observed (N)

Mark date and code

3 to 4 years

Strands		Things to Consider	OBSERVATION Dates	Code
Early Math	24 Recognizes numerals that label, i.e., room numbers, page numbers	Increasing awareness that numerals in the environment have a purpose.	1 2 3 4	
	25 Touches and counts increasing number of objects (record the number below)	He may count higher but does not yet understand one to one correspondence correctly so he may skip objects and numbers.	1 2 3 4	
	26 Matches one-to-one, e.g., one plate, one spoon on each place mat	One-to-one correspondence is an important math skill that will help later in counting and adding skills.	1 2 3 4	
Science	27 Describes or shows what things do	She shows a growing ability to describe and discuss living things and things familiar to her.	1 2 3 4	

Comment:

Figure 1. Preschool TOP and Activity Card 27 from 3-4 years section. (From Larsen et al. [2003]. *New Portage Guide Birth to Six* [p. 15]. Portage, WI: Cooperative Educational Service Agency 5, reprinted by permission.)

Collaboration

The *TOP* can be completed by one or more teachers in the group care setting. In the home-based setting, the teacher can complete the form alone or with the child's parents. The *Child Planning and Family Partnership Document* provides a structure for conferencing with parents about their children's assessment results (see Figure 2). It includes space to list ideas for supporting skill development in each domain—both at home and in group settings.

I. What the family has observed: Strengths and Hopes

II. Skills the Child is Developing

Areas of Development/Skills	Ideas to support these skills at the center:	Ideas to support these skills at home:
COMMUNICATION/LANGUAGE/LITERACY Strengths: Working on:		
SOCIAL EMOTIONAL DEVELOPMENT Strengths: Working on:		

NEW PORTAGE GUIDE: BIRTH TO SIX   continued on next page   © 2003 Portage Project

Figure 2. Child Planning and Family Partnership Document. (From Larson et al. [2003]. *New Portage Guide Birth to Six* [p. 1]. Portage, WI: Cooperative Educational Services Agency 5, reprinted by permission.)

Evidence Base

Brue, A., & Oakland, T. (2001). The Portage Guide to Early Intervention: An evaluation of published evidence. *School Psychology International, 22*(3), 243–252.

Provides a summary of research on the first edition of the *Portage Guide;* includes anecdotal information from parents and professionals as well as empirical data from five studies.

Considerations and Recommendations

- The *NPG* can be used by a wide range of early childhood professionals, particularly those without a strong foundation in development and/or developmentally appropriate practices for young children.

- A review of the literature indicates that research on the first edition was meager, and although the authors state that the *NPG* was developed using current research in early childhood and feedback from users, no published research could be found on the *NPG*.

Close Up on next page

The Oregon Project for Preschool Children who are Blind or Visually Impaired, 6th edition (The OR Project)

The Oregon Project
For Preschool Children
Who are Blind or Visually Impaired
Skills Inventory
Sixth Edition

Author(s): S. Anderson, S. Boigon, K. Davis, and C. DeWaard

Publication date: 2007

Publisher: Southern Oregon Education Service District

Web site(s): http://www.soesd.k12.or.us

Cost: $160.00 per kit (includes Manual, 5 Skills Inventories, and Resource CD-ROM)

Assessment type: Curriculum-embedded assessment

Age range: Birth to 6 years, or any child functioning at developmental levels between birth and 6 years

Domains/subtests: Cognitive, Language, Social Vision, Compensatory Skills, Self-Help, Fine Motor, and Gross Motor

Population targeted: Children who are blind or visually impaired

Technology features: *Resource CD* (includes Excel Scoring; *OR Project* forms in PDF form; links to web sites; *OR Project* activity templates; and worksheets and articles detailing best practices, vision information, health conditions, child development, and activities)

Translations: None

MNO

Other features	Rating	Standard	Rating
Validated purposes	Low	Acceptability	◑
Curricular links	High	Authenticity	◑
Comprehensive coverage	High	Collaboration	◑
Graduated scoring	Low	Evidence	◑
Progress monitoring	Medium	Multifactors	◑
Standards alignment	Medium	Sensitivity	◐
Diversity features	Low	Universality	◑
Family engagement	High	Utility	◑
Teamwork	High		
Professional development	Medium	OVERALL	◑
Technology	Medium		

The Oregon Project for Preschool Children who are Blind or Visually Impaired, 6th edition (The OR Project)

Author(s): S. Anderson, S. Boigon, K. Davis, and C. DeWaard

About the Measure

The OR Project is a comprehensive assessment and programming system for children who are blind or visually impaired and functioning at developmental levels between birth and 6 years.

The OR Project was one of the first practical, developmental frameworks to assist parents, teachers, and children with visual impairments, and this latest revision contains additional skills and resources.

The system consists of four component parts: the Manual, Teaching Activities, Reference Section, and *Skills Inventory*.

Authenticity

The OR Project includes more than 800 distinct developmental skills, each with corresponding Teaching Activities. The curriculum stresses observation of natural, adaptive behaviors of children in everyday settings, routines, and activities. Everything about assessing the child is individualized, including how the family chooses to participate, where to begin the assessment, and the order in which to continue. Although some items may require presentation of materials, there are no scripted instructions, so the assessor can use language, reinforcement, and materials that are available and motivating to the child.

Assessing children who are blind or have visual impairments requires additional considerations. A unique feature of *The OR Project* is a section entitled Compensatory, which includes skills that the child needs to learn to compensate for the inability to obtain information visually. Figure 1 contains a sample from the Compensatory section of Teaching Activities.

Compensatory	Birth-One Year

1   Quiets to sound; appears comforted by human voice

> Television or radio noise should not be a constant background. Similarly, wind-up musical toys are great once in a while, but not all the time. Sound should elicit an "Oh! What's that? That is so interesting!" reaction.

Make sure all family members have frequent opportunities to talk to the baby individually. Voices are one of the major ways he will come to recognize people.

2   Responds differently to tactile sensations: temperature or texture

The baby's daily routine will expose her to warm or cool bath water, cotton or velour towels, cloth or disposable diapers, thermal or flannel blankets, and a variety of textures of baby clothing. As family members interact with the baby, she will be exposed to several sets of hands, all of which are different temperature and textures. Watch for indications that the baby is alert to these changes.

Rub the child's cheek gently with different textures: cotton ball, the side of a warm bottle, the sleeve of a furry robe. Gently pull different cloth materials through her hands and fingers (a warm washcloth, a silk scarf, a wool scarf).

3   Enjoys being touched and handled by familiar people ®

The child who has a visual impairment may not make eye contact, but he comes to know the differences in people by their voices, the way they smell, and the way they handle him. Watch for indications that the baby is starting to recognize people.

Hold your baby often in your arms or use an infant Snuggly so that you can hold the baby while you are walking around. Let him fall asleep in your arms, on his dad's chest, or across your lap as you stroke his back and legs.

Infant massage is a relaxing activity for both you and the child.

Figure 1.   Sample from Compensatory section of Teaching Activities. (From Anderson, S., Boigon, S., Davis, K., & DeWaard, C. [2007]. *The Oregon Project for Preschool Children who are Blind or Visually Impaired, 6th edition*. Medford, OR: Southern Oregon Education Service District; reprinted by permission.)

M
N
O

Utility

The *Skills Inventory* booklet is to be used throughout the child's preschool years to assess the child's development over time, determine goals and objectives, and record the child's acquisition of new skills. Teaching activities and 200 skills have been added to the sixth edition.

Skills are organized by domain and age in a developmental sequence. A symbol is placed beside the item number indicating skills that may develop significantly later for a child who is blind. Beside each skill in the inventory is a grid for three dates and a square that reads *Has skill*; this component is useful for progress monitoring. The Implementation section includes lists of materials needed for assessment by age level and developmental area. Following the assessment of each of the developmental domains is a blank page for notetaking.

Another useful component is the computer graphing of an individual child's profile to clearly depict the child's strengths and areas for instruction. The Student Profile (see Figure 2) pro-

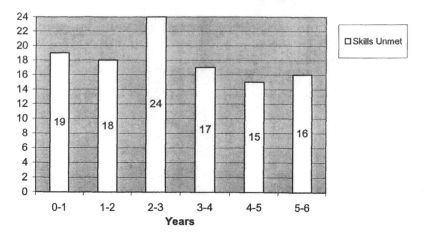

Student Profile: Language

Figure 2. Example of Student Profile for language. (From Anderson, S., Boigon, S., Davis, K., & DeWaard, C. [2007]. *The Oregon Project for Preschool Children who are Blind or Visually Impaired, 6th edition*. Medford, OR: Southern Oregon Education Service District; reprinted by

vides a visual representation of the child's progress over time relative to age and other skill areas.

In addition to the *Skills Inventory*, *The OR Project* includes 12 different forms that are useful for documentation of information gathered. Another distinctive feature of *The OR Project* is the Resource Section, which includes an extensive list of educational materials, a list of agencies serving children who are blind or visually impaired, and a glossary for users.

Collaboration

The OR Project overview includes a section on the parent–teacher/specialist partnership. The *Skills Inventory* begins by stressing the importance of establishing rapport and finding out what the family's priorities are for the child. It advises the professional to spend time getting to know the child in the context of the family. The family members have a say in how they prefer to participate in the assessment, including choosing objectives and goals on which to focus instruction.

A *Consultation Form* assists teams in maintaining communication with families, and the *Transition Plan* documents what is needed and who is responsible for planning and implementing transition activities.

Evidence Base

Shearer, D. (1976). *Portage Guide to Early Education*. Portage, WI: Cooperative Educational Service Agency No. 12.

The model for *The OR Project* is based on the first edition of the *Portage Guide*, which includes anecdotal information from parents and professionals as well as empirical data from five studies.

Hamilton, D.A. (1995). *The utility of the Assessment Evaluation Programming System in the development of quality IEP goals and objectives for young children, birth to three, with visual impairments* (Doctoral dissertation, University of Oregon). Retrieved from Dissertations & Theses: A&I (Pub. No. AAT 9541906)

The study compared the efficacy of the *Assessment, Evaluation, and Programming System for Infants and Children* (*AEPS*®) with that of *The OR Project* to determine which assessment best creates quality educational goals and objectives.

Considerations and Recommendations

- *The OR Project* is the premier system for assessing children who are blind or visually impaired.

- The authors are advised to conduct research to document the efficacy of using *The OR Project* with children who are blind and also to align the content with Office of Special Education Programs (OSEP) indicators as a way to further promote the system's legitimate use for accountability with this population.

MNO

Close Up on next page

The Ounce Scale

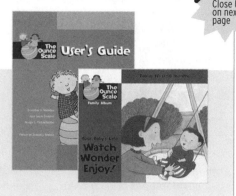

Author(s): Samuel J. Meisels, Dorothea B. Marsden, Amy Laura Dombro, Donna R. Weston, and Abigail M. Jewkes

Publication date: 2003

Publisher: NCS Pearson

Web site(s): http://psychcorp.pearsonassessments .com

Cost: $131.75 for the kit (includes Standards, User's Guide, Reproducible Masters, and one of each Observation Record and Family Album)

Assessment type: Curriculum-referenced assessment

Age range: Birth to 42 months

Domains/subtests: Social and Emotional Development (Personal Connections, Feelings About Self, Relationships with Other Children), Communication and Language (Understanding and Communication), Cognitive Development (Exploration and Problem Solving), and Physical Development (Movement and Coordination)

Population targeted: Typically developing children, those at risk, and children with diagnosed disabilities; used in Early Head Start; field validation: *n* = 250

Technology features: Web-based data entry and electronic scoring

Translations: Spanish

Other features	Rating	Standard	Rating
Validated purposes	Low	Acceptability	◐
Curricular links	High	Authenticity	◕
Comprehensive coverage	High	Collaboration	◐
Graduated scoring	Medium	Evidence	◕
Progress monitoring	Medium	Multifactors	◕
Standards alignment	High	Sensitivity	◔
Diversity features	Low	Universality	◐
Family engagement	High	Utility	◑
Teamwork	High		
Professional development	Medium	OVERALL	◐
Technology	Medium		

The Ounce Scale

Author(s): Samuel J. Meisels, Dorothea B. Marsden,
Amy Laura Dombro, Donna R. Weston, and Abigail M. Jewkes

About the Measure

The Ounce Scale is an ecologically sound, authentic assessment and an instructional tool that promotes understanding of child development.

The Ounce Scale can be used with children who are at risk, typically developing children, and children with delays and diagnosed disabilities.

Authenticity

The Ounce Scale provides a structure that helps parents and caregivers evaluate the growth and development of infants and toddlers. This tool offers a holistic picture of a child's development by observing behaviors in natural contexts on an ongoing basis. See Figure 1 for a sample of how the *Observation Record* is organized by area of development, probing observation questions, age-level expectations, space to make comments, and examples of how children might demonstrate the skills related to the particular area.

In addition to evaluating a child's growth and helping to plan intervention activities and goals, *The Ounce Scale* truly is a resource that serves to further parents' and caregivers' understanding of development. *The Ounce Scale* centers on six areas of development and contains observation questions, examples, and rationales of child behavior in each age level. Explanations of development and examples of behavior emphasize the individual and reinforce the idea that children demonstrate a range of behaviors and that there is no one "correct" response. The focus is on the child's personal strengths, areas of difficulty, expression, and learning style.

MNO

The Ounce Scale Babies III Developmental Profile

Child _____

Date of birth _____ Age _____

Teacher/Home Visitor _____

Assessment completed by _____

Today's date _____

12 Months

SOCIAL and EMOTIONAL

I. Personal Connections: It's About Trust
1. Shows preference for familiar adults (p. 23)
2. Reacts to unfamiliar adults (p. 24)

II. Feelings About Self: Learning About Me
1. Shows likes and dislikes (p. 24)
2. Tries to manage own behavior in different situations (p. 25)

III. Relationships With Other Children: Child to Child
1. Demo___ awareness ___ther chil___ (p. 26)

COMMU___ICATION and ___GUA___

IV. Underst___ ___ Co___ni___ing: ___y ___lk
1. Sh___ underst___lin___ and ___ord___ (p. ___
2. Uses ___t so___ds, verbal e___ssions, a___ gestures to communicate (p. 27)

COGNITIVE DEVELOPMENT

V. Exploration and Problem Solving: Baby Discoveries
1. Shows understanding of things in the environment during exploration (p. 28)
2. Demonstrates memory (p. 28)
3. Makes expected things happen (p. 29)

PHYSICAL DEVELOPMENT

VI. Movement and Coordination: Babies in Motion
1. Changes position and begins to move from place to place (p. 30)
2. Coordinates eyes with hands while holding and exploring objects (p. 30)

Comments: _____

Parent signature _____ Date _____

The Developmental Profiles should be used in conjunction with observations made over time, as documented in the Observation Records and matched to the age-level descriptions in the Standards for the Developmental Profiles.

MNO

Figure 1. Sample of an Observation Record. (*The Ounce Scale*. Copyright © 2003. NCS Pearson, Inc. Reprinted with permission. All rights reserved.)

Utility

The Ounce Scale consists of three unique and interrelated elements: 1) *Observation Records*, 2) *Family Albums*, and 3) *Developmental Profiles*.

The *Observation Records* are divided into eight age levels at 4-month intervals and six areas of development with a particular focus on the social and emotional development of infants and toddlers. Assessment of a child with delays would begin at a lower age level.

The *Family Album* provides a venue for families to document child behavior. Information from the *Observation Record* and *Family Album* informs the *Developmental Profile* of the child.

The *Developmental Profile* is used to evaluate growth at the end of each of the eight age levels. The profile allows comparison with age-level standards and results in a rating that is based on what has been learned about the child. Each item on the profile corresponds to the same item in the standards. The information is particularly useful for caregivers with less training or experience in assessment. The standards assist in determining ratings by describing behavior indicators and providing examples illustrating the two rating categories (*Developing as expected* or *Needs development*). Those indicators on which the child is not meeting expectations can be carried over to the next age level and targeted for intervention.

Collaboration

The Ounce Scale is written in family-friendly language and incorporates both parent and caregiver perspectives. Like the *Observation Record*, the *Family Album* (see Figure 2) is organized by area of development and contains probing observation questions, age-level expectations, space to make comments, and examples of how children might demonstrate skills related to particular areas.

Figure 2. Sample of a Family Album. (*The Ounce Scale*. Copyright © 2003. NCS Pearson, Inc. Reprinted with permission. All rights reserved.)

In addition, the *Family Album* serves to promote relationships, discussion, and understanding of the child's development. A section entitled Try This and See What Happens in the *Family Album* offers suggestions of activities for parents and children that support development. Pages in the album are available for the family to add drawings, photos, written documentation, and mementos. Because *the Family Album* belongs to the family, participation in and ownership of the assessment and planning process are encouraged.

Evidence Base

Meisels, S.J., Beachy-Quick, K., & Wen, X. (2008). *Ounce scale validation project.* Retrieved February 11, 2010, from http://www.erikson.edu/default/research/facpresentations.aspx

Describes a study of 287 children enrolled in Chicago-area Early Head Start programs. Several components of reliability and validity including internal reliability, interrater reliability, concurrent validity, convergent validity, predictive validity, social validity, and treatment validity were examined. The report further describes an analysis of the sensitivity and specificity of the measure.

Considerations and Recommendations

- *The Ounce Scale* is an exemplar of a truly family-friendly measurement tool that promotes collaboration among parents and professionals and clear, mutual understanding of the child's characteristics and needs.
- *The Ounce Scale* can be used to meet IDEA Part C early intervention eligibility criteria by structuring clinical judgment or informed opinions of parents and professionals as an authentic avenue for supporting the need for services and support.
- Additional research is needed to validate use for eligibility and accountability, particularly with children with disabilities.

M N O

Close Up on next page

Partners in Play
Assessing Infants and Toddlers in Natural Contexts

Author(s): Gail Ensher, Tasia P. Bobish, Eric Gardner, Carol L. Reinson, Deborah A. Bryden, and Danial J. Foertsch

Publication date: 2007

Publisher: Delmar, Cengage Learning

Web site(s): http://www.delmarlearning.com

Cost: $28.95

Assessment type: Curriculum-referenced assessment

Age range: Birth through 3 years of age

Domains/subtests: Neuromotor Domain, Sensory-Perceptual Domain, Cognitive Domain, Language Domain, Social and Emotional Behavior; medical history, health, and family/environmental factors are recorded on the *Parent Interview Record Form*

Population targeted: Infants and toddlers at risk for or with delays and disabilities

Technology features: *The Online Companion™* includes chapter reviews and study questions, learning activities with scoring rubrics, suggested readings, web links for parents and professionals, and a sample course syllabus for curriculum planning

Translations: None

Other features	Rating		Standard	Rating
Validated purposes	Low		Acceptability	◕
Curricular links	Medium		Authenticity	◕
Comprehensive coverage	High		Collaboration	◕
Graduated scoring	High		Evidence	◑
Progress monitoring	Medium		Multifactors	◕
Standards alignment	Medium		Sensitivity	◕
Diversity features	Medium		Universality	◕
Family engagement	High		Utility	●
Teamwork	High			
Professional development	Medium		OVERALL	◕
Technology	Low			

PQRS

Partners in Play
Assessing Infants and Toddlers in Natural Contexts

Author(s): Gail Ensher, Tasia P. Bobish, Eric Gardner,
Carol L. Reinson, Deborah A. Bryden, and Danial J. Foertsch

About the Measure

By viewing the child in play and in social contexts, *Partners in Play* (*PIP*), an authentic, curriculum-embedded system, provides a wealth of information to guide eligibility decisions and also a means to monitor progress and guide intervention.

In addition to information gleaned from interviewing the caregiver, the child is observed in three contexts: unstructured child–caregiver play, unstructured examiner–child play, and structured examiner–child interaction.

As stated so eloquently in the Foreword, *PIP* gives professionals a way to document clinical opinion through a "playful approach that accommodates and honors differences" (Ensher et al., 2007, p. v).

Authenticity

The goal of *PIP* is to assess young children with flexible procedures, both formal and informal in natural environments, to elicit their best responses. Beginning with the *Initial Caregiver Interview* form, information on the child's birth and medical history is collected. Next, using the *Caregiver Report of Child Development,* the assessor is able to get a picture of the child's developmental status in key areas through 47 items. By beginning with the interview, the child is afforded time to adjust to the evaluators. The Unstructured Caregiver–Child Play section follows with 13 clusters of 59 items, allowing the assessor to observe the child as he or she typically interacts with family. The assessor/facilitator then engages in unstructured play with the child (see Figure 1), revealing how the child relates to an unfamiliar adult, and follows the free play with more directed activities across 50 items. Information from the caregiver report is substantiated during unstructured and structured play, and these different sources of information allow for a more thorough depiction of the child's status and needs.

The items on the Structured and Unstructured Caregiver–Child Play and Structured and Unstructured Examiner–Child Play items are scored on a 4-point Likert scale (see items in Figure 1). On the *Caregiver Report of Child Development,* the 4-point Likert scale is used in some instances. For other items, a point is given for each item the child can perform (e.g., if the child vocalizes to communicate or if he or she is able to act out a familiar routine). In recognition of the uneven skill development in children with disabilities, there are no basal or ceiling determinants; children are given credit on the basis of observations or responses to items.

Unstructured Caregiver-Child Play

L1. Strategies for Communication

a. Differential vocalization
(1 month – 6 months)

Circle One	
Not evident	1
Emerging	2
Developing	3
Well developed	4

b. Vocal play
(3 months – 18 months)

Circle One	
Not evident	1
Emerging	2
Developing	3
Well developed	4

c. Reduplicated babbling
(9 months – 18 months)

Circle One	
Not evident	1
Emerging	2
Developing	3
Well developed	4

d. Variegated babbling
(9 months – 18 months)

Circle One	
Not evident	1
Emerging	2
Developing	3
Well developed	4

e. Using gestures
(9 months – 36 months)

Circle One	
Not evident	1
Emerging	2
Developing	3
Well developed	4

f. Jargon-like vocalizations
(9 months – 36 months)

Circle One	
Not evident	1
Emerging	2
Developing	3
Well developed	4

g. Making requests
(11 months – 36 months)

Circle One	
Not evident	1
Emerging	2
Developing	3
Well developed	4

h. Using single words
(11 months – 36 months)

Circle One	
Not evident	1
Emerging	2
Developing	3
Well developed	4

i. Putting 2 words together
(11 months – 36 months)

Circle One	
Not evident	1
Emerging	2
Developing	3
Well developed	4

j. Putting 3 or more words together
(11 months – 36 months)

Circle One	
Not evident	1
Emerging	2
Developing	3
Well developed	4

k. Initiating/engaging in dialogue/discourse
(17 months – 36 months)

Circle One	
Not evident	1
Emerging	2
Developing	3
Well developed	4

L2. Communication of Needs/Intent

a. Making basic needs known (e.g., fatigue, hunger, change of position)
(1 month – 36 months)

Circle One	
Never/rarely	1
Sometimes	2
Usually/frequently	3
Most of the time/always	4

b. Making social needs known (e.g., desire to be picked up, to engage in play)
(1 month – 36 months)

Circle One	
Never/rarely	1
Sometimes	2
Usually/frequently	3
Most of the time/always	4

Notes:
_____
_____
_____
_____
_____
_____
_____

Figure 1. Items sampled from the Unstructured Caregiver–Child Play section. (From ENSHER/BOBISH/GARDNER/BRYDEN/FOERTSCH. *Partners in Play, 1E.* © 2007 Wadsworth, a part of Cengage Learning, Inc. Reproduced by permission. www.cengage.com/permissions)

PQRS

Utility

Having different vantage points from which to view the child's development yields a wealth of assessment information, which can ultimately inform interventions. A complete description of the evaluation process as well as detailed items and scoring guidelines make *PIP* a valuable tool.

The authors devote a substantial portion of the assessment directions to discussion of the importance of having an in-depth understanding of the family's culture. The discussion includes consideration of assessing children with cultural and language differences and the importance of understanding perceptions of acceptable behavior and disability. Another useful feature concerns considerations for assessing infants, toddlers, and children with specific challenges such as a short attention span, hyperactivity, sensory sensitivities, issues with coordination, and motor impairments. Suggestions are provided to minimize the effects of the particular area of deficit. The manual recommends, for example, that when assessing a child with a short attention span, external stimuli in the room should be limited, the child should be seated and given frequent breaks, and tasks involving movement should be interspersed.

A section in the appendix is devoted to a quick reference of milestones. It is easy to understand why this tool is useful not only for assessing infants and young children but also for training professionals in transdisciplinary team assessment.

Collaboration

PIP was developed to encourage and facilitate transdisciplinary team assessment. The team is encouraged to plan appropriately for the family visit. One person is chosen to act as the examiner/facilitator while the other team members observe and take notes. The facilitator is selected by the team and ideally has expertise in the area of the child's delay or problem. The authors suggest that another team member may carry out the interviews, giving the facilitator time to establish rapport with the infant or young child. The parent is an active participant and is available for the child throughout the assessment. All members provide their perceptions of the child's strengths and needs.

There are also two caregiver record forms; the first includes the medical history of the child and mother, and the second includes development of the child in all domains. For the Structured Examiner–Child Play Scoring Worksheets (see Figure 2), a list of activities is provided and is followed on subsequent pages by detailed descriptions of each activity, suggested materials, administration procedures, recording instructions, and a visual of that activity on the scoring form. The appendices include all forms; sample forms that are already completed are provided for quick reference.

C30. ATTENTION TO FACES AND DESIGNS

Observation	Age Range	Score
a. Attends to human face	1–6 months	
b. Attends to checkerboard	1–6 months	
c. Attends to schematic face	1–6 months	
d. Responds to real image in mirror	3–18 months	
e. Shows early responses to baby doll	5–18 months	

SP31. TRACKING

Observation	Age Range	Score
a. Tracks horizontally	1–36 months	
b. Tracks in circle	1–36 months	
c. Shows smooth eye movement	1–36 months	
d. Shows coordinated eye movement	1–36 months	

Figure 2. Selected items from the Structured Examiner–Child Play Scoring Worksheets. (From ENSHER/ BOBISH/GARDNER/BRYDEN/FOERTSCH. *Partners in Play, 1E.* © 2007 Wadsworth, a part of Cengage Learning, Inc. Reproduced by permission. www.cengage.com/permissions)

Evidence Base

PIP is an outgrowth of the *Syracuse Dynamic Assessment (SDA)* (1998). The *SDA* has been in development since 1979 by a multidisciplinary team of professionals representing the disciplines of communication sciences and disorders, developmental psychology, early childhood special education, occupational therapy, physical therapy, and psychological measurement. The items and activities included in *PIP* have been developed on the basis of clinical and field testing.

For more than 15 years, the *SDA* has been used in Onondaga County, New York, to determine eligibility for early intervention services.

Ensher, G.L., Clark, D.A., & Songer, N.S. (2009). *Families, infants, and young children at risk: Pathways to best practice*. Baltimore: Paul H. Brookes Publishing Co.

Provides discussion of various supportive interventions and includes discussion of the *PIP* in action.

Considerations and Recommendations

- The authors advise two to three sessions to cover all aspects of this assessment, depending on how quickly the child becomes fatigued.

- The *PIP* can be used in early intervention programs for children ages 0–3 years to unify the eligibility, planning, and parent engagement processes rather than separating the purposes through different and often conflicting instruments and styles.

- The publishers would serve this tool well by redesigning the cover for durability.

PQRS

Close Up on next page

The Pediatric Evaluation of Disability Inventory (PEDI™)

Pediatric Evaluation of Disability Inventory (PEDI)

Author(s): Stephen M. Haley, Wendy J. Coster, Larry H. Ludlow, Jane T. Haltiwanger, and Peter J. Andrellos

Publication date: 1992

Publisher: CRE Care

Web site(s): http://www.crecare.com

Cost: $42.75 for 25 forms; $122.25 for manual; $262.00 for software

Assessment type: Curriculum-referenced assessment with norms

Age range: 6 months to 7.5 years, or children who function below 7.5 years developmentally

Domains/subtests: Assessment of children's key functional capabilities and performances; Part I measures current capabilities; Part II measures caregiver assistance; Part III measures modifications necessary to support functioning; domains include Self-Care, Mobility, and Social Function

Population targeted: Children with neurophysiological concerns and/or combined physical and cognitive deficit; normed group: $n = 412$

Technology features: Software for data entry, scoring, and generation of individual summary score profiles

Translations: Translated internationally (i.e., Turkey, Spain, Norway, the Netherlands, China)

PQRS

Other features	Rating	Standard	Rating
Validated purposes	High	Acceptability	◕
Curricular links	Medium	Authenticity	◕
Comprehensive coverage	Medium	Collaboration	◕
Graduated scoring	Low	Evidence	◕
Progress monitoring	Low	Multifactors	◕
Standards alignment	Low	Sensitivity	◑
Diversity features	High	Universality	◔
Family engagement	High	Utility	◑
Teamwork	Medium		
Professional development	Medium	OVERALL	◕
Technology	Medium		

The Pediatric Evaluation of Disability Inventory (PEDI™)

Author(s): Stephen M. Haley, Wendy J. Coster,
Larry H. Ludlow, Jane T. Haltiwanger, and Peter J. Andrellos

About the Measure

The *PEDI™* is unique among authentic, curriculum-referenced assessments with norms because of its specific design, development, and field validation on infants, toddlers, and preschoolers with physical impairments and associated neurodevelopmental deficits.

The *PEDI™* was one of the first measures to emphasize the identification of the child's functional capabilities in critical self, social, and movement domains and then link these assessments with individual rehabilitation goals, services, and supports to promote independent functioning.

Its creative blend of authentic, functional, and adaptive features buttressed with pooled normative data make it a highly useful measure.

Authenticity

Through the Functional Skills scales, the *PEDI™* samples critical functional capabilities (capable/unable) that link directly to intervention rather than measures of categorical disability. The content of the *PEDI™* emphasizes real-life "survival" skills in adaptive, motor, self-help, and social communication functions. In these domains, all competencies rely on observations of the child's functioning in the daily demands of everyday settings and routines. See Figure 1 for sample items.

UNABLE / CAPABLE — 0 1

C. Functional Use of Communication — 0 1

11. Names things
12. Uses specific words or gestures to direct or request action by another person
13. Seeks information by asking questions
14. Describes an object or action
15. Tells about own feelings or thoughts

D. Complexity of Expressive Communication — 0 1

16. Uses gestures with clear meaning
17. Uses single word with meaning
18. Uses two words together with meaning
19. Uses 4-5 word sentences
20. Connects two or more thoughts to tell a simple story

E. Problem-resolution — 0 1

21. Tries to show you the problem or communicate what is needed to help the problem
22. If upset because of a problem, child must be helped immediately or behavior deteriorates
23. If upset because of a problem, child can seek help and wait if it is delayed a short time
24. In ordinary situations, child can describe the problem and his/her feelings with some detail (usually does not act out)
25. Faced with an ordinary problem, child can join adult in working out a solution

F. Social Interactive Play (Adults) — 0 1

26. Shows awareness and interest in others
27. Initiates a familiar play routine
28. Takes turn in simple play when cued for turn
29. Attempts to imitate adult's previous action during a play activity
30. During play child may suggest new or different steps, or respond to adult suggestion with another idea

G. Peer Interactions: (Child of similar age) — 0 1

31. Notices presence of other children, may vocalize and gesture toward peers
32. Interacts with other children in simple and brief episodes
33. Tries to work out simple plans for a play activity with another child
34. Plans and carries out cooperative activity with other children; play is sustained and complex
35. Plays activities or games that have rules

H. Play with Objects — 0 1

36. Manipulates toys, objects or body with intent
37. Uses real or substituted objects in simple pretend sequences
38. Puts together materials to make something
39. Makes up extended pretend play routines involving things the child knows about
40. Makes up elaborate pretend sequences from imagination

Comments

I. Self-Information — 0 1

41. Can state first name
42. Can state first and last name
43. Provides names and descriptive information about family members
44. Can state full home address; if in hospital, name of hospital and room number
45. Can direct an adult to help child return home or back to the hospital room

J. Time Orientation — 0 1

46. Has a general awareness of time of mealtimes and routines during the day
47. Has some awareness of sequence of familiar events in a week
48. Has very simple time concepts
49. Associates a specific time with actions/events
50. Regularly checks clock or asks for the time in order to keep track of schedule

K. Household Chores — 0 1

51. Beginning to help care for own belongings if given constant direction and guidance
52. Beginning to help with simple household chores if given constant direction and guidance
53. Occasionally initiates simple routines to care for own belongings; may require physical help or reminders to complete
54. Occasionally initiates simple household chores; may require physical help or reminders to complete
55. Consistently initiates and carries out at least one household task involving several steps and decisions; may require physical help

L. Self-Protection — 0 1

56. Shows appropriate caution around stairs
57. Shows appropriate caution around hot or sharp objects
58. When crossing the street with an adult present, child does not need prompting about safety rules
59. Knows not to accept rides, food or money from strangers
60. Crosses busy street safely without an adult

M. Community Function — 0 1

61. Child may play safely at home without being watched constantly
62. Goes about familiar environment outside of home with only periodic monitoring for safety
63. Follows guidelines/expectations of school and community setting
64. Explores and functions in familiar community settings without supervision
65. Makes transaction in neighborhood store without assistance

SOCIAL FUNCTION DOMAIN SUM

PLEASE BE SURE YOU HAVE ANSWERED ALL ITEMS.

Figure 1. Sample items from the *PEDI™*. (From Haley, S.M., Costar, W.J., Ludlow, L.H., Haltiwanger, J.T., & Andrellos, P.J. [1992]. *Pediatric Evaluation of Disability Inventory [PEDI™]*. Upper Saddle River, NJ: Pearson; reprinted by permission.)

PQRS

Utility

With the *Functional Skills* scale as the basis (Part I), parents and professionals complete the *Caregiver Assistance* scale (Part II) to profile the extent of help needed in daily functioning in each functional competency area; this forms the basis of an individualized rehabilitation plan. In conjunction with Part II, the *Modifications* scale (Part III) enables teams to reach consensus on the degree of modifications necessary to promote functional competence for each child (see Figure 2). Overall, this three-step system effectively links assessment and intervention in a noncurricular format by focusing on common functional competencies and intervention methods for children.

Parts II and III: Caregiver Assistance and Modification

Circle the appropriate score for Caregiver Assistance and Modification for each item.

	Caregiver Assistance Scale						Modification Scale			
	Independent	Supervision	Minimal	Moderate	Maximal	Total	None	Child	Rehab	Extensive
SELF-CARE DOMAIN	5	4	3	2	1	0	N	C	R	E
A. **Eating:** eating and drinking regular meal; do not include cutting steak, opening containers or serving food from serving dishes	5	4	3	2	1	0	N	C	R	E
B. **Grooming:** brushing teeth, brushing or combing hair and caring for nose	5	4	3	2	1	0	N	C	R	E
C. **Bathing:** washing and drying face and hands, taking a bath or shower; do not include getting in and out of a tub or shower, water preparation, or washing back or hair	5	4	3	2	1	0	N	C	R	E
D. **Dressing Upper Body:** all indoor clothes, not including back fasteners; include help putting on or taking off splint or artificial limb; do not include getting clothes from closet or drawers	5	4	3	2	1	0	N	C	R	E
E. **Dressing Lower Body:** all indoor clothes; include putting on or taking off brace or artificial limb; do not include getting clothes from closet or drawers	5	4	3	2	1	0	N	C	R	E
F. **Toileting:** clothes, toilet management or external device use, and hygiene; do not include toilet transfers, monitoring schedule, or cleaning up after accidents	5	4	3	2	1	0	N	C	R	E
G. **Bladder Management:** control of bladder day and night, clean-up after accidents, monitoring schedule	5	4	3	2	1	0	N	C	R	E
H. **Bowel Management:** control of bowel day and night, clean-up after accidents, monitoring schedule	5	4	3	2	1	0	N	C	R	E
Self-Care Totals **SELF-CARE SUM** ☐										Self-Care Modification Frequencies
MOBILITY DOMAIN										
A. **Chair/Toilet Transfers:** child's wheelchair, adult-sized chair, adult-sized toilet	5	4	3	2	1	0	N	C	R	E
B. **Car Transfers:** mobility within car/van, seat belt use, transfers, and opening and closing doors	5	4	3	2	1	0	N	C	R	E
C. **Bed Mobility/Transfers:** getting in and out and changing positions in child's own bed	5	4	3	2	1	0	N	C	R	E
D. **Tub Transfers:** getting in and out of adult-sized tub	5	4	3	2	1	0	N	C	R	E
E. **Indoor Locomotion:** 50 feet (3-4 rooms); do not include opening doors or carrying objects	5	4	3	2	1	0	N	C	R	E
F. **Outdoor Locomotion:** 150 feet (15 car lengths) on level surfaces; focus on physical ability to move outdoors (do not consider compliance or safety issues such as crossing streets)	5	4	3	2	1	0	N	C	R	E
G. **Stairs:** climb and descend a full flight of stairs (12-15 steps)	5	4	3	2	1	0	N	C	R	E
Mobility Totals **MOBILITY SUM** ☐										Mobility Modification Frequencies
SOCIAL FUNCTION DOMAIN										
A. **Functional Comprehension:** understanding of requests and instructions	5	4	3	2	1	0	N	C	R	E
B. **Functional Expression:** ability to provide information about own activities and make own needs known; include clarity of articulation	5	4	3	2	1	0	N	C	R	E
C. **Joint Problem Solving:** include communication of problem and working with caregiver or other adult to find a solution; include only ordinary problems occurring during daily activities; (for example, lost toy; conflict over clothing choices.)	5	4	3	2	1	0	N	C	R	E
D. **Peer Play:** ability to plan and carry out joint activities with a familiar peer	5	4	3	2	1	0	N	C	R	E
E. **Safety:** caution in routine daily safety situations, including stairs, sharp or hot objects and traffic	5	4	3	2	1	0	N	C	R	E
Social Function Totals **SOCIAL FUNCTION SUM** ☐										Social Function Modification Frequencies

Figure 2. Sample of Parts II and III: Caregiver Assistance and Modification. (From Haley, S.M., Costar, W.J., Ludlow, L.H., Haltiwanger, J.T., & Andrellos, P.J. [1992]. *Pediatric Evaluation of Disability Inventory [PEDI™]*. Upper Saddle River, NJ: Pearson; reprinted by permission.)

The *PEDI*™ combines norm-referenced scores and functional data to fulfill major early childhood assessment purposes: eligibility, programming, and progress monitoring.

Perhaps the most unique aspect of the *PEDI*™ is that the child's functional capabilities and caregiver assistance and modifications are profiled by normative data. The norming of caregiver assistance and modifications enables team members to compare the adaptations needed for an individual with those needed for a child of his or her age with a particular severity of functional impairment.

PQRS

Collaboration

The *PEDI*™ was designed and developed by interdisciplinary professionals. The entire basis of the *PEDI*™ supports interdisciplinary collaboration in assessment and intervention in both hospital and community early childhood intervention settings. The *PEDI*™ uses common language accessible both to parents and diverse interdisciplinary professionals. It accomplishes this through the overarching structure of functional capabilities that eschews disciplinary jargon and targets the child's observational skills and needs. Parents and all professionals collaborate in making consensus decisions about functioning across settings and about intervention strategies that work.

Like the *Adaptive Behavior Assessment System-Second Edition (ABAS-II)*, the *PEDI*™ has the capability to generate item cross-walks with the *International Classification of Functioning, Disability and Health: Children and Youth Version (ICF-CY)* to make the *ICF* more practical in its use and to serve as the common language for interdisciplinary and international functional classification and decision making.

Evidence Base

The *PEDI*™ is widely used and is often cited as the comparison measure in studies of other tools. There are several studies that have investigated translations of the *PEDI*™ in Scandinavia, Turkey, and Puerto Rico. The following provides a brief overview of the research on the technical adequacy of the *PEDI*™.

- Four studies examined the reliability of the *PEDI*™, including interrater reliability, internal consistency, and test–retest reliability (McCarthy et al., 2002; Nicholas & Case-Smith, 1996; Sundberg, 1992; Trzyna, 1996).

- Seven studies analyzed the validity of the *PEDI*™, including concurrent construct, content, and discriminant validity (Boschen & Wright, 1994; Feldman, Haley, & Coryell, 1990; Haley, Coster, & Fass, 1991; McCarthy et al., 2002; Nicholas & Case-Smith, 1996; Schultz, 1992; Wright & Boschen, 1994).

- Four studies investigated the *PEDI*™'s ability to detect change over time (Knox & Usen, 1998; Nordmark, Jarnlo, & Hagglund, 2000; Tokcan, 2000; Vos-Vromans, Ketelaar, & Gorter, 2005).

Considerations and Recommendations

- The *PEDI*™ is regarded as one of the most valuable and technically adequate measures of functional and adaptive behaviors of young children.

- The *PEDI*™ creatively combines the best of authentic, curriculum-referenced, adaptive, and normative features in an easily used, accessible, and practical format. The *PEDI*™ can serve as a model for test development in the disability field.

- The *PEDI*™ can be improved by infusing additional item content that is universally designed and functional and may not require adaptations.

PQRS

Close Up on next page

Preschool and Kindergarten Behavior Scales—Second Edition (PKBS-2)

Author(s): Kenneth W. Merrell

Publication date: 2002

Publisher: PRO-ED

Web site(s): http://www.proedinc.com

Cost: $124.00 per kit (includes test manual and 50 forms)

Assessment type: Curriculum-referenced assessment with norms

Age range: 3–6 years

Domains/subtests: *Social Skills Scale* includes Social Cooperation, Social Interaction, and Social Independence. *Problem Behavior Scale* comprises Externalizing (Self-Centered/Explosive, Attention Problems/Overactive, and Antisocial/Aggressive) and Internalizing Behaviors (Social Withdrawal and Anxiety/Somatic Problems)

Population targeted: All children including children with concerning behaviors; two normative samples: n = 3,313 (original edition n = 2,855; 458 added to original sample for second edition); field-validated in numerous longitudinal studies in early childhood intervention including Head Start

Technology features: None

Translations: Spanish-language rating form

Other features	Rating		Standard	Rating
Validated purposes	Medium		Acceptability	◑
Curricular links	High		Authenticity	◑
Comprehensive coverage	Low		Collaboration	◑
Graduated scoring	High		Evidence	◑
Progress monitoring	Medium		Multifactors	◑
Standards alignment	Medium		Sensitivity	◐
Diversity features	Medium		Universality	◑
Family engagement	High		Utility	◐
Teamwork	High			
Professional development	Low		OVERALL	◑
Technology	Low			

PQRS

Cover image from Merrell, K. (2002). *Preschool and Kindergarten Behavior Scales–Second Edition Complete Kit*. Austin, TX: *PRO-ED*; used with permission.

Preschool and Kindergarten Behavior Scales— Second Edition (PKBS-2)

Authors(s): Kenneth W. Merrell

About the Measure

The *PKBS-2* is the essence of simplicity, research rigor, practicality, and utility for the assessment of social-behavioral competencies in preschool children; its track record marks it as the standard in this area.

Among its many uses, the *PKBS-2* is an assessment instrument for the early detection of social-emotional and behavior problems in young children for purposes of prevention and early intervention.

The strengths of the *PKBS-2* are apparent in its ease of use by both parents and professionals and the usefulness of the information so that teams can make decisions with confidence regarding functional diagnosis, eligibility, planning, and progress monitoring.

Authenticity

The *PKBS-2* Summary/Response Form (see Figure 1) can be completed by a variety of caregivers across various settings. Ratings are based on the raters' knowledge of the child over the 3 months preceding assessment. Raters rely on natural observations of naturally occurring behaviors in everyday routines. Each item is rated on a 4-point Likert scale. Separate score conversion tables are included in the *PKBS-2 Examiner's Manual* so that school-based raters are compared only with other school-based raters and home-based raters are compared with like raters as well.

Social Skills Scale

	Never	Rarely	Sometimes	Often	Scoring Key		
1. Works or plays independently	0	1	2	3			
2. Is cooperative	0	1	2	3			
3. Smiles and laughs with other children	0	1	2	3			
4. Plays with several different children	0	1	2	3			
5. Tries to understand another child's behavior ("Why are you crying?")	0	1	2	3			
6. Is accepted and liked by other children	0	1	2	3			
7. Follows instructions from adults	0	1	2	3			
8. Attempts new tasks before asking for help	0	1	2	3			
9. Makes friends easily	0	1	2	3			
10. Shows self-control	0	1	2	3			

Problem Behavior Scale

	Never	Rarely	Sometimes	Often	Scoring Key	
1. Acts impulsively without thinking	0	1	2	3		
2. Becomes sick when upset or afraid	0	1	2	3		
3. Teases or makes fun of other children	0	1	2	3		
4. Does not respond to affection from others	0	1	2	3		
5. Clings to parent or caregiver	0	1	2	3		
6. Makes noises that annoy others	0	1	2	3		
7. Has temper outbursts or tantrums	0	1	2	3		
8. Wants all the attention	0	1	2	3		
9. Is anxious or tense	0	1	2	3		
10. Will not share	0	1	2	3		
11. Is physically aggressive (hits, kicks, pushes)	0	1	2	3		
12. Avoids playing with other children	0	1	2	3		
13. Yells or screams when angry	0	1	2	3		
14. Takes things away from other children	0	1	2	3		
15. Has difficulty concentrating or staying on task	0	1	2	3		

Figure 1. Sample of items from the Social Skills Scale of the Summary/Response Form and sample of items from the Problem Behavior Scale of the Summary/Response Form. (From Merrell, K.W. [2002]. *Preschool and Kindergarten Behavior Scales–Second Edition [PKBS-2]*. Austin: TX: PRO-ED; reprinted by permission.)

Utility

The *PKBS*-2 was designed and field-validated for multiple purposes in early childhood intervention. When it is used as a screener, cut-off scores can be used to identify children who are at risk for behavioral problems and who may need further appraisal. The scale can be used in conjunction with other assessments to determine eligibility for special education and wrap-round behavioral support services. Similarly, the content of the *PKBS*-2 is functional and direct, leading to tangible and measurable intervention goals. Finally, the *PKBS-2* is sensitive to children's progress over time in response to intervention (RTI)–based prevention and intervention programs.

The *Examiner's Manual* lists three ways to link assessment results with intervention planning

1. Use risk level indicators to select children for intervention whose scores show moderate to significant deficits or problems

2. Use the specific wording of scale items to develop individualized education program (IEP) goals; the *Examiner's Manual* provides specific instructions to guide users in developing IEP goals based on test items.

3. Use the subscale cut-off scores to identify specific clusters or skill deficits that need attention

The Social Skills and Problem Behavior scales within the *PKBS-2* include eight discrete subscales that can be analyzed individually to identify targeted intervention needs for children who may have a significant deficit or problem in one area but whose overall score is unremarkable.

The format of the *PKBS-2* has been simplified from the original version. First, the Problem Behavior scoring has been changed so that three scores can be used for routine purposes: Externalizing Problems, Internalizing Problems, and a Composite score. Five supplemental scales can be used to identify specific symptoms of emotional and behavioral problems in young children. These include Self-Centered/Explosive, Attention Problems/Overactive, Antisocial/Aggressive, Social Withdrawal, and Anxiety/Somatic problems (see Figure 2).

In addition, risk levels have been incorporated to assist in interpreting the *PKBS-2* scores. For both the Social Skills and Problem Behavior Scales, scores at the end of the distribution representing problem areas are classified into High Risk or Moderate Risk levels. Results from the *PKBS-2* during intervention often demonstrate an inverse relationship between increasing social skills and decreasing problem behaviors (i.e., demonstrating that by targeting prosocial responses, problem behaviors are decreased).

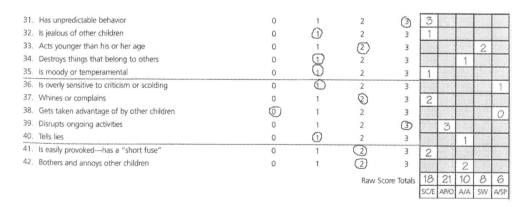

Figure 2. Sample of the completed Supplemental Problem Behavior Subscales Scoring Key. (From Merrell, K.W. [2002]. Preschool and Kindergarten Behavior Scales–Second Edition [PKBS-2]. Austin: TX: PRO-ED; reprinted by permission.)

Collaboration

The *PKBS-2* encourages partnership between families, caregivers, and professionals, particularly when it is used for determining eligibility. For eligibility determination, the authors recommend using the *PKBS-2* as a component of a multisource approach to comprehensive assessment. When using the *PKBS-2*, professionals and parents are likely to maintain their primary role identity during all phases of assessment, planning, and intervention.

The terminology used in the *PKBS-2* is accessible and nonthreatening, which is important for facilitating collaboration and accuracy among professionals and with families. The manual is also user friendly. For example, the chapter on interpreting the *PKBS-2* provides information on general use of test scores and issues in understanding behavior rating scales. Strategies are given for interpreting results, and case studies are included as an example of how the interpretations can be applied.

Evidence Base

A wide variety of psychometric evidence for *PKBS-2* included in the *Examiner's Manual* demonstrates acceptable internal consistency, test-retest, and interrater reliability as well as validity focused on content, internal structure, relations to other variables, and consequences of assessment.

Independent research on the *PKBS-2* includes two studies: 1) a dissertation examining the discriminant and concurrent validity of the *PKBS-2* (Edwards, 2009) and 2) a study investigating the validity and reliability of a condensed Spanish version of the *PKBS-2* (Reyna & Brussino, 2009).

A number of researchers have used the *PKBS-2* in their research to study early childhood behavior and language competencies (Rinaldi, Rogers-Adkinson, & Arora, 2009), school readiness, (Marquez, 2006), social and learning related skill constructs (Sok Mui, Rodger, & Brown, 2010), teacher and parent perceptions of behavior (Cho, 2007; Winsler & Wallace, 2002), impact of parenting behaviors of low-income families (Whiteside-Mansell, Bradley, & McKelvey, 2009), and intervention efficacy (Pickens, 2009; Watson, 2007).

Specifically, the *PKBS-2* was one of several measures used to document the impact and outcomes of a high-profile model early care and education effort in the Pittsburgh region over 3 years. High-risk preschoolers in the Early Childhood Initiative (ECI) model showed dramatic improvements in social-behavioral competencies and successful transition to kindergarten based on the sensitivity of the *PKBS-2* pre-post progress and accountability assessments (Bagnato, 2002).

Due to the nature of the revisions to the *PKBS-2*, research on the first edition remains relevant. Several studies documented the construct validity of the *PKBS* (Carney & Merrell, 2005; Jentzsch & Merrell, 1996; Merrell, 1995a, 1995b, 1996; Merrell & Holland, 1997). Researchers have also examined the reliability of the *PKBS* (Carney & Merrell, 2002; Edwards, Whiteside-Mansell, Conners & Deere, 2003).

Considerations and Recommendations

- The *PKBS* has been field-validated broadly in Head Start and prekindergarten programs and with children in inclusive classrooms.

- The *PKBS* shows the outcome studies listed in the evidence section to underpin its use for major early childhood intervention purposes including progress monitoring and accountability.

- The structure of the measure supports its use as an efficient metric for documenting program impact regarding the complex interrelationship among mentoring teachers in positive behavioral support practices leading to increasing social skills and decreasing behavior problems (Bagnato, 2008).

- The *PKBS-2* was developed specifically for the 3- to 6-year-old population and is not a downward extension of a school-age assessment.

PQRS

Scales of Independent Behavior-Revised™ (SIB-R™)

Author(s): Robert H. Bruininks, Richard W. Woodcock, Richard R. Weatherman, and Bradley K. Hill

Publication date: 1996

Publisher: Riverside Publishing

Web site(s): http://www.riversidepublishing.com

Cost: $283.00 (includes all pieces required for the assessment)

Assessment type: Curriculum-referenced assessment with norms

Age range: Birth through adult (80+ years)

Domains/subtests: Motor Skills, Social Interaction and Communication Skills, Personal Living Skills, Community Living Skills, Internalized Maladaptive Behavior, Asocial Maladaptive Behavior, and Externalized Maladaptive Behavior

Population targeted: Individuals with delays or deficits in adaptive functioning; n = 2,182 stratified to reflect 1990 U.S. Census

Technology features: CD-ROM scoring and reporting program

Translations: Short form available for individuals with visual impairments

Other features	Rating	Standard	Rating
Validated purposes	Medium	Acceptability	◑
Curricular links	Medium	Authenticity	●
Comprehensive coverage	Medium	Collaboration	◐
Graduated scoring	Medium	Evidence	◐
Progress monitoring	Medium	Multifactors	◐
Standards alignment	Medium	Sensitivity	◐
Diversity features	Medium	Universality	◐
Family engagement	Low	Utility	◐
Teamwork	Low		
Professional development	Low	OVERALL	◑
Technology	Medium		

PQRS

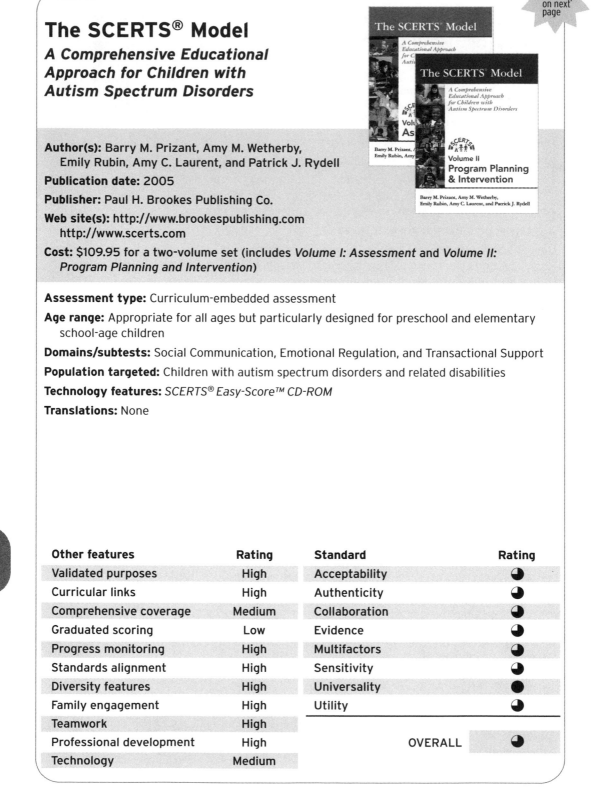

Close Up on next page

The SCERTS® Model
A Comprehensive Educational Approach for Children with Autism Spectrum Disorders

Author(s): Barry M. Prizant, Amy M. Wetherby, Emily Rubin, Amy C. Laurent, and Patrick J. Rydell

Publication date: 2005

Publisher: Paul H. Brookes Publishing Co.

Web site(s): http://www.brookespublishing.com
http://www.scerts.com

Cost: $109.95 for a two-volume set (includes *Volume I: Assessment* and *Volume II: Program Planning and Intervention*)

Assessment type: Curriculum-embedded assessment

Age range: Appropriate for all ages but particularly designed for preschool and elementary school-age children

Domains/subtests: Social Communication, Emotional Regulation, and Transactional Support

Population targeted: Children with autism spectrum disorders and related disabilities

Technology features: *SCERTS® Easy-Score™ CD-ROM*

Translations: None

PQRS

Other features	Rating	Standard	Rating
Validated purposes	High	Acceptability	◖
Curricular links	High	Authenticity	◖
Comprehensive coverage	Medium	Collaboration	◖
Graduated scoring	Low	Evidence	◖
Progress monitoring	High	Multifactors	◖
Standards alignment	High	Sensitivity	◖
Diversity features	High	Universality	●
Family engagement	High	Utility	◖
Teamwork	High		
Professional development	High	OVERALL	◖
Technology	Medium		

The SCERTS® Model

A Comprehensive Educational Approach for Children with Autism Spectrum Disorders

Author(s): Barry M. Prizant, Amy M. Wetherby, Emily Rubin, Amy C. Laurent, and Patrick J. Rydell

About the Measure

Grounded in sound theory and research, *The SCERTS® Model* exemplifies contemporary approaches to addressing the communication and social-emotional abilities of children with autism spectrum disorders (ASDs) and their families.

Organized around social communication, emotional regulation, and transactional support, authentic assessment items link directly to strategies for individualized program planning and intervention in a curriculum-based format.

SCERTS® supports the development of pragmatic communication competencies by creating social to language to conversational partnerships; this sequence and its focus make the system usable for children with diverse functional needs.

Authenticity

The *SCERTS®* assessment is used to evaluate a child's functioning in the social communication, emotional regulation, and transactional support domains. Information is collected from parents and individuals familiar with the child in a variety of settings by asking them to complete the *SCERTS® Assessment Process Report* form (SAP-R). The *SAP-R* forms for each of the three communication stages can be found in Appendix A of Volume I. The *SAP-R* can be used as a questionnaire that is filled out independently by the family, or it can be used as part of an interview. The *SAP-R* forms also include a needs assessment for the family to identify significant family needs, significant strengths and needs that the family members observe in the child, opportunities to see the child at his or her "best" and "worst," and information regarding the child's typical social partners. The information gathered from the *SAP-R* form can be used to plan the observation.

The *SCERTS® Assessment Process Observation (SAP-O)* is designed to gather information about a child's range of abilities and needs in the context of natural environments. Figure 1 is from the *SAP-O* and provides specific examples of authentic assessment items.

To ensure that the observation is representative of the child's behavior, six variables believed to influence a child's behavior are considered: natural contexts, length of observation, partners, group size, activity variables, and transitions. Guidelines for addressing each of these variables during the observation are described in the manual on pages 148–150. For example, for the natural context variable, the guidelines recommend that children should be observed in at least two settings (e.g., home and educational setting). If multiple observations cannot be completed, information from the *SAP-R* form and/or from video of the child in other natural contexts can provide evidence of consistent functioning across settings. In the event that the reports do not demonstrate consistent functioning across settings, observations in multiple setting must be completed. After completing the *SAP-O,* family members are asked to validate the results of the assessment findings by completing the Family Perception and Priorities section of the *SAP Summary Form (SAP SUM).*

PQRS

P Q R S

SCERTS™

SAP-OBSERVATION FORM: Social Partner Stage (page 7)
Transactional Support

Child's name: _____

				LEARNING SUPPORT
Qtr 1	Qtr 2	Qtr 3	Qtr 4	
				1 Partner structures activity for active participation
				LS1.1 Defines clear beginning and ending to activity
				LS1.2 Creates turn-taking opportunities and leaves spaces for child to fill in
				LS1.3 Provides predictable sequence to activity
				LS1.4 Offers repeated learning opportunities
				LS1.5 Offers varied learning opportunities
				2 Partner uses augmentative communication support to foster development
				LS2.1 Uses augmentative communication support to enhance child's communication and expressive language
				LS2.2 Uses augmentative communication support to enhance child's understanding of language and behavior
				LS2.3 Uses augmentative communication support to enhance child's expression and understanding of emotion
				LS2.4 Uses augmentative communication support to enhance child's emotional regulation
				3 Partner uses visual and organizational support
				LS3.1 Uses support to define steps within a task
				LS3.2 Uses support to define steps and time for completion of activities
				LS3.3 Uses visual support to enhance smooth transitions between activities
				LS3.4 Uses support to organize segments of time across the day
				LS3.5 Uses visual support to enhance attention in group activities
				LS3.6 Uses visual support to foster active involvement in group activities
				4 Partner modifies goals, activities, and learning environment
				LS4.1 Adjusts social complexity to support organization and interaction
				LS4.2 Adjusts task difficulty for child success
				LS4.3 Modifies sensory properties of learning environment
				LS4.4 Arranges learning environment to enhance attention
				LS4.5 Arranges learning environment to promote child initiation
				LS4.6 Designs and modifies activities to be developmentally appropriate
				LS4.7 Infuses motivating materials and topics in activities
				LS4.8 Provides activities to promote initiation and extended interaction
				LS4.9 Alternates between movement and sedentary activities as needed
				LS4.10 "Ups the ante" or increases expectations appropriately

SCORING KEY: 2, criterion met consistently (across two partners in two contexts);
1, criterion met inconsistently or with assistance; **0**, criterion not met

SCERTS™

SAP-OBSERVATION FORM: Social Partner Stage (page 5)
Emotional Regulation

Child's name: _____

				SELF-REGULATION
Qtr 1	Qtr 2	Qtr 3	Qtr 4	
				1 Demonstrates availability for learning and interacting
				SR1.1 Notices people and things in the environment
				SR1.2 Shows interest in a variety of sensory and social experiences
				SR1.3 Seeks and tolerates a variety of sensory experiences
				SR1.4 Initiates bids for interaction (= JA1.2)
				SR1.5 Engages in brief reciprocal interaction (= JA1.3)
				SR1.6 Engages in extended reciprocal interaction (= JA1.4)
				SR1.7 Responds to sensory and social experiences with differentiated emotions
				2 Uses behavioral strategies to regulate arousal level during familiar activities
				SR2.1 Uses behavioral strategies to regulate arousal level during solitary activities (↔ SU3.1)
				SR2.2 Uses behavioral strategies to regulate arousal level during social interactions
				SR2.3 Uses behavioral strategies modeled by partners to regulate arousal level
				SR2.4 Uses behavioral strategies to engage productively in an extended activity
				3 Regulates emotion in new and changing situations
				SR3.1 Anticipates another person's actions in familiar routines (= SU2.1)
				SR3.2 Participates in new and changing situations
				SR3.3 Uses behavioral strategies to regulate arousal level in new and changing situations
				SR3.4 Uses behavioral strategies to regulate arousal level during transitions
				4 Recovers from extreme dysregulation by self
				SR4.1 Removes self from overstimulating or undesired activity
				SR4.2 Uses behavioral strategies to recover from extreme dysregulation
				SR4.3 Reengages in interaction or activity after recovery from extreme dysregulation
				SR4.4 Decreases amount of time to recover from extreme dysregulation
				SR4.5 Decreases intensity of dysregulated state

SCORING KEY: 2, criterion met consistently (across two partners in two contexts);
1, criterion met inconsistently or with assistance; **0**, criterion not met

Figure 1. Examples of assessment items from *SAP-O*. (From Prizant, B.M., Wetherby, A.M., Rubin, E., Laurent, A.C., & Rydell, P.J. [2006]. *The SCERTS® Model: A Comprehensive Educational Approach for Children with Autism Spectrum Disorders: Vol. I. Assessment*. Baltimore: Paul H. Brookes Publishing Co.; reprinted by permission.)

Utility

The *SCERTS®* Assessment process is designed to give information that can be directly linked to educational programming and takes into consideration needs expressed by the family. Information is gathered in the social communication (child's social communication abilities including joint attention and symbol use), emotional regulation (attention, arousal, and establishment of social relationships), and transactional support (a child's needs in interpersonal support and learning support, as well as support to families and professionals) domains.

The *SAP Map* is used for planning the assessment. The *SAP Map* assists in identifying the assessment team members, their roles and responsibilities, where the observation will take place, and who will plan the observation.

The *SAP SUM* provides a format to summarize the child's strengths and needs that were identified during the *SAP-O* and the family's perceptions for the *SAP-O* results and priorities for goal setting.

SAP Activity Planning Forms can be used to plan daily activities for the target child. The *SAP Activity Planning Form* (see Figure 2) identifies meaningful and purposeful activities, the lev-

SAP Activity Planning Form

Child's name: Jason **Communication stage:** Social Partner **Date:** 11-14-05 **Page #:** 1 (A.M.)

Team members and partners: Social worker (SW), occupational therapist (OT), speech-language pathologist (SLP), paraprofessional (P), mom (M), dad (D), aunt (A), uncle (U), cousin (C)

Activity/time	Social complexity	Group size	Team members and partners	Weekly child objectives: Jason will respond to bids for interaction.	Jason will request desired food or objects.	Jason will request social games.	Jason will use conventional contact gestures.	Jason will engage when alerted by partners.	Jason will respond to partners' use of behavioral strategies.	Jason will notice people and things in the environment.	Jason will seek and tolerate a variety of sensory experiences.	Weekly partner objectives: Partner will follow Jason's focus of attention.	Partner will attune to Jason's emotion and pace.	Partner will recognize signs of dysregulation and offer support.	Partner will offer choices nonverbally or verbally.	Partner will use appropriate proximity and nonverbal behavior to encourage interaction.	Partner will define a clear beginning and ending to activities.	Partner will create turn-taking opportunities and leave spaces for Jason to fill in.	Partner will modify sensory properties of learning environment.	Sample transactional supports
Breakfast (MOD) 9:00 A.M.–9:30 A.M.	1:1	3–4	M, P, SLP/OT		X			X				X	X			X				(LS) While seated in a highchair, food items will be offered in see-through containers that are difficult to open.
Morning play (PAR, ENG) 9:30 A.M.–10:15 A.M.	1:1	3–4	M, P, SLP/OT	X		X			X		X				X			X	X	(IS) Partners will offer frequent choices of toys and will pair play routines with songs.
Diaper change (NAT) 10:15 A.M.–10:30 A.M.	1:1	2–3	M, SW					X		X				X			X		X	(IS) Sensory-motor play and singing will be incorporated during the diaper change.
Morning play (PAR & ENG) 10:30 A.M.–11:15 A.M.	1:1	3–4	M, P, SW		X		X					X				X				(LS) In Jason's backyard, a see-through bin will be placed in the sandbox to entice Jason's interest in preferred cause-effect toys.
Lunch (MOD) 11:15 A.M.–12:00 A.M.	1:1	2–3	M, P				X		X					X	X					(LS) At a child-size table, choices of food items will be offered in see-through containers that are difficult to open.

Instructions: Write the weekly Social Communication and Emotional Regulation objectives for the child and the Transactional Support objectives for the partner in the vertical boxes across the top. In the far right vertical box at the upper right-hand corner, list the team members and the child's partners and numbers or initials for each team member or partner. In each row below the column headings, write a brief description of the activity and the time, the ratio for social complexity, the group size, and the number or initials of the team members or partners participating in that activity. Then check off all of the objectives that will be targeted in each activity. Write in a brief description of sample transactional support used in each activity.

Figure 2. SAP Activity Planning Form. (From Prizant, B.M., Wetherby, A.M., Rubin, E., Laurent, A.C., & Rydell, P.J. [2006]. *The SCERTS® Model: A Comprehensive Educational Approach for Children with Autism Spectrum Disorders: Vol. II. Program Planning and intervention.* Baltimore: Paul H. Brookes Publishing Co.; reprinted by permission.)

els of support needed in the activities, roles and responsibilities of educational team members, and family partners who will play a role in service provision. The *SAP Daily Tracking Log* and *SAP Weekly Tracking Log* can be used for progress monitoring and to determine the effectiveness of program implementation.

Collaboration

The *SCERTS®* is completed through an assessment team, which is created for each child through completion of the *SAP Map*. The assessment team can include any relevant professionals (speech therapists, occupational therapists, teachers, intervention specialists, psychologists, and/or an applied behavior analysts). The *SAP Map* may identify the need for collaboration with outside experts as well (e.g., a neurologist or behavior specialist).

The *SCERTS® Model* uses information reported by family members or teachers who know the child well, who spend time with the child in different settings, and who are familiar with the child's development over time. Information is gathered through completion of the *SAP-R* form, which can be administered as a questionnaire or as an interview. The *SAP-R* also allows professional team members to gather information about family questions and concerns. The families' observations and comments about their children's functioning are included directly in the assessment reports to validate the importance of family input in the assessment process.

The *SCERTS® Model* recognizes that professionals and other service providers may face challenges when implementing an intensive educational program; therefore, the *SCERTS® Support Plan for Professionals and Service Providers* can be developed by the team pertaining to each child. The plan addresses activities to target both educational (e.g., team meetings, regularly scheduled staff in-service training sessions, consultation time for professional-to-professional exchange of ideas) and emotional needs (e.g., scheduled sharing opportunities at the end of the school day, crisis meetings, regularly scheduled staff retreats outside the school setting).

Evidence Base

Wetherby, A.M., Rubin, E., Laurent, A.C., Prizant, B.M., & Rydell, P.J. (2006). *Summary of research supporting the SCERTS® Model*. Retrieved February 12, 2010, from http://www.scerts.com/docs/ResearchSupportingtheSCERTSModel10-7-06.pdf

Extensive research (including 60 studies) has been conducted on the three *SCERTS®* domains, documenting treatment validity, social validity, and utility.

- Experimental studies with randomized clinical trials to document treatment effects of *SCERTS®* interventions under controlled conditions.

- Quasi-experimental studies that demonstrate the feasibility of implementing *The SCERTS® Model* and measuring related treatment effects.

- Single-subject experimental studies that examine specific intervention strategies that are incorporated in *The SCERTS® Model*.

- Descriptive studies that document core deficits of ASDs or significant predictors of outcomes for individuals with ASDs that are targeted in *The SCERTS® Model*.

Considerations and Recommendations

- *The SCERTS® Model* is rooted in a set of principles regarding the importance of developing success, independence, and functional skills, in which all behaviors demonstrated are viewed as having or serving a communicative function for the child; this logical and functional approach makes the *SCERTS®* one of the premier systems for children with social-communication needs, especially children with ASDs.

- *The SCERTS® Model* includes sample educational and emotional support activities for families to implement at home and also includes a form (Family Support and Planning Form, Vol. II, p. 77) to facilitate planning and implementing activities that provide educational and emotional support to families.

- The Program Planning and Intervention component of *The SCERTS® Model* could be expanded to include more detailed examples of how to make the link from assessment to program planning and intervention.

PQRS

Close Up on next page

School Function Assessment (SFA)

Author(s): Wendy Coster, Theresa Deeney, Jane Halti-wanger, and Stephen Haley

Publication date: 1998

Publisher: NCS Pearson

Web site(s): http://psychcorp.pearsonassessment.com

Cost: $210.00 for kit

Assessment type: Curriculum-referenced assessment

Age range: Kindergarten through Grade 6

Domains/subtests: Measures performance of functional tasks that support participation in the academic and social aspects of elementary school programs; areas include Participation and Task Supports, Activity Performance including Physical Tasks and Cognitive/Behavioral Tasks, and an Adaptations Checklist

Population targeted: Children in an elementary school environment with functional developmental disabilities

Technology features: None

Translations: None

Other features	Rating	Standard	Rating
Validated purposes	Medium	Acceptability	◑
Curricular links	High	Authenticity	◑
Comprehensive coverage	High	Collaboration	◑
Graduated scoring	Medium	Evidence	◕
Progress monitoring	High	Multifactors	◑
Standards alignment	Medium	Sensitivity	●
Diversity features	Medium	Universality	○
Family engagement	Low	Utility	◐
Teamwork	Medium		
Professional development	Low	OVERALL	◑
Technology	Low		

School Function Assessment (SFA)

Author(s): Wendy Coster, Theresa Deeney, Jane Haltiwanger, and Stephen Haley

About the Measure

The *SFA* is an authentic, curriculum-referenced measure (with national norms) that emphasizes a functional appraisal of physical and cognitive academic/behavioral competencies as prerequisite skills to succeed in school.

The *SFA* (a loose, upward extension of the *Pediatric Evaluation of Disability Inventory* [*PEDI*]) involves a comprehensive appraisal of the individual's context including education settings, extent of general education participation, task engagement, and adaptations for functional impairments.

The *SFA* results in a functional profile that highlights both individual strengths and needs and comparisons with other individuals who show typical and atypical performances. Few authentic assessment measures are available for school-age children, but the *SFA* sets the example and a "high bar" for future developments in this high-need area.

Authenticity

Authentic assessments with the *SFA* encompass functional appraisals in four parts, which link the individual's capabilities with the ecological context of school and community: Participation, Task Supports, Activity Performance, and Adaptations/Assistance. Although the Activity Performance competencies in several functional areas are exemplary (e.g., maintains adequate posture to complete seat work; operates computers using simple switches; communicates where something is located; asks permission; refrains from provoking others; finishes project that takes several days; offers help to other person; demonstrates understanding of instructions), the most notable aspect of the *SFA* is its ecological appraisal of the contextual features that are necessary to foster independent functioning. See Figure 1 for sample items from the Participation rating scale, highlighting contextual features.

PQRS

Rate ALL of the following settings.	
Playground/Recess: Free time spent in the classroom, gym, or on the playground (excluding structured P.E. classes) including both physical and social-emotional aspects of participation. Includes playing games involving physical activity, using playground equipment, following rules, and playing cooperatively with peers. If the student has recess in a place separate from all or most peers, the student's participation should be rated as "1—Participation extremely limited."	1 2 3 4 5 6
Transportation: Getting to and from school under all conditions (such as weather or traffic) using one or more methods (e.g., bus, car, van, walking). Includes moving in and out of vehicles, entering and exiting the school building, and maintaining appropriate social behavior both while on vehicles as well as transitioning into and out of the build... *(Traveling ... in the s... is addres... in Tr...ing.)*	1 2 3 4 5 6
Bathroom/Toileting: ...ting tasks pe...rm... in a b...om en...en... includi...han...ing clothing using a catheter or diapers, flus...he t...t, ta...ca...of p...so...h...ene...e, ...ing h...ds), and the... physical acts of getting ...from th...bath...om and t.../o...he t... If t...stud...never uses t...bathroom, the student's participation...be r...d as "1—P...icipation ...remely limit..."	1 2 3 4 5 6
Transitions: Moving from one area or room of the school to another, including lining up, moving in crowded corridors or aisles, negotiating doorways, following directions and rules, and maintaining appropriate social behavior. *(Note: Transitioning from activity to activity within the classroom is addressed in the Classroom setting.)*	1 2 3 4 5 6
Mealtime/Snack Time: Tasks and activities associated with eating at school, whether eating occurs in the cafeteria or classroom, such as obtaining or organizing lunch or snack, eating and cleaning up, and maintaining appropriate social appearance and behavior while eating. If the student is tube fed, rate the extent of his or her participation in the regular mealtime/snack time environment. If the student eats or is fed in a place separate from peers, the student's participation should be rated as "1—Participation extremely limited."	1 2 3 4 5 6
Respondent's Initials	**Participation Raw Score (sum of six ratings)**	

Figure 1. Sample items from Participation rating scale. (School Function Assessment [SFA]. Copyright © 1998 NCS Pearson Inc. Reproduced with permission. All rights reserved.)

Utility

The *SFA* fulfills the major purposes in early childhood intervention in a functional approach, including eligibility, programming, and performance monitoring. The *SFA* also focuses on the essential features of activity performance and participation within the demands of real-life routines. In this respect, the *SFA* merges with the *International Classification of Functioning, Disability and Health: Children and Youth Version (ICF-CY)* in terms of its focuses on activity, participation, and environmental supports that promote progress.

The *SFA* item content matches well with many of the *ICF-CY* individual and environmental codes. The Participation features focus on the capacity to perform major life tasks in real-life circumstances. In each of these respects, the *SFA* is a mini–*ICF-CY* and thus promotes the use of the functional classification system.

Collaboration

The *SFA Manual* suggests gathering information from multiple individuals (called *respondents*) who have observed the student on several occasions in school, who understand the typical range of development for the particular skill being assessed, and who know what supports are available to the student. Respondents could be general education teachers, special education teachers, related service providers, or teacher aides.

PQRS

The authors offer three possible methods for completing the *SFA* scales: Coordinator Method, Collaborative Effort Method, and Single Respondent Method. Using the Coordinator Method, one individual coordinates the distribution, collection, and results tabulation of the *Record Forms* from each respondent. All respondents confer to discuss the results of the assessment after all data have been collected. For the Collaborative Effort Method, all respondents meet together to complete the Record Form through discussion and analyze the results together. The Single Respondent Method is only recommended when an individual wants information about one particular component of the *SFA* and has sufficient knowledge of the student to complete the assessment individually.

Evidence Base

Coster, W., Deeney, T., Haltiwanger, J., & Haley, S. (1998). *School Function Assessment: User's manual*. San Antonio, TX: The Psychological Corporation.

  The *SFA* manual describes the outcomes of three development and validation studies conducted on the Pilot, Tryout, and Standardized versions of the *SFA*. The report includes data on test–retest reliability, internal consistency, content validity, and construct validity.

Coster, W., Mancini, M., & Ludlow, L. (1999). Factor structure of the School Function Assessment. *Educational & Psychological Measurement*, 59(4), 665.

  Examines the factor structure of the *Activity Performance* scales component of the *SFA*.

Davies, P., Lee Soon, P., Young, M., & Clausen-Yamaki, A. (2004). Validity and reliability of the School Function Assessment in elementary school students with disabilities. *Physical & Occupational Therapy in Pediatrics*, 24(3), 23–43.

  Examines the interrater reliability and validity of score interpretation.

Hwang, J.L., & Davies, P.L. (2009). Rasch analysis of the School Function Assessment provides additional evidence for the internal validity of the activity performance scales. *American Journal of Occupational Therapy*, 63(3), 369–373.

  Examines the internal construct validity of the *Activity Performance* scales component of the *SFA*.

Hwang, J., Davies, P., Taylor, M., & Gavin, W. (2002). Validation of School Function Assessment with elementary school children. *OTJR: Occupation, Participation and Health*, 22(2), 48–58.

  Examines the *SFA*'s convergent validity with the *Vineland Adaptive Behavior Scales (Classroom Edition)*, construct validity, and discriminant validity.

Ogonowski, J., Kronk, R., Rice, C., & Feldman, H. (2004). Inter-rater reliability in assigning ICF codes to children with disabilities. *Disability & Rehabilitation*, 26(6), 353–361.

  Examines the interrater reliability of several assessments including the *SFA*.

PQRS

Considerations and Recommendations

- The *SFA* is the premier measure for functional assessment in school settings for individuals with significant disabilities and for programs that do not use a functional curriculum but require a measure that links to intervention directly.

- The system is ripe for fundamental research on its treatment validity, particularly as the field attempts to implement "response-to-intervention" models.

SKI-HI Language Development Scale, 2nd Edition

Author(s): Susan Watkins

Publication date: 2004

Publisher: HOPE

Web site(s): http://hopepubl.com
http://www.skihi.org

Cost: *SKI-HI Language Development Scale Instructional Manual* $5.00
SKI-HI Curriculum $290.00

Assessment type: Curriculum-referenced assessment

Age range: Birth to 5 years

Domains/subtests: Receptive and expressive language

Population targeted: Infants and young children with hearing impairments;
developed for children from birth to 3 years, but suitable for children up to age 5

Technology features: None

Translations: Spanish

Other features	Rating	Standard	Rating
Validated purposes	Low	Acceptability	◗
Curricular links	Medium	Authenticity	◗
Comprehensive coverage	Low	Collaboration	◖
Graduated scoring	Low	Evidence	◔
Progress monitoring	Low	Multifactors	○
Standards alignment	Low	Sensitivity	◐
Diversity features	Medium	Universality	◐
Family engagement	High	Utility	◐
Teamwork	Medium		
Professional development	High	OVERALL	◐
Technology	Low		

235

Social Skills Improvement System Rating Scales (SSIS™ Rating Scales)

Author(s): Frank M. Gresham and Stephen N. Elliott

Publication date: 2007

Publisher: NCS Pearson

Web site(s): http://psychcorp.pearsonassessments.com

Cost: $245.80 for the Hand-Scored Starter Set in English (includes manual and one package of 25 of each of the forms)

Assessment type: Curriculum-referenced assessment with norms

Age range: 3–18 years

Domains/subtests: Social Skills, Problem Behaviors, and Academic Competence

Population targeted: Students at risk for academic or social behavior difficulties; norm group: *n* = 4,700, ages 3–18; *n* = 600, preschool

Technology features: *ASSIST™* software (purchased separately) provides computer scoring and reporting, including individual, progress, and multirater reports and a direct link to interventions with the *SSIS Intervention Guide*

Translations: Spanish versions of parent and student forms

Other features	Rating	Standard	Rating
Validated purposes	High	Acceptability	◑
Curricular links	High	Authenticity	◑
Comprehensive coverage	Low	Collaboration	◑
Graduated scoring	Medium	Evidence	◑
Progress monitoring	Medium	Multifactors	◑
Standards alignment	Medium	Sensitivity	◔
Diversity features	High	Universality	◐
Family engagement	High	Utility	◐
Teamwork	High		
Professional development	Medium	OVERALL	◐
Technology	Medium		

Temperament and Atypical Behavior Scale (TABS)

Early Childhood Indicators of Developmental Dysfunction

Author(s): Stephen J. Bagnato, John T. Neisworth, John J. Salvia, and Frances M. Hunt

Publication date: 1999

Publisher: Paul H. Brookes Publishing Co.

Web site(s): http://www.brookespublishing.com

Cost: $95.00 (includes Manual, 50 Screeners, and 30 Assessments)

Assessment type: Curriculum-referenced assessments with norms

Age range: 11–71 months

Domains/subtests: Detached, Hypersensitive/Active, Underreactive, and Dysregulated; 55-item full measure; 15-item screener

Population targeted: Children who may be at risk for later developmental delay; n ≥ 1,000; pooled norm group of children with typical development and disorders; used in several National Institutes of Health (NIH) studies of neurological and genetic disorders including fragile X syndrome and autism; recommended as a premier instrument for use by physicians by the American Academy of Pediatrics

Technology features: None

Translations: None

Other features	Rating	Standard	Rating
Validated purposes	High	Acceptability	◑
Curricular links	High	Authenticity	◑
Comprehensive coverage	Low	Collaboration	◐
Graduated scoring	Medium	Evidence	◕
Progress monitoring	Medium	Multifactors	◐
Standards alignment	Medium	Sensitivity	◔
Diversity features	Low	Universality	◐
Family engagement	High	Utility	◔
Teamwork	High		
Professional development	Low	OVERALL	◐
Technology	Low		

T U V

237

Close Up on next page

Transdisciplinary Play-Based Assessment, Second Edition (TPBA2), *and* Transdisciplinary Play-Based Intervention, Second Edition (TPBI2)

Author(s): Toni Linder, with invited contributors

Publication date: 2008

Publisher: Paul H. Brookes Publishing Co.

Web site(s): http://www.brookespublishing.com

Cost: $54.95 for *TPBA2*; $59.95 for *TPBI2*; $54.95 for *Administration Guide*

Assessment type: Curriculum-embedded assessment

Age range: Birth to 6 years

Domains/subtests: Sensorimotor, Emotional and Social, Communication, and Cognitive; *TPBA2* also includes tools for evaluating children's vision, hearing, and emerging literacy skills, though these tools are not considered an official component of the overall assessment

Population targeted: Children who are typically developing, advanced, and at risk as well as children with disabilities

Technology features: CD-ROM with forms and Office of Special Education Programs (OSEP) child outcomes reporting tool; *Observing Kassandra* DVD

Translations: None

Other features	Rating	Standard	Rating
Validated purposes	Medium	Acceptability	◑
Curricular links	High	Authenticity	◑
Comprehensive coverage	High	Collaboration	◑
Graduated scoring	High	Evidence	◑
Progress monitoring	High	Multifactors	◑
Standards alignment	Medium	Sensitivity	◑
Diversity features	High	Universality	◑
Family engagement	High	Utility	◑
Teamwork	High		
Professional development	Medium	OVERALL	◑
Technology	Medium		

TUV

Transdisciplinary Play-Based Assessment, Second Edition (TPBA2)

Author(s): Toni Linder, with invited contributors

About the Measure

The *TPBA2* is the premiere, play-based, curriculum-embedded assessment that relies on rich narratives of children during daily activities to determine their strengths and to identify functional intervention targets.

Building on the strengths of the original *TPBA*, the *TPBA2* continues with its tradition of functional developmental content, integral involvement by caregivers, and emphasis on transdisciplinary teaming.

A team completes every aspect of the decision-making process, including planning, conducting assessment, interpreting results, and providing instruction.

Authenticity

The *TPBA2* observational assessment occurs during a 1- to 1½-hour time period either at the child's home or in a play setting. During the assessment, the child is observed interacting with toys and materials. As needed, the assessor manipulates the environment to elicit behaviors in specific areas of functioning that have not yet been observed. For example, the assessor may place a puzzle in the setting to encourage independent play or provide balls to encourage social play.

The *TPBA2* does not require the use of a standard set of toys or materials. Before the assessment, parents complete the *Family Assessment of Child Functioning* form that provides information about the child's interests and preferences. The team uses this information to choose both preferred and nonpreferred toys, materials, and activities. If the child is assessed at home, the team would bring toys and materials to ensure the child has the ability to demonstrate skills targeted in each developmental domain.

During the assessment, the professional who is most familiar to the child serves as the play facilitator. Parents may also serve as play facilitators in addition to the professional play facilitator. (See the Collaboration section for more information about parent and professional roles during the assessment.)

Utility

The *TPBA2* offers significant guidance for users in transferring the assessment results to intervention goals and objectives in the form of a 12-step cyclic plan for assessment, goal development, intervention, and progress monitoring. Figure 1 shows the 12-step process along with a descriptive example of each step.

Table 9.2. Overview of the TPBI 12-step plan for Jamal

Step	Example
1. Identify strengths, needs, and desired global outcomes (GO).	A global outcome selected by Jamal's family was that Jamal have positive social relations. They also wanted him to be able to communicate effectively.
2. Identify priority subcategories contributing to outcomes.	Jamal's family chose Attention, Behavioral Regulation, and Language Production as key subcategories or areas for intervention.
3. Determine baseline of child's performance using Goal Attainment. Scales with the Functional Outcomes Rubric (FOR)	Jamal's parents circled *3* on Attention ("Selective focus of attention . . . only pays attention only to specific interests"); *3* on Behavioral Regulation ("Beginning to understand what not to do, but does it anyway"); and *1* on Language Production ("Expresses needs by crying, facial expression, and body movement").
4. Write functional intervention targets (FITs) or objectives.	For the targeted area of Attention, home and school, the team identified as a functional objective that "During play, Jamal will attend to the adult's face when he or she is talking to him for at least 5 seconds three times during each play time for a week, without verbal prompting."
5. Select activities, settings, and routines.	One of the routines selected by Jamal's family was play routines, because Jamal tends to play by himself and not interact with others. This is not a stressful or a pleasurable time, but they would like for him to enjoy playing with others.
6. Complete the Team Intervention Plan.	The following steps can be done in the same meeting, if time permits, or a meeting can be held at another time. The next steps require sufficient time for the team to thoroughly discuss issues and strategies.
7. Identify or create strategies.	One of the interpersonal strategies identified for Jamal was that his parents would position themselves in front of Jamal and get down on his level in front of his face and wait for him to look up before trying to talk to him. This would give him a visual focus of attention, in addition to the verbal input, making it more likely that he would attend to the message.
8. Individualize environmental and interpersonal strategies using TIP Strategies Checklists for ideas.	Jamal has favorite toys, foods, and routines. A plan was developed to make a picture schedule for Jamal of his daily routines, including pictures of his favorite things. His favorite objects and foods also would be put on picture cards and would be used for choice making and practice in labeling.
9. Write concrete examples.	"When giving Jamal a choice, hold up the actual objects (e.g., truck or ball) or a picture of the objects (e.g., bed or book) by your face to encourage him to look at you, and ask him in a short phrase, 'Jamal. Do you want the truck or the ball?'"
10. Determine how information will be shared.	The team provided the family with information on how to make picture schedules, recommended an upcoming class on encouraging turn-taking and language production, and gave them contacts for a parent support group.
11. Implement intervention.	The speech-language pathologist was the primary interventionist for Jamal. She met weekly with the team to discuss intervention strategies, obtain suggestions and feedback, and offer support. She made weekly consultation visits to the home and school, where she observed, coached, and provided demonstrations of intervention strategies. She frequently took another team member with her to provide an additional perspective and give her transdisciplinary input.
12. Evaluate progress and revise the plan.	After 4 months, the team had Jamal's parents and teacher once again complete the Goal Attainment Scales for the areas they had selected. All areas showed that he had increased his skills, and thus new targets were determined.

Figure 1.   Overview of TPBI 12-step plan. (From Linder, T. [2008]. *Transdisciplinary Play-Based Assessment, Second Edition [TPBA2]*. Baltimore: Paul H. Brookes Publishing Co.; reprinted by permission.)

Detailed examples of how teachers can support general development in each subdomain are provided in the *TPBI2* along with specific intervention strategies. In addition, intervention strategies focus on modifications to typical daily routines and activities rather than on discrete trial teaching of skills. For example, as a strategy to support emergent literacy in infants and toddlers, the *TPBI2* recommends that a caregiver name the foods a child is eating during mealtime or comment on the child's food.

A brief *Goal Attainment Scale* is provided for each subcategory in the *TPBI2;* this scale serves as a measure for progress monitoring. Figure 2 provides an example of the *Goal Attainment Scale* for the Strategies for Improving Attention subdomain of Cognitive Development.

When the *TPBA2* (assessment) and *TPBI2* (intervention) are used in tandem, the process of planning instruction and interventions based on assessment results is seamless and easy to follow.

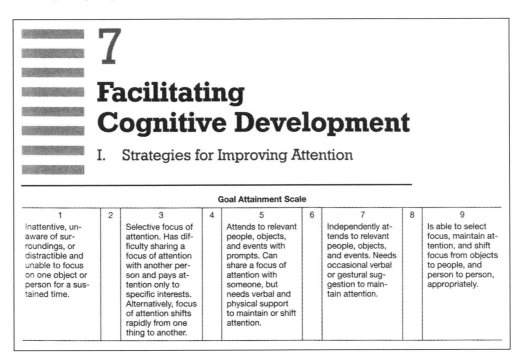

7

Facilitating Cognitive Development

I. Strategies for Improving Attention

Goal Attainment Scale

1	2	3	4	5	6	7	8	9
Inattentive, un-aware of sur-roundings, or distractible and unable to focus on one object or person for a sus-tained time.		Selective focus of attention. Has dif-ficulty sharing a focus of attention with another per-son and pays at-tention only to specific interests. Alternatively, focus of attention shifts rapidly from one thing to another.		Attends to relevant people, objects, and events with prompts. Can share a focus of attention with someone, but needs verbal and physical support to maintain or shift attention.		Independently at-tends to relevant people, objects, and events. Needs occasional verbal or gestural sug-gestion to main-tain attention.		Is able to select focus, maintain at-tention, and shift focus from objects to people, and person to person, appropriately.

Figure 2. Example of a Goal Attainment Scale. (From Linder, T. [2008]. *Transdisciplinary Play-Based Intervention, Second Edition [TPBI2]*. Baltimore: Paul H. Brookes Publishing Co.; reprinted by permission.)

Collaboration

The *TPBA2* requires a team approach to assessment, incorporating professional, parent, and caregiver information and participation. During the assessment, each professional team member serves as the expert in his or her specialty area. Each professional team member also serves in a non–discipline-specific role during the assessment as assigned by the team before the assessment. Non–discipline-specific roles include family facilitator, play facilitator, videographer, and observer. The *Administration Guide* suggests team members consider pro-fessionals' knowledge of the child and/or family, relationship with the child and/or family, per-sonalities, and conversational styles when assigning non–discipline-specific roles.

Parents are involved in many steps of the *TPBA2* assessment process. Information is ob-tained from the family and caregivers regarding the child's current functioning, health, and relevant history by completing the *Family Assessment of Child Functioning* and the *Child and Family History Questionnaire*. The family facilitator acts as an advocate for the family during the assessment process to ensure that the family members' input, values, and priorities are considered. Figure 3 describes strategies and rationale for including families in the assess-ment process. For example, the table offers the strategy, "Summarize the findings," and pro-vides the related rationale, "Reduces the large amount of information produced to an un-derstandable level and helps families prioritize what is most important."

T U V

Table 6.2. Family facilitation strategies and rationale

Strategy	Rationale
Feelings should be acknowledged.	Encourages families to share and discuss emotional effects of events; helps families know that professionals care.
Open-ended questions, supportive comments should be used.	Encourages families to share more information and to pursue a topic in their own direction rather than being led to a simple response.
Respect diverse cultures, including values, attitudes, and languages.	Encourages families to share information and be willing to incorporate a range of options in problem solving.
Follow-up is important.	Gives families an opportunity to comment, provide more information, and ask questions. It shows interest and encourages collaboration.
Attend to the family's priorities for their child.	Encourages team members to frame their observations and recommendations in terms of what is important to families, thus motivating collaboration.
Moderate pace and amount of information.	Helps families be able to hear what is most important and gives them time to process information and ask questions.
Illustrate what is meant with functional examples.	Makes the observations meaningful in relation to the lives and routines of the children and families, and thus promotes understanding and collaboration.
Listen to perceptions, and *Look* for positives.	Helps the team understand the child within the context of the family and helps families reframe a negative characteristic or behavior into something they can cope with in a more acceptable way.
Interpret findings in family-friendly terms.	Promotes understanding, acceptance, and adaptation to individual differences.
Encourage collaborative problem solving.	Increases likelihood that parents will follow through on recommendations when they have input into defining, exploring, and producing possible solutions that might work for their family.
Summarize the findings.	Reduces the large amount of information produced to an understandable level and helps families prioritize what is most important.

Figure 3. Family facilitation strategies and rationale. (From Linder, T. [2008]. *Transdisciplinary Play-Based Assessment, Second Edition [TPBA2]*. Baltimore: Paul H. Brookes Publishing Co.; reprinted by permission.)

Evidence Base

DeBruin, K.A. (2005). *A validation study of TPBA-R with the BDI-2*. Unpublished doctoral dissertation, University of Denver, Colorado.

The study sample included 45 children from 30 to 60 months who were eligible for IDEA services. Social validity and concurrent validity compared the *TPBA-R* with the *Battelle Developmental Inventory–2* were examined.

Linder, T.W. (2005). *Interrater reliability of the revised Transdisciplinary Play-Based Assessment*. Unpublished manuscript, University of Denver, Colorado.

A study of 55 individuals ranging from students in school psychology to experts in early childhood education and related fields (e.g., speech language pathology, occupational therapy) rated children using video footage of four previously administered *TPBA* assessments. Interobserver agreement was calculated for five subgroups of observers. The results ranged from 0.75 to 1.00, with the highest agreement from a team of experts who had completed numerous assessments together across several years using the *TPBA*.

Linder, T., Goldberg, G., & Goldberg, M. (2007). *The validity of the transdisciplinary construct for assessment*. Unpublished manuscript, University of Denver Colorado.

The authors completed a survey of 12 child development experts, three in each of four developmental domains. The survey measured the experts' perceptions of how problems in one subcategory of child development influenced perceptions of problems in another subcategory.

TUV

Linder, T., & Linas, K. (2009). A functional, holistic approach to developmental assessment through play. *Zero to Three, 30*(1), 28–33.

> The authors provide a summary of research on the *TPBA* and *TPBA2* in the context of current best-practice theories in early childhood assessment. The authors cite three additional studies that examined various aspects of validity of the *TPBA* and/or *TPBA2* (Cornett, 1998; Friedli, 1994; Linas, 2009).

Three additional studies examine reliability and validity of a play-based assessment system that is based on components of the TPBA (Kelly-Vance, Needleman, Troia, & Oliver, 1999; Kelly-Vance & Ryalls, 2005; Kelly-Vance, Ryalls, & Glover, 2002).

Note: *TPBA-R* and *TPBA2* are the same. *TPBA2* was called *TPBA-R* while under development.

Considerations and Recommendations

- The *TPBA2* is a continuation of a groundbreaking tradition by Linder that emphasizes play as the foundation for developmentally appropriate measurement of young children's learning through natural interactions with people and objects in the environment; the *TPBA2* is the exemplar of this approach.

- Each step of the assessment (e.g., Team Planning, Team Assessment, Team Analysis) and intervention (e.g., writing functional intervention targets; selecting activities, settings, and routines) processes is clearly and simply defined.

- The *TPBA2* needs research to support all intended and promoted purposes (e.g., identifying intervention targets, eligibility determination, Office of Special Education Programs [OSEP] child outcomes reporting).

T U V

Vineland Adaptive Behavior Scales, Second Edition (Vineland™-II)

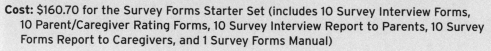

Author(s): Sara S. Sparrow, Domenic V. Cicchetti, and David A. Balla

Publication date: 2005

Publisher: NCS Pearson

Web site(s): http://psychcorp.pearsonassessments.com

Cost: $160.70 for the Survey Forms Starter Set (includes 10 Survey Interview Forms, 10 Parent/Caregiver Rating Forms, 10 Survey Interview Report to Parents, 10 Survey Forms Report to Caregivers, and 1 Survey Forms Manual)

Assessment type: Curriculum-referenced assessment with norms

Age range: *Survey Interview Form, Parent/Caregiver Rating Form, Expanded Interview Form:* Birth to 90 years
Teacher Rating Form: 3 years to 21 years, 11 months

Domains/subtests: Receptive and Expressive Communication, Daily Living (personal, domestic, and community), Social Skills and Relationships (interpersonal, play, and leisure), Gross and Fine Motor Skills, Problem Behaviors; links with International Classification of Functioning, Disability and Health: Children and Youth Version (ICF-CY) and makes it easier to use for applied purposes

Population targeted: Especially suitable for assessing individuals with mental retardation or who have difficulty performing in structured and contrived situations; normative sample: *n* = 1,200 (birth to 5 years, 11 months); *n* = 3,000 (birth to 18 years, 11 months); field-validated on various disability groups

Technology features: *ASSIST™* scoring software available for Mac and Windows for the *Interview Edition* (Expanded and Survey Forms) and for Windows only for the *Classroom Edition*

Translations: Spanish

Other features	Rating	Standard	Rating
Validated purposes	High	Acceptability	◑
Curricular links	Medium	Authenticity	◐
Comprehensive coverage	High	Collaboration	◐
Graduated scoring	Medium	Evidence	◑
Progress monitoring	Medium	Multifactors	◑
Standards alignment	Medium	Sensitivity	◐
Diversity features	Medium	Universality	◐
Family engagement	High	Utility	◐
Teamwork	High		
Professional development	Low	OVERALL	◑
Technology	Medium		

Close Up on next page

Vineland Social Emotional Early Childhood Scales (Vineland™ SEEC)

VINELAND Social-Emotional Early Childhood Scales

Author(s): Sara S. Sparrow, David A. Balla, and Domenic V. Cicchetti

Publication date: 1998

Publisher: NCS Pearson

Web site(s): http://psychcorp.pearsonassessments.com

Cost: $95.00 for kit (includes Manual and 25 Record Forms); $279.15 for CD Kit; $39.90 for 25 Record Forms

Assessment type: Curriculum-referenced assessment with norms

Age range: Birth through 5 years, 11 months

Domains/subtests: Interpersonal Relationships, Play and Leisure Time, and Coping Skills; these scores combine to yield a Social-Emotional Composite score

Population targeted: Children in need of social-emotional behavioral assessment or intervention; assessment is derived from Socialization component of the *Vineland Adaptive Behavior Scales, Expanded Form,* and shares its early childhood age norms: *n* = 3,000 including 200 individuals per age group through 11 years

Technology features: *Vineland SEEC ASSIST™* scoring and reporting software

Translations: Spanish

Other features	Rating	Standard	Rating
Validated purposes	Low	Acceptability	◐
Curricular links	Medium	Authenticity	◔
Comprehensive coverage	Medium	Collaboration	◐
Graduated scoring	Medium	Evidence	◔
Progress monitoring	Medium	Multifactors	◔
Standards alignment	Medium	Sensitivity	◐
Diversity features	Medium	Universality	◑
Family engagement	High	Utility	◑
Teamwork	Medium		
Professional development	Low	OVERALL	◐
Technology	Medium		

T U V

Vineland Social Emotional Early Childhood Scales (Vineland™ SEEC)

Author(s): Sara S. Sparrow, David A. Balla, and Domenic V. Cicchetti

About the Measure

The *Vineland Social Emotional Early Childhood Scales (Vineland™ SEEC)* is one of the best authentic and curriculum-referenced assessments with norms and emphasizes a developmental orientation to social-emotional progress expressed in real-life settings and routines.

The *Vineland™ SEEC* comprises infancy and early childhood competencies and normative data extracted from the *Vineland Adaptive Behavior Scales, Second Edition (Vineland™-II)*, and packaged in a more usable format for early childhood intervention.

Authenticity

Vineland™ SEEC domains are organized into Interpersonal Relationships, Play & Leisure Time, and Coping Skills. The clusters or subdomains organize specific competencies under important strands such as recognizing emotions, initiating social communication, following rules, and sharing and cooperating. Figure 1 illustrates the *Vineland™ SEEC*'s organization using the Coping Skills Scale as an example.

Skills measured in the *Vineland™ SEEC* can only be accurately observed and recorded by familiar and knowledgeable caregivers in a child's life and within a child's everyday settings and routines. The skills measured by the *Vineland™ SEEC* have been shown in various research studies to be building blocks or predictors of early school success.

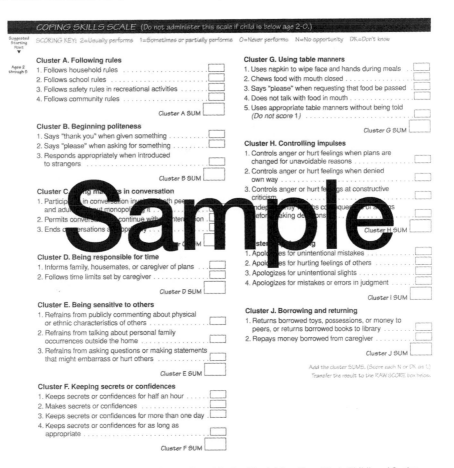

Figure 1. Coping Skills Scale sample items. (From *Vineland Social Emotional Early Childhood Scales [Vineland™ SEEC]*. Copyright © 1998 NCS Pearson, Inc. Reproduced with permission. All rights reserved.)

Utility

On the back of the scoring sheet, a *Program Planning Profile* can be found that provides a visual map of skills that the child has mastered (see Figure 2). This tool can aid users by clearly displaying a child's strengths and weaknesses relative to each other and to the norm group.

The competencies contained within the *Vineland™ SEEC* are phrased positively rather than being viewed as behavior problems. This aspect, along with the *Program Planning Profile*, enables teams to use the *Vineland™ SEEC* to create positively oriented, individualized intervention plans to build social-emotional competencies and prerequisite skills for early school success.

The *Vineland™ SEEC* ratings (2, 1, 0, *No opportunity*) provide a relatively graduated method to identify goals. The *Vineland™ SEEC* can be a core component to link to a program's general curriculum and to specifically promote social-emotional competence while having a balanced developmental approach.

T U V

247

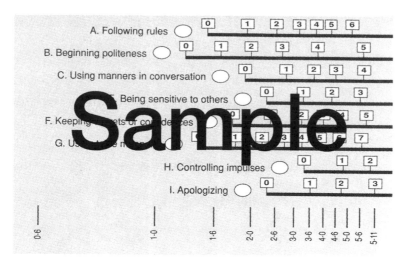

Figure 2. Sample of the Program Planning Profile. (From *Vineland Social Emotional Early Childhood Scales [Vineland™ SEEC]*. Copyright © 1998 NCS Pearson, Inc. Reproduced with permission. All rights reserved.)

The *Vineland™ SEEC* has national norms, which include individuals with disabilities, making the *Vineland™ SEEC* useful for eligibility determination and potentially for accountability purposes to meet Office of Special Education Programs (OSEP) mandates regarding child outcomes.

Collaboration

Completion of the *Vineland™ SEEC* requires parents and professionals to collaborate on rating the child's individual acquisition of specific competencies. Moreover, the program planning phase envisions parents and professionals cocreating the plan, goals, and strategies to promote these skills in home, preschool, and community contexts.

Evidence Base

The *Vineland™ SEEC* manual (Sparrow, Balla, & Cicchetti, 1998) includes descriptions and references to studies regarding the technical adequacy of the *Vineland™ SEEC* with children ages 6 months to 18 years.

- Altman and Mills (1990) examined the validity and sensitivity in a study of socialization scores on the *Vineland™ SEEC* for infants ages 18 and 24 months.

- Goldstein, Smith, Waldrep, and Inderbitzen (1987) examined the convergent validity of the *Vineland ABS Survey Form** compared with the *Scales of Independent Behavior Early Development Scale* and the *Scales of Independent Behavior Short Form*.

- Johnson, Cook, and Kullman (1992) studied the concurrent and convergent validity of the *Vineland ABS Survey Form* Socialization domain* through a comparison of *Battelle Inventory* scores for 67 children with motor delays.

- Numerous studies document the validity of the *Vineland™ SEEC* by identifying social-emotional scoring patterns for different developmental delays (Loveland & Kelley, 1991; Mayes, Volkmar, Hooks, & Cicchetti, 1993; Rodriguez, Morgan, & Geffken, 1991; Shonkoff, Hauser-Cram, Krauss, & Upshur, 1992; Sparrow & Cicchetti, 1987; Sparrow et al., 1986; Vig & Jedrysec, 1995; Volkmar et al., 1987).

- Payne, McGee-Brown, Taylor, and Dukes (1993) examined the predictive validity of *Vineland™ SEEC* results for 4-year-olds in school readiness preparation programs.

- Sparrow, Balla, and Cicchetti (1998) investigated the discriminiant validity of the *Vineland™ SEEC* scales by comparing it with the *Peabody Picture Vocabulary Test–Revised*.

- In a longitudinal study of 11 children with pervasive development disorder and 14 children who were typically developing, Sparrow et al. (1986) found similar cognitive and academic achievement scores between groups and statistically significantly different social-emotional scores on the *Vineland ABS*.

- In a study of 83 children ages 4–6 with developmental delays, Szatmari, Archer, Fisman, and Streiner (1994) examined parent and teacher correlations on the Socialization domain.

*The Socializalition domain in the *Vineland™ SEEC* is a replication of the Socialization domain in the *Vineland ABS* for birth to age 5 years, 11 months.

Considerations and Recommendations

- Arguably the most strength-based, positive, and comprehensive social-emotional scale for young children.

- National norms support use with diverse developmental disabilities/disorders.

- Although not a curriculum, the *Vineland™ SEEC* has many curricular qualities that enable its use for goal planning and general sequencing.

- With norms, the *Vineland™ SEEC* fulfills early childhood intervention purposes well for eligibility determination in the social-emotional domain, goal planning, and performance monitoring.

TUV

Vulpe Assessment Battery-Revised

Developmental Assessment • Performance Analysis • Individualized Programming for the Atypical Child

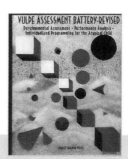

Author(s): Shirley German Vulpé

Publication date: 1994

Publisher: Slosson Educational Publications

Web site(s): http://www.slosson.com

Cost:: :$170.25

Assessment type: Curriculum-referenced assessment

Age range: Children functioning developmentally between birth and 6 years of age

Domains/subtests: Gross Motor, Fine Motor, Language, Cognitive Processes and Specific Concepts, Adaptive Behaviors, Activities of Daily Living, Assessment of the Environment, and Basic Senses and Functions

Population targeted: Children with atypical developmental patterns related to medical or social conditions that affect development; field tested in Australia, Canada, England, Ireland, South Africa, and the United States

Technology features: None

Translations: None

Other features	Rating	Standard	Rating
Validated purposes	Medium	Acceptability	◑
Curricular links	Medium	Authenticity	◐
Comprehensive coverage	High	Collaboration	◐
Graduated scoring	High	Evidence	◐
Progress monitoring	High	Multifactors	◑
Standards alignment	Medium	Sensitivity	◐
Diversity features	Low	Universality	◐
Family engagement	Medium	Utility	◑
Teamwork	High		
Professional development	Low	OVERALL	◑
Technology	Low		

TUV

Close Up
on next
page

The Work Sampling System®

Author(s): Samuel J. Meisels,
Dorothea B. Marsden, Judy R. Jablon,
Aviva B. Dorfman, and Margo K. Dichtelmiller

Publication date: 2004

Publisher: NCS Pearson

Web site(s): http://psychocorp.pearsonassessments.com

Cost: $208.00 for the kit (Manual, Guidelines, 30 Checklists, Rubrics, Wall Charts,
and Reproducible Summary Report and Documentation Masters)

Assessment type: Curriculum-referenced assessment

Age range: Prekindergarten through Grade 5

Domains/subtests: Personal and Social, Language and Literacy, Mathematical Thinking,
Scientific Thinking, Social Studies, The Arts, and Physical Development

Population targeted: Young children including children of diverse abilities and various cultural,
linguistic, economic, and social backgrounds; field validation over several studies: $n \geq 3{,}270$

Technology features: Online scoring (online annual license fee per child); training available
via *WebEx* and via DVD for the paper-and-pencil version

Translations: Summary Report Forms for parents are available in Spanish.

Other features	Rating	Standard	Rating
Validated purposes	Medium	Acceptability	◐
Curricular links	High	Authenticity	●
Comprehensive coverage	High	Collaboration	◕
Graduated scoring	High	Evidence	◑
Progress monitoring	High	Multifactors	◕
Standards alignment	High	Sensitivity	◔
Diversity features	Low	Universality	◕
Family engagement	Low	Utility	◑
Teamwork	Medium		
Professional development	Medium	OVERALL	◕
Technology	High		

W X Y Z

The Work Sampling System®

Author(s): Samuel J. Meisels, Dorothea B. Marsden,
Judy R. Jablon, Aviva B. Dorfman, and Margo K. Dichtelmiller

About the Measure

The *The Work Sampling System® (WSS)* provides an excellent structure for implementing developmentally appropriate programs for young children of all developmental levels. It exemplifies authentic assessment for classroom settings.

It is based on national and state standards and covers the domains of personal and social development, language and literacy, mathematical thinking, scientific thinking, social studies, the arts, and physical development.

The *WSS* incorporates different types of information to assist the teacher in deciphering the child's strengths and planning appropriate instruction.

Authenticity

The *WSS* uses teachers' perceptions to document child abilities, behavior, and knowledge across multiple areas of growth and development. The assessment focuses on developmentally appropriate curricular tasks across time and within the child's natural environment. Based on the premise that children have diverse learning styles, backgrounds, and needs, the flexible framework encourages teachers to recognize limitations and nurture strengths.

The checklist (see Figure 1) is completed on the basis of the child's performance on activities that are integrated into typical routines. Examples of ways the child might demonstrate a skill are provided, but instructions in the guidelines stress that the list is not exhaustive of all the ways the skill may be observed. Teachers can use methods relevant to children's needs, interests, and settings to plan individual and group lessons.

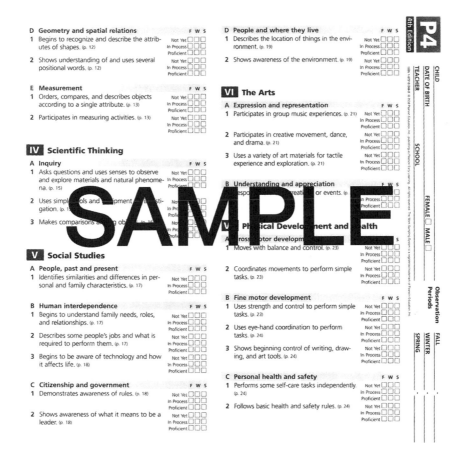

Figure 1. Sample of checklist. (From Preschool 3 and Preschool 4, *The Work Sampling System*®. Copyright © 2003 NCS Pearson, Inc. Reproduced with permission. All rights reserved.)

Utility

The *WSS* provides a systematic way of organizing and managing information collected from multiple sources. Through developmental guidelines, checklists, and portfolios, teachers are assisted in summarizing and recording their observations to monitor child progress and individualize instruction.

The developmental guidelines are broken down into separate booklets by year (e.g., *Preschool 3, Preschool 4, Kindergarten, First Grade*). The guidelines present developmentally appropriate expectations for children in each age/grade range. The guidelines are also represented in a separate text, the *Omnibus Guidelines,* allowing teachers the opportunity to view the developmental continuum of the system. Checklists are used to record observations. Portfolio development involves the child and illustrates the individuality and progression of his or her work over time. The portfolio also chronicles those instructional strategies and materials that are particularly effective for individual children.

The *WSS* is a valuable tool in helping children make the transition to kindergarten programs. Portfolios of children's work and developmental checklists provide information on specific competencies in domains relevant to kindergarten curricula.

In addition to paper administration, an online version is available that summarizes ongoing assessment three times annually for each child in a report that families can readily understand. Online training is also available.

Collaboration

The *Checklist* and *Summary Reports* are completed three times annually (fall, winter, and spring), facilitating communication between classroom teachers, special education teachers, consultants, and family members. Teachers and specialists are encouraged to collaborate when assessing and planning instruction. The system can be used to report progress to families, educators, and the community and to monitor progress and inform instruction.

Evidence Base

Gallant, D. (2009). Predictive validity evidence for an assessment program based on the Work Sampling System in mathematics and language and literacy. *Early Childhood Research Quarterly, 24*(2), 133–141.

A study of 1,281 elementary students examined the predictive validity of the *WSS* by comparing teacher ratings in first grade to student performance on a statewide assessment in third grade.

Meisels, S., Liaw, F., Dorfman, A., & Nelson, R. (1995). The Work Sampling System: Reliability and validity of a performance assessment for young children. *Early Childhood Research Quarterly, 10*(3), 277–296.

Investigated internal reliability, interrater reliability, concurrent validity, predictive validity, and criterion validity of the field test version of the *WSS* using a sample of 100 kindergarten-age children.

Four studies addressed various aspects of validity, including social and predictive validity, (Miesels et al., 2003; Miesels, Xue, Bickel, Nicholson, & Atkins-Burnett, 2001; Miesels, Xue, & Shamblott, 2008; Nicholson, 2000). Miesels et al. (2008) also addressed the reliability of the *WSS*.

Considerations and Recommendations

- Like the *Ounce Scale,* the *WSS* is an exemplar of an authentic assessment system that promotes collaboration among parents and professionals in sensible and friendly ways.

- The *WSS* is used as a measure for Office of Special Education Programs (OSEP) child outcome reporting in several states; therefore, evidence of validity and reliability for this purpose—and particularly for use with children with disabilities—is critical. Such evidence is needed to ensure the credibility of the *WSS* in the emerging integrated state early childhood education systems.

References

Abbott-Shim, M. (2000). *Sure Start Effectiveness Study: Final Report.* Atlanta: Quality Assist.

Allen, K., & Cowen, R. (2008). Using naturalistic procedures to teach children with autism. In J. Luiselli, D. Russo, W. Christian, & S. Wilczynski (Eds.), *Effective practices for children with autism. Educational and behavioral support interventions that work.* New York: Oxford University Press.

Altepeter, T.S., Moscato, E.M., & Cummings, J.A. (1986). Comparison of scores of hearing-impaired children on the Vineland Adaptive Behavior Scales and the Vineland Social Maturity Scale. *Psychological Reports, 59*(2), 635–639.

Altman, J., & Mills, B. (1990). Caregivers' behaviors and adaptive behaviors in home care and daycare. *Early Childhood Development and Care, 62,* 87–92.

Aman, M.G., Novotny, S., Samango-Sprouse, C., Lecavalier, L., Leonard, E., Gadow, K.D., et al. (2004). Outcome measures for clinical drug trials in autism. *CNS Spectrums, 9*(1), 36–47.

Anderson, S., Boigon, S., Davis, K., & deWaard, C. (2007). *The Oregon Project for Preschool Children who are Blind or Visually Impaired, Sixth Edition.* Medford: Southern Oregon Education Service District.

Arick, J., Nave, G., & Hoffman, T., (2000). *The Extended Career and Life Role Assessment System.* Salem: Oregon Department of Education.

Arick, J., Nave, G., Hoffman, T., & Krug, D.A. (2004). *FACTER: Functional Assessment and Curriculum for Teaching Everyday Routines.* Austin, TX: PRO-ED.

Atkinson, L. (1990). Standard errors of prediction for the Vineland Adaptive Behavior Scales. *Journal of School Psychology, 28,* 355–359.

Atkinson, L., Bevc, I., Dickens, S., & Blackwell, J. (1992). Concurrent validities of the StanfordBinet (fourth edition), Leiter, and Vineland with developmentally delayed children. *Journal of School Psychology, 30,* 165–173.

Ausubel, C. (1965). *Theory and problems of child development* (2nd ed.). New York: Grune and Stratton.

Bagnato, S.J. (2002). *Quality early learning—Key to school success: A first-phase 3-year program evaluation research report for Pittsburgh's Early Childhood Initiative, final report.* Available online at http://uclid.org:8080/uclid/pdfs/ecp_final_report.pdf

Bagnato, S.J. (2007). *Authentic assessment for early childhood intervention: Best practices.* New York: Guilford Press.

Bagnato, S.J. (2008). *Positive impact of a prevention approach to early childhood behavioral support on children's social and self-control skills and teacher interactions.* Pittsburgh, PA: Early Childhood Partnerships, HealthyCHILD. Retrieved from http://www.earlychildhoodpartnerships.org

Bagnato, S.J., Blair, K., Slater, J., McNally, R., Mathew, J., & Minzenberg, B. (2004). Developmental healthcare partnerships in inclusive early childhood intervention settings: The HealthyCHILD Model. *Infants and Young Children, 17*(4), 301–317.

Bagnato, S.J., Fevola, A.F., Hawthorne, C., Suen, H.K., & McKeating-Esterle, E. (2006). *The Pennsylvania Early Intervention Outcomes Study (PEIOS): An authentic assessment and program evaluation research and outcomes initiative—Final program evaluation outcomes research report.* Pittsburgh, PA: Children's Hospital of Pittsburgh, University of Pittsburgh, Early Children's Partnerships.

Bagnato, S.J., Fevola, A., Suen, H., Hawthorne, C., & McKeating-Esterle, E. (2006). *The Pennsylvania Early Intervention Outcomes Study (PEIOS): An authentic assessment and program evaluation outcomes and research initiative—Program outcomes research report.* Pittsburgh, PA: Children's Hospital of Pittsburgh, University of Pittsburgh, Early Children's Partnerships.

Bagnato, S., & Yeh Ho, H. (2006). High stakes testing with preschool children: Violation of professional standards for evidence based practice in early childhood intervention. *KEDI Journal of Educational Policy, 3*(1), 23–43. (Retrieved from Education Research Complete database.)

Bagnato, S.J., Macey, M., Salaway, J., & Lehman, C. (2007a). *Research foundations for authentic assessment for early intervention eligibility determination.* Washington, DC: U.S. Department of Education, Office of Special Education Programs, TRACE Center for Excellence.

Bagnato, S.J., Macey, M., Salaway, J., & Lehman, C. (2007b). *Research foundations for conventional tests and testing for early intervention eligibility determination.* Washington, DC: U.S. Department of Education, Office of Special Education Programs, TRACE Center for Excellence.

Bagnato, S.J., & McKeating-Esterle, E. (2007). *Research foundations for team assessment models in early intervention.* Washington, DC: U.S. Department of Education, Office of Special Education Programs, TRACE Center for Excellence.

Bagnato, S.J., McKeating-Esterle, E., & Bartolomasi. (2007). *Evidence-base for team assessment practices in early intervention.* Washington, DC: U.S. Department of

Education, Office of Special Education Programs, TRACE Center for Excellence.

Bagnato, S.J., McKeating-Esterle, E., Fevola, A., & Bortolomasi, P. (2008). Valid use of clinical judgment (informed opinion) for early intervention eligibility: Evidence base and practice characteristics. *Infants & Young Children, 21*(4), 334–349.

Bagnato, S.J., McKeating-Esterle, E., Fevola, A., & Hawthorne, C. (2007). *A comparison of clinical judgment (informed opinion) with performance-based assessment to document early intervention status in Pennsylvania.* Unpublished research manuscript.

Bagnato S.J., & Murphy, J.P., (1989). Validity of curriculum-based scales with young neurodevelopmentally disabled children: Implications for team assessment. *Early Education and Development, 1*(1), 50–63.

Bagnato, S.J., & Neisworth, J.T. (1981). *LINKing developmental assessment and curricula: Prescriptions for early intervention.* Rockville, MD: Aspen Publishers.

Bagnato, S.J., & Neisworth, J.T. (1990). *System to Plan Early Childhood Services (SPECS).* Circle Pines, MN: American Guidance Service.

Bagnato, S.J., & Neisworth, J.T. (1991). *Assessment for early intervention: Best practices for professionals.* New York: Guilford.

Bagnato, S.J., & Neisworth, J.T. (1995). A national study of the social and treatment "invalidity" of intelligence testing in early intervention. *Social Psychology Quarterly, 9*(2), 81–102.

Bagnato, S., Neisworth, J., & Munson, S. (1997). *LINKing assessment and early intervention: An authentic curriculum-based approach.* Baltimore: Paul H. Brookes Publishing Co.

Bagnato, S.J., Neisworth, J.T, Salvia, J.J., & Hunt, F.M. (1999). *Temperament and Atypical Behavior Scale (TABS): Early childhood indicators of developmental dysfunction.* Baltimore: Paul H. Brookes Publishing Co.

Bagnato, S.J., Smith-Jones, J., Matesa, M., & McKeating-Esterle, E. (2006). Research foundations for using clinical judgment (informed opinion) for early intervention eligibility determination. *Cornerstones, 2*(3), 1–14.

Bagnato, S.J., Suen, H., Brickley, D., Jones, J., & Dettore, E. (2002). Child developmental impact of Pittsburgh's Early Childhood Initiative (ECI) in high-risk communities: First-phase authentic evaluation research. *Early Childhood Research Quarterly, 17*(4), 559–589.

Bailey, E., & Bricker, D. (1986). A psychometric study of a criterion-referenced assessment instrument designed for infants and young children. *Journal of the Division of Early Childhood, 10*(2), 124–134.

Balboni, G., Pedrabissi, L., Molteni, M., & Villa, S. (2001). Discriminant validity of the Vineland Scales: Score profiles of individuals with mental retardation and a specific disorder. *American Journal on Mental Retardation, 106*(2), 162–172.

Bamburg, J.W., Cherry, K.E. , Matson, J.L., & Penn, D. (2001). Assessment of schizophrenia in persons with severe and profound mental retardation using the Diagnostic Assessment for the Severely Handicapped (DASH-II). *Journal of Developmental and Physical Disabilities, 13,* 319–332.

Benn, R. (1994). Conceptualizing eligibility for early intervention services. In D.M. Bryant & M.A. Graham (Eds.), *Implementing early intervention* (pp. 18–45). New York: Guilford Press.

Bergan, J.R., Bergan, J.R., Rattee, M., Field, J.K., Smith, K., Cunningham, K., et al. (2003). *The Galileo System for the Electronic Management of Learning.* Retrieved on

October 14, 2009, from the Assessment Technology, Inc., web site: http://www .ati-online.com/galileoPreschool/PreWelcomeTechManual.html

Bergan, J.R., Burnham, C.G., Feld, J.K., & Bergan, J.R. (2009). *The Galileo Pre-K On-line System for the Electronic Management of Learning.* Retrieved on October 14, 2009, from the Assessment Technology, Inc., web site: http://www.ati-online .com/pdfs/researchPreschool/GalileoTechManual.pdf

Blair, J.D. (2003). *Factor structure of the Devereux Early Childhood Assessment (DECA): Differences by age, race, gender, and rater.* Doctoral dissertation, University of South Florida.

Boschen, K.A., & Wright, V. (1994). The Pediatric Evaluation of Disability Inventory (PEDI): Results of a validity study in cerebral palsy. Part 1: Poster presented at the Annual meeting of the American Academy for Cerebral Palsy and Developmental Medicine. *Developmental Medicine and Child Neurology, 36*(7), 37.

Bredekamp, S. (1987). *Developmentally appropriate practice in early childhood programs serving children from birth through age 8.* Washington, DC: National Association for the Education of Young Children.

Bredekamp, S., & Copple, C. (2009). *Developmentally appropriate practice in early childhood programs* (3rd ed.). Washington, DC: National Association for the Education of Young Children.

Bricker, D. (Ed.). (2002). *Assessment, Evaluation, and Programming System for Infants and Children (AEPS®)* (2nd ed.). Baltimore: Paul H. Brookes Publishing Co.

Bricker, D., Bailey, E., & Slentz, K. (1990). Reliability, validity, and utility of the Evaluation and Programming System for Infants and Young Children (EPS-I). *Journal of Early Intervention, 14*(2), 147–160.

Bricker, D., Clifford, J., Yovanoff, P., Pretti-Frontczak, K., Waddell, M., Allen, D., et al. (2008). Eligibility determination using a curriculum-based assessment: A further examination. *Journal of Early Intervention, 31*(1), 3–21.

Bricker, D., & Pretti-Frontczak, K. (1997). *A study of psychometric properties of the Assessment, Evaluation, and Programming Test for Three to Six Years.* Unpublished report, Center on Human Development, Early Intervention Program, University of Oregon, Eugene.

Bricker, D., Yovanoff, P., Capt, B., & Allen, D. (2003). Use of a curriculum-based measure to corroborate eligibility decisions. *Journal of Early Intervention, 26*(1), 20–30.

Bronfenbrenner, U. (1979). *The ecology of human development: Experiments by nature and design.* Cambridge, MA: Harvard University Press.

Brue, A., & Oakland, T. (2001). The Portage Guide to Early Intervention: An evaluation of published evidence. *School Psychology International, 22*(3), 243–252.

Bruininks, R.H., Hill, B.H., Weatherman, R.F., & Woodcock, R.W. (1986). *Inventory for Client and Agency Planning.* Chicago: Riverside.

Burchinal, M., & Roberts, J. (1996). Quality of center child care and infant cognitive and language Development. *Child Development, 67*(2), 606–620.

California Department of Education, Special Education Division. (2008). *Reliability and validity of the Desired Results Developmental Profile access (DRDP access): Results of the 2005–2006 Calibration Study.* Retrieved August 17, 2009, from http:// www.draccess.org/assessors/Reliability/AnValidity.html

Campbell, F., & Ramey, C. (1995). Cognitive and school outcomes for high risk African-American students at middle adolescence: Positive effects of early intervention. *American Educational Research Journal, 32*(4), 743–772.

Canivez, G.L., & Bordenkircher, S.E. (2002). Convergent and divergent validity of the Adjustment Scales for Children and Adolescents and the Preschool and Kindergarten Behavior Scales. *Journal of Psychoeducational Assessment, 20,* 30.

Carney, A., & Merrell, K. (2002). Reliability and comparability of a Spanish-language form of the Preschool and Kindergarten Behavior Scales. *Psychology in the Schools, 39*(4), 367.

Carney, A., & Merrell, K. (2005). Teacher ratings of young children with and without ADHD: Construct validity of two child behavior rating scales. *Assessment for Effective Intervention, 30*(3), 65–75.

Carter, A.S., Volkmar, F.R., Sparrow, S.S., Wang, J.J., Lord, C., Dawson, G., et al. (1998). The Vineland Adaptive Behavior Scales: Supplementary norms for individuals with Autism. *Journal of Autism and Developmental Disorders, 28*(4), 287–302.

Cho, A. (2007). *The relationship between maternal stress and mothers' perceptions of their preschool children's social behaviors: A cross-cultural study of immigrant Korean mothers in the United States and Korean mothers in Korea* (Doctoral Dissertation, University of North Texas). Retrieved from Proquest Digital Dissertations (AAT 3288252).

Commission on Behavioral and Social Sciences and Education. (2002). *Minority students in special and gifted education.* Washington, DC: National Academies Press.

Committee on Disability in America, Jette, A., & Field, M. (2007). *The future of disability in America.* Washington, DC: National Academies Press.

Copple, C., & Bredekamp, S. (1997). *Developmentally appropriate practice in early childhood programs.* Washington, DC: National Association for the Education of Young Children.

Copple, C., & Bredekamp, S. (2008). Professional development: Getting clear about developmentally appropriate practice. *Young Children, 63*(1), 54–55.

Cornett, J.Y. (1998). *An investigation of the reliability and validity of two Transdisciplinary Play-Based Assessment methods: The open-ended and objective-based observation coding procedures* (Doctoral dissertation, Illinois State University). Retrieved from Dissertations & Theses: A&I (Pub. No. AAT 9924345)

Coster, W., Deeney, T., Haltiwanger, J., & Haley, S. (1998). *School Function Assessment: User's manual.* San Antonio, TX: The Psychological Corporation.

Coster, W., Mancini, M., & Ludlow, L. (1999). Factor structure of the school functional assessment. *Educational & Psychological Measurement, 59*(4), 665.

Cripe, J.J. (1990). *Evaluating the effectiveness of training procedures in a linked system approach to individual family service plan development* (Doctoral dissertation). Retrieved from Dissertations & Theses: A&I (Pub. No. AAT 9111099)

Cwik, M., & Espy, K. (2003). External validity of the *BRIEF®-P* in normally developing preschoolers. *Journal of the International Neuropsychological Society, 9,* 297.

Davies, P., Lee Soon, P., Young, M., & Clausen-Yamaki, A. (2004). Validity and reliability of the School Function Assessment in elementary school students with disabilities. *Physical & Occupational Therapy in Pediatrics, 24*(3), 23–43.

Day, P. (1974). *Validity of the ordinality of items in four subscales of the Callier-Azusa Scale (Edition E).* Unpublished manuscript, University of Texas at Dallas.

Day, P., & Stillman, R. (1974). *Interobserver reliability of the Callier-Azusa Scale.* Unpublished manuscript, University of Texas at Dallas.

de Bildt, A., Kraijer, D., Sytema, S., & Minderaa, R. (2005). The psychometric properties of the Vineland Adaptive Behavior Scales in children and adolescents with mental retardation. *Journal of Autism and Developmental Disorders, 35*(1), 53–62.

DeBruin, K.A. (2005). *A validation study of TPBA-R with the BDI-2.* Unpublished doctoral dissertation, University of Denver, Colorado.

Del Giudice, E., Titomanlio, L., Brogna, G., Bonaccorso, A., Romano, A., Mansi, G., et al. (2006). Early intervention for children with Down syndrome in southern Italy: The role of parent-implemented developmental training. *Infants & Young Children, 19*(1), 50–58.

Deno, S.L. (2003). *Curriculum-based measures: Development and perspectives: Assessment for effective intervention.* Retrieved on December 9, 2009, from http://www.progressmonitoring.net/CBM_Article_Deno.pdf.pdf

Desired Results *access* Project. (2007). *Desired Results Developmental Profile.* Available online at http://www.draccess.org

Desired Results *access* Project. (2010). *DRDP access manual.* Sacramento: California Department of Education, Special Education Division.

D'Eugenio, D.B., & Moersch, M.S. (Eds.). (1981). *Developmental Programming for Infants and Young Children: Preschool Developmental Profile.* Ann Arbor: University of Michigan Press.

Division for Early Childhood, Council for Exceptional Children. (2007). *Promoting positive outcomes for children with disabilities: Recommendations for curriculum, assessment and program evaluation.* Missoula, MT: Author.

Docette, J., & Freeman, R. (1980). Progress tests for the developmentally disabled: An introduction. *Exceptional Children, 52,* 199–204.

Dodge, D.T., Colker, L.J., & Heroman, C. (2010). *The Creative Curriculum for Preschool: Vol. 2. Interest areas* (5th ed.). Washington, DC: Teaching Strategies.

Doyle, A., Ostrander, R., Skare, S., Crosby, R.D., & August, G. (1997). Convergent and criterion-related validity of the Behavior Assessment System for Children Parent Rating Scales. *Journal of Clinical Child Psychology, 26,* 276–284.

Edwards, M. (2009). *Identifying at risk young children: A comparison of the Preschool and Kindergarten Behavior Scales, Second Edition and the Behavior Assessment System for Children, Second Edition* (Doctoral dissertation, Capella University). Available from Dissertations & Theses: A&I (AAT 3379265).

Edwards, M.C., Whiteside-Mansell, L., Conners N.A., & Deere, D. (2003). The Unidimensionality and reliability of the Preschool and Kindergarten Behavior Scales. *Journal of Psychoeducational Assessment, 21,* 16–31.

Ensher, G., Bobish, T.P., Gardner, E., Reinson, C.L., Bryden, D.A., & Foertsch, D.J. (2007). *Partners in Play: Assessing infants and toddlers in natural contexts.* Florence, KY: Cengage Learning.

Ensher, G.L., Clark, D.A., & Songer, N.S. (2009). *Families, infants, and young children at risk: Pathways to best practice.* Baltimore: Paul H. Brookes Publishing Co.

Feldman, B., Haley, S.M., & Coryell, J. (1990). Concurrent and construct validity of the Pediatric Evaluation of Disability. *Physical Therapy, 70*(10), 602–610.

Fenton, G., DArdia, C., Valente, D., DelVecchio, I., Fabrizi, A., & Bernabei, P. (2003). Vineland Adaptive Behavior profiles in children with autism and moderate to severe developmental delay. *Autism, 7*(3), 269–287.

Fevola, A., Bagnato, S.J., & Kronk, B. (2009). Authentic assessment of the social participation of young children with special needs: Promoting a universal social health vision through the ICF-CY. In R. Simeonsson (Ed.), *International issues in early childhood intervention.* New York: Oxford University Press.

Fevola, A.F., Bagnato, S.J., & Kronk, B. (2010). Authentic assessment of the social participation of young children with special needs: Promoting a universal social health vision through the ICF-CY. In F. Peterander, E. Bjorck-Akesson, & R.J. Simeonsson (Eds.), *Dimensions of early childhood intervention: Transatlantic perspectives.* Baltimore: Paul H. Brookes Publishing Co.

Fevola, A.F., Bagnato, S.J., Matesa, M., & Lehman, C. (2006). *Research review for characteristics of presumptive eligibility promoting early intervention.* Washington, DC: U.S. Department of Education, Office of Special Education Programs, TRACE Center for Excellence.

Foegen, A., & Deno, S. (1997). *General outcome measures in secondary mathematics: An exploration of relations to the NCTM goals.* (Retrieved from ERIC database.)

Frankenburg, W.K., & Dodds, J.B. (1969). *The Denver Developmental Screening Test.* Denver: University of Colorado Medical Center.

Freeman, B.J., DelHomme, M., Guthrie, D., & Zhang, F. (1999). Vineland Adaptive Behavior Scale scores as a function of age and initial IQ in 210 autistic children. *Journal of Autism and Developmental Disorders, 29*(5), 379–384.

Friedli, C.R. (1994). *Transdisciplinary Play-Based Assessment: A study of reliability and validity* (Doctoral dissertation, University of Colorado at Boulder). Retrieved from Dissertations & Theses: A&I (Pub. No. AAT 9506333)

Fujiura, G., & Yamaki, K. (1997). An analysis of ethnic variations in developmental disability prevalence and household economic status. *Mental Retardation, 35,* 286–294.

Fujiura, G.T., & Yamaki, K. (2000). Trends in the demography of childhood poverty and disability. *Exceptional Children, 66*(2), 187–199.

Gallant, D. (2009). Predictive validity evidence for an assessment program based on the Work Sampling System in mathematics and language and literacy. *Early Childhood Research Quarterly, 24*(2), 133–141.

Gao, X. (2008). *Validity of an authentic assessment in order to report young children's accountability data on early language, literacy and pre-math areas.* Unpublished doctoral dissertation, University of Kentucky, Lexington.

Gilbert, S.L. (1997). *Parent and teacher congruency on variations of a screening assessment: An examination (Report No. H023B50009).* Auburn, AL: Auburn University. Retrieved November 27, 2009, from http://www.eric.ed.gov/ERICDocs/data/ericdocs2sql/content_storage_01/0000019b/80/15/0e/46.pdf

Gioia, G.A., Espy, K., & Isquith, P.K. (2003). *BRIEF-P: Behavior Rating Inventory of Executive Function–Preschool version: Professional manual.* Lutz, FL: Psychological Assessment Resources.

Gioia, G.A., Isquith, P.K., & Espy, K. (2003). Construct validity of the Behavior Rating Inventory of Executive Function–Preschool version. *Journal of the International Neuropsychological Society, 9,* 297.

Goldstein, D.J., Smith, K.B., Waldrep, E.L., & Inderbitzen, H.M. (1987). Comparison of the Woodcock-Johnson Scales of Independent Behavior and Vineland Adaptive Behavior Scales in infant assessment. *Journal of Psychoeducational Assessment, 5,* 1–6.

Gould, J. (1981). *The mismeasure of man.* New York: W.W. Norton & Co.

Greenwood, C., Carta, J., Walker, D., Hughes, K., & Weathers, M. (2006). Preliminary investigations of the application of the early communication indicator (ECI) for infants and toddlers. *Journal of Early Intervention, 28*(3), 178–196.

Grisham-Brown, J., Hallam, R., & Pretti-Frontczak, K. (2008). Preparing Head Start personnel to use a curriculum based assessment: A model for implementation in the age of accountability. *Journal of Early Intervention (Innovative Practices)*.

Haley, S.M., Coster, J., & Fass, R.M. (1991). A content validity study of the Pediatric Evaluation of Disability Inventory. *Pediatric Physical Therapy 3*, 177–184.

Haley, S.M., Costar, W.J., Ludlow, L.H., Haltiwanger, J.T., & Andrellos, P.J. (1992). *Pediatric Evaluation of Disability Inventory (PEDI)*. Upper Saddle River, NJ: Pearson.

Halle, T., & Vick, J. E. (2007). *Quality in early childhood care and education settings: A Compendium of measures*. Washington, DC: U.S. Department of Health and Human Services.

Hamilton, D.A. (1995). *The utility of the Assessment Evaluation Programming System in the development of quality IEP goals and objectives for young children, birth to three, with visual impairments* (Doctoral dissertation, University of Oregon). Retrieved from Dissertations & Theses: A&I (Pub. No. AAT 9541906)

Hamilton, M.L. (1995). *A normative study of the Diagnostic Assessment for the Severely Handicapped (DASH) scale* (Doctoral dissertation, Louisiana State University and Agricultural & Mechanical College). Retrieved from Dissertations & Theses: A&I (Pub. No. AAT 9609090)

Hammill, D.D., Leigh, J.E., Pearson, N.A., & Maddox, T. (1998). *Basic School Skills Inventory–Third Edition (BSSI-3)*. Austin, TX: PRO-ED.

Harbin, G., Rous, B., & McLean, M. (2005). Issues in designing state accountability systems. *Journal of Early Intervention, 27*(3), 137–164.

Harrison, P.L., & Oakland T. (2003). *Adaptive Behavior Assessment System, Second Edition (ABAS-II)*. San Antonio, TX: Harcourt Assessment.

Hart, B., & Risley, T. (1995). *Meaningful differences in the everyday experience of young American children*. Baltimore: Paul H Brookes Publishing Co.

Hartford Foundation for Public Giving. (October 2004). *Hartford children are learning by leaps and bounds: Achievements of children involved in Brighter Futures Child Care Enhancement Project*. Hartford, CT: Author.

Head Start Bureau. (1992). *Head Start program performance standards* (DHHS Publication No. ACF92-31131). Washington, DC: U.S. Department of Health and Human Services.

Heroman, C., Burts, D.C., Berke, K., & Bickart, T.S. (2010). *Teaching Strategies GOLD™ Objectives for Development & Learning: Birth through kindergarten*. Washington, DC: Teaching Strategies.

HighScope Educational Research Foundation. (2002). Development and validation. In *User guide: Child Observation Record for Infants and Toddlers* (pp. 31–36). Ypsilanti, MI: High/Scope Press.

HighScope Educational Research Foundation. (2003). Preschool COR development and validation. In *User guide: Preschool Child Observation Record* (pp. 29–35). Ypsilanti, MI: High/Scope Press.

Holt, T., Gilles, J., Holt, A., & Davids, V. (2004). *HELP®—the Hawaii Early Learning Profile® for Preschoolers*. Palo Alto, CA: Vort Corporation.

Horowitz, S.H. (2006). *Recognition and response: RTI goes to preschool*. Available online at http://www.ncld.org/at-school/general-topics/early-learning-aamp-literacy/recognition-a-response-rti-goes-to-preschool

Hresko, W., Miguel, S., Sherbenou, R., & Burton, S. (1994). *Developmental Observation Checklist System*. Austin, TX: PRO-ED.

Hsia, T. (1993). *Evaluating the Psychometric Properties of the Assessment, Evaluation, and Programming System for Three to Six Years: AEPS Test.* Unpublished doctoral dissertation, University of Oregon, Eugene.

Hutchinson, K.T. (1999). The relationship between the affective processing capabilities and social skills functioning of children with Attention Deficit Hyperactivity Disorder (Doctoral dissertation, Columbia University). *Dissertation Abstracts International, 59*(10-B), 5566.

Hwang, J.L., & Davies, P.L. (2009). Rasch analysis of the School Function Assessment provides additional evidence for the internal validity of the activity performance scales. *American Journal of Occupational Therapy, 63*(3), 369–373.

Hwang, J., Davies, P., Taylor, M., & Gavin, W. (2002). Validation of School Function Assessment with elementary school children. *OTJR: Occupation, Participation and Health, 22*(2), 48–58.

Individuals with Disabilities Education Act Amendments of 1997, PL 105-17, 20 U.S.C. §§ 1400 *et seq.*

Individuals with Disabilities Education Act (IDEA) of 1990, PL 101-476, 20 U.S.C. §§ 1400 *et seq.*

Individuals with Disabilities Education Improvement Act (IDEA) of 2004, PL 108-446, 20 U.S.C. 1400 *et seq.*

Isquith, P.K., Crawford, J.S., Espy, K.A., & Gioia, G.A. (2005). Assessment of executive function in preschool-aged children. *Mental Retardation and Developmental Disabilities Research Reviews, 11,* 209–215.

Jaberg, P.E., Dixon, D.J., & Weis, G.M. (2009). Replication evidence in support of the psychometric properties of the Devereux Early Childhood Assessment. *Canadian Journal of School Psychology, 24*(2), 158–166.

Jain, M., Turner, D., & Worrell, T. (1994). The Vulpe Assessment Battery and the Peabody Developmental Motor Scales: A preliminary study of concurrent validity between gross motor sections. *Physical & Occupational Therapy in Pediatrics, 14*(1), 23–34.

Janus, M., & Offord, D. (2000). *The Early Development Instrument.* Montreal, Canada: McMaster University.

Jentzsch, C., & Merrell, K. (1996). An investigation of the construct validity of the Preschool and Kindergarten Behavior Scales. *Assessment for Effective Intervention, 21*(2), 1–15.

Johnson, L.J., Cook, M.J., & Kullman, A.J. (1992). An examination of the concurrent validity of the Battelle Developmental Inventory as compared with the Vineland Adaptive Scales and the Bayley Scales of Infant Development. *Journal of Early Intervention, 16*(4), 353–359.

Johnson-Cramer, N.L. (1998). *Assessment of school-aged children with comorbidity of attention deficit hyperactivity disorder and low birth weight classifications* (Doctoral dissertation, The University of Wisconsin–Madison). Retrieved from Dissertations & Theses: A&I (Pub. No. AAT 9829136)

Johnson-Martin, N.M., Attermeier, S.M., & Hacker, B.J. (2004a). *Assessment Log and Development Progress Charts for the Carolina Curriculum.* Baltimore: Paul H. Brookes Publishing Co.

Johnson-Martin, N.M., Attermeier, S.M., & Hacker, B.J. (2004b). *The Carolina Curriculum for Infants and Toddlers with Special Needs (CCITSN)* (3rd ed.). Baltimore: Paul H. Brookes Publishing Co.

Johnson-Martin, N.M., Hacker, B.J., & Attermeier, S.M., (2004). *The Carolina Curriculum for Preschoolers with Special Needs (CCPSN)* (2nd ed.). Baltimore: Paul H. Brookes Publishing Co.

Jones, A.B., Jr. (1999). *A three-tiered nosology for developmentally disabled adults living in a rural community.* (Doctoral dissertation, The Union Institute, Ohio). Retrieved from Dissertations & Theses: A&I (Pub. No. AAT 9916982)

Jones, S.C. (2003). *Childhood depression and resiliency: An evaluation of the Devereux Early Childhood Assessment Program.* Doctoral dissertation, University of Northern Iowa, Cedar Falls, IA.

Kamphaus, R.W. (1987). Defining the construct of adaptive behavior by the Vineland Adaptive Behavior Scales. *Journal of School Psychology, 25,* 97–100.

Kamphaus, R.W., Jiménez, M.E., Pineda, D.A., Rowe, E.W., Fleckenstein, L., Restrepo, M.A., et al. (2000). Análisis transcultural de un instrumento de dimensiones múltiples en el diagnóstico del déficit de atención. *Revista de Neuropsicología, Neuropsyqiatría y Neurociencias, 2,* 51–63.

Kaplan, A. (1964). *The conduct of inquiry.* San Francisco: Chandler Publishing.

Kelly-Vance, L., Needleman, H., Troia, K., & Oliver, B. (1999). Early childhood assessment: A comparison of the Bayley Scales of Infant Development and Play-Based Assessment in two-year-old at-risk children. *Developmental Disabilities Bulletin, 27,* 1–15.

Kelly-Vance, L., & Ryalls, B.O. (2005). A systematic, reliable approach to play assessment in preschoolers. *School Psychology International, 26*(4), 398–412.

Kelly-Vance, L., Ryalls, B.O., & Glover, K.G. (2002). The use of play assessment to evaluate the cognitive skills of two- and three-year-old children. *School Psychology International, 23,* 169–185.

Kim, Y. (1997). *Activity-Based Assessment: A Functional Approach to Determining Eligibility of Young Children.* Unpublished doctoral dissertation, University of Oregon, Eugene.

Knox, V., & Usen Y. (1998). Clinical review of the pediatric Evaluation of Disability Inventory. *British Journal of Occupational Therapy, 63,* 29–32.

Koralek, D. (1999). *Classroom strategies to promote children's social and emotional development.* Lewisville, NC: Kaplan Early Learning Company.

Korsten, J.E., Dunn, D., Foss, T.V., & Francke, M.K. (1993). *Every Move Counts.* Tucson, AZ: Therapy Skill Builders.

Kronk, B. (2004). *Mapping the ICF content to the VABS and ABAS-II.* Unpublished manuscript, University of Pittsburg.

Krug, D.A., Arick, J.R., & Almond, P.J. (2008). *Autism Screening Instrument for Educational Planning, Third Edition.* Austin, TX: PRO-ED.

Lambert, R.G. (n.d.). *The Developmental Continuum Assessment System for Ages 3 to 5: The assessment component of The Creative Curriculum for Preschool technical report.* Retrieved from http://www.teachingstrategies.com/content/ pageDocs/Dev_Continuum_Technical_Report.pdf

Lambert, R.G., & Capizzano, J. (2005). *Preschool curriculum evaluation research: US Department of education institute for educational sciences evaluation of the Creative Curriculum for Preschool.* Paper presented at the American Education Research Association conference. Retrieved from http://www.teachingstrategies.com/content/pageDocs/Lambert%20AERA%20Conference%20Paper.pdf

Lambert, R.G., & Capizzano, J. (2007). *The Creative Curriculum Developmental Continuum for Infants, Toddlers & Twos: The assessment component of the Creative Cur-*

riculum for Infants, Toddlers & Twos technical report. Retrieved from http://www
.teachingstrategies.com/content/pageDocs/Lambert%20Technical%20Report
%20Developmental%20Continuum%20for%20Infants,%20Toddlers%20&%20T
wos.pdf

Lapierre, C.B. (1999). *A comparison of the DASH-II (Diagnostic assessment for the Severely Handicapped-II) to pre-existing psychological diagnosis* (Doctoral dissertation, Texas A&M University). ProQuest Information & Learning (Pub. No. AAT 9943521)

Larson et al. (2003). *New Portage Guide Birth to Six.* Portage, WI: Cooperative Educational Service Agency.

Layburn, K.A. (2004). *An evaluation of an early childhood assessment program and its effect on preschool children* (Doctoral dissertation). Available from ProQuest Dissertations and Thesis database.

LeBuffe, P.A., & Naglieri, J.A. (1999). *Devereux Early Childhood Assessment.* Lewisville, NC: Kaplan Early Learning Company.

LENA Foundation. (2008). *Language Environment Analysis (LENA) System.* Boulder, CO: Author.

Lett, N.J., & Kamphaus, R.W. (1997). Differential validity of the BASC Student Observation System and the BASC Teacher Rating Scales. *Canadian Journal of School Psychology, 13,* 1–14.

Lewit, E., & Baker, L. (1996). Children in special education. *Future of Children, 6*(1), 139–151.

Lien, M.T., & Carlson, J. (2009). Psychometric properties of the Devereux Early Childhood Assessment in a Head Start sample. *Journal of Psychoeducational Assessment, 27*(5), 386–396.

Linas, K. (2009). *Concurrent validity of the Transdisciplinary Play Based Assessment-2* (Doctoral dissertation, University of Denver). Retrieved from Dissertations & Theses: A&I (Pub. No. AAT 3372480)

Linder, T.W. (2005). *Interrater reliability of the revised Transdisciplinary Play-Based Assessment.* Unpublished manuscript, University of Denver, Colorado.

Linder, T. (2008). *Transdisciplinary Play-Based Assessment* (2nd ed.). Baltimore: Paul H. Brookes Publishing Co.

Linder, T., & Linas, K. (2009). A functional, holistic approach to developmental assessment through play. *Zero to Three, 30*(1), 28–33.

Linder, T., Goldberg, G., & Goldberg, M. (2007). *The validity of the transdisciplinary construct for assessment.* Unpublished manuscript, University of Denver Colorado.

Lollar, D.J., & Simeonsson, R.J. (2005). Diagnosis to function: classification for children and youths. *Developmental and Behavioral Pediatrics, 26,* 323–330.

LoMurray, M. (2007). *The fidelity of DECA program implementation by the BECEP Head Start Program* (Master's thesis). Bismarck, ND: Minot State University.

Louisiana Department of Education. (2001). *Evaluation of the Starting Points Preschool Program: A follow-up study.* Retrieved from http://www.doe.state.la
.us/lde/ uploads/3006.pdf

Loveland, K.A., & Kelley, M.L. (1991). Development of adaptive behavior in preschoolers with autism or Down syndrome. *American Journal on Mental Retardation, 96,* 13–20.

Lowther, T.L. (2004). *The impact of a social skills intervention of the development of resiliency in preschool children* (Master's thesis). Available from ProQuest Dissertations and Thesis database (UMI 1424930).

Macey, M., Bagnato, S.J., Lehman, C., & Salaway, J. (2007). *Research foundations of authentic assessments ensure accurate and representative early intervention eligibility.* Pittsburgh, PA: UCLID Center.

Macy, M.G., Bricker, D.D., & Squires, J.K. (2005). Validity and reliability of a curriculum-based assessment approach to determine eligibility for part C services. *Journal of Early Intervention, 28*(1), 1–16.

Mahone, E.M., & Hoffman, J. (2007). Behavior ratings of executive function among preschoolers with ADHD. *The Clinical Neuropsychologist, 21*, 569–586.

Marquez, H.B. (2006). *School readiness: Kindergartners' social development and developmentally appropriate classrooms* (Doctoral Dissertation, Kansas State University). Retrieved from Proquest Digital Dissertations (AAT 3234509).

Matson, J.L., Hamilton, M., Duncan, D., Bamburg, J., Smiroldo, B., & Others, A. (1997). Characteristics of stereotypic movement disorder for self-injurious behavior assessed with the diagnostic assessment for the severely handicapped (DASH-II). *Research in Developmental Disabilities, 18*, 457–469.

Matson, J.L., Kiely, S.L., & Bamburg, J.W. (1997). The effect of stereotypes on adaptive skills as assessed with the DASH-II and Vineland Adaptive Behavior Scales. *Research in Developmental Disabilities, 18*(6), 471–476.

Matson, J.L., & Malone, C.J. (2006). Validity of the sleep subscale of the Diagnostic Assessment for the Severely Handicapped-II (DASH-II). *Research in Developmental Disabilities: A Multidisciplinary Journal, 27*(1), 85–92.

Matson, J.L., & Others, A. (1996). Characteristics of autism as assessed by the Diagnostic Assessment for the Severely Handicapped-II (DASH-II). *Research in Developmental Disabilities, 17*(2), 135–143.

Matson, J.L., Rush, K.S., Hamilton, M., Anderson, S.J., Bamburg, J.W., Baglio, C.S., et al. (1999). Characteristics of depression as assessed by the diagnostic assessment for the severely handicapped-II (DASH-II). *Research in Developmental Disabilities, 20*(4), 305–313.

Matson, J.L., & Smiroldo, B.B. (1997). Validity of the mania subscale of the diagnostic assessment for the severely handicapped-II (DASH-II). *Research in Developmental Disabilities, 18*(3), 221–225.

Matson, J.L., Smiroldo, B.B., & Hastings, T.L. (1998). Validity of the Autism/Pervasive Developmental Disorder subscale of the Diagnostic Assessment for the Severely Handicapped-II. *Journal of Autism and Developmental Disorders, 28*(1), 77–81.

Mayes, L., Volkmar, F., Hooks, M., & Cicchetti, D. (1993). Differentiating pervasive developmental disorder not otherwise specified from autism and language disorders. *Journal of Autism and Developmental Disorders, 23*(1), 79–90.

McCarthy, M.L., Silberstein, C.E., Atkins, E.A., Harryman, S.E., Sponseller, P.D., & Hadley-Miller, N.A. (2002). Comparing reliability and validity of pediatric instruments for measuring health and well-being of children with spastic cerebral palsy. *Developmental Medicine & Child Neurology, 44*(7), 468–476.

McCathren, R.B. (2000). Testing predictive validity of the communication composite of the Communication and Symbolic Behavior Scales. *Journal of Early Intervention, 23*(1), 36–46.

McConnell, S., McEvoy, M., & Priest, J. (2002). "Growing" measures for monitoring progress in early childhood education: A research and development process for individual growth and development indicators. *Assessment for Effective Intervention, 27*(4), 3–14.

Mcgrew, K.S., Bruininks, R.H., & Thurlow, M.L. (1992). Relationship between Measures of Adaptive Functioning and Community Adjustment for Adults with Mental Retardation. *Exceptional Children, 58*(6), 517–529.

Meisels, S.J., Beachy-Quick, K., & Wen, X. (2008). *Ounce scale validation project.* Retrieved February 11, 2010, from http://erikson.edu/default/research/facpresentations.aspx

Meisels, S.J., Atkins-Burnett, S., Xue, Y., Nicholson, J., Bickel, D., & Son, S. (2003). Creating a system of accountability: The impact of instructional assessment on elementary children's achievement test scores. *Education Policy Analysis Archives, 11*(9).

Meisels S., Liaw, F., Dorfman, A., & Nelson, R. (1995). The Work Sampling System: Reliability and validity of a performance assessment for young children. *Early Childhood Research Quarterly, 10*(3), 277–296.

Meisels, S.J., Marsden, D.B., Jablon, J.R., Dorfman, A.B., & Dichtelmiller, M.K. (1998). *The Work Sampling System.* San Antonio, TX: Pearson.

Meisels, S.J., Xue, Y., Bickel, D., Nicholson, J., & Atkins-Burnett, S. (2001). Parental reactions to authentic performance assessment. *Educational Assessment, 7*(1), 61–85.

Meisels, S.J., Xue, Y., & Shamblott, M. (2008). Assessing language, literacy and mathematics skills with Work Sampling for Head Start. *Early Education and Development, 19*(6), 963–981.

Merrell, K.W. (1995a). An investigation of the relationship between social skills and internalizing problems in early childhood: Construct validity of the Preschool and Kindergarten Behavior Scales, *Journal of Psychoeducational Assessment, 13,* 230–240.

Merrell, K.W. (1995b). Relationships among early childhood behavior rating scales: Convergent and discriminant construct validity of the Preschool and Kindergarten Behavior Scales. *Early Education and Development 6,* 253–264.

Merrel, K.W. (1996). Assessment of social skills and behavior problems in early childhood: The Preschool and Kindergarten Behavior Scales. *Journal of Early Intervention, 20,* 132–145.

Merrell, K. (2003). *Preschool and Kindergarten Behavior Scales–Second Edition.* Austin, TX: PRO-ED.

Merrell, K., & Holland, M. (1997). Social-emotional behavior of preschool-age children with and without developmental delays. *Research in Developmental Disabilities, 18*(6), 393–405.

Middleton, H.A., Keene, R.G., & Brown, G.W. (1990). Convergent and discriminant validities of the Scales of Independent Behavior and the revised Vineland Adaptive Behavior Scales. *American Journal on Mental Retardation, 94,* 669–673.

Mihaylov, S., Jarvis, S., Clover, A., & Beresford, B. (2004). Identification and description of environmental factors that influence participation of children with cerebral palsy. *Developmental Medicine and Child Neurology, 46*(5), 299–304.

Morgan, F.T. (2005). Development of a measure to screen for reactive attachment disorder in children 0–5 years. Doctoral dissertation, Alliant International University, Fresno, CA. *Proquest Dissertations , 81,* AAT 3173576.

Morgan, G., Shinn, T., Shea, L.M., & Sholes, S. (2002). *A research study on the generalization of functional routines.* Portland, OR: Portland State University.

Murphy, S.B. (2000). *The role of student and teacher ethnicity in the assessment of emotional and behavioral disorders: Examining ratings of student behavior on the Behavior Assessment System for Children* (BASC). Unpublished manuscript.

National Association for the Education of Young Children. (2003, November). *Early childhood curriculum, assessment, and program evaluation: Building an effective, accountable system in programs for children birth to age 8. A joint position statement of the National Association for the Education of Young Children (NAEYC) and the National Association of Early Childhood Specialists in State Departments of Education (NAECS/SDE).* Available online at http://www.naeyc.org/files/naeyc/file/positions/pscape.pdf

Neisworth, J.T., & Bagnato, S.J. (2004). The mismeasure of young children: The authentic assessment alternative. *Infants and Young Children, 17*(3), 198–212.

Nelson, B., Martin, R.P., Hodge, S., Havill, V., & Kamphaus, R. (1999). Modeling the prediction of elementary school adjustment from preschool temperament. *Personality and Individual Differences, 26,* 687–700.

Newborg, J. (2004). *Battelle Developmental Inventory–Second Edition (BDI-2).* Itasca, IL: Riverside.

Nicholas, D.S., & Case-Smith, J. (1996). Reliability and validity of the Pediatric Evaluation of Disability Inventory. *Pediatric Physical Therapy,* 15–24.

Nicholson, J.M. (2000). *Examining evidence of the consequential aspects of validity in a curriculum-embedded performance assessment* (Doctoral dissertation, University of Michigan). Retrieved from Dissertations & Theses: A&I. (Pub. No. AAT 9990953)

Niemeyer, J., & Scott-Little, C. (2002). *Assessing kindergarten children: A compendium of assessment instruments.* Retrieved July 1, 2009, from the SERVE: South Eastern Regional Vision for Education web site: http://www.serve.org/Assessment/assessment-publicationh.php

No Child Left Behind (NCLB) Act of 2001, PL 107-110, 115 Stat. 1425, 20 U.S.C. §§ 6301 *et seq.*

Noh, J. (2005). *Examining the psychometric properties of the second edition of the Assessment, Evaluation, and Programming System for Three to Six Years: AEPS Test 2nd Edition (3–6).* Unpublished doctoral dissertation, University of Oregon, Eugene.

Nordmark, E., Jarnlo, G.B., & Hagglund, G. (2000). Comparison of the Gross Motor Function Measure and Pediatric Evaluation of Disability Inventory in assessing motor function in children undergoing selective dorsal rhizotomy. *Developmental Medicine & Child Neurology, 42,* 245–252.

Notari, A., & Bricker, D. (1990). The utility of a curriculum-based assessment instrument in the development of individualized education plans for infants and young children. *Journal of Early Intervention, 14*(2), 117–132.

Notari, A., & Drinkwater, S.G. (1991). Best practice for writing child outcomes: An evaluation of two methods. *Topics in Early Childhood Special Education, 11*(3), 92–106.

Offord Centre for Child Studies. (2007/2008). *Early Development Instrument: A population-based measure for communities.* Available online at http://www.offord centre.com/readiness/files/EDI_2008_General_CON.PDF

Ogonowski, J., Kronk, R., Rice, C., & Feldman, H. (2004). Inter-rater reliability in assigning ICF codes to children with disabilities. *Disability & Rehabilitation, 26*(6), 353–361.

Ostrander, R., Weinfurt, K.P., Yarnold, P.R., & August, G.J. (1998). Diagnosing attention deficit disorders with the Behavioral Assessment System for Children and the Child Behavior Checklist: Test and construct validity analyses using optimal discriminant classification trees. *Journal of Consulting and Clinical Psychology, 66,* 660–672.

Ostrom, R.M. (1995). *Concurrent validation of the affective scale of the Diagnostic Assessment for the Severely Handicapped (DASH) scale* (Doctoral dissertation, George Fox University, Oregon). Retrieved from Dissertations & Theses: A&I (Pub. No. AAT 9613024)

Paclawskyj, T.R., Matson, J.L., Bamburg, J.W., & Baglio, C.S. (1997). A comparison of the Diagnostic Assessment for the Severely Handicapped-II (DASH-II) and the aberrant behavior checklist (ABC). *Research in Developmental Disabilities, 18*(4), 289–298.

Parks, S. (2007). *HELP®—the Hawaii Early Learning Profile® (0–3)*. Palo Alto, CA: Vort Corporation.

Payne, D., McGee-Brown, M., Taylor, P., & Dukes, M. (1993). Development and validation of a family environment checklist for use in selecting at-risk participants for innovative educational preschool programs. *Educational and Psychological Measurement, 53*(4), 1079–1084.

Pearson Education, Inc. (2009). *BASC and BASC-2 research bibliography*. Retrieved on July 31, 2009, from http://pearsonassess.com/NR/rdonlyres/45A61151-4AAC-412F-BB91-8CAE5F6FA7E6/0/BASC_BASC2_bib.pdf

Perenboom, R., & Chorus, A. (2003). Measuring participation according to the International Classification of Functioning, Disability and Health (ICF). *Disability & Rehabilitation, 25*(11/12), 577.

Perry, A., & Factor, D.C. (1989). Psychometric validity and clinical usefulness of the Vineland Adaptive Behavior Scales and the AAMD Adaptive Behavior Scale for an autistic sample. *Journal of Autism and Developmental Disorders, 19*(1), 41–55.

Pickens, J. (2009). Socio-emotional programme promotes positive behaviour in preschoolers. *Care in Practice, 15*(4), 261–278.

Pretti-Frontczak, K., & Brewer, D. (2005). *Early childhood assessment in an age of accountability*. Kent, OH: Kent State University.

Pretti-Frontczak, K., & Bricker, D. (2000). Enhancing the quality of individualized education plan (iep) goals and objectives. *Journal of Early Intervention, 23*(2), 92–105.

Prizant, B.M., Wetherby, A.M., Rubin, E., Laurent, A.C., & Rydell, P.J. (2006a). *The SCERTS® Model: A comprehensive educational approach for children with autism spectrum disorders: Vol. I. Assessment*. Baltimore: Paul H. Brookes Publishing Co.

Prizant, B.M., Wetherby, A.M., Rubin, E., Laurent, A.C., & Rydell, P.J. [2006b]. *The SCERTS® Model: A comprehensive educational approach for children with autism spectrum disorders: Vol. II. Program planning and intervention*. Baltimore: Paul H. Brookes Publishing Co.

Raggio, D.J., & Massingale, T.W. (1990). Comparability of the Vineland Social Maturity Scale and the Vineland Adaptive Behavior Scale-Survey form with infants evaluated for developmental delay. *Perceptual and Motor Skills, 71*, 415–418.

Raggio, D.J., & Massingale, T.W. (1993). Comparison of the Vineland Social Maturity Scale, the Vineland Adaptive Behavior Scales–Survey Form, and the Bayley Scales of Infant Development with infants evaluated for developmental delay. *Perceptual and Motor Skills, 77*, 931–937.

Raggio, D.J., Massingale, T.W., & Bass, J.D. (1994). Comparison of Vineland Adaptive Behavior Scales–Survey Form age equivalent and standard scores with the Bayley Mental Development Index. *Perceptual and Motor Skills, 79*, 203–206.

Redding, M.M. (1997). *Construct and criterion-related validity of the Diagnostic Assessment for the Severely Handicapped (DASH) scale* (Doctoral dissertation, Mississippi

State University). Retrieved from Dissertations & Theses: A&I (Pub. No. AAT 9818701)

Research Department, Florida Children's Forum. (2004). *Birth to three screening and assessment resource guide.* Retrieved July 1, 2009, from http://www.floridajobs .org/earlylearning/documents/resource.pdf.

Reyna, C., & Brussino, S. (2009). Psychometric Properties of the Preschool and Kindergarten Behavior Scales in a sample of Argentinean children from 3 to 7 years old. (Abstract). *Psykhe, 18*(2), 127–140.

Reynolds, C.R., & Kamphaus, R.W. (1992). *Behavior Assessment System for Children* (BASC). Circle Pines, MN: American Guidance Service.

Reynolds, C.R., & Kamphaus, R.W. (2002). *The clinician's guide to the behavior assessment system for children.* New York: The Guilford Press.

Reynolds, C.R., & Kamphaus, R.W. (2004). *Behavior Assessment System for Children, Second Edition (BASC™-2).* Upper Saddle River, NJ: Pearson.

Rinaldi, C., Rogers-Adkinson, D., & Arora, A. (2009). An exploratory study of the oral language and behavior skills of children with identified language and emotional disabilities in preschool. *International Journal of Early Childhood Special Education, 1*(1), 32–45.

Rodriguez, J.R., Morgan, S.B., & Geffken, G.R. (1991). A comparative evaluation of adaptive behavior in children and adolescents with autism, Down syndrome, and normal development. *Journal of Autism and Developmental Disorders, 21,* 187–196.

Ronka, C.S., & Barnett, D. (1986). A comparison of adaptive behavior ratings: Revised Vineland and AAMD ABS-SE. *Special Services in the Schools, 2*(4), 87–96.

Rosenbaum, P., Saigal, S., Szatmari, P., & Hoult L. (1995). Vineland Adaptive Behavior Scales as a summary of functional outcome of extremely low-birthweight children. *Developmental Medicine and Child Neurology, 37,* 577–586.

Rowland, C. (Ed.). (2009). *Assessing communication and learning in young children who are deafblind or who have multiple disabilities.* Portland: Oregon Health & Science University.

Sameroff, A., & Chandler, M. (1975). Transactional models in early social relations. *Human Development, 18,* 65–79.

Sandall, S., Hemmeter, M.L., Smith, B., & McLean, M. (2005). *DEC recommended practices in early intervention/early childhood special education* (2nd ed.). Longmont, CO: Sopris West.

Sandall, S., McClean, M., & Smith, B. (2005). *DEC recommended practices in early intervention/early childhood special education.* Arlington, VA: Council Exceptional Children.

Sanford, A.R., Zelman, J.G., Hardin, B.J., & Peisner-Feinberg, E.S. (2004). *Learning Accomplishment Profile, Third Edition (LAP-3).* Lewisville, NC: Kaplan Press.

Schultz, C.I. (1992) *Concurrent Validity of the Pediatric Evaluation of Disability Inventory.* Unpublished doctoral dissertation, Tufts University, Medford, MA.

Schultz, T., & Kagan, S.L. (2007). *Taking stock: assessing and improving early childhood learning and program quality. The report of the National Early Childhood Accountability Task Force.* Available online at http://www.pewtrusts.org/our_work_report_ detail.aspx?id=30962

Schwartz, I.S., Boulware, G.L., McBride, B.M., Sandall, S.R. (2001). Functional assessment strategies for young children with autism. *Focus on Autism and Developmental Disabilities, 16,* 222–231.

Schweinhart, L., & McNair, S. (1993). Observing young children in action to assess their development: The High/Scope Child Observation Record study. *Educational & Psychological Measurement, 53*(2), 445–455.

Sevin, J.A. (1993). *Dual diagnosis in persons with severe or profound mental retardation: A reliability study of the DASH* (Doctoral dissertation, Louisiana State University and Agricultural & Mechanical College). Retrieved from Dissertations & Theses: A&I (Pub. No. AAT 9405422)

Shearer, D. (1976). *Portage Guide to Early Education.* Portage, WI: Cooperative Educational Service Agency No. 12.

Shelby, M., Nagle, R., Barnett-Queen, L., Quattlebaum, P., & Wuori, D. (1998). Parental reports of psychosocial adjustment and social competence in child survivors of acute lymphocytic leukemia. *Children's Health Care, 27*(2), 113–129.

Sher, N. (1999). *Activity-based assessment: Facilitating curriculum linkage between eligibility evaluation and intervention.* Unpublished doctoral dissertation, University of Oregon, Eugene.

Shonkoff, J.P., Hauser-Cram, P., Krauss, M.W., & Upshur, C.C. (1992). Development of infants with disabilities and their families: Implications for theory and service delivery. *Monographs of the Society for Research in Child Development, 57*(6, Serial No. 230).

Shonkoff, J., & Meisels, S. (1991). Defining eligibility for services under PL 99-457. *Journal of Early Intervention, 15*(1), 21–25.

Simeonsson, R.J. (2006). *Children's rights and ICF-CY documentation.* Geneva: World Health Organization.

Simeonsson, R.J., & Bailey, D.B. (1991). *ABILITIES Index.* Chapel Hill: University of North Carolina at Chapel Hill.

Slentz, K. (1986). Evaluating the instructional needs of young children with handicaps: Psychometric adequacy of the Evaluation and Programming System–Assessment Level II (Doctoral dissertation). *Dissertation Abstracts International, 47*(11), 4072A.

Smith, R.L. (1978). *A study of the interrater reliability of the Behavioral Characteristics Progression* (Doctoral dissertation). Retrieved December 4, 2009, from Dissertations & Theses: A&I (Pub. No. AAT 7911092)

Snow, C.E., & Van Heme, S.B. (Eds.). (2008). *Early childhood assessment: Why, what, and how.* Washington, DC: National Academies Press.

Sok Mui, L., Rodger, S., & Brown, T. (2010). Learning related and interpersonal social skills constructs in two existing social skills assessments. *Occupational Therapy in Mental Health, 26*(2), 131–150.

Sparrow, S.S., Balla, D.A., & Cicchetti, D.V. (1998). *Vineland SEEC: Social Emotional Early childhood scales* (Manual). Circle Pines, MN: American Guidance Service.

Sparrow, S.S., & Cicchetti, D.V. (1985). Diagnostic uses of the Vineland Adaptive Behavior Scales. *Journal of Pediatric Psychology, 10*(2), 215–225.

Sparrow, S.S., & Cicchetti, D.V. (1987). Adaptive behavior and the psychologically disturbed child. *Journal of Special Education, 21*(1), 89–100.

Sparrow, S., Cicchetti, D., & Balla, D. (2005). *Vineland Adaptive Behavior Scales* (2nd ed.). Minneapolis, MN: Pearson Assessment.

Sparrow, S.S., Rescorla, L.A., Provence, S., Condon, S.O., Goudreau, D., & Cicchetti, D. (1986). Follow-up of "typical" children—A brief report. *Journal of the American Academy of Child and Adolescent Psychiatry, 25,* 181–185.

Stanford, A.R., Zelman, J.G., Hardin, B.J., & Peisner-Feinberg, E.S. (2004). *Learning Accomplishment Profile, Third Edition (LAP-3)*. Lewisville, NC: Kaplan Press.

Squires, J., & Bricker, D. (2009). *Ages & Stages Questionnaires®, Third Edition (ASQ-3™): A Parent-Completed Child-Monitoring System*. Baltimore: Paul H. Brookes Publishing Co.

Squires, J., Bricker, D., & Twombly, E. (2002). *Ages & Stages Questionnaires®: Social-Emotional (ASQ:SE): A parent-completed, child-monitoring system for social-emotional behaviors*. Baltimore: Paul H. Brookes Publishing Co.

Stevens, G.D. (1962). *A taxonomy in special education for children with body disorders.* Pittsburgh, PA: Department of Special Education and Rehabilitation.

Stillman, R. (1973). *Measuring progress in deaf-blind children: Use of the "Azusa Scale."* Dallas, TX: Callier Center for Communication Disorders. (ERIC Document Reproduction Service No. ED084729)

Stillman, R. (1974). *Callier-Azusa Scale: Assessment of Deaf-Blind Children*. Dallas, TX: Callier Center for Communication Disorders.

Straka, E. (1994). Assessment of young children for communication delays. *Dissertation Abstracts International, 56*(02), 456A. (UMI No. AAT95-19689)

Sturmey, P. (2001). An Exploratory Factor Analysis of the ICAP Maladaptive Behavior Items. *Journal of Developmental and Physical Disabilities, 13*(2), 137–140.

Sturmey, P., Matson, J.L., & Lott, J.D. (2004). The factor structure of the DASH-II. *Journal of Developmental and Physical Disabilities, 16*(3), 247–255.

Suen, H., Logan, C., Neisworth, J., & Bagnato, S. (1995). Parent–professional congruence: Is it necessary? *Journal of Early Intervention, 19*(3), 243–52.

Sundberg, K.B. (1992). *Inter-rater reliability of the Pediatric Evaluation of Disability Inventory: Parental and professional agreement*. Unpublished doctoral dissertation, Tufts University, Medford, MA.

Szatmari, P., Archer, L., Fisman, S., & Streiner, D.L. (1994). Parent and teacher agreement in the assessment of pervasive developmental disorders. *Journal of Autism and Developmental Disorders, 24*(6), 703–717.

Taylor, R.L., Richards, S.B., & Moody, S.L. (1990). Concurrent validity of the motor domain of the Vineland Adaptive Behavior Scales. *Perceptual and Motor Skills, 71*, 685–686.

Thompson, L., Combs, C., Shroeder, S., Morgan, & Feinstein, J. (2002). *A research study of pre-teaching essential core steps within functional routines*. Portland, OR: Portland State University.

Thorpe, J., Kamphaus, R.W., Rowe, E.W., & Fleckenstein, L. (2000, August). *Longitudinal effects of child adaptive competencies and, externalizing and internalizing behavior problems on behavioral and academic outcomes*. Paper presented at the meeting of the American Psychological Association, Washington, DC.

Tokcan, G. (2000). Functional recovery of children and adolescents with brain injury in an inpatient setting: Responsiveness of the Pediatric Evaluation of Disability Inventory. *Dissertation Abstracts International, 79* (AAT 1398029).

Trzyna, J. (1996). The test-retest reliability of the Pediatric Evaluation Disability Inventory. *Dissertation Abstracts International, 85* (AAT 1378586).

United Nations. (1998). *Convention on the rights of the child* (1577 U.N.T.S.3). Geneva: Author.

Vacca, M.M., & Koralek, D. (1999). *Devereux Early Childhood Assessment observation journal: A planning resource for the comprehensive DECA program*. Lewisville, NC: Kaplan Early Learning.

Valdovinos, M.G., Zarcone, J.R., Hellings, J.A., Kim, G., & Schroeder, S.R. (2004). Using the Diagnostic Assessment of the Severely Handicapped-II (DASH-II) to measure the therapeutic effects of risperidone. *Journal of Intellectual Disability Research, 48*(1), 53–59.

Van Leeuwen, S. (2007). *Validity of the Devereux Early Childhood Assessment instrument.* Dissertation University of British Columbia, Victoria.

VanDerHeyden, A.M. (2005). Intervention assessment practices in early childhood intervention: Measuring what is possible instead of what is present. *Journal of Early Intervention, 28*, 28–33.

Vaughn, M.L., Riccio, C.A., Hynd, G.W., & Hall, J. (1997). Diagnosing ADHD (predominantly inattentive and combined type subtypes): Discriminant validity of the Behavior Assessment System for Children and the Achenbach Parent and Teacher Rating Scales. *Journal of Clinical Child Psychology, 2*, 349–357.

Verhulst, F.C., Koot, H.M., & Van der Ende, J. (1994). Differential predictive value of parents' and teachers' reports of children's problem behaviors: A longitudinal study. *Journal of Abnormal Child Psychology, 22*, 531–546.

Vig, S., & Jedrysek, E. (1995). Adaptive behavior of young urban children with developmental disabilities. *Mental Retardation, 33*, 90–98.

Voelker, S.L., Johnston, T.C., Agar, C., Gragg, M., & Menna, R. (2007). Vineland survey: Self-administered checklist format for teachers of young children in rehabilitation. *Journal of Developmental and Physical Disabilities, 19*(3), 177–186.

Volkmar, F.R., Sparrow, S.S., Goudreau, D., Cicchetti, D.V., Paul, R., & Cohen, D.J. (1987). Social deficits in autism: An operational approach using the Vineland Adaptive Behavior Scales. *Journal of American Academy of Child and Adolescent Psychiatry, 26*, 156–161.

Vos-Vromans D.C., Ketelaar, M., & Gorter, J.W. (2005). Responsiveness of evaluative measures for children with cerebral palsy: The Gross Motor Function Measure and the Pediatric Evaluation of Disability Inventory. *Disability and Rehabilitation, 27*(20), 1245–1252.

Vulpe, S.G. (1977). Vulpe performance analysis scale: An inter-rater reliability study. In S.G. Vulpe, *The Vulpe Assessment Battery–Revised.* Aurora, NY: Slosson Educational.

Vulpe, S. (1994). *Vulpe Assessment Battery, Revised.* East Aurora, NY: Slosson Educational Publications.

Warren, S.F., Yoder, P.J. & Leew, S.V. (2002). *Promoting social-communicative development in infants and toddlers.* In H. Goldstein, L.A. Kaczmarek, & K.M. English (Vol. Eds.) & S.F. Warren & M.E. Fey (Series Eds.), *Communication and language intervention series: Vol. 10. Promoting social communication: Children with developmental disabilities from birth to adolescence* (pp. 121–149). Baltimore: Paul H. Brookes Publishing Co.

Watson, D.L. (2007). *An early intervention approach for students displaying negative externalizing behaviors associated with childhood depression: A study of the efficacy of play therapy in the school.* (Doctoral Dissertation, Capella University). Retrieved from Proquest Digital Dissertations (AAT 3266269).

Wetherby, A.M., Allen, L., Cleary, J., Kublin, K., & Goldstein, H. (2002). Validity and reliability of the Communication and Symbolic Behavior Scales Developmental Profile with very young children. *Journal of Speech, Language & Hearing Research, 45*(6), 1203–1218.

Wetherby, A.M., & Prizant, B.M. (2002). Technical characteristics. In *Communication and Symbolic Behaviors Scales Developmental Profile* (pp. 87–118). Baltimore: Paul H. Brookes Publishing Co.

Wetherby, A.M., & Prizant, B.M. (2003). *CSBS™™ Caregiver Questionnaire.* Baltimore: Paul H. Brookes Publishing Co.

Wetherby, A.M., Rubin, E., Laurent, A.C., Prizant, B.M., & Rydell, P.J. (2006). *Summary of research supporting the SCERTS® Model.* Retrieved February 12, 2010, from http://www.scerts.com/docs/ResearchSupportingtheSCERTSModel10-7-06.pdf

Whiteside-Mansell, L., Bradley, R.H., & McKelvey, L. (2009). Parenting and preschool child development: Examination of three low-income U.S. cultural groups. *Journal of Child and Family Studies, 18,* 48–60.

Wilcox, M., & Shannon, M. (Vol. Eds.). (1998). *Communication and language series: Vol. 5. Prelinguistic communication: Facilitating the transition from prelinguistic to initial linguistic communication.* Baltimore: Paul H. Brookes Publishing Co.

Winsler, A., & Wallace, G. (2002). Behavior problems and social skills in preschool children: parent-teacher agreement and relations with classroom observations. *Early Education and Development, 13*(1), 41-58.

World Health Organization. (2001). *International classification of functioning, disability and health.* Geneva: Author.

World Health Organization. (2007a). *International classification of functioning, disability and health: Children and youth version.* Geneva: Author.

World Health Organization. (2007b). *International statistical classification of diseases and related health problems* (10th rev.). Geneva: Author.

Wright, V., & Boschen, K.A. (1994). The Pediatric Evaluation of Disability Inventory (PEDI): Results of a reliability study in cerebral palsy, Part 2. *Developmental Medicine and Child Neurology, 36*(7), 37.

Yeh Ho, H., & Bagnato, S.J. (2007). *Research foundations for the use of social-emotional indicators to determine access to early intervention services.* Washington, DC: U.S. Department of Education, Office of Special Education Programs, TRACE Center for Excellence.

Youhua, W., Oakland, T., & Algina, J. (2008). Multigroup Confirmatory Factor Analysis for the Adaptive Behavior Assessment System-II Parent Form, Ages 5–21. *American Journal on Mental Retardation, 113*(3), 178–186.

Zaslow, M., Calkins, J., Halle, T., Zaff, J., & Margie, N.G. (2000). *Community-level school readiness: Definitions, assessments.* Washington, DC: Child Trends, Knight Foundations. Ausubel, C. (1965). *Theory and problems of child development* (2nd ed.). New York: Grune and Stratton.

Appendixes

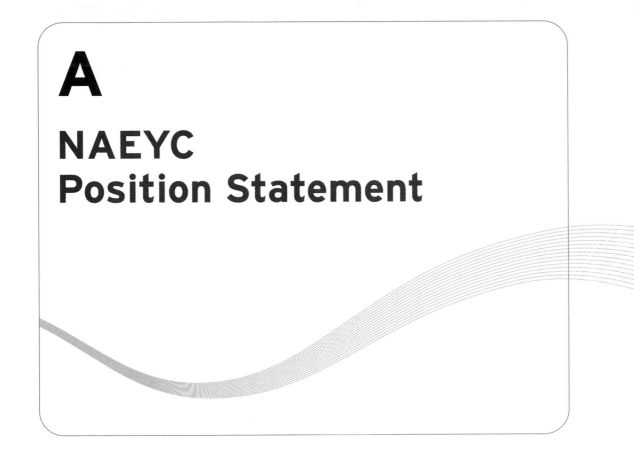

A

NAEYC
Position Statement

**POSITION STATEMENT
WITH EXPANDED RESOURCES**

Early Childhood Curriculum, Assessment, and Program Evaluation

Building an Effective, Accountable System in Programs for Children Birth through Age 8

This resource is based on the 2003 Joint Position Statement of the **National Association for the Education of Young Children** (NAEYC) and the **National Association of Early Childhood Specialists in State Departments of Education** (NAECS/SDE). It includes the statement of position, recommendations, and indicators of effectiveness of the position statement, as well as an overview of relevant trends and issues, guiding principles and values, a rationale for each recommendation, frequently asked questions, and developmental charts.

Introduction

High-quality early education produces long-lasting benefits (Schweinhart & Weikart 1997; National Research Council & Institute of Medicine 2000; Peisner-Feinberg et al. 2000; National Research Council 2001; Reynolds et al. 2001; Campbell et al. 2002). With this evidence, federal, state, and local decision makers are asking critical questions about young children's education. What should children be taught in the years from birth through age eight? How would we know if they are developing well and learning what we want them to learn? And how could we decide whether programs for children from infancy through the primary grades are doing a good job?

Answers to these questions—questions about *early childhood curriculum, child assessment,* and *program evaluation*—are the foundation of the joint position statement from the National Association for the Education of Young Children (NAEYC) and the National Association of Early Childhood Specialists in State Departments of Education (NAECS/SDE).

Overview

This document begins by summarizing the position of NAEYC and NAECS/SDE about what is needed in an effective system of early childhood education—a system that supports a reciprocal relationship among curriculum, child assessment, and program evaluation. Next, the document outlines the position statement's background and intended effects. It describes the major trends, new understandings, and contemporary issues that have influenced the position statement's recommendations. With this background, the document then outlines the principles and values that guide an interconnected system of curriculum, child assessment, and program evaluation. We emphasize that such a system must be linked to and guided by early learning standards and early childhood program standards that are consistent with professional recommendations (NAEYC & NAECS/SDE 2002; NAEYC 2003).

Next, key recommendations, rationales, and indicators of effectiveness are presented for each of these components, accompanied by frequently asked questions. Although the recommendations and indicators will generally apply to children across the birth–eight age range, in many cases the recommendations need developmental adaptation and fine-tuning. Where possible, the position statement notes these adaptations or special considerations. To further illustrate these developmental considerations, each component is accompanied by a chart (pp. 19-26) that gives examples of how the recommendations would be implemented with infants and toddlers, preschoolers, and kindergarten-primary grade children. This resource concludes by describing examples of the support and resources needed to develop effective systems of curriculum, child assessment, and program evaluation.

Position Statement Adopted November 2003

2

The Position

The National Association for the Education of Young Children and the National Association of Early Childhood Specialists in State Departments of Education take the position that policy makers, the early childhood profession, and other stakeholders in young children's lives have a shared responsibility to

• construct comprehensive systems of curriculum, assessment, and program evaluation guided by sound early childhood practices, effective early learning standards and program standards, and a set of core principles and values: belief in civic and democratic values; commitment to ethical behavior on behalf of children; use of important goals as guides to action; coordinated systems; support for children as individuals and members of families, cultures,[1] and communities; partnerships with families; respect for evidence; and shared accountability.

• implement curriculum that is thoughtfully planned, challenging, engaging, developmentally appropriate,[2] culturally and linguistically responsive, comprehensive, and likely to promote positive outcomes for all young children.

• make ethical, appropriate, valid, and reliable assessment a central part of all early childhood programs. To assess young children's strengths, progress, and needs, use assessment methods that are developmentally appropriate, culturally and linguistically responsive, tied to children's daily activities, supported by professional development, inclusive of families, and connected to specific, beneficial purposes: (1) making sound decisions about teaching and learning, (2) identifying significant concerns that may require focused intervention for individual children, and (3) helping programs improve their educational and developmental interventions.

• regularly engage in program evaluation guided by program goals and using varied, appropriate, conceptually and technically sound evidence, to determine the extent to which programs meet the expected standards of quality and to examine intended as well as unintended results.

• provide the support, professional development, and other resources to allow staff in early childhood programs to implement high-quality curriculum, assessment, and program evaluation practices and to connect those practices with well-defined early learning standards and program standards.

Position Statements' Intended Effects

In developing and disseminating position statements, NAEYC, NAECS/SDE, and their partner organizations aim to

• take informed positions on significant, controversial issues affecting young children's education and development[3] —in this case, issues related to curriculum development and implementation, the purposes and uses of assessment data, and benefits and risks in accountability systems for early childhood programs.

• promote broad-based dialogue on these issues, within and beyond the early childhood field.

• create a shared language and evidence-based frame of reference so that practitioners, decision makers, and families may talk together about early childhood curriculum, assessment, and program evaluation and their relationship to early learning standards and program standards.

• influence public policies—in this case, those related to early childhood curriculum development, adoption, and implementation; child assessment practices; and program evaluation practices—one by one and as these fit together into a coherent educational system linked to child outcomes or standards.

• stimulate investments needed to create accessible, affordable, high-quality learning environments and professional development that support the implementation of excellent early childhood curriculum, assessment, and program evaluation.

• build more satisfying experiences and better educational and developmental outcomes for all young children.

---

[1] The term *culture* includes ethnicity, racial identity, economic class, family structure, language, and religious and political beliefs, which profoundly influence each child's development and relationship to the world.

[2] NAEYC defines *developmentally appropriate practices* as those that "result from the process of professionals making decisions about the well-being and education of children based on at least three important kinds of information or knowledge: what is known about child development and learning...; what is known about the strengths, interests, and needs of each individual child in the group...; and knowledge of the social and cultural contexts in which children live" (Bredekamp & Copple 1997, 8–9).

[3] In this context, *development* is defined as the social, emotional, physical, and cognitive changes in children stimulated by biological maturation interacting with experience.

3

Trends and Issues

Since 1990, significant trends and contemporary issues, research findings, and new understandings of and changes in practice have influenced early childhood education. Many changes have had positive effects on the field and on the infants, toddlers, preschoolers, and kindergarten-primary children who are enrolled in early childhood programs. Other changes are less positive, raising concerns about how they may affect children's development, learning, and access to services.

To provide a context for the recommendations that follow, we outline some of these issues.

1. The contexts and needs of children, families, programs, and early childhood staff have changed significantly.

A snapshot taken today of the children and families served by our country's early childhood programs would look very different from one taken in 1990. Many more children would appear in the picture, as ever-higher proportions of children attend child care, Head Start, preschool, family child care, and other programs (Lombardi 2003; NIEER 2003). In more and more families, both parents work, further increasing the demand for child care, especially for infants and toddlers (Paulsell et al. 2002; Lombardi 2003). These changes in families' needs have influenced staffing patterns, hours of care, and other characteristics of programs for children before school entry, while also affecting the experiences children bring with them to kindergarten, first grade, and beyond.

The diversity of the U.S. population continues to expand, creating a far more multiethnic, multiracial, multireligious, and multicultural context for early childhood education. By the year 2030, 40 percent of all school-age children will have a home language other than English (Thomas & Collier 1997). Early childhood programs now include large numbers of immigrant children and children born to new immigrant parents, young children whose home language is not English, children living in poverty, and children with disabilities (Brennan et al. 2001; DHHS 2002; Rosenzweig, Brennan, & Ogilvie 2002; Annie E. Casey Foundation 2003; Hodgkinson 2003; U.S. Census Bureau 2003). These demographic trends have implications for decisions about curriculum, assessment practices, and evaluations of the effectiveness of early childhood programs.

Over the past decade, programs serving young children and families have also changed. Full-day and full-year child care and Head Start programs have expanded. Early Head Start did not exist in 1990, and few states offered prekindergarten programs either on a universal or targeted basis. In contrast, Early Head Start

in 2003 served approximately 62,000 low-income children from birth through age three (3 percent of the eligible children) and their families (ACF 2003), and 42 states and the District of Columbia had invested in prekindergarten programs based in or linked with public schools (Mitchell 2001), although most served relatively small numbers of children identified as living in poverty and at risk of school failure. Full-day kindergarten is now common in many school districts; in 2002, 25 states and the District of Columbia funded full-day kindergarten, at least in districts that chose to offer these services (Quality Counts 2002). Head Start programs increasingly collaborate with other early education programs, including state-funded prekindergarten programs, community-based child care providers, and local elementary schools (Head Start Program Performance Standards 1996; Lombardi 2003). Any new recommendations with respect to early childhood curriculum, child assessment, and program evaluation must take this expanded scope into account and must recognize the difficulties of coordinating and evaluating such a diverse array of programs.

National reports and government mandates have raised expectations for the formal education and training of early childhood teachers, especially in Head Start and in state-funded prekindergarten programs (National Research Council 2001; ASPE 2003). Teachers today are expected to implement more effective and challenging curriculum in language, literacy, mathematics, and other areas and to use more complex assessments of children's progress (National Research Council 2001). Both preschool teachers and teachers in kindergarten and the primary grades are expected to introduce academic content and skills to ever-younger children. These expectations, and the expanding number of early childhood programs, make the field's staffing crisis even more urgent, since the increased expectations have not been matched by increased incentives and opportunities for professional development.

The early childhood field lacks adequate numbers of qualified and sufficiently trained staff to implement appropriate, effective curriculum and assessment. Turnover continues to exceed 30 percent annually (Whitebook et al. 2001; Lombardi 2003), and compensation for early childhood educators continues to be inadequate and inequitable (Laverty et al. 2001). The staff turnover rate is greatly affected by a number of program characteristics, including the adequacy of compensation. All early childhood settings—including public-school-based programs—are experiencing critical shortages and turnover of qualified teachers, especially in areas that serve children who are at the highest risk for negative outcomes and who most need outstanding teachers (Keller 2003; Quality Counts 2003).

4

2. Evidence has accumulated about the value of high-quality, well-planned curriculum and child assessment.

In recent years, national reports and national organizations' position statements have sounded a consistent theme: Although children's fundamental needs are the same as ever, children, including the youngest children, are capable of learning more—and more complex—language, concepts, and skills than had been previously thought (National Research Council 2000; National Research Council & Institute of Medicine 2000; National Research Council 2001; Committee for Economic Development 2002).

We now have a better understanding of the early foundations of knowledge in areas such as literacy, mathematics, visual and performing arts, and science. In each of these areas, new research (for example, NAEYC & IRA 1998; National Research Council 1998; NAEYC & NCTM 2002) has begun to describe the sequences in which children become more knowledgeable and competent. This research is increasingly useful in designing and implementing early childhood curriculum. Well-planned, evidence-based curriculum, implemented by qualified teachers who promote learning in appropriate ways, can contribute significantly to positive outcomes for all children. Yet research on the effectiveness of specific curricula for early childhood remains limited, especially with respect to curriculum effects on specific domains of development and learning and curriculum to support young children whose home language is not English and children with disabilities.

3. State and federal policies have created a new focus on early childhood standards, curriculum, child assessment, and evaluation of early childhood programs.

Today, every state has K–12 standards specifying what children are expected to know and be able to do in various subject matter and/or developmental areas (Align to Achieve 2003). Head Start now has a Child Outcomes Framework (Head Start Bureau 2001), and a recent survey (Scott-Little, Kagan, & Frelow 2003) found that 39 states had or were developing standards for children below kindergarten age. As in the K–12 standards movement, states are beginning to link curriculum frameworks to early childhood standards (Scott-Little, Kagan, & Frelow 2003). Especially in the arena of literacy, both federal and state expectations emphasize the need for "scientifically based research" to guide curriculum adoption and evaluations of curriculum effectiveness.

The trend toward systematic use of child assessments and program evaluations has also led to higher stakes being attached to these assessments—in prekindergarten and Head Start programs as well as in kindergarten and the primary grades, where state accountability systems often dominate instruction and assessment. State investments in pre-K programs often come with clear accountability expectations. At every level of education, in an increasingly high-stakes climate, programs unable to demonstrate effectiveness in improving readiness or creating positive child outcomes may be at risk of losing support.

4. Attention to early childhood education has sometimes led to misuses of curriculum, assessment, and program evaluation.

Good intentions can backfire (Meisels 1992). In response to expectations that all programs should have a formal or explicit curriculum, programs sometimes adopt curricula that are of poor quality; align poorly with children's age, culture, home language (Tabors 1997; Fillmore & Snow 2000), and other characteristics; or focus on unimportant, intellectually shallow content (National Research Council 2001; Espinosa 2002). In other cases, a curriculum may be well designed but may be implemented with teaching practices ill suited to young children's characteristics and capacities (Bredekamp & Copple 1997). And few programs, districts, or states that adopt a particular curriculum track to see whether that curriculum is being implemented as intended and with good early childhood pedagogy.

Assessment practices in many preschools, kindergartens, and primary grade programs have become mismatched to children's cultures or languages, ages, or developmental capacities. In an increasingly diverse society, interpretations of assessment results may fail to take into account the unique cultural aspects of children's learning and relationships. As with curriculum, assessment instruments often focus on a limited range of skills, causing teachers to narrow their curriculum and teaching practices (that is, to "teach to the test"), especially when the stakes are high. An unintended result is often the loss of dedicated time for instruction in the arts or other areas in which high-stakes tests are not given.

In the press for results and accountability, basic tenets of appropriate assessment, as expressed by national professional organizations (for example, NASP 2002; AERA 2000; AERA, APA, & NCME 1999), are often violated. Assessments or screening tools may fail to meet adequate technical standards (Glascoe & Shapiro

5

2002), or assessments designed for one purpose (such as to guide teaching strategies) may be used for entirely different and incompatible purposes (NAEYC & NAECS/SDE 2002; Scott-Little, Kagan, & Clifford 2003). An example is the use of screening results to evaluate program effectiveness or to exclude children from services.

Summary

In the years since the publication of NAEYC's and NAECS/SDE's original position statement on early childhood curriculum and assessment (1990), much more has become known about the power of high-quality curriculum, effective assessment practices, and ongoing program evaluation to support better outcomes for young children. Yet the infrastructure of the early childhood education system, within and outside the public schools, has not allowed this knowledge to be fully used—resulting in curriculum, assessment systems, and program evaluation procedures that are not of consistently high quality. An overarching concern is that these elements of high-quality early education—curriculum, child assessment, and program evaluation—are often addressed in disconnected and piecemeal fashion.

The promise of a truly integrated, effective system of early childhood curriculum, assessment, and program evaluation is great. Although much is not yet known, greater research knowledge exists than ever before, and policy makers are convinced that early education is the key to later success, especially for our most vulnerable children. Despite disagreements about how best to use this key, early childhood educators today have unprecedented opportunities.

In taking advantage of these opportunities, clear principles and values are essential guides. Before turning to specific recommendations, the next section of this document proposes nine such principles.

Guiding Principles and Values

• Belief in civic and democratic values

The values of a democratic society guide the position statement's recommendations. Respect for others; equality, fairness, and justice; the ability to think critically and creatively; and community involvement are valued outcomes in early childhood programs. Decisions that affect young children, families, and programs involve stakeholders in democratic, respectful ways.

• Commitment to ethical behavior on behalf of children

NAEYC's Code of Ethical Conduct (NAEYC 1998) emphasizes that decisions about curriculum, assessment, and program evaluation must "first, do no harm"—never denying children access to services to which they are entitled and always creating opportunities for children, families, and programs to experience beneficial results.

• Use of important goals as guides to action

Clear, well-articulated goals that are developmentally and educationally significant—including early learning standards and program standards—direct the design and implementation of curriculum, assessment, and evaluation. These goals are public and are understood by all those who have a stake in the curriculum/assessment/evaluation design and implementation.

• Coordinated systems

The desired outcomes and content of the curriculum, the ways in which children's progress is assessed, and the evaluation of program effectiveness are coordinated and connected in a positive, continuous way.

• Support for children as individuals and as members of families, cultures, and communities

Curriculum, assessment, and program evaluation support children's diversity, which includes not only children's ages, individual learning styles, and temperaments but also their culture, racial identity, language, and the values of their families and communities.

• Respect for children's abilities and differences

All children—whatever their abilities or disabilities—are respected and included in systems of early education. Curriculum, assessment, and program evaluation promote the development and learning of children with and without disabilities.

• Partnerships with families

At all ages, but especially in the years from birth through age eight, children benefit from close partnerships and ongoing communication between their families and their educational programs.

• Respect for evidence

An effective system of curriculum, assessment, and program evaluation rests on a strong foundation of evidence. "Evidence" includes empirical research and well-documented professional deliberation and consensus, with differing weights given to differing types of evidence.

• Shared accountability

NAEYC and NAECS/SDE believe that professionals are indeed accountable to the children, families, and communities they serve. Although many aspects of children's lives are outside the influence of early

6

childhood programs, staff and administrators—as well as policy makers—must hold themselves accountable for providing all children with opportunities to reach essential developmental and educational goals.

Recommendations

This section presents recommendations for each of three critical elements of an effective system: curriculum, child assessment, and program evaluation. Each recommendation is followed by a rationale or justification. Next are listed indicators of effectiveness—what someone would be likely to see if the recommendation were well implemented. Because the position statement addresses the full birth–eight age range, appropriate distinctions are made wherever possible about how the recommendation or related indicators would be implemented with infants and toddlers, preschoolers, and kindergarten-primary children. A set of frequently asked questions is presented for each recommendation, and developmental charts provide examples that further elaborate these points.

Curriculum

Key Recommendation

Implement curriculum that is thoughtfully planned, challenging, engaging, developmentally appropriate, culturally and linguistically responsive, comprehensive, and likely to promote positive outcomes for all young children.

Rationale

Curriculum is more than a collection of enjoyable activities. *Curriculum* is a complex idea containing multiple components, such as goals, content, pedagogy, or instructional practices. Curriculum is influenced by many factors, including society's values, content standards, accountability systems, research findings, community expectations, culture and language, and individual children's characteristics.

Definitions and issues about the sources and purposes of curriculum have been debated for many years (Hyson 1996; Dahlberg, Moss, & Pence 1999; Marshall, Schubert, & Sears 2000; Goffin & Wilson 2001; Eisner 2002). Whatever the definition, good, well-implemented early childhood curriculum provides developmentally appropriate support and cognitive challenges and,

therefore, is likely to lead to positive outcomes (Frede 1998). A recurring theme in recent research syntheses has been that curriculum in programs for infants through the primary grades must be comprehensive, including attention to social and emotional competence and positive attitudes or approaches to learning (Peth-Pierce 2001; Raver 2002). Another emphasis is on the implementation of curricula providing cultural and linguistic continuity for young children and their families.

The position statement reflects the view that "curriculum that is goal oriented and incorporates concepts and skills based on current research fosters children's learning and development" (Commission on NAEYC Early Childhood Program Standards and Accreditation Criteria 2003). But what should children *learn* through this curriculum? The answer is influenced by children's ages and contexts. For example, for babies and toddlers, the curriculum's heart is relationships and informal, language-rich, sensory interactions. For second graders, relationships continue to be important as a foundation for building competencies such as reading fluency and comprehension. And for young children of all ages, the curriculum needs to build on and respond to their home languages and cultures.

Researchers have found that young children with and without disabilities benefit more from the curriculum when they are engaged or involved (Raspa, McWilliam, & Ridley 2001; NCES 2002). Particularly for younger children, firsthand learning—through physical, mental, and social activity—is key. At every age from birth through age eight (and beyond), play can stimulate children's engagement, motivation, and lasting learning (Bodrova & Leong 2003). Learning is facilitated when children can "choose from a variety of activities, decide what type of products they want to create, and engage in important conversations with friends" (Espinosa 2002, 5).

Widespread agreement exists that curriculum—including early childhood curriculum—should be based on evidence and evaluated for its effectiveness (National Research Council 2001). However, claims that specific curricula are *research based*—that is, evidence exists that these curricula are effective—are often not supported. A program can select a specific "research-based curriculum" for use with its enrolled children—confident that it is the right choice, when in reality the curriculum was shown to be effective with children who are older or younger, or who differ in culture or language, from the children for whom the curriculum is now being adopted. Other programs or school districts may adopt a curriculum for one specific area, such as reading or mathematics, with little regard for how that

7

curriculum aligns with, or is conceptually consistent with, other aspects of the program. The National Research Council (2001) warns that such a piecemeal approach can result in a disconnected conglomeration of activities and teaching methods, lacking focus, coherence, or comprehensiveness.

However, a body of longitudinal evidence does describe the long-term effects of some specific curriculum models or approaches—with benefits identified for curricula that emphasize child initiation (Schweinhart & Weikart 1997; Marcon 1999, 2002) and curricula that are planned, coherent, and well implemented (Frede 1998; National Research Council 2001). Evidence is also accumulating about development, learning, and effective early childhood curriculum in specific areas such as language and literacy (Hart & Risley 1995; Whitehurst & Lonigan 1998; Dickinson & Tabors 2001) and mathematics (NAEYC & NCTM 2002). Despite this evidence, there is still much we do not know. The forthcoming results of several federally funded programs of research on early childhood curriculum and other studies may help educators make better-informed decisions when adopting or developing curriculum. The goal is not to identify one "best" curriculum—there is no such thing—but rather to identify what features of a curriculum may be most effective for which outcomes and under which conditions.

Indicators of Effectiveness

• *Children are active and engaged.*

Children from babyhood through primary grades—and beyond—need to be cognitively, physically, socially, and artistically active. In their own ways, children of all ages and abilities can become interested and engaged, develop positive attitudes toward learning, and have their feelings of security, emotional competence, and linkages to family and community supported.

• *Goals are clear and shared by all.*

Curriculum goals are clearly defined, shared, and understood by all stakeholders (for example, program administrators, teachers, and families). The curriculum and related activities and teaching strategies are designed to help achieve these goals in a unified, coherent way.

• *Curriculum is evidence-based.*

The curriculum is based on evidence that is developmentally, culturally, and linguistically relevant for the children who will experience the curriculum. It is organized around principles of child development and learning.

• *Valued content is learned through investigation, play, and focused, intentional teaching.*

Children learn by exploring, thinking about, and inquiring about all sorts of phenomena. These experiences help children investigate "big ideas," those that are important at any age and are connected to later learning. Pedagogy or teaching strategies are tailored to children's ages, developmental capacities, language and culture, and abilities or disabilities.

• *Curriculum builds on prior learning and experiences.*

The content and implementation of the curriculum builds on children's prior individual, age-related, and cultural learning, is inclusive of children with disabilities, and is supportive of background knowledge gained at home and in the community. The curriculum supports children whose home language is not English in building a solid base for later learning.

• *Curriculum is comprehensive.*

The curriculum encompasses critical areas of development, including children's physical well-being and motor development; social and emotional development; approaches to learning; language development; cognition and general knowledge; and subject matter areas such as science, mathematics, language, literacy, social studies, and the arts (more fully and explicitly for older children).

• *Professional standards validate the curriculum's subject-matter content.*

When subject-specific curricula are adopted, they meet the standards of relevant professional organizations (for example, the American Alliance for Health, Physical Education, Recreation and Dance [AAHPERD], the National Association for Music Education [MENC]; the National Council of Teachers of English [NCTE]; the National Council of Teachers of Mathematics [NCTM]; the National Dance Education Organization [NDEO]; the National Science Teachers Association [NSTA]) and are reviewed and implemented so that they fit together coherently.

• *The curriculum is likely to benefit children.*

Research and other evidence indicates that the curriculum, if implemented as intended, will likely have beneficial effects. These benefits include a wide range of outcomes. When evidence is not yet available, plans are developed to obtain this evidence.

8

Early Childhood CURRICULUM: Frequently asked questions

1. What are curriculum goals?

The goals of a curriculum state the essential desired outcomes for children. When adopting a curriculum, it is important to analyze whether its goals are consistent with other goals of the early childhood program or with state or other early learning standards, and with program standards. Curriculum goals should support and be consistent with expectations for young children's development and learning.

2. What is the connection between curriculum and activities for children?

Whether for toddlers or second graders, a good curriculum is more than a collection of activities. The goals and framework of the curriculum do suggest a coherent set of activities and teaching practices linked to standards or expectations—although not in a simple fashion: Good activities support multiple goals. Together and over time, these activities and practices will be likely to help all children develop and learn the curriculum content. Standards and curriculum can give greater focus to activities, helping staff decide how these activities may fit together to benefit children's growth. Appropriate curriculum also promotes a balance between planned experiences—based on helping children progress toward meeting defined goals—and experiences that emerge as outgrowths of children's interests or from unexpected happenings (for example, a new building is being built in the neighborhood). While these experiences are not planned, they are incorporated into the program in ways that comply with standards and curriculum goals.

3. What are the most important things to consider in making a decision about adopting or developing a curriculum?

It is important to consider whether the curriculum (as it is or as it might be adapted) fits well with (a) broader goals, standards, and program values (assuming that those have been thoughtfully developed), (b) what research suggests are the significant predictors of positive development and learning, (c) the sociocultural, linguistic, and individual characteristics of the children for whom the curriculum is in-

tended, and (d) the values and wishes of the families and community served by the program. While sometimes it seems that a program's decision to develop its own curriculum would ensure the right fit, caution is needed regarding a program's ability to align its curriculum with the features of a high-quality curriculum (that is, to address the recommendation and indicators of effectiveness of the position statement). Considerable expertise is needed to develop an effective curriculum—one that incorporates important outcomes and significant content and conforms with research on early development and learning and other indicators noted in the position statement—and not merely a collection of activities or lesson plans (see also FAQ #7 in this section).

4. What should be the connection between curriculum for younger children and curriculum they will encounter as they get older?

Early childhood curriculum is much more than a scaled-back version of curriculum for older children. As emphasized in Early Learning Standards (NAEYC & NAECS/SDE 2002), earlier versions of a skill may look very different from later versions. For example, one might think that knowing the names of two U.S. states at age four in preschool is an important predictor of knowing all 50 states in fourth grade. However, knowing two state names is a less important predictor than gaining fundamental spatial and geographic concepts. Resources, including those listed at the end of this document, can help teachers and administrators become more aware of the curriculum in later years. With this knowledge, they can think and collaborate about ways for earlier and later learning to connect. Communication about these connections can also support children and parents as they negotiate the difficult transitions from birth–three to preschool programs and then to kindergarten and the primary grades.

5. Is there such a thing as curriculum for babies and toddlers?

Indeed there is, but as the developmental chart about curriculum suggests, curriculum for babies and toddlers looks very different from curriculum for preschoolers or

(continued on page 9)

9

Early Childhood CURRICULUM: FAQ (cont'd)

first-grade children. High-quality infant/toddler programs have clear goals, and they base their curriculum on knowledge of very early development. Thus a curriculum for children in the first years of life is focused on relationships, communicative competencies, and exploration of the physical world, each of which is embedded in daily routines and experiences. High-quality infant/toddler curriculum intentionally develops language, focusing on and building on the home language; promotes security and social competence; and encourages understanding of essential concepts about the world. This lays the foundation for mathematics, science, social studies, literacy, and creative expression without emphasizing disconnected learning experiences or formal lessons (Lally et al. 1995; Lally 2000; Semlak 2000).

6. When should the early childhood curriculum begin to emphasize academics?

There is no clear dividing line between "academics" and other parts of a high-quality curriculum for young children (Hyson 2003a). Children are learning academics from the time they are born. Even infants and toddlers are beginning—through play, relationships, and informal opportunities—to develop the basis of later knowledge in areas such as mathematics, visual and performing arts, social studies, science, and other areas of learning. As children transition into K–3 education, however, it is appropriate for the curriculum to pay focused attention to these and other subject matter areas, while still emphasizing physical, social, emotional, cognitive, and language development, connections across domains, and active involvement in learning.

7. Should programs use published curricula, or is it better for teachers to develop their own curriculum?

The quality of the curriculum—including its appropriateness for the children who will be experiencing it—should be the important question. If a published, commercially available curriculum—either a curriculum for one area such as literacy or mathematics or a comprehensive curriculum—is consistent with the position statement's recommendations and the program's goals and values, appears well suited to the children and families served by the program, and can be imple-

mented effectively by staff, then it may be worth considering, especially as a support for inexperienced teachers. To make a well-informed choice, staff (and other stakeholders) need to identify their program's mission and values, consider the research and other evidence about high-quality programs and curricula, and select a curriculum based on these understandings. Some programs may determine that in their situation the best curriculum would be one developed specifically for that program and the children and families it serves. In that case—if staff have the interest, expertise, and resources to develop a curriculum that includes clearly defined goals, a system for ensuring that these goals are shared by stakeholders, a system for determining the beneficial effects of the curriculum, and other indicators of effectiveness—then the program may conclude that it should take that route.

8. Is it all right to use one curriculum for mathematics, another for science, another for language and literacy, another for social skills, and still another for music?

If curricula are adopted or developed for distinct subject matter areas such as literature or mathematics, coherence and consistency are especially important. Are the goals and underlying philosophy of each curriculum consistent? What will it feel like for a child in the program? Will staff need to behave differently as they implement each curriculum? What professional development will staff need to make these judgments?

9. What's needed to implement a curriculum effectively?

Extended professional development, often with coaching or mentoring, is a key to effective curriculum implementation (National Research Council 2001). Well-qualified teachers who understand and support the curriculum goals and methods are more likely to implement curriculum effectively. So-called scripted or teacher-proof curricula tend to be narrow, conceptually weak, or intellectually shallow. Another key to success is assessment. Ongoing assessment of children's progress in relation to the curriculum goals gives staff a sense of how their approach may need to be altered for the whole group or for individual children.

10

Assessment of Young Children

Key Recommendation

Make ethical, appropriate, valid, and reliable assessment a central part of all early childhood programs. To assess young children's strengths, progress, and needs, use assessment methods that are developmentally appropriate, culturally and linguistically responsive, tied to children's daily activities, supported by professional development, inclusive of families, and connected to specific, beneficial purposes: (1) making sound decisions about teaching and learning, (2) identifying significant concerns that may require focused intervention for individual children, and (3) helping programs improve their educational and developmental interventions.

Rationale

Assessment components and purposes. Often people think of assessment as formal testing only, but assessment has many components and many purposes. Assessment methods include observation, documentation of children's work, checklists and rating scales, and portfolios, as well as norm-referenced tests. Consensus has developed around the four primary and distinctive purposes of early childhood assessment, best articulated in the work of the National Education Goals Panel (Shepard, Kagan, & Wurtz 1998). Issues concerning two of these purposes are the focus of this section of the position statement: (1) assessment to support learning and instruction and (2) assessment to identify children who may need additional services (Kagan, Scott-Little, & Clifford 2003). Two other purposes—assessment for program evaluation and monitoring trends and assessment for high-stakes accountability—will be discussed in the next recommendation, on Program Evaluation and Accountability.

High-quality programs are "informed by ongoing systematic, formal, and informal assessment approaches to provide information on children's learning and development. These assessments occur within the context of reciprocal communications with families and with sensitivity to the cultural contexts in which children develop" (Commission on NAEYC Early Childhood Program Standards and Accreditation Criteria 2003, np). For young bilingual children, instructionally embedded assessments using observational methods and samples of children's performance can provide a much fuller and more accurate picture of children's abilities than other methods. Individually, culturally, and linguistically appropriate assessment of all children's strengths, developmental status, progress, and needs provides

essential information to early childhood professionals as they attempt to promote children's development and learning (Meisels & Atkins-Burnett 2000; Stiggins 2001, 2002; McAfee & Leong 2002; Jones 2003).

When assessment is directed toward a narrow set of skills, programs may ignore the very competencies that have been shown to build a strong foundation for success in areas including but not limited to academics (National Research Council & Institute of Medicine 2000; Raver 2002). Furthermore, poor quality or poorly administered assessments, or assessments that are culturally inappropriate, may obscure children's true intellectual capacities. Many factors—anxiety, hunger, inability to understand the language of the instructions, culturally learned hesitation in initiating conversation with adults, and so on—may influence a child's *performance,* creating a gap between that performance and the child's actual ability, and causing staff to draw inaccurate conclusions that can limit the child's future opportunities.

Screening considerations. Research demonstrates that early identification and intervention for children with or at risk for disabilities can significantly affect outcomes (Shonkoff & Meisels 2000). Thus, early childhood programs play an important part in helping to identify concerns. Brief screening measures have been shown to be helpful in selecting children who may need further evaluation (Meisels & Fenichel 1996), but only if the screening tools meet high technical standards and if they are linked to access to further professional assessment.

Considerations in using individual norm-referenced tests. In general, assessment specialists have urged great caution in the use and interpretation of standardized tests of young children's learning, especially in the absence of complementary evidence and when the stakes are potentially high (National Research Council 1999; Jones 2003; Scott-Little, Kagan, & Clifford 2003). All assessment activities should be guided by ethical principles (NAEYC 1998) and professional standards of quality (AERA, APA, & NCME 1999). The issues are most pressing when individual norm-referenced tests are being considered as part of an assessment system. In those cases, the standards set forth in the joint statement of the American Educational Research Association, the American Psychological Association, and the National Center for Measurement in Education (AERA, APA, & NCME 1999) provide essential technical guidance. The "Program Evaluation and Accountability" section of this revised position statement discusses these issues in more detail.

11

Improving teachers' and families' assessment literacy. Teacher expertise is critical to successful assessment systems, yet such expertise is often lacking (Horton & Bowman 2002; Hyson 2003b; Scott-Little, Kagan, & Clifford 2003). Assessment literacy has been identified as a major gap in the preservice and inservice preparation of teachers (Stiggins 1999, 2002; Barnett 2003). Families are frequently given too little information about the purposes and interpretation of assessments of their children's development and learning (Popham 1999, 2000; Horton & Bowman 2002; Lynch & Hanson 2004).

Indicators of Effectiveness

• *Ethical principles guide assessment practices.*

Ethical principles underlie all assessment practices. Young children are not denied opportunities or services, and decisions are not made about children on the basis of a single assessment.

• *Assessment instruments are used for their intended purposes.*

Assessments are used in ways consistent with the purposes for which they were designed. If the assessments will be used for additional purposes, they are validated for those purposes.

• *Assessments are appropriate for ages and other characteristics of children being assessed.*

Assessments are designed for and validated for use with children whose ages, cultures, home languages, socioeconomic status, abilities and disabilities, and other characteristics are similar to those of the children with whom the assessments will be used.

• *Assessment instruments are in compliance with professional criteria for quality.*

Assessments are valid and reliable. Accepted professional standards of quality are the basis for selection, use, and interpretation of assessment instruments, including screening tools. NAEYC and NAECS/SDE support and adhere to the measurement standards set forth by the American Educational Research Association, the American Psychological Association, and the National Center for Measurement in Education (AERA, APA, & NCME 1999). When individual norm-referenced tests are used, they meet these guidelines.

• *What is assessed is developmentally and educationally significant.*

The objects of assessment include a comprehensive, developmentally, and educationally important set of goals, rather than a narrow set of skills. Assessments are aligned with early learning standards, with program goals, and with specific emphases in the curriculum.

• *Assessment evidence is used to understand and improve learning.*

Assessments lead to improved knowledge about children. This knowledge is translated into improved curriculum implementation and teaching practices. Assessment helps early childhood professionals understand the learning of a specific child or group of children; enhance overall knowledge of child development; improve educational programs for young children while supporting continuity across grades and settings; and access resources and supports for children with specific needs.

• *Assessment evidence is gathered from realistic settings and situations that reflect children's actual performance.*

To influence teaching strategies or to identify children in need of further evaluation, the evidence used to assess young children's characteristics and progress is derived from real-world classroom or family contexts that are consistent with children's culture, language, and experiences.

• *Assessments use multiple sources of evidence gathered over time.*

The assessment system emphasizes repeated, systematic observation, documentation, and other forms of criterion- or performance-oriented assessment using broad, varied, and complementary methods with accomodations for children with disabilities.

• *Screening is always linked to follow-up.*

When a screening or other assessment identifies concerns, appropriate follow-up, referral, or other intervention is used. Diagnosis or labeling is never the result of a brief screening or one-time assessment.

• *Use of individually administered, norm-referenced tests is limited.*

The use of formal standardized testing and norm-referenced assessments of young children is limited to situations in which such measures are appropriate and potentially beneficial, such as identifying potential disabilities. (See also the indicator concerning the use of individual norm-referenced tests as part of program evaluation and accountability.)

• *Staff and families are knowledgeable about assessment.*

Staff are given resources that support their knowledge and skills about early childhood assessment and their ability to assess children in culturally and linguistically appropriate ways. Preservice and inservice training builds teachers' and administrators' "assessment literacy," creating a community that sees assessment as a tool to improve outcomes for children. Families are part of this community, with regular communication, partnership, and involvement.

12

Child ASSESSMENT: Frequently asked questions

1. What is the connection between curriculum and assessment?

Curriculum and assessment are closely tied. Classroom- or home-based assessment tells teachers what children are like and allows them to modify curriculum and teaching practices to best meet the children's needs. Curriculum also influences what is assessed and how; for example, a curriculum that emphasizes the development of self-regulation should be accompanied by assessments of the children's ability to regulate their attention, manage strong emotions, and work productively without a great deal of external control.

2. What should teachers be assessing in their classrooms? When and why?

The answers to these questions depend, again, on the program's goals and on the curriculum being used. But all teachers need certain information in order to understand children's individual, cultural, linguistic, and developmental characteristics and to begin to recognize and respond to any special needs or concerns. The most important thing is to work with other staff and administrators to develop a systematic plan for assessment over time, using authentic measures (those that reflect children's real-world activities and challenges) and focusing on outcomes that have been identified as important. The primary goal in every case is to make the program (curriculum, teaching practices, and so on) as effective as possible so that every child benefits.

3. How is assessment different for children of varying ages, cultures, languages, and abilities?

The younger the child, the more difficult it is to use assessment methods that rely on verbal ability, on focused attention and cooperation, or on paper-and-pencil methods. The selection of assessments should include careful attention to the ages for which the assessment was developed. Even with older children (kindergarten–primary age), the results of single assessments are often unreliable for individuals, since children may not understand the importance of "doing their best" or may be greatly influenced by fatigue, temporary poor health, or other distractions. Furthermore, in some cultures competition and individual accomplishment are discouraged, making it difficult to validly assess young

children's skills. For young children whose home language is not English, assessments conducted in English produce invalid, misleading results. Finally, children with disabilities benefit from in-depth and ongoing assessment, including play-based assessment, to ensure that their individual needs are being met. When children with disabilities participate in assessments used for typically developing classmates, the assessments need adaptation in order for all children to demonstrate their competence (Meisels & Atkins-Burnett 2000; Sandall, McLean, & Smith 2000; McLean, Bailey, & Wolery 2004).

4. How should specific assessment tools or measures be selected? Is it better to develop one's own assessments or to purchase them?

Thorough discussion of early learning standards, program goals and standards, and the curriculum that the program is using will guide selection of specific assessment measures. In a number of cases, curriculum models are already linked to related assessments. It is important to think systemically so that assessments address all important areas of development and learning. This may seem overwhelming, but the same assessment tool or strategy often gives helpful information about multiple aspects of children's development. Other important considerations are whether a particular assessment tool or system will create undue burdens on staff or whether it will actually contribute to their teaching effectiveness. Issues of technical adequacy are also important to examine, especially for assessments used for accountability purposes. Special attention should be given to whether an assessment was developed for and tested with children from similar backgrounds, languages, and cultures as those for whom the assessment will be used. When selecting assessments for children whose home language is not English, additional questions arise; for example, are the assessment instruments available in the primary languages of the children who are to be assessed? Given these challenges, it seems tempting to develop an assessment tailored to the unique context of a particular program. However, beyond informal documentation, the difficulty of designing good assessments multiplies. Those who plan to develop their own assessment tools

(continued on page 13)

13

Child ASSESSMENT: FAQ (cont'd)

need to be fully aware of the challenges of standardizing and validating these assessments.

5. What is screening and how should it be used?

Screening is a quickly administered assessment used to identify children who may benefit from more in-depth assessment. Although screening tools are brief and appear simple, they must meet strict technical standards for test construction and be culturally and linguistically relevant. Only staff with sufficient training should conduct screening; families should be involved as important sources of information about the child; and, when needed, there should always be referrals to further specialized assessment and intervention. Screening is only a first step. Screening may be used to identify children who should be observed further for a possible delay or problem. However, screening should not be used to diagnose children as having special needs, to prevent children from entering a program, or to assign children to a specific intervention solely on the basis of the screening results. Additionally, screening results should not be used as indicators of program effectiveness.

6. What kind of training do teachers and other staff need to conduct assessments well?

Professional development is key to effective child assessment. Positive attitudes about assessment and "assessment literacy" (knowledge of assessment principles, issues, and tools) are developed through collaboration and teamwork, in which all members of an early childhood program come to agree on desired goals, methods, and processes for assessing children's progress. In addition, preservice programs in two- and four-year higher education institutions should provide students with research-based information and opportunities to learn and practice observation, documentation, and other forms of classroom-level assessment (Hyson 2003b). Understanding the purposes and limitations of early childhood norm-referenced tests, including their use with children with disabilities, is also part of assessment literacy, even for those not trained to administer such tests.

7. How should families be involved in assessment?

Ethically, families have a right to be informed about the assessment of their children. Families' own perspectives about their child are an important resource for staff. Additionally, families of young children with disabilities have a legal right to be involved in assessment decisions (IDEA 1997). Early childhood program staff and administrators share the results of assessments—whether informal observations or more formal test results—with families in ways that are clear, respectful, culturally responsive, constructive, and use the language that families are most comfortable with.

14

Program Evaluation and Accountability

Key Recommendation

Regularly evaluate early childhood programs in light of program goals, using varied, appropriate, conceptually and technically sound evidence to determine the extent to which programs meet the expected standards of quality and to examine intended as well as unintended results.

Rationale

With increased public investments in early childhood education come expectations that programs should be accountable for producing positive results (Scott-Little, Kagan, & Clifford 2003). The results of carefully designed program evaluations can influence better education for young children and can identify social problems that require public policy responses if children are to benefit. Program evaluations vary in scope from a relatively informal, ongoing evaluation that a child care center might conduct to improve its services, to large scale studies of the impact of statewide prekindergarten initiatives (Gilliam & Zigler 2000; Schweinhart 2003), to district and statewide evaluations of children's progress in the early grades of school. As part of this effort, program monitoring is an important tool for judging the quality of implementation and modifying how the program is being implemented.

The higher the stakes for programs and public investments, the more critical and rigorous should be the standards for evaluation design, instrumentation, and analysis, although this is not always the case (Henry 2003; Scott-Little, Kagan, & Clifford 2003). Evaluation specialists (for example, Shepard, Kagan, & Wurtz 1998; Jones 2003) emphasize that the goals of program evaluation are different from the goals of classroom-level assessment intended to improve teaching and learning. These specialists further emphasize that many instruments originally designed for one purpose cannot be validly used for other purposes. When such efforts are undertaken, special attention is needed to issues of sampling and aggregation (Horm-Wingerd, Winter, & Plocfchan 2000; Scott-Little, Kagan, & Clifford 2003).

Of particular importance is the issue of alignment—in this case, alignment of evaluation instruments with the identified goals of the program and with the curriculum or intervention that is being evaluated. Mismatches between program goals and evaluation design and instruments may lead to erroneous conclusions about the effectiveness of particular interventions (Yoshikawa & Zigler 2000; Muenchow 2003).

More and more states are using data about children's outcomes as part of a system to evaluate the effectiveness of prekindergarten and other programs. In this climate, clear guidelines are essential—guidelines about the technical properties of the measures to be used as well as the place of child-level data within a larger system that includes other data sources, such as assessments of classroom quality, parent interviews, or community-level data (Love 2003). Several issues have been discussed extensively: (1) the risk of misusing child outcome data to penalize programs serving the most vulnerable children, especially when no information is available about the gains children have made while in the program (Muenchow 2003); (2) the potential misuse of individually administered, norm-referenced tests with very young children as a substitute for, and as the sole indicator of, program effectiveness (Yoshikawa & Zigler 2000); (3) the risk of using data from assessments designed for English-speaking, European American children to draw conclusions about linguistically and culturally diverse groups of children; and (4) the risk of conducting poor quality evaluations because little investment has been made in training, technical assistance, and data analysis capabilities. Any effective system of program evaluation and accountability must take these issues into consideration.

Indicators of Effectiveness

• *Evaluation is used for continuous improvement.*

Programs undertake regular evaluation, including self-evaluation, to document the extent to which they are achieving desired results, with the goal of engaging in continuous improvement. Evaluations focus on processes and implementation as well as outcomes. Over time, evidence is gathered that program evaluations do influence specific improvements.

• *Goals become guides for evaluation.*

Evaluation designs and measures are guided by goals identified by the program, by families and other stakeholders, and by the developers of a program or curriculum, while also allowing the evaluation to reveal unintended consequences.

• *Comprehensive goals are used.*

The program goals used to guide the evaluation are comprehensive, including goals related to families, teachers and other staff, and community as well as child-oriented goals that address a broad set of developmental and learning outcomes.

• *Evaluations use valid designs.*

Programs are evaluated using scientifically valid designs, guided by a "logic model" that describes ways

15

in which the program sees its interventions having both medium- and longer-term effects on children and, in some cases, families and communities.

• *Multiple sources of data are available.*

An effective evaluation system should include multiple measures, including program data, child demographic data, information about staff qualifications, administrative practices, classroom quality assessments, implementation data, and other information that provides a context for interpreting the results of child assessments.

• *Sampling is used when assessing individual children as part of large-scale program evaluation.*

When individually administered, norm-referenced tests of children's progress are used as part of program evaluation and accountability, matrix sampling is used (that is, administered only to a systematic sample of children) so as to diminish the burden of testing on children and to reduce the likelihood that data will be inappropriately used to make judgments about individual children.

• *Safeguards are in place if standardized tests are used as part of evaluations.*

When individually administered, norm-referenced tests are used as part of program evaluation, they must be developmentally and culturally appropriate for the particular children in the program, conducted in the language children are most comfortable with, with other accommodations as appropriate, valid in terms of the curriculum, and technically sound (including reliability and validity). Quality checks on data are conducted regularly, and the system includes multiple data sources collected over time.

• *Children's gains over time are emphasized.*

When child assessments are used as part of program evaluation, the primary focus is on children's gains or progress as documented in observations, samples of classroom work, and other assessments over the duration of the program. The focus is not just on children's scores upon exit from the program.

• *Well-trained individuals conduct evaluations.*

Program evaluations, at whatever level or scope, are conducted by well-trained individuals who are able to evaluate programs in fair and unbiased ways. Self-assessment processes used as part of comprehensive program evaluation follow a valid model. Assessor training goes beyond single workshops and includes ongoing quality checks. Data are analyzed systematically and can be quantified or aggregated to provide evidence of the extent to which the program is meeting its goals.

• *Evaluation results are publicly shared.*

Families, policy makers, and other stakeholders have the right to know the results of program evaluations.

PROGRAM EVALUATION and ACCOUNTABILITY:
Frequently asked questions

1. What is the purpose of evaluating early childhood programs?

The primary purpose of program evaluation is to improve the quality of education and other services provided to young children and their families.

2. What is accountability?

The term *accountability* refers to the responsibility that programs have to deliver what they have been designed to do and, in most cases, what they have been funded to do. Accountability usually is emphasized when programs such as prekindergartens, public school programs, or Head Start have received local, state, or federal funds. In those cases the public has a legitimate interest in receiving information about the results obtained.

3. What standards of quality should be used in evaluating programs that serve young children?

Attention should be given to the goals that the program itself has identified as important. National organizations (such as NAEYC through its accreditation standards and criteria), state departments of education, and others have developed more general standards of quality. In addition, comprehensive observation instruments and other rating scales are widely used to obtain data on program quality. The advantage of using such measures, or participating in a national accreditation system, is that the program is evaluated against a broad set of criteria that have been developed with expert input.

(continued on page 16)

16

PROGRAM EVALUATION and ACCOUNTABILITY: FAQ (cont'd)

4. Is it necessary for all programs serving young children to be evaluated?

Programs differ in size, scope, and sponsorship. For some, regular evaluation is a requirement and condition of continued support. However, all programs serving young children and their families should undergo some kind of regular evaluation in order to engage in continuous self-study, reflection, and improvement. In large-scale state assessments (for example, of state prekindergarten programs), some data may be collected from all programs, while a smaller sample may participate in an intensive scientific evaluation with appropriate comparison groups (Schweinhart 2003).

5. What components should a program evaluation include?

Evaluation should always begin with a review of the program's goals and, where relevant, its mandated scope and mission. In every case the evaluation should address all components of the program as designed and as delivered. In other words, evaluation should include attention to the processes by which services and educational programs are delivered as well as to the outcomes or results. Outcomes, especially child outcomes, cannot be understood without knowing how effectively educational and other services were actually implemented.

6. Who should conduct program evaluations?

This depends on the scope and purpose of the evaluation. In some cases, program staff themselves are able to gather the information needed for review and improvement. However, greater objectivity is obtained when evaluations are conducted by others, often through in-depth interviews or discussions with staff and families. In high-stakes situations, it is not desirable for those who have a direct investment in the outcome of the evaluation to be involved in collecting and analyzing data.

7. What kinds of support are needed to conduct a good evaluation?

Adequate resources are essential, so that program evaluation does not drain resources from the actual delivery of services. Consultation about the design of the evaluation is helpful, as is assistance in gathering and interpreting data. Print and Web-based resources are available to those just getting started in thinking about program evaluation (ACYF 1997; Gilliam & Leiter 2003; McNamara 2003; Stake 2003). Support systems or facilitation projects are available to help programs that are preparing for accreditation or other evaluative reviews.

8. How should data gathered in a program evaluation be analyzed?

Once again, the purpose of the evaluation and the scope of the program and the evaluation itself will influence the answer to this question. Both quantitative and qualitative methods are appropriate and useful, depending on the questions being asked. Returning to the central questions of the evaluation will guide analysis decisions, since the results will help answer those questions.

9. How should information from a program evaluation be used?

As described earlier, program evaluation data are intended to improve program quality. In an open process, results are shared with stakeholders, who may include families, staff, community members, funders, and others. Objective discussion of strengths and needs in light of the program's goals and mission will help guide decisions about changes that would create even higher quality and more effective service delivery.

17

Data from program monitoring and evaluation, aggregated appropriately and based on reliable measures, should be made available and accessible to the public.

Creating Change through Support for Programs

Implementing the preceding recommendations for curriculum, child assessment, and program evaluation requires a solid foundation of support. Calls for better results and greater accountability from programs for children in preschool, kindergarten, and the primary grades have not been backed up by essential supports. All early childhood programs need greater resources and supportive public policies to allow the position statement's recommendations to have their intended effects.

The overarching need is to create an integrated, well-financed system of early care and education that has the capacity to support learning and development in all children, including children living in poverty, children whose home language is not English, and children with disabilities. Unlike many other countries (OECD 2001), the United States continues to have a fragmented system for educating children from birth through age eight, under multiple auspices, with greatly varying levels of support, and with inadequate communication and collaboration (Lombardi 2003). Several examples illustrate the kinds of supports that are needed.

Teachers as the key. As expectations for professional preparation and for implementing high-quality curriculum and assessment systems rise (National Institute on Early Childhood Development and Education 2000; National Research Council 2001), the early childhood field faces persistent low wages and high turnover (National Research Council 2001; Whitebook et al. 2001; Quality Counts 2002; Lombardi 2003). Yet research continues to underscore the role of formal education and specialized training in producing positive outcomes for children (National Research Council 2001), as well as less tangible teacher qualifications such as curiosity about children, willingness to engage in collaborative inquiry, and skilled communication with culturally and linguistically diverse families and administrators. Finding and keeping these highly qualified professionals, and ensuring a diverse and inclusive work force, will require significant public investment.

Standards for preparing new teachers. NAEYC's standards for early childhood professional preparation (Hyson 2003b) describe the knowledge, skills, and dispositions that higher education programs should develop in those preparing to teach young children. Those standards are fully consistent with and support the position statement's recommendations concerning curriculum and assessment. Expanded professional development resources will help better prepare higher education faculty to develop these competencies, using current, evidence-based information and practices. Strong accreditation systems create incentives for institutions to align their two-year, four-year, and graduate programs with these kinds of national standards.

The value of ongoing professional development. Although not replacing formal education, ongoing professional development is another key to helping staff implement evidence-based, effective curriculum and assessment systems for all children, responding to children's diverse needs, cultures, languages, and life situations. All staff—paraprofessionals as well as teachers and administrators—need access to professional development and to professional time and opportunities for collaboration that enable them to develop, select, implement, and engage in ongoing critique of curriculum and assessment practices that meet young children's learning and developmental needs. Time and resources for collaborative professional development now are often limited, both in public schools and in child care settings.

Research has identified many characteristics of effective staff development (National Research Council 2000; NAESP 2001; NSDC 2001; Education World 2003), yet much "training" still consists of one-time workshops with little follow-up, coaching, or mentoring (National Research Council 2000). The design and delivery of professional development often ignore the diversity of adult learners who vary in prior experience, culture, and education. In addition, little time is available for program staff—teachers, administrators, and others—to meet around critical issues of curriculum and assessment, or to prepare for program evaluations in a thoughtful way (National Research Council 2000). And once program evaluations are completed and results are available, public policies often fail to support needed improvements and expansion of services at the program, district, or state level—especially if the costs of the assessments themselves are absorbing resources needed in cash-strapped states and cities (Muenchow 2003).

Even well-qualified staff need ongoing, job-embedded professional development to help them better understand the curriculum, adapt curriculum to meet the learning needs of culturally and linguistically diverse children and children with disabilities, and design more effective approaches to working with all children. A key issue is creating genuine "learning communities" of

18

staff, within and across programs, who can support and learn from one another and from the wider professional environment as they implement integrated systems of curriculum and assessment. Resources beyond early education settings (for example, community cultural and civic resources such as arts organizations and libraries) can be tapped to supplement and enrich staff professional development opportunities.

Administrators' needs. Whether they are elementary school principals, child care directors, or Head Start coordinators, administrators hold the key to effective systems of curriculum, assessment, and program evaluation. Administrators are often the primary decision makers in adopting curriculum and assessment systems, arranging for staff development, and planning program evaluations. For administators, intensive and

ongoing professional development is essential—often participating in the same training provided to staff to create a shared frame of reference. This professional development needs to address administrators' varied backgrounds, work settings, and needs. For example, some elementary school administrators have not yet had opportunities to gain insights into the learning and developmental characteristics of young children. Others may be well grounded in infant/toddler or preschool education yet have had little opportunity to communicate with and collaborate with other administrators whose programs serve children as they transition from Head Start or child care into public schools.

A shared commitment. As these examples show, many challenges face those who want to provide all young children with high-quality curriculum, assessment, and evaluation of early childhood programs. Public commitment, along with significant investments in a well-financed system of early childhood education and in other components of services for young children and their families, will make it possible to implement these recommendations fully and effectively.

Developmental Charts

Although the recommendations in the position statement are applicable to all programs serving children from birth through age eight, some of the specifics may differ. Therefore, the next section contains developmental charts that provide brief but not exhaustive examples of ways in which each recommendation of the position statement would be implemented in programs for infants and toddlers, preschoolers, and kindergarten-primary age children.

The following charts are included:

• Curriculum in Programs for Infants, Toddlers, Preschoolers, Kindergartners, and Primary Grade Children

• Assessment in Programs for Infants, Toddlers, Preschoolers, Kindergartners, and Primary Grade Children

• Program Evaluation and Accountability in Programs for Infants, Toddlers, Preschoolers, Kindergartners, and Primary Grade Children

---

Position Statement Revisions Committee

Lindy Buch, *Co-chair*
Maurice Sykes, *Co-chair*
Susan Andersen
Elena Bodrova
Jerlean Daniel
Linda Espinosa
Dominic Gullo
Marlene Henriques
Jacqueline Jones
Mary Louise Jones
Deborah Leong
Ann Levy
Christina Lopez Morgan
Joyce Staples
Marilou Hyson, NAEYC Staff
Peter Pizzolongo, NAEYC Staff

CURRICULUM in programs for infants, toddlers, preschoolers, kindergartners, and primary grade children

19

POSITION STATEMENT RECOMMENDATION: Implement curriculum that is thoughtfully planned, challenging, engaging, developmentally appropriate, culturally and linguistically responsive, comprehensive, and likely to promote positive outcomes for all young children.

Curriculum that is thoughtfully planned: Whatever the children's ages, curriculum goals link with important developmental tasks and are comprehensive in scope. Teaching strategies are tailored to children's ages, developmental capacities, language and culture, and abilities or disabilities. A major shift as children move into kindergarten and the primary grades is toward greater focus on subject matter areas, without ignoring their developmental foundations.

Infants/Toddlers	Preschoolers	Kindergarten/Primary
Goals focus on children's development as they learn about themselves and others, as well as ways to communicate, think, and use their muscles.	Goals focus on children's exploration, inquiry, and expanding vocabularies.	Goals focus on children's emergent knowledge and skills in all subject matter areas, including language and literacy, mathematics, science, social studies, health, physical education, and the visual and performing arts.
Goals for infants address security, responsive interactions with caregivers, and exploration.	Goals address children's physical well-being and motor development; social and emotional development; approaches to learning; language development; and cognition and general knowledge.	Goals continue to address all developmental areas including socioemotional development. and approaches to learning ("habits of mind").
Goals for toddlers address independence, need for control, discovery, and beginning social interactions.	Experiences provide for knowledge and skill learning in literacy, mathematics, science, social studies, and the visual and performing arts.	

Curriculum that is challenging and engaging: For all ages the curriculum leads children from where they are to new accomplishments while maintaining their interest and active involvement. Content that is engaging for children of different ages changes with development and with new experiences, requiring careful observation and adaptation.

Infants/Toddlers	Preschoolers	Kindergarten/Primary
Children can use their whole bodies and their senses as they manipulate toys and other safe objects and engage in play alone, with a primary caregiver, and at times with or near other infants.	Curriculum facilitates children's construction of knowledge through their interactions with materials, each other, and adults.	Curriculum promotes children's developing attitudes as "learners"—using their curiosity, creativity, and initiative.
Children's enthusiasm for exploring is supported by matching their interests with challenging curricula.	Curriculum promotes experiences in which children's thinking moves from the simple to the complex, from the concrete to the abstract.	Curriculum provides experiences in which children use oral and written language, mathematical and scientific thinking, and investigatory skills to build a knowledge base across disciplines and expand their skills repertoire.
For toddlers, curriculum also focuses on their emerging abilities to play with other children.	Curriculum provides opportunities for children to initiate activities, as well as for teacher initiation and scaffolding.	Curriculum leads to children's recognition of their own competence.
	Curriculum leads to children's recognition of their own achievements.	

(chart continued on page 20)

The information in this chart is based on the recommendations of the NAEYC-NAECS/SDE Position Statement on Curriculum, Assessment, and Program Evaluation (www.naeyc.org/resources/position_statements/pscape.pdf). The chart provides examples of ways in which the recommendations of the NAEYC-NAECS/SDE Position Statement on Curriculum, Assessment, and Program Evaluation can be implemented in programs for infants/toddlers, preschoolers, and kindergarten/primary age children. The examples can best be understood within the context of the full position statement.

20

CURRICULUM chart (cont'd)

Infants/Toddlers	Preschoolers	Kindergarten/Primary
Curriculum that is developmentally appropriate and culturally and linguistically responsive: Whatever the children's ages, curriculum fits well with their developmental levels, abilities and disabilities, individual characteristics, families and communities, and cultural contexts. Curriculum supports educational equity for children who are learning a second language. Curriculum for younger children makes cultural connections primarily through relationships, daily routines, and "rituals"; older children benefit from more explicit incorporation of culturally relevant materials and from topic-centered as well as integrated learning opportunities.		
Curriculum addresses the wide variations in infants' and toddlers' interests, temperaments, and patterns of growth and development. Curriculum planning and implementation emphasize understanding of and respect for home culture, efforts to incorporate home values and practices, and discussion with families about differences between their expectations and those of the program.	Integration across subject matter areas is high, while some "focusing" is appropriate (e.g., experiences devoted to learning about print and numbers). Curriculum planning and implementation—including the use of "props" for play and other representations—emphasize experiences that reflect the children's cultures and cultural values.	Curriculum focuses on a continuum of learning in topic areas and integration across disciplines. The curriculum also facilitates adaptation of instruction for children who are having difficulty and for those needing increasing challenges. Children learn ways to develop constructive relationships with other people and respect for individual and cultural differences.
Curriculum that is comprehensive: Whatever the children's ages, the curriculum attends to a broad range of developmental and learning outcomes—across domains and subject matter areas and including experiences that promote children's nonviolent behavior and conflict resolution. For older children, the curriculum pays greater attention to specific content areas but without ever ignoring some domains in favor of a narrow set of other outcomes.		
Curriculum incorporates children's relationships with their caregivers and routines (e.g., sleeping, diapering/toileting) as opportunities for learning, as well as through experiences in which children play with objects, their caregivers, and (increasingly) each other. Curriculum provides a context in which teachers use their knowledge about each child to plan opportunities for learning across domains—physical well-being and motor development; social and emotional development; approaches to learning; language development; and cognition and general knowledge.	Curriculum facilitates children's learning through individual and small and large group experiences that promote physical well-being and motor development; social and emotional development; approaches to learning; language development, including second-language development; and cognition and general knowledge. Curriculum provides a context in which children learn through meaningful everyday experiences, including play. Within this context, various academic disciplines are addressed—including mathematics, literacy, science, social studies, and the arts.	Curriculum and related instruction are increasingly focused on helping children acquire deeper understanding of information and skills in subject areas (e.g., language and literacy, science, mathematics, social studies, and visual and performing arts) within a comprehensive set of developmental outcomes. Curriculum helps children recognize the connections between and across disciplines and domains. Curriculum-based experiences encompass a variety of active strategies in which individuals or small groups explore, inquire, discover, demonstrate, and solve problems.

(continued on page 21)

CURRICULUM chart (cont'd)

Infants/Toddlers	Preschoolers	Kindergarten/Primary
	Curriculum that promotes positive outcomes: Whatever the children's ages, the curriculum is selected, adapted, and revised to promote positive outcomes for children. Outcomes include both immediate enjoyment and nurturance and longer-term benefits. Curriculum for younger children pays special attention to those key developmental outcomes shown to be essential to later success—not focusing simply on earlier versions of specific academic skills.	
Curriculum promotes experiences that lead to documented evidence that infants and toddlers are learning about themselves and others, communicating their needs to responsive adults, gaining understandings of basic concepts, and developing motor and coordination skills appropriate for their ages. Outcomes also include evidence that each child is developing a sense of trust, security, and, increasingly, independence.	Curriculum provides experiences that lead to documented evidence that preschoolers are acquiring and applying knowledge and skills in physical well-being and motor development; social and emotional development; approaches to learning; language development; and cognition and general knowledge—as well as more specific skills important for later school success. Children demonstrate positive attitudes toward learning and their increasing abilities to represent their experiences in a variety of ways (e.g., through drawing/painting, dictating/writing, and dramatic play).	Curriculum provides experiences that lead to documented evidence that children are acquiring important competencies in literacy, mathematics, science, visual and performing arts, and other subject matter areas—as well as continuing to develop cognitive, physical, and socioemotional competencies. These outcomes are appropriate for children's ages as well as their interests and the communities in which they live. Children demonstrate positive attitudes toward learning and their increasing understanding of key concepts, skills, and tools of inquiry of the subject matter areas; their application of these understandings to various situations; and their understanding of the connections across disciplines.

21

22

ASSESSMENT in programs for infants, toddlers, preschoolers, kindergartners, and primary grade children

POSITION STATEMENT RECOMMENDATION: Make ethical, appropriate, valid, and reliable assessment a central part of all early childhood programs. To assess young children's strengths, progress, and needs, use methods that are developmentally appropriate, culturally and linguistically responsive, tied to children's daily activities, supported by professional development, inclusive of families, and connected to specific, beneficial purposes: making sound decisions about teaching and learning; identifying significant concerns that may require focused intervention for individual children; and helping programs improve their educational and developmental interventions

Assessment that is developmentally appropriate and culturally and linguistically responsive: Whatever the children's ages, the focus of the assessment is consistent with the program's goals for children. The assessment system incorporates methods that have been validated for use with children whose ages, cultures, home languages, socioeconomic status, abilities and disabilities, and other characteristics are similar to those of the children with whom the assessments will be used. Assessment methods include accommodations for children with disabilities, when appropriate. Assessment of older children relies more on direct measures and formal methods.

Infants/Toddlers	Preschoolers	Kindergarten/Primary
Assessments focus on children's status and progress in their abilities to learn about themselves and others, communicate, think, and use their muscles.	Assessments focus on children's exploration, inquiry across disciplines, and expanding vocabularies.	Assessments continue to address broad dimensions of development yet are increasingly focused on the continuum of learning in topic areas as well as integration across disciplines—language and literacy, mathematics, science, social studies, health, physical education, and visual and performing arts.
Assessment measures ensure teachers' recognition of similar knowledge and skills across differences in cultural representation and incorporate families' home values, languages, experiences, and rituals.	Assessment measures address children's physical well-being and motor development; social and emotional development; approaches to learning; language development; and cognition and general knowledge.	Teachers involve children in evaluating their own work.
	Measures also ensure teachers' recognition of similar knowledge and skills across differences in cultural representation and incorporate culturally based experiences, including family values and languages.	Assessment measures ensure teachers' recognition of similar knowledge and skills across differences in cultural representation and incorporate culturally based experiences, including family values and languages.

The information in this chart is based on the recommendations of the NAEYC-NAECS/SDE Position Statement on Curriculum, Assessment, and Program Evaluation (www.naeyc.org/resources/position_statements/pscape.pdf). The chart provides examples of ways in which the recommendations of the NAEYC-NAECS/SDE Position Statement on Curriculum, Assessment, and Program Evaluation can be implemented in programs for infants/toddlers, preschoolers, and kindergarten/primary age children. The examples can best be understood within the context of the full position statement.

(chart continued on page 23)

ASSESSMENT chart (cont'd)

23

Infants/Toddlers	Preschoolers	Kindergarten/Primary
Assessment that is tied to children's daily activities: Whatever the children's ages, assessment incorporates teachers' observation recordings and other documentation, obtained during regular classroom activities, collected systematically at regular intervals. Whatever the children's ages, teachers observe both what children can do on their own and what they can do with skillful adult prompting and support. For younger children, assessment is primarily incorporated with their play and interactions; for older children, assessment methods may be more clearly defined, separate from other activities, and include some paper-and-pencil methods.		
Assessments include teachers' observation recordings of children's performance during routines and activities, as well as other documentation (e.g., photographs or videotapes of children playing; samples of drawings).	Assessments include teachers' observation recordings of children's performance during classroom experiences, as well as other documentation (e.g., photographs of children's block constructions; samples of easel paintings).	Assessments include teachers' observation recordings of children's performance during instructional activities, as well as other documentation (e.g., children's written records of their knowledge and skill acquisition, samples of work completed).
Assessment that is supported by professional development: For teachers of all children from birth through age eight, professional development incorporates research-based information regarding assessment systems and measures and includes opportunities for teachers to refine their assessment and analysis skills. Professional development needs for teachers of younger and older children change from a more exclusive focus on informal, play-based assessment to include knowledge of formal assessments connected to learning standards.		
Assessments address observation recordings and other play- and interaction-focused measures.	Assessments address observation recordings and other forms of documentation regarding children's play and interactions (e.g., children's writing samples, graphs representing children's experiences with quantities).	Assessments address observation recordings, collections of children's work, and more formal assessment methods (e.g., teachers asking children questions regarding their knowledge of topics, children's performance on problem-solving tasks).
Assessment that is inclusive of families: Families are informed about the assessment of their children (at all ages). Teachers obtain information from parents and share information about children in ways that are clear, respectful, and constructive. With younger children, the information that is shared focuses primarily on health and development. As children become older, families share information that also includes children's progress in academic domains as assessed in more formal and often state-mandated ways.		
Teachers and parents share information periodically about children's engagement in routines (e.g., being fed or eating) and experiences (e.g., playing peekaboo or looking for hidden objects). For infants, parents also receive daily information about children's eating, sleeping, and eliminating.	Teachers and parents share information periodically about children's progress in all domains. Teachers and parents work together to make decisions regarding children's learning goals and approaches to learning.	Teachers and parents share information periodically about children's progress in all domains and disciplines. Assessment measures might include letter or numerical grades; when such grades are used, reports to parents also include narrative comments regarding children's learning across disciplines. Teachers inform parents about the meaning, uses, and limitations of the results of large-scale assessments.

(continued on page 24)

24

ASSESSMENT chart (cont'd)

Infants/Toddlers	Preschoolers	Kindergarten/Primary
Assessment that is used to make sound decisions about teaching and learning: Whatever the children's ages, assessment information is used to support learning, consistent with the goals of the curriculum. For younger children, information about each child's growth and development is used to make decisions regarding possible changes to the environment, interactions, and experiences. With older children, assessment information is also used for making decisions about each child's current understanding and skills in content areas, what he or she should be ready to learn next, and instructional methods that help the children meet important developmental and learning goals		
Assessment addresses children's abilities to learn about themselves and others, communicate, think, and use their muscles. Teachers adjust their routines and experiences for each child based on assessment of the child's skill acquisition, temperament, interests, and other factors.	Assessment addresses children's physical well-being and motor development; social and emotional development; approaches to learning; language development; and cognition and general knowledge. Teachers develop short- and long-range plans for each child and the group based on children's knowledge and skills, interests, and other factors.	The teaching and learning decisions that are made on the basis of assessment results increasingly include a focus on how best to promote acquisition of literacy, mathematics, and other content-specific areas—yet with broader assessment results continuing to have a strong influence on instructional decisions. Teachers use assessment information to determine which teaching approaches are working, as well as adaptations needed for individual children who are having difficulty and for those needing increasing challenges.
Assessment that is used to identify significant concerns that may require focused intervention: Whatever the children's ages, health and developmental screening is used to identify those children who may benefit from more in-depth assessment. Very young children may be screened regularly for potential health problems and developmental delays. For older children, screening and follow-up assessment may lead to identification of disabilities or other specific concerns that were not apparent when children were younger. When disabilities or other problems are diagnosed, appropriate interventions are planned and implemented.		
Assessments focus on health needs and acquisition of normal developmental milestones. Screening may be conducted as part of a child's well-baby or well-child care and/or through participation in Early Head Start or other group programs.	Assessments continue to focus on health needs and possible developmental delays. Screening typically is conducted as children enter Head Start and other preschool programs. Often, staff from these programs receive specific training for conducting the assessments.	Assessments, including vision and hearing screening, typically are conducted for all children entering kindergarten. Formal school-district or state-mandated screening and referral protocols are followed for all children.

(continued on page 25)

ASSESSMENT chart (cont'd)

Infants/Toddlers	Preschoolers	Kindergarten/Primary
	Assessment that is used to help programs improve their educational and developmental interventions: In all early childhood programs, information is used to help teachers and program administrators maintain an awareness of the effects of program activities on the children and families served. With this awareness, improvements to programs can be made. Assessment information for younger children predominantly addresses physical characteristics and health issues, moving toward more direct measures of older children's knowledge and skills (e.g., paper-and-pencil tests that are discipline specific).	
Assessment data are collected regarding immunizations, well-baby care received, and sensory and perceptual capacities.	Assessment information is gathered regarding physical well-being and motor development; social and emotional development; approaches to learning; language development; and cognition and general knowledge.	Assessment information is gathered primarily through direct measures (across disciplines).
Analysis of assessment information may lead to changes in primary caregiver responsibilities, styles of interactions, strategies to promote language development, indoor and outdoor environments, and/or other aspects of the program.	Analysis of assessment information may lead to changes in the daily schedule, curriculum and teaching strategies, styles of interaction, interest area arrangements, outdoor play area resources, and/or other aspects of the program.	Analysis of assessment information may lead to changes in teaching approaches for the whole group, design and implementation of activities for small groups of children, and/or other aspects of the program.

26

PROGRAM EVALUATION and ACCOUNTABILITY
in programs for infants, toddlers, preschoolers, kindergartners, and primary grade children

POSITION STATEMENT RECOMMENDATION: Regularly evaluate early childhood programs in light of program goals, using varied, appropriate, conceptually and technically sound evidence to determine the extent to which programs meet the expected standards of quality and to examine intended as well as unintended results.

Infants/Toddlers	Preschoolers	Kindergarten/Primary
	Effective program evaluation and accountability: Programs serving children of all ages engage in ongoing evaluation in light of their identified goals and are accountable for producing beneficial results. Although many similarities are found across all high-quality early childhood programs, the specific standards of quality used to evaluate programs (e.g., program standards and early learning standards), issues about the kinds of evidence that are most appropriate, and specific risks inherent in accountability systems vary depending on the ages of the children served. Programs for older children are more likely to be mandated to participate in large-scale evaluations using norm-referenced assessments; in those cases, multiple safeguards should be in place, ensuring that the tests are developmentally appropriate, conducted in the language children are most comfortable with, and employ other accommodations as appropriate. Aggregated, not individual, data should be used as part of an accountability system, and gain scores should be emphasized rather than "snapshots" of scores upon exit from a program.	
Program evaluation and accountability uses standards of quality (program and early learning standards) that are specific to infants and toddlers and address the developmental domains (physical well-being and motor development; social and emotional development; approaches to learning; language development; and cognition and general knowledge), as well as those that are relevant to all programs.

In evaluating program effectiveness, great importance is placed on family-related goals and outcomes because of their critical developmental significance for infants and toddlers.

Use of children's gain scores as part of an accountability system, while preferable over other types of comparisons, still warrant caution because of the wide variability and unevenness of early development. | Program evaluation and accountability attends to a comprehensive range of developmental and learning outcomes, both in identifying program goals and in evaluating effectiveness.

As preschool programs increasingly become part of state accountability systems, outcomes should not be limited to academic disciplines but should include developmental domains—physical well-being and motor development; social and emotional development; approaches to learning; language development; and cognition and general knowledge—as well as address adherence with applicable program standards.

Given the difficulty of using formal standardized assessments with preschool children, alternate methods and sampling procedures should be emphasized. | Program evaluation and accountability in programs serving kindergarten and primary-age children is typically conducted within a system of federal, state, and district expectations.

Although more capable of participating in some kinds of formal assessments, children six to eight may still fail to show their level of competence under testing conditions, leading to erroneous conclusions about programs as well as individual children.

Accountability systems for children this age run the risk of reinforcing a narrow range of program goals; special attention is needed to maintain a comprehensive, developmentally appropriate system that focuses on program standards as well as learning standards.

Assessment of kindergarten and primary grade children using formal standardized assessments continues to be problematic. Alternate methods of sampling procedures should be emphasized. |

The information in this chart is based on the recommendations of the NAEYC-NAECS/SDE Position Statement on Curriculum, Assessment, and Program Evaluation (www.naeyc.org/resources/position_statements/pscape.pdf). The chart provides examples of ways in which the recommendations of the NAEYC-NAECS/SDE Position Statement on Curriculum, Assessment, and Program Evaluation can be implemented in programs for infants/toddlers, preschoolers, and kindergarten/primary age children. The examples can best be understood within the context of the full position statement.

27

Glossary

This glossary includes brief definitions of some key terms used in the position statement and in this resource. Definitions are based on common usage in the fields of early education, child development, assessment, and program evaluation. Terms with asterisks are adapted from a recent glossary of standards and assessment terms (see below).

Aggregation: A process of grouping distinct information or data (for example, combining information about individual schools or programs into a data set describing an entire school district or state).

Alignment: In this context, coherence and continuity among goals, standards, desired results, curriculum, and assessments, with attention to developmental differences as well as connections across ages and grade levels. Alignment includes attention to developmental differences as well as connections.

*Assessment: A systematic procedure for obtaining information from observation, interviews, portfolios, projects, tests, and other sources that can be used to make judgments about children's characteristics.

Assessment Literacy: Professionals', students', or families' knowledge about the goals, tools, and appropriate uses of assessment.

Child Development: In this early childhood context, development is defined as the social, emotional, physical, and cognitive changes in children stimulated by biological maturation interacting with experience.

Cognition: Includes processes for acquiring information, inquiring, thinking, reasoning, remembering and recalling, representing, planning, problem solving, and other mental activities.

*Criterion or Performance-Oriented Assessment: Assessment in which the person's performance (that is, score) is interpreted by comparing it with a prespecified standard or specific content and/or skills.

Culturally and Linguistically Responsive: In this instance, development and implementation of early childhood curriculum, assessment, or program evaluation that is attuned to issues of values, identity, worldview, language, and other culture-related variables.

* Terms adapted from "The Words We Use: A Glossary of Terms for Early Childhood Education Standards and Assessments," developed by the State Collaborative on Assessment and Student Standards (SCASS). Glossary online: www.ccsso.org/projects/SCASS/projects/early_childhood_education_assessment_consortium/publications_and_products/2838.cfm.

Culture: Includes ethnicity, racial identity, economic class, family structure, language, and religious and political beliefs.

Data: Factual information, especially information organized for analysis or used to make decisions.

Developmentally Appropriate: NAEYC defines developmentally appropriate practices as those that "result from the process of professionals making decisions about the well-being and education of children based on at least three important kinds of information or knowledge: what is known about child development and learning…; what is known about the strengths, interests, and needs of each individual child in the group…; and knowledge of the social and cultural contexts in which children live" (Bredekamp & Copple 1997, 8–9).

*Documentation: The process of keeping track of and preserving children's work as evidence of their progress or of a program's development.

*Early Learning Standards: Statements that describe expectations for the learning and development of young children.

Implementation: In this context, the process of taking a planned curriculum, assessment system, or evaluation design and "making it happen" in ways that are consistent with the plan and desired results.

Logic Model: A model of how components of a program or service effect changes that move participating children and families toward desired outcomes.

Matrix Sampling: An approach to large-scale assessment in which only part of the total assessment is administered to each child.

*Norm-Referenced: A standardized testing instrument by which the person's performance is interpreted in relation to the performance of a group of peers who have previously taken the same test—a "norming" group.

Observational Assessment: Assessment based on teachers' systematic recordings and analysis of children's behavior in real-life situations.

Outcomes: In this case, desired results for young children's learning and development across multiple domains.

Pedagogy: A variety of teaching methods or approaches used to help children learn and develop.

Program Evaluation: A systematic process of describing the components and outcomes of an intervention or service.

28

Program Monitoring: A tool for judging the quality of program implementation and modifying how the program is being implemented. Frequently part of a regulatory process.

*Program Standards: Widely accepted expectations for the characteristics or quality of early childhood settings in schools, early childhood centers, family education homes, and other education settings.

Referral: In this context, making a recommendation or actual linkage of a child and family with other professionals, for the purpose of more in-depth assessment and planning. Usually follows screening or other preliminary information gathering.

Reliability: The consistency of an assessment tool; important for generalizing about children's learning and development.

Sampling: In this instance, the use of a smaller number of children or programs (often randomly selected) in large-scale assessments in order to statistically estimate the characteristics of a larger population.

*Screening: The use of a brief procedure or instrument designed to identify, from within a large population of children, those children who may need further assessment to verify developmental and/or health risks.

Significance (goals/content/assessment): "Significant" curriculum goals, content, or objects of assessment are those that have been found to be critically important for children's current and later development and learning. (In other contexts, it refers to *statistical* significance or the likelihood that a research finding was not produced by chance.)

Stakeholders: Those who have a shared interest in a particular activity, program, or decision.

Standardized: An assessment with clearly specified administration and scoring procedures and normative data.

Unintended Consequences: In this context, the results of a particular intervention or assessment that were not intended by the developers and that may have potential—and sometimes negative—impact.

Validity: The extent to which a measure or assessment tool measures what it was designed to measure.

References

ACF (Administration for Children and Families, U.S. Department of Health and Human Services). 2003. Head Start program fact sheet. Washington, DC: Author.

ACYF (Administration on Children, Youth and Families). 1997. *The program manager's guide to evaluation.* Washington, DC: Author.

AERA (American Educational Research Association). 2000. *Position statement concerning high-stakes testing in preK–12 education.* Washington, DC: Author.

AERA, APA (American Psychological Association), & NCME (National Council on Measurement in Education). 1999. *Standards for educational and psychological testing.* Washington, DC: AERA.

ASPE (Office of the Assistant Secretary for Planning and Evaluation, U.S. Department of Health and Human Services). 2003. *Strengthening Head Start: What the evidence shows.* Washington, DC: Author.

Align to Achieve. 2003. *The standards database.* Watertown, MA: Author. Online: www.aligntoachieve.org/AchievePhaseII/basic-search.cfm

Annie E. Casey Foundation. 2003. *KIDS COUNT data book.* Baltimore: Author.

Barnett, W.S. 2003. Better teachers, better preschools: Student achievement linked to teacher qualifications. *NIEER Policy Briefs* 2. Online: http://nieer.org/resources/policybriefs/2.pdf

Bodrova, E., & D. Leong. 2003. Chopsticks and counting chips: Do play and foundational skills need to compete for the teacher's attention in an early childhood classroom? *Young Children* 58 (3): 10–17.

Bredekamp, S, & C. Copple, eds. 1997. *Developmentally appropriate practice in early childhood programs.* Rev. ed. Washington, DC: NAEYC.

Brennan, E., E. Caplan, S. Ama, & O. Warfield. 2001. *Child care: Inclusion as enrichment.* Focal Point. Portland, OR: Regional Research Institute for Human Services, Portland State University. Online: www.rtc.pdx.edu/FPinHTML/FocalPointFA01/pgFPfa01Inclusive.shtml

Campbell, F.A., C.T. Ramey, E.P. Pungello, J. Sparling, & S. Miller-Johnson. 2002. Early childhood education: Young adult outcomes from the Abecedarian Project. *Applied Developmental Science 6:* 42–57.

Commission on NAEYC Early Childhood Program Standards and Accreditation Criteria. 2003. Draft NAEYC early childhood program standards. Online: www.naeyc.org/accreditation/nextera.asp

Committee for Economic Development. 2002. *Preschool for all: Investing in a productive and just society.* New York: Author.

DHHS (U.S. Department of Health and Human Services). 2002. *Specialized child care.* Washington, DC: Author. Online: http://aspe.hhs.gov/hsp/isp/ancillary/CHCare.htm

Dahlberg, G., P. Moss., & A. Pence. 1999. *Beyond quality in early childhood education and care: Postmodern perspectives.* Philadelphia: Falmer.

Dickinson, D.K., & P.O. Tabors, eds. 2001. *Beginning literacy with language: Young children learning at home and school.* Baltimore: Brookes.

Education World. 2003. *Knowledge loom: Professional development.* Wallingford, CT: Author. Online: www.educationworld.com/a_curr/index.shtml

Eisner, E.W. 2002. *The educational imagination: On the design and evaluation of school programs.* Upper Saddle River, NJ: Merrill/Prentice Hall.

Espinosa, L. 2002. High quality preschool: Why we need it and what it looks like. *NIEER Policy Briefs* 1. Online: http://nieer.org/resources/policybriefs/1.pdf

Fillmore, L.W., & C. Snow. 2000. *What teachers need to know about language.* Washington, DC: U.S. Department of Education, Office of Educational Research and Improvement, Education Resources Information Center.

29

Frede, E.C. 1998. Preschool program quality in programs for children in poverty. In *Early care and education for children in poverty: Promises, programs, and long-term outcomes,* eds. W.S. Barnett & S.S. Boocock. Buffalo, NY: State University of New York Press.

Gilliam, W.S., & V. Leiter. 2003. Evaluating early childhood programs: Improving quality and informing policy. *Zero to Three* 23 (6): 6–13.

Gilliam, W.S., & E.F. Zigler. 2000. A critical meta-analysis of all evaluations of state-funded pre-school from 1977 to 1998: Implications for policy, service delivery and program evaluation. *Early Childhood Research Quarterly* 15 (4): 441–72.

Glascoe, F., & H. Shapiro. 2002. Developmental screening. *Pediatric Development and Behavior.* Online: www.dbpeds.org/articles/detail.cfm?id=5

Goffin, S.G., & C. Wilson. 2001. *Curriculum models and early childhood education: Appraising the relationship,* 2d ed. Upper Saddle River, NJ: Merrill/Prentice Hall.

Hart, B., & T.R. Risley. 1995. *Meaningful differences in the everyday experience of young American children.* Baltimore: Brookes.

Head Start Bureau. 2001. Head Start child outcomes framework. *Head Start Bulletin* 70: 44–50.

Head Start Program Performance Standards. 1996. 45 CFR Part 1304. Online: www.acf.hhs.gov/programs/hsb/performance/index.htm

Henry, G.T. 2003. Assessing school readiness: System design framework and issues. In *Assessing the state of state assessments: Perspectives on assessing young children,* eds. C. Scott-Little, S.L. Kagan, & R.M. Clifford, 25–35. Greensboro, NC: SERVE.

Hodgkinson, H. 2003. *Leaving too many children behind: A demographer's view on the neglect of America's youngest children.* Washington, DC: Institute for Educational Leadership.

Horm-Wingerd, D.M., P.C. Winter, & P. Plocfchan. 2000. *Primary level assessment for IASA Title 1: A call for discussion.* Washington, DC: Council of Chief State School Officers.

Horton, C., & B. Bowman. 2002. *Child assessment at the preprimary level: Expert opinion and state trends.* Chicago: Erikson Institute.

Hyson, M. 1996. Theory: An analysis (Part 2). In *Advances in early education and day care,* eds. J. Chafel & S. Reifel, 41–89. Greenwich, CT: JAI.

Hyson, M. 2003a. Putting early academics in their place. *Educational Leadership* 60 (7): 20–23.

Hyson, M., ed. 2003b. *Preparing early childhood professionals: NAEYC's standards for programs.* Washington, DC: NAEYC.

IDEA (Individuals with Disabilities Act) Amendments. 1997. 20 U.S.C. 1400 et seq.

IES (Institute of Education Sciences, U.S. Department of Education). 2003. *Preschool curriculum evaluation research.* Online: http://pcer.rti.org

Jones, J. 2003. *Early literacy assessment systems: Essential elements.* Princeton, NJ: Educational Testing Service.

Kagan, S.L., C. Scott-Little, & R.M. Clifford. 2003. Assessing young children: What policymakers need to know and do. In *Assessing the state of state assessments: Perspectives on assessing young children,* eds. C. Scott-Little, S.L. Kagan, & R.M. Clifford, 5–11. Greensboro, NC: SERVE.

Keller, B. 2003. Question of teacher turnover sparks research interest. *Education Week* 22 (33): 8.

Lally, J.R. 2000. Infants have their own curriculum: A responsive approach to curriculum planning for infants and toddlers. *Head Start Bulletin* 67: 6–7.

Lally, J.R., A. Griffen, E. Fenichel, M. Segal, E. Szanton, & B. Weissbourd. 1995. *Caring for infants and toddlers in groups: Developmentally appropriate practice.* Washington, DC: ZERO TO THREE.

Laverty, K., A. Burton, M. Whitebook, & D. Bellm. 2001. *Current data on child care salaries and benefits in the United States.* Washington, DC: Center for the Child Care Workforce.

Lombardi, J. 2003. *Time to care: Redesigning child care to promote education, support families, and build communities.* Philadelphia: Temple University Press.

Love, J.M. 2003. Instrumentation for state readiness assessment: Issues in measuring children's early development and learning. In *Assessing the state of state assessments: Perspectives on assessing young children,* eds. C. Scott-Little, S.L. Kagan, & R.M. Clifford, 43–55. Greensboro, NC: SERVE.

Lynch, E., & M. Hanson. 2004. Family diversity, assessment, and cultural competence. In *Assessing infants and preschoolers with special needs,* 4th ed., eds. M. McLean, D. Bailey, & M. Wolery. Columbus, OH: Merrill.

MENC (National Association for Music Education). 1996. *The performance standards for music: Strategies and benchmarks for assessing progress toward the national standards, grades preK–12.* Reston, VA: Author. Online: www.menc.org/publication/books/performance_standards/contents.html

Marcon, R.A. 1999. Differential impact of preschool models on development and early learning of inner-city children: A three-cohort study. *Developmental Psychology* 35 (2): 358–75. EJ 582 451.

Marcon, R.A. 2002. Moving up the grades: Relationship between preschool model and later school success. *Early Childhood Research and Practice* 4 (1). Online: http://ecrp.uiuc.edu/v4n1/index.html

Marshall, D., W. Schubert, & J. Sears. 2000. *Turning points in curriculum.* Upper Saddle River, NJ: Merrill/Prentice Hall.

McAfee, O., & D. Leong. 2002. *Assessing and guiding young children's development and learning,* 3d ed. Boston: Allyn & Bacon.

McLean, M., D. Bailey, & M. Wolery, eds. 2004. *Assessing infants and preschoolers with special needs.* 4th ed. Columbus, OH: Merrill.

McNamara, C. 2003. *Field guide to nonprofit program design, marketing, and evaluation.* Minneapolis, MN: Authenticity Consulting.

Meisels, S.J. 1992. Doing harm by doing good: Iatrogenic effects of early childhood enrollment and promotion policies. *Early Childhood Research Quarterly* 7 (2): 155–74.

Meisels, S.J., & S. Atkins-Burnett. 2000. The elements of early childhood assessment. In *Handbook of early childhood intervention.* 2d ed., eds. J.P. Shonkoff & S.J. Meisels, 387–415. New York: Cambridge University Press.

Meisels, S.J., & E. Fenichel, eds. 1996. *New visions for the developmental assessment of infants and young children.* Washington, DC: ZERO TO THREE.

Mitchell, A. 2001. *Prekindergarten programs in the states: Trends and issues.* Vienna, VA: National Child Care Information Center.

Muenchow, S. 2003. A risk management approach to readiness assessment: Lessons from Florida. In *Assessing the state of state assessments: Perspectives on assessing young children,* eds. C. Scott-Little, S.L. Kagan, & R.M. Clifford, 13–23. Greensboro, NC: SERVE.

NAESP (National Association of Elementary School Principals). 2001. *Leading learning communities: Standards for what principals should know and be able to do.* Alexandria, VA: Author. Online: www.naesp.org/llc.pdf

NAEYC. 1998. *Code of ethical conduct.* Position statement. Washington, DC: Author.

NAEYC & IRA (International Reading Association). 1998. *Learning to read and write: Developmentally appropriate practices for young children.* Joint Position Statement. Washington, DC: Author.

NAEYC & NAECS/SDE (National Association of Early Childhood Specialists in State Departments of Education). 1990. *Guidelines for appropriate curriculum content and assessment in programs serving children ages 3 through 8.* Joint position statement. Washington, DC: NAEYC.

NAEYC & NAECS/SDE. 2002. *Early learning standards: Creating the conditions for success.* Joint position statement. Washington, DC: NAEYC.

NAEYC & NCTM (National Council of Teachers of Mathematics). 2002. *Early childhood mathematics: Promoting good beginnings.* Joint position statement. Washington, DC: NAEYC.

30

NASP (National Association of School Psychologists). 2002. *Position statement on early childhood assessment.* Bethesda, MD: Author. Online: www.nasponline.org/information/pospaper_eca.html

NCES (National Center for Education Statistics). 2002. *Children's reading and mathematics achievement in kindergarten and first grade.* Washington, DC: Author. Online: http://nces.ed.gov/pubs2002/2002125.pdf

NIEER (National Institute for Early Education Research). 2003. Fast facts: National early education and care enrollment trends—Overview. New Brunswick, NJ: Author. Online: http://nieer.org/resources/facts/index.php?FastFactID=7

NSDC (National Staff Development Council). 2001. *Standards for staff development.* Rev. ed. Oxford, OH: Author.

National Research Council. 1998. *Preventing reading difficulties in young children.* Committee on the Prevention of Reading Difficulties in Young Children, eds. C.E. Snow, M.S. Burns, & P. Griffin, Board on Children, Youth, and Families, Commission on Behavioral and Social Sciences and Education. Washington, DC: National Academy Press.

National Research Council. 1999. *High stakes: Testing for tracking, promotion, and graduation.* Committee on Appropriate Test Use, eds. J.P. Heubert & R.M. Hauser. Washington, DC: National Academy Press.

National Research Council. 2000. *How people learn: Brain, mind, experience, and school.* Committee on Developments in the Science of Learning, eds. J. Bransford, A. Brown, & R. Cocking, Commission on Behavioral and Social Sciences and Education. Washington, DC: National Academy Press.

National Research Council. 2001. *Eager to learn: Educating our preschoolers.* Committee on Early Childhood Pedagogy, eds. B. Bowman, M. Donovan, & M. Burns, Commission on Behavioral and Social Sciences and Education. Washington, DC: National Academy Press.

National Research Council & Institute of Medicine. 2000. *From neurons to neighborhoods: The science of early childhood development.* Committee on Integrating the Science of Early Childhood Development, eds. J. Shonkoff & D. Phillips, Board on Children, Youth, and Families, Commission on Behavioral and Social Sciences and Education. Washington, DC: National Academy Press.

Neuman, S.B., & D.K. Dickinson. 2001. *Handbook of early literacy research.* New York: Guilford.

New, R.S. 1999. *An integrated early childhood curriculum: Moving from the "what" and the "how" to the "why."* 3d ed. New York: Teachers College Press.

OECD (Organization for Economic Co-operation and Development). 2001. *Starting strong: Early education and care.* Paris, France: Author.

Paulsell, D., J. Cohen, A. Stieglitz, E. Lurie-Hurvitz, E. Fenichel, & E. Kisker. 2002. *Partnerships for quality: Improving infant-toddler child care for low-income families.* Washington, DC: ZERO TO THREE; Princeton, NJ: Mathematica Policy Research.

Peisner-Feinberg, E., M. Burchnal, R. Clifford, M. Culkin, C. Howes, S. Kagan, N. Yazejian, P. Byler, J. Rustici, & J. Zelazo. 2000. *The children of the Cost, Quality, and Outcomes Study go to school: Technical report.* Chapel Hill: University of North Carolina, Frank Porter Graham Child Development Center.

Peth-Pierce, R. 2001. *A good beginning: Sending America's children to school with the social and emotional competence they need to succeed.* Monograph based on two papers commissioned by the Child Mental Health Foundations and Agencies Network (FAN). Chapel Hill: University of North Carolina.

Popham, W.J. 1999. *Classroom assessment: What teachers need to know.* 2d ed. Boston: Allyn & Bacon.

Popham, W.J. 2000. *Testing! Testing! What every parent should know about school tests.* Boston: Allyn & Bacon.

Quality Counts. 2002: Building blocks for success—State efforts in early childhood education. *Education Week* 21 (17).

Quality Counts. 2003. The teacher gap. *Education Week* 22 (17).

Raspa, M.J., R.A. McWilliam, & S.M. Ridley. 2001. Child care quality and children's engagement. *Early Education and Development* 12: 209–24.

Raver, C. 2002. Emotions matter: Making the case for the role of young children's emotional development for early school readiness. *SRCD Social Policy Report* 16 (3). Ann Arbor, MI: Society for Research in Child Development.

Reynolds, A.J., J.A. Temple, D.L. Robertson, & E.A. Mann. 2001. Long-term effects of an early childhood intervention on educational achievement and juvenile arrest: A 15-year follow-up of low-income children in public schools. *Journal of the American Medical Association* 285 (18): 2339–46.

Rosenzweig, J., E. Brennan, & A. Ogilvie. 2002. Work-family fit: Voices of parents of children with emotional and behavioral disorders. *Social Work* 47 (4): 415–24.

Sandall, S., M. McLean, & B. Smith. 2000. *DEC recommended practices in early intervention/early childhood special education.* Longmont, CO: Sopris West.

Schweinhart, L.J. 2003. Issues in implementing a state preschool program evaluation in Michigan. In *Assessing the state of state assessments: Perspectives on assessing young children,* eds. C. Scott-Little, S.L. Kagan, & R.M. Clifford, 37–42. Greensboro, NC: SERVE.

Schweinhart, L.J., & D.P. Weikart. 1997. The High/Scope pre-school curriculum comparison study through age 23. *Early Childhood Research Quarterly* 12: 117–43.

Scott-Little, C., S.L. Kagan, & R.M. Clifford, eds. 2003. *Assessing the state of state assessments: Perspectives on assessing young children.* Greensboro, NC: SERVE.

Scott-Little, C., S.L. Kagan, & V. Frelow. 2003. *Standards for preschool children's learning and development: Who has standards, how were they developed, and how are they used?* Greensboro, NC: SERVE.

Semlak, S. 2000. Curriculum in Early Head Start. *Head Start Bulletin* 69: 14–15.

Shepard, L.A. 1994. The challenges of assessing young children appropriately. *Phi Delta Kappan* 76: 206–12.

Shepard, L., S.L. Kagan, & E. Wurtz. 1998. *Principles and recommendations for early childhood assessments.* Washington, DC: National Education Goals Panel.

Shonkoff, J.P., & S.J. Meisels, eds. 2000. *Handbook of early childhood intervention,* 2d ed., 387–415. New York: Cambridge University Press.

Stake, R.E. 2003. *Standards-based and responsive evaluation.* Thousand Oaks, CA: Sage.

Stiggins, R. 1999. Evaluating classroom assessment training in teacher education programs. *Educational Measurement: Issues and Practice* 18 (1): 23–27.

Stiggins, R. 2001. The unfulfilled promise of classroom assessment. *Educational Measurement: Issues and Practice* 20 (3): 5–15.

Stiggins, R. 2002. Assessment for learning. *Education Week* 21 (26): 30: 32–33.

Tabors, P.O. 1997. *One child, two languages: A guide for preschool educators of children learning English as a second language.* Baltimore: Brookes.

Thomas, W.P., & V.P. Collier. 1997. *School effectiveness for language minority students.* Washington, DC: National Clearinghouse for Bilingual Education.

U.S. Census Bureau. 2003. Child care arrangements for preschoolers by family characteristics and employment status of mother: Spring 1999. *Survey of income and program participation.* Washington, DC: Author.

Whitebook, M., L. Sakai, E. Gerber, & C. Howes. 2001. *Then and now: Changes in child care staffing, 1994–2000.* Washington, DC: Center for the Child Care Workforce.

Whitehurst, G.J., & C.J. Lonigan. 1998. Child development and emergent literacy. *Child Development* 69: 848–72.

Yoshikawa, H., & E. Zigler. 2000. Mental health in Head Start: New directions for the twenty-first century. *Early Education and Development* 11: 247–64.

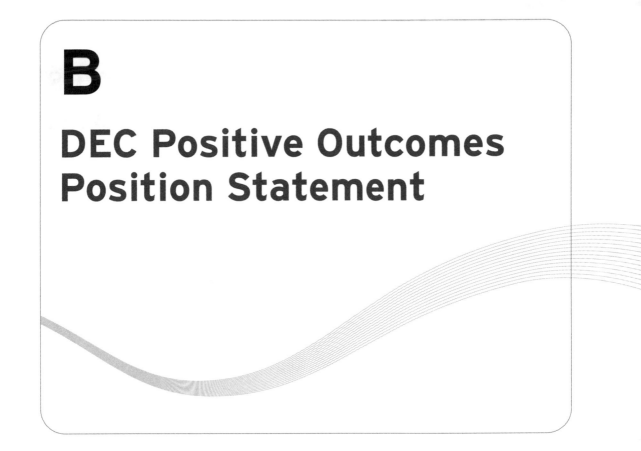

B

DEC Positive Outcomes Position Statement

Promoting Positive Outcomes for Children with Disabilities:

Recommendations for Curriculum, Assessment, and Program Evaluation

Developed by the Division for Early Childhood of the Council for Exceptional Children

Endorsed by the National Association for the Education of Young Children, March 2007.

DIVISION FOR EARLY CHILDHOOD • 27 Fort Missoula Road, Suite 2 • Missoula, MT 59804
Phone: 406-543-0872 FAX: 406-543-0887 E-mail: dec@dec-sped.org

DEC. (2007). Promoting positive outcomes for children with disabilities:
Recommendations for curriculum, assessment, and program evaluation. Missoula, MT: Author.

Promoting Positive Outcomes for Children with Disabilities:

Recommendations for Curriculum, Assessment, and Program Evaluation

Promoting Positive Outcomes for Children with Disabilities: Recommendations for Curriculum, Assessment, and Program Evaluation (2007) has been developed by the Division for Early Childhood (DEC) of the Council for Exceptional Children to serve as a companion document to a 2003 joint position statement, Early Childhood Curriculum, Assessment, and Program Evaluation—Building an Effective, Accountable System in Programs for Children Birth Through Age 8, created by the National Association for the Education of Young Children (NAEYC) and the National Association of Early Childhood Specialists in State Departments of Education (NAECS/SDE). The DEC document includes three sections: "Curriculum"; "Assessment"; and "Program Evaluation." The intended audiences for the document include early childhood administrators and personnel who work with young children with disabilities. Teacher educators, those providing professional development, family members, and state and federal policy makers will also benefit from these materials.

Background, History, and Context

The NAEYC-NAECS/SDE position statement.

As described in the NAEYC and NAECS/SDE document (2003), a number of converging factors led to the development of the two organizations' joint position statement. NAEYC and NAECS/SDE had previously published a joint position statement on early childhood curriculum and assessment (1990). Since then:

> Much more has become known about the power of high-quality curriculum, effective assessment practices, and ongoing program evaluation to support better outcomes for young children. Yet the infrastructure of the early childhood education system, within and outside the public schools, has not allowed this knowledge to be fully used—resulting in curriculum, assessment systems, and program evaluation procedures that are not of consistently high quality. (NAEYC & NAECS/SDE, 2003, p. 5)

These and other issues prompted the decision to create a new position statement and to form a working group including leaders from both organizations and other experts. As part of this process, the two organizations sought the views of other stakeholders, including the leadership of DEC. Drafts were placed on the NAEYC and NAECS/SDE Web sites and sent to experts for feedback; conference sessions invited further discussion of the position statement's recommendations. The

result of these efforts was a document that was approved both by NAEYC's Governing Board and by the membership of NAECS/SDE.

Connections between this document and the NAEYC-NAECS/SDE position statement.

After the NAEYC-NAECS/SDE position statement (2003) was approved by the NAEYC Board, the DEC Executive Board endorsed the paper. They also approved the development of a companion paper to the NAEYC-NAECS/SDE position statement. A workgroup was formed that included experts in curriculum, assessment, and program evaluation, as well as a liaison from the DEC Executive Board and NAEYC. The specific charge to the workgroup was to review the general recommendations from the NAEYC-NAECS/SDE position statement (2003) and consider them in light of specific issues for programs serving young children with disabilities and their families. These issues included:

1. Significant increases in accountability evaluation in the area of early intervention and early childhood special education (EI/ECSE) through both the No Child Left Behind Act (NCLB) of 2001 and the Individuals with Disabilities Education Improvement Act (IDEA) of 2004. This included the identification of child outcomes that were to be measured by all Part C and Preschool Special Education Programs under IDEA.

2. An increase in the mandates in IDEA related to inclusive settings, including serving children in natural environments for early intervention, and access to the general curriculum for preschool children with disabilities.

3. Increased attention to quality in inclusive settings, as evidenced in DEC Recommended Practices: A Comprehensive Guide for Practical Application (Sandall, Hemmeter, Smith, & McLean, 2005) and the NAEYC revised program standards and accreditation criteria.

The recommendations in the NAEYC-NAECS/SDE position statement (2003) explicitly included and made reference to children with disabilities. For example, with respect to curriculum, the 2003 position statement stated, "The content and implementation of the curriculum builds on children's prior . . . learning, is inclusive of children with disabilities, and is supportive of background knowledge gained at home and in the community" (NAEYC & NAECS/SDE,

p. 7). Similarly, the "Assessment" section of the 2003 position statement recommends that "Assessments are designed for and validated for use with children whose ages, cultures, home languages, socioeconomic status, abilities and disabilities, and other characteristics are similar to those of the children with whom the assessments will be administered" (NAEYC & NAECS/SDE, p. 11).

DEC intends that this document be read and used in conjunction with the NAEYC-NAECS/SDE position statement (2003), which puts forth general recommendations and guidance intended to apply to curriculum, assessment, and program evaluation practices for all young children, including those with disabilities. The recommendations in this DEC document are not alternatives, nor do they contradict the NAEYC-NAECS/SDE recommendations. Rather, they extend, more specifically apply, and further explicate the recommendations in the more general position statement. By reading and implementing both sets of recommendations, practitioners and policy makers will have the benefit of complementary perspectives and expertise.

Guiding Principles and Values

Besides convergence in the two documents' recommendations, both have been guided by similar principles and values. As articulated in the NAEYC-NAECS/SDE position statement (2003), these include:

- A belief in civic and democratic values, including respect, equality, and a participatory approach to decision making;
- A commitment to ethical behavior on behalf of children;
- The use of educationally and developmentally significant goals as guides in designing and implementing curriculum, assessment, and program evaluation;
- Coordinated systems that connect curriculum, assessment, and program evaluation;
- Support for children as individuals and as members of families, cultures, and communities;
- Respect for children's abilities and differences, so that systems of curriculum, assessment, and program evaluation promote the development and learning of all children;
- Partnerships and communication with families;
- Respect for evidence, including research as well as professional consensus; and
- Shared accountability for giving all children opportunities to reach essential goals—including accountability of programs, staff, administrators, and policy-makers.

Readers will see these principles and values repeatedly emphasized and applied in this document's recommendations, as they were in the NAEYC-NAECS/SDE position statement (2003). These principles and values are also consistent with and support the values embodied in DEC Recommended Practices: A Comprehensive Guide for Practical Application

(Sandall et al., 2005), which are designed to guide educators, other practitioners, families, and administrators in providing high-quality services for young children with disabilities. Of great importance within these contexts are values related to collaboration and teaming; participatory decision making; and the rights of all children to participate actively and meaningfully within their families and communities, with additional consideration for universal access or universal design.

Organization of this Document

This document is organized into three major sections that parallel and are consistent with the organization of the NAEYC-NAECS/SDE position statement (2003): Curriculum, Assessment, and Program Evaluation. Each section begins with a key recommendation, followed by the rationale for the recommendation, key issues for children with disabilities, specific indicators of effectiveness, and frequently asked questions. Additional resources are included in the Appendix, including examples of specific activities to support the rationale and/or indicators, and references.

Desired Effects of this Document

The DEC anticipates that Promoting Positive Outcomes for Children with Disabilities: Recommendations for Curriculum, Assessment, and Program Evaluation (2007) will have a number of positive effects on the profession and on young children and their families.

First, DEC offers information about issues that are both high-stakes and controversial, such as how to include children with disabilities when decisions about curriculum, assessment, and program evaluation are being made. Answers are not always clear, and yet the experts who wrote the paper drew together a significant body of evidence that should help provide guidance to those making these decisions.

As this document becomes widely disseminated, DEC also anticipates that it will promote critical dialogue and reflection both about its recommendations and about effective ways to implement the recommendations. Because of the multidisciplinary nature of our field, this dialogue should be especially productive, cutting across disciplines and traditional academic fields.

By building on and referring back to the general position statement from NAEYC-NAECS/SDE (2003), this document will also help create a common language and frame of reference across the fields of early childhood education and ECSE. For example, the concept of "universal design" can be a powerful idea for all those involved in working with young children, although its use has often been limited to those in special education.

Consistent with one of the major goals of DEC, we hope the recommendations and related evidence put forth in this document will influence national and state policies. The reauthorization of IDEA has created both new opportunities and challenges. At the same time, broader state systems of standards, assessment, and accountability in pre-k, early childhood special education, and other early childhood initiatives have major implications for young children with disabilities. This is especially important as programs around the country begin to provide national data on the extent to which young children with disabilities are meeting the three national child outcomes required by the Office of Special Education Programs for children served under IDEA.

Of course, the ultimate goal of this document is to create conditions that will allow all children to experience joyful, nurturing environments that produce positive outcomes in all aspects of their development and learning.

What Else Is Needed?

For the desired effects outlined in this document to be realized, additional supports will be needed. As pointed out in all three sections of this document, capacity building is essential. This includes an enhanced emphasis on professional development, both at the pre-service and in-service levels, so that higher education faculty, trainers, teachers, and administrators have the knowledge and skills to implement the recommendations. In addition, the multidisciplinary nature of EI/ECSE requires special attention to the needs of therapists and specialists who are part of the child's team to ensure they have access to professional development and support needed to both understand and meaningfully participate in the curriculum, assessment, and program evaluation processes.

Capacity building is also needed within programs. This includes ensuring that ratios and class sizes are structured to allow teachers to implement the kinds of curriculum and assessment practices recommended in this document. In addition, the field also needs to develop the capacity of early childhood practitioners (both generalists and specialists in ECSE) to articulate and advocate for the practices recommended here. In many cases, this means advocating for new public policies consistent with the document's recommendations, and the resources to implement those policies.

The mission of DEC is to promote policies and practices that support families and enhance the optimal development of children. This document provides one mechanism for accomplishing this mission by providing specific recommendations on how families, teachers, providers, and administrators can meaningfully include young children with disabilities in curriculum, assessment, and program evaluation efforts so that positive outcomes can be achieved.

CURRICULUM

Key Recommendation

To benefit all children, including those with disabilities and developmental delays, it is important to implement an integrated, developmentally appropriate, universally designed curriculum framework that is flexible, comprehensive, and linked to assessment and program evaluation activities. Such a curriculum framework can help ensure successful access, which in turn facilitates participation and learning of all children and families regardless of need, ability, or background.

A comprehensive curriculum framework encompasses four elements: assessment; scope and sequence; activities and intervention strategies; and progress monitoring. A curriculum framework is a dynamic system that should guide all aspects of a high quality program.

Rationale

The NAEYC-NAECS/SDE position statement on early childhood curriculum, assessment, and program evaluation makes clear that curriculum is more than a collection of enjoyable activities (2003). Curriculum is a complex idea containing multiple components including goals, content, pedagogy, and instructional practices. Curriculum should serve as a comprehensive guide for instruction and day-to-day inter-actions with young children (Branscombe, Castle, Dorsey, Sur-beck, & Taylor, 2003; Davis, Kilgo, & Gamel-McCormick, 1998; Dodge & Bickart, 2003; Goffin & Wilson, 2001; Hass, 2000; Hitchcock, Meyer, Rose, & Jackson, 2002; Karger & Hitchcock, 2003; Sands, Adams, & Stout, 1995; Wolery & Sainato, 1996).

Key Issues in Curriculum for Young Children with Disabilities

The purpose of this section is to describe a comprehensive curriculum framework that is built on the principles of universal design as a means of ensuring access, participation, and progress for all learners. Further, a curriculum framework as described here provides a set of recommended practices for (a) promoting active engagement and learning; (b) individualizing and adapting practices for each child based on ongoing data; (c) providing opportunities for children's learning within regular routines; and (d) working collaboratively and sharing responsibilities among families and professionals (Sandall et al, 2005).

Universal design for learning.

The 2004 amendments to IDEA require that all children, regardless of ability, have access to the general curriculum, and have the opportunity to participate and make progress in the general curriculum. While the mandate is not new, many providers working with young children continue to struggle with understanding how to make each component of the mandate a reality.

Access and participation mean more than placing children in child care programs, preschools, or primary classrooms. Although a child may be present in these programs or classrooms, cognitive, sensory, affective, physical, linguistic, or cultural barriers impact the degree to which a curriculum is truly accessible to them. In addition, a curriculum that is effective for some children may not result in positive outcomes for others.

An accessible curriculum means that all aspects of the curriculum (i.e., the environment, the goals, the content, the instructional methods and interactions, the assessments, and the toys/materials) invite active participation of all children, regardless of disability or special needs. But how can access and participation be achieved for all?

Educators, caregivers, and therapists work diligently to make the curriculum accessible to children with disabilities by varying content, providing instructional support, designing developmentally appropriate activities, and adapting toys or materials. For example, they may add a switch to allow a child with physical impairments to operate a toy, or create a series of picture cards to clarify the daily schedule for a child with communication delays. However, these efforts to make the curriculum accessible and encourage active participation are generally geared toward a single child (i.e., designed for one child at a time) and are added after the fact. While critical to meeting the needs and interests of the individual child, making the curriculum accessible after the fact can be time consuming, challenging for the educator or caregiver, and beneficial to only a small number of children at a given time or within a given activity.

The practice of making adaptations to an existing curriculum framework is like adding a wheelchair ramp to an existing building rather than designing the ramp during construction. The after-the-fact method is more expensive, takes more time, and may be awkward and unsightly. Today's architects, operating from a universal design perspective, build in access from the design stage, creating ramps, rails, and manageable entrances from the inception. Not only are these adaptations attractive, they are useful for individuals with and without disabilities, thereby benefiting many people simultaneously.

A curriculum framework can be designed in the same way. That is, the curriculum developer builds in universal access from the beginning rather than as an after-the-fact adaptation. When a curriculum framework is being designed, the full range of diversity represented in the children and families who may participate should be considered.

Universally designed daily activities, instructional supports, and toys/materials help ensure that all children have meaningful and successful access to and participation in the curriculum (Karger & Hitchcock, 2003). Considering children's individual

needs and interests from the beginning decreases the likelihood that an adaptation will draw unwanted attention to a child. A universal perspective to curriculum design also increases the likelihood that all children will achieve positive outcomes.

There are three essential principles of universal design for learning that have been identified (Blackhurst et al., 1999; CAST, 2004; Orkwis, 1999; Orkwis & McLane, 1998). A universally designed curriculum framework provides:

- Multiple means of representation. This principle ensures instruction, questions, expectations, and learning opportunities are provided in various formats and at different levels of complexity, addressing a range of ability levels and visual, auditory, and kinesthetic needs. (This principle is reflected in the activities listed in Table 1A in the Appendix.)

- Multiple means of engagement. This principle ensures various opportunities are presented for arousing children's attention, curiosity, and motivation, addressing a wide range of interests, preferences, and personal styles. Engagement is then maintained by providing various levels of scaffolding, repetition, and appropriate challenges to ensure successful learning. (This principle is reflected in the activities listed in Table 1B in the Appendix.)

- Multiple means of expression. This principle ensures children have a variety of formats for responding, demonstrating what they know, and for expressing ideas, feelings, and preferences. In addition, children have options in their use of resources, toys, and materials, addressing individual strengths, preferences, and abilities. (This principle is reflected in the activities listed in Table 1C in the Appendix.)

These principles of universal design for learning are essential for ensuring both physical access and meaningful participation across daily routines and activities for all young children (e.g., children with diverse cultural or linguistic backgrounds, children who have identified disabilities, or children who need additional support to master content). Even with thoughtful design, teams may find it necessary to make accommodations and modifications to meet the individual needs of particular children and/or families. Built upon definitions provided by Wrightslaw (2003), we define accommodations as acts made to level the playing field and provide equal access and opportunity without substantially altering what children are expected to learn and be able to do. Examples of accommodations include altering instruments, toys/materials, allowing various response formats, and/or altering the settings or timing. Modifications are defined as substantial changes in practices and expectations. Examples of modifications include changes in instructional level, content, and performance criteria, and changes in test form or format including alternate assessments.

Regardless of the setting in which early care and education services are provided or the model for providing the service, the principles of universal design for learning are at the heart of an effective curriculum framework and articulate a comprehensive approach to meet the needs of all young children. The following section describes the integrated elements of a cohesive, universally designed curriculum framework. This is followed by a discussion of the need for collaboration and partnerships among service providers, families, and community members.

Curriculum framework.

Developing, implementing, and evaluating a curriculum framework can be complex and at times challenging. Yet a curriculum framework is important in ensuring:

• Access to and full participation by all children;

• Adherence to the program's mission and goals;

• Assurance that individual children's and families' needs are met; and

• Accountability to agency and state standards/mandates.

Consistent with the NAEYC-NAECS/SDE position statement (2003), an effective curriculum framework emphasizes the interrelated and cyclical relationships between assessment and curriculum and does not necessarily have a specific beginning or ending point. In other words, a comprehensive and universally designed curriculum framework creates feedback spirals that allow teams to inform and change practice (Dodge, 2000; Grisham-Brown & Pretti-Frontczak, 2003; Helm & Gronlund, 2000; McAfee & Leong, 2002). Feedback spirals encourage teams to see change as a necessary process to quality instruction and programming. Feedback spirals also encourage teams to engage in ongoing data gathering, analysis, reflection, and revision. Therefore, it is critical for teams to have a clear idea of intended outcomes.

The specific elements of a cohesive, universally designed curriculum framework include assessment and progress monitoring, scope and sequence strategies, and activities and intervention strategies; these elements also require collaboration with other members of the team. These specific elements, described more fully in the following section, must also take into consideration universal design for learning, the essential need of partnering, and an understanding that providers will need to be flexible when implementing a curriculum framework, and provide accommodations and modification as needed.

Assessment and progress monitoring.

It is important that teams conduct comprehensive, universally designed, and authentic assessment and ongoing monitoring of all children's development and learning. Team members need a clear understanding of all children's current skills and abilities to ensure access and participation, and to develop appropriate learning opportunities.

As teams implement assessment/progress monitoring, there may be times when accommodations to toys/materials, procedures, and items are necessary to obtain accurate information about what a child knows, can do, and is starting to do. Examples of accommodations that can be made during assessment/progress monitoring include:

• Extended wait or performance time;

• Presentation of information verbally and/or visually;

• Increased size of print/pictures; and

• Presentation of toys/materials that are adjustable and flexible in how they are used.

Teams may also find it necessary to provide more individualized or specialized practices for some children. For example, they need to modify or change their assessment/progress monitoring practices to ensure all children are able to participate and that children are not penalized for having a disability. Modifications may include (a) using an alternative measure, (b) changing how a child demonstrates or performs a skill or task, (c) assessing underlying, earlier, or prerequisite skills, and/or (d) reducing the number of items assessed/monitored. A more detailed examination of assessment and progress monitoring is provided in the Assessment section of this paper. Examples of how assessment/progress monitoring can go from generic practices to highly individualized interventions are provided in Table 2A.

Scope and sequence.

Scope refers to broad, often-integrated areas of development (e.g., motor, communication, adaptive, social) and/or content areas (e.g., mathematics, science, literacy). Sequence refers to the order (ages/stages/grade levels) in which the content will be taught and learned and is often specified in a developmental hierarchy (from easier to more difficult) or by grade level.

Over the last several years, policy, public interest, and research have led to the development of state and/or program standards (Schumacher, Irish, & Lombardi, 2003). A standard is defined as a "general statement that represents the information, skills, or both, that students should understand and be able to do" (Bodrova, Leong, Paynter, & Semenov, 2000, p. 33). Standards (sometimes referred to as content standards, child or learning outcomes, and indicators) are designed to organize, prioritize, and frame what children are to learn at various stages or ages of development/education (Kurtenbach, 2000; McLaughlin & Shepard, 1995). For scope and sequence, broad outcomes for all learners are often set by state and/or program standards and these standards may serve as the common scope and sequence for all learners in a particular state, region, or program.

When federal, state, or program standards are used as a common scope and sequence, it is important to note that in some cases they may not include all skills and knowledge important for early development (e.g., some standards documents may not address social, adaptive, or motor development) (NAEYC & NAECS/SDE, 2003; Scott-Little, Kagan & Frelow, 2005), either in general or specifically in terms of children with disabilities. Therefore, the scope and sequence for young children should include all areas of development and learning, not just those areas covered in federal, state, or program standards.

For some children, teams may find that accommodations are needed to ensure children are progressing through the scope and sequence outlined. The main concepts or ideas embedded within the standards are targeted for all, but teams may need to alter the learning environment, provide additional supports, and/or allow children to use alternative communication devices to demonstrate knowledge and skill.

Individually targeted skills may also be needed within the scope and sequence and are identified based upon the unique needs of children. These skills are often documented in individualized family service plans (IFSPs) and individualized education plans (IEPs) for children with identified disabilities (Grisham-Brown, Hemmeter, & Pretti-Frontczak, 2005). Individually targeted skills, while remaining aligned with common standards for all children, represent a substantial modification or change in terms of expectations, performance criteria, and/or form or format. Individually targeted skills should not be simply a restatement of what is being addressed for all learners, but rather the underlying, earlier, or prerequisite skills that are necessary for a child to have access to and participate fully in the curriculum. Examples of how the scope and sequence can go from generic practices to highly individualized practices are illustrated in Table 2B in the Appendix.

Activities and intervention strategies.

Young children's learning occurs as a part of the routines and activities of daily life and play (Sandall et al., 2005). This is true of all children; as stated in the NAEYC-NAECS/SDE position statement (2003), "Researchers have found that young children with and without disabilities benefit more from the curriculum when they are engaged or involved" (p. 6), and the point is underscored in this document with respect to young children with disabilities. Learning opportunities are created by adults, peers, and the environment itself. Thus children's learning can be enhanced by ensuring that daily activities and routines are rich with learning opportunities, rather than being created during contrived situations directed by adults (Horn, Lieber, Li, Sandall, & Schwartz, 2000; Sandall et al., 2002). The use of daily routines and activities as the context for learning in a universally designed curriculum framework ensures that standards and

individually targeted skills are addressed in a manner that expands, modifies, or is integral to the activity in a meaningful way (Pretti-Frontczak & Bricker, 2004).

High quality learning contexts that incorporate the three principles of universal design serve as the foundation for intervention planning for all children. For children with disabilities that need additional support, accommodations are provided to ensure that these children are progressing (Robertson, Green, Schloss, & Kohler, 2003; Sandall et al., 2002; Vaughn, Ae-Hwa, Morris-Sloan, Hughes, Batya, & Dheepa, 2003). To make such accommodations, teams can:

- Provide social supports (e.g., peer-mediated intervention strategies, cooperative learning);
- Use visual, auditory, and kinesthetic methods (e.g., use pictures and models when explaining);
- Use a range of reinforcers (e.g., smiles, hugs, praise, provision of desired toy/object, continuing play);
- Adapt toys/materials to allow children to use a variety of movements in different positions;
- Alter the physical, social, or temporal environment;
- Alter the schedule of activities and routines;
- Adjust the amount and type of support provided; and
- Divide an activity into smaller steps.

Similarly, individualized instructional opportunities and modifications should be provided as necessary to meet a child's unique learning needs (Sandall et al., 2002). For example, the team might plan specific teaching episodes or embedded learning opportunities (ELOs) to address the individual child's specific learning priorities within the context of the ongoing routines and activities (Horn et al., 2000). ELOs should be created by service providers, family members, and community members and should encourage children to actively explore the environment through participation in daily activities.

When creating ELOs, teams should use a variety of strategies that fall on a continuum from (a) non-directive: an adult or peer serves as a facilitator in supporting a child's participation during usual routines and activities, to (b) mediating: adults and peers model and provide scaffolding to maintain children's interest and motivation, and promote learning, to (c) directive: adults and peers guide or lead the interaction (Bredekamp & Rosegrant, 1992, 1995; Grisham-Brown et al., 2005; Sandall et al., 2005; Widerstrom, 2005). A teaching continuum implies that teams are purposeful in making decisions about how to provide support to young children. Regardless of the part of the continuum used, three over-arching principles should be applied to fully implement a universally designed curriculum framework.

First, teams should use the full continuum of teaching strategies. As stated in the NAEYC-NAECS/SDE position statement

(2003), in implementing effective curriculum, "pedagogy or teaching strategies are tailored to children's ages, developmental capacities, language and culture, and abilities or disabilities" (p. 7). When teams focus only on one end of the continuum (e.g., nondirective instruction) or another (e.g., directive instruction), it is difficult to meet the full range of children's needs.

Second, teams need to be systematic in their selection, development, and use of the supports they provide young children. To do this, teams need to determine which skills require specific support, what type of support children need to move toward learning, and the circumstances under which support will be provided (e.g., how long a caregiver waits before providing the support). It is important to understand that systematic teaching applies to all strategies along the continuum and should be employed by all members of the team (Grisham-Brown et al., 2005).

Third, it is important to remember the critical role adults play in responding to, expanding, and supporting children's communicative attempts, play, and interactions. Examples of how the activities and intervention strategies panel can go from generic practices to highly individualized practices are provided on Table 2C in the Appendix.

Feedback spirals: Revisiting assessment and progress monitoring practices.

Assessment/progress monitoring helps ensure continuous feedback spirals. Feedback spirals are necessary to inform and change practice, guide interactions and the selection of toys/materials, and inform decision making regarding all aspects of the program (e.g., goals, instructional efforts, professional development, expenditures). This requires the use of a variety of methods to ensure collection of reliable, valid, and useful assessment/progress monitoring data (Branscombe, Castle, Dorsey, Surbeck, & Taylor, 2003; Helm, Beneke, & Steinheimer, 1998; Wolery, 2004) and adequate and collaborative time to review and interpret the data to inform and change practice (Dodge, 2000; Grisham-Brown & Pretti-Frontczak, 2003; Helm & Gronlund, 2000; McAfee & Leong, 2002).

Collaboration and partnering.

Collaboration and partnerships between program personnel and families or other members of the community serve as the structure and support for a curriculum framework. Collaborative efforts or partnerships are formed between a teacher and an assistant, a home visitor and a caregiver, or a child care provider and an itinerant teacher. These types of partnerships happen routinely for most, if not all, children.

In some instances it may be necessary to increase the number of members of the collaborative partnership, the intensity of the partnership, and/or the expertise of the members to address the needs of a child with a disability. For example,

if a child presents challenging behaviors, team members may include the family, child care providers, an intervention specialist, a communication specialist, and a behavior specialist. These team members may need to communicate often as they develop, implement, and evaluate a plan to address the child's challenging behaviors

Regardless of type or intensity of the partnerships, collaboration is not only desirable, but also necessary in providing services to young children that (a) are accessible, (b) ensure full participation, and (c) promote progress (Sandall et al., 2005). Collaboration should be sought in the design, implementation, and evaluation of a curriculum framework.

Indicators of Effectiveness

All learners have access to and participate in the curriculum through multiple means of representation, engagement, and expression.

This indicator is especially critical for children who have disabilities or other special learning needs.

Multiple means of representation are provided so that the curriculum is accessible to all children regardless of ability, needs, or background.

When multiple means of representation are provided, the presentation of the instruction, the interactions between adults and children, the materials and toys, and the environment are all designed to offer different and various opportunities that allow children to participate most effectively. This built-in flexibility ensures that the curriculum framework is both challenging and attainable for children functioning at different levels. Just as stairs and ramps allow people to arrive at the same destination, using a variety of formats in the design and implementation of a curriculum framework allows children to arrive at the same desired destination.

An example of a curriculum framework with multiple means of representation is one where adults use practices such as differentiated instruction and the development of learning opportunities at different levels of complexity. For instance, the teacher gives children options for learning about the moon from a collection of books that range from easy to difficult, videos, Internet sites, models, or planetarium visits. These options accommodate a range of ability levels as well as visual, auditory, and kinesthetic needs. Another example is the use of strategies such as scaffolding, in which the adults build on what children already know and guide them to the next level. For example, a caregiver knows that some of the infants in her care will be able to hold objects in one hand but not both. Anticipating their needs, she plans learning opportunities that can occur during activities throughout the day, such as providing pull-apart toys and toys with two easy-grip handles or giving children two crackers at the same time.

Further, since some children may do better when they hear information while others need to see it, adults should provide multi-sensory options in different formats, such as giving instructions with both words and pictures. For example, a daily schedule can be written, and pictures or objects can be provided for children with visual impairments. Flexible practices and multiple formats give children alternative ways to access and participate in the curriculum regardless of their background, experience, prior knowledge, or physical challenges. See Table 1A in the Appendix for additional examples.

Multiple means of engagement are available so that children fully participate in the curriculum regardless of ability, needs, or background.

Since children's interests and abilities vary, the curriculum framework should provide flexible options that appeal to children with different abilities, developmental levels, preferences, and cultural backgrounds. The combination of optional supports and various levels of challenges should facilitate children's engagement where novelty (randomness and surprise) is balanced with familiarity (repetition and predictability). Such practices should appeal to individual differences and help children maintain engagement.

An example of a curriculum framework with multiple means of engagement is one in which children may select toys/materials that are creative and open-ended or structured and controlled. They may choose to work in bright and noisy areas or places that are dim and quiet, with groups or individually. They may take advantage of the optional supports, such as handles on puzzle pieces or an easy setting on an interactive early reading software program, or select from a range of challenges appropriate for different levels. See Table 1B in the Appendix for additional examples.

Multiple means of expression are supported so that children can demonstrate what they know and are able to do regardless of ability, needs, or background.

A flexible curriculum framework encourages all children to communicate and show what they know and are able to do using any method they can or prefer. In general, children should be encouraged to use a variety of verbal and non-verbal expressions to demonstrate the skills and concepts they have acquired, those that are emerging, and those that team members need to continue to support and provide practice opportunities for. Adults should encourage and support any form of expression, including the use of speech, signs, gestures, pictures, objects, writing, art, and assistive technology. By allowing children to express themselves in multiple ways, children will have greater independence and success in getting their wants and needs met and in sharing their ideas. See Table 1C in the Appendix for additional examples.

Programs adopt curriculum goals that are clear and shared by all.

As emphasized in the NAEYC-NAECS/SDE position statement (2003), common goals (also referred to as outcomes or standards) should stem from critical concepts and skills deemed important for all young children to acquire (i.e., for children with disabilities, children at risk, and children without identified disabilities). At times, particular children may need more individualized goals (often identified on an individualized family service plan/individualized education plan). Individualized plans help team members address the possible reasons a child is having difficulty accessing and participating in daily activities and routines and making progress toward the common goals in the general curriculum. Individualized needs for children should represent underlying, earlier, or prerequisite concepts and skills that once obtained will enhance a child's access, participation, and progress in daily activities and the general curriculum.

Curriculum is comprehensive.

Programs should have a curriculum framework that is well understood by all stakeholders and covers all areas of growth and development considered important for young children, and one that addresses federal, state, or agency standards (NAEYC & NAECS/SDE, 2003). A comprehensive, universally designed curriculum ensures that children are exposed to and participate in a wide variety of experiences. A comprehensive curriculum should employ a continuum of teaching strategies from adult-directed, to mediated, to child-directed to ensure children's individual needs are met. Feedback spirals within the curriculum framework allow teams to inform and change practice, responding promptly to children's needs.

Programs strive to build and maintain successful partnerships as curriculum is implemented.

A curriculum framework is only as strong as the partnerships that support it. All young children should be served by community, school, and family members who share a common vision for supporting their health, growth, and development. Programs serving young children are strengthened by collaborative relationships among program personnel, families, and community members. Collaboration occurs when individuals interact and engage in shared decision making in an effort to achieve a common goal. Effective collaborative partners have a shared vision and jointly assume responsibility for serving children. Partnerships vary both in frequency and formality. Regardless of the frequency or formality of collaboration, open communication, mutual trust, and shared values are essential for successful partnerships.

Frequently Asked Questions

1. *Why are the principles of universal design for learning important for all programs and people working with young children? For example, what do the principles mean for a mom interacting with her baby, for those providing home visits, for child care providers in community settings, for an inclusive preschool special education teacher, or for a general education 1st grade teacher?*

Whether someone is working with infants, toddlers, preschoolers, or students in the elementary grades, the principles of universal design for learning provide a foundation for ensuring full access and active participation for all learners. Regardless of the setting, children are more likely to thrive when they are given a variety of supports and opportunities to meet their diverse needs.

For example, a mom's interaction with her baby would include rich and varied forms of communication, including singing, talking, sharing books, making faces, using gestures, playing simple games, dancing, showing pictures, and playing with toys or other materials. Home visitors would be prepared to offer an abundant repertoire of activities and strategies appropriate for different levels of difficulty, sensitive to different cultures, and adaptable for the different settings in which they would be practiced.

Child care providers and educators, whether in a home or center-based setting, design the environment, instructional strategies, activities, materials, and resources to meet the needs of the diverse groups of children and/or families they might serve. The principles of universal design for learning ensure that the learning needs of all children with and without identified disabilities are addressed using multiple means of representation, engagement, and expression to create various opportunities for children to learn and develop.

2. *What is the "general curriculum" for young children?*

The general curriculum includes activities, interactions, and learning opportunities provided for young children throughout their daily routines. The general curriculum should be consistent with young children's development and state/program standards. However, the general curriculum should be thought of as more than any single set of standards or developmental expectations, single resource (e.g., DAP guidelines), or single textbook.

Curriculum for young children is highly complex and, as presented here, composed of many elements. The primary purpose of a curriculum is to guide learning activities and provide consistency of expectations, content, methods, and outcomes (Karger & Hitchcock, 2003). It is critical that the same curriculum established for young children without disabilities be afforded to young children with disabilities.

3. *Are national, state, district, or program standards along with professional organization guidelines (e.g., DAP, recommended practices), commercially published curricula, or a child's individualized plan sufficient for ensuring access to participation in the general curriculum?*

Ensuring access to and participation in the general curriculum requires programs to design or select, implement, and evaluate a curriculum framework consistent with principles of universal design. These principles provide a foundation for and collaboration among personnel, families, and community members.

National, state, district, or program standards along with commercial materials or a child's individualized plan are important, but not sufficient to ensure that a comprehensive curriculum framework is in place. The standards and the individualized plan provide scope and sequence, while commercially available materials may provide ideas regarding activities and instructional strategies but do not complete the curriculum framework. The principles of universal design and collaboration are still needed, along with assessment and progress monitoring practices.

4. *How can individualized plans (e.g., IFSPs and IEPs), written using domains of development (e.g., fine motor, gross motor, adaptive, cognition, social communication, social) be aligned with standards organized by content area (e.g., literacy, mathematics, science, social studies)?*

A primary concern for those working with young children with disabilities is that the areas of literacy, mathematics, science, and social studies or other content areas targeted in standards will become the sole focus of intervention efforts. Teachers and others involved in providing services are concerned that if they target the critical skills such as feeding, walking, expressing wants and needs, getting along with others, or playing with toys that they will not be able to show alignment with and progress toward content area standards.

It is important to understand that various states and programs define alignment differently (Nolet & McLaughlin, 2000). Some will interpret alignment between individualized plans and standards as parallel—a more one-to-one notion—while others suggest there should be reference from the individualized plan back to standards. Despite how alignment is defined, standards are designed to organize, prioritize, and frame what children are to learn at various stages or ages of development/education (e.g., Kurtenbach, 2000; McLaughlin & Shepard, 1995), not to dictate or limit what is taught. Further, standards are only one part of a curriculum framework, which should be comprehensive and integrated across all areas of learning.

Individualized plans (particularly IFSPs and IEPs) are designed to help teams understand and address what is needed in order for the child to access and participate in the general curriculum. Individualized plans should not be restatements of the general curriculum. Rather, IFSPs and IEPs should emphasize those things a child and/or family needs to ensure access and participation. Individualized plans should include a focused, coherent sequence of intentionally designed intervention to efficiently address a child's and family's needs.

Therefore, there are times when individualized plans may closely align with standards. For example, most states have standards related to reading comprehension. A child's individualized plan can have a target skill that addresses the need to improve reading comprehension. This is especially true if a child's challenges, with respect to this skill, are keeping the child from accessing and participating in the general curriculum and requires specially designed instruction. There may be times when the alignment is not as close (i.e., when it is necessary to address underlying or prerequisite skills not directly found in standards). For example, if a child presents several challenging behaviors, the individualized plan should address such behaviors as helping the child learn to express his or her wants and needs and play appropriately with toys and others. Such specific skills may not be directly noted or found in state/program standards, but they are critical for ensuring a child has access to and can participate in the general curriculum and attain the skills specified by standards.

5. *Who is responsible for ensuring a universally designed curriculum framework is in place?*

The saying "it takes a village to raise a child" is applicable to assigning responsibility for ensuring that a comprehensive and universally designed curriculum framework is in place. All team members need to understand which practices are in place for all children and determine when more individualized efforts are required. Further, all team members need to understand what is expected of and developmentally appropriate for young children.

Given that programs serving young children are becoming more diverse and are under increasing pressure to be accountable regarding child outcomes, curriculum planning needs to concurrently address (a) what children should learn, (b) what they already know and can do, (c) how they will be taught, and (d) the activities and interactions that will be used to facilitate learning (e.g., Helm & Gronlund, 2000; Meisels, 2000). Further, collaborative planning time needs to include:

• Reflection and discussion;

• Interpretation of data patterns; and

• Consideration by all team members for needed changes.

Lastly, the involvement of all team members helps ensure that multiple and varied learning opportunities occur across a child's daily routine using a variety of strategies.

6. *How can I use this document to improve services for young children?*

It is important that teams understand and support the curriculum practices described. Becoming knowledgeable may involve taking the following steps:

a. Engage in self-study and reflection. Begin by reflecting on the overall recommendations in the NAEYC-NAECS/SDE position statement (2003), considering the practices in this document within this broader foundation. Then, consider whether the practices described in this paper (e.g., principles of universal design, elements of a curriculum framework, the need for collaboration) are present, and to what extent, in your own practice and within your program/agency.

b. Engage in discussion among team members about which features are not in place and how changes can be made. Remember to start small by improving one practice at a time. Form a study group with colleagues, families, or other members of your community to discuss and learn more about the practices presented here. For example, select recent journal articles describing effective or innovative practices (e.g., articles published in the Journal of Early Intervention or Early Childhood Research Quarterly) or the practices described in the DEC Recommended Practices: A Comprehensive Guide for Practical Application (Sandall et al., 2005) and try them out and then discuss what worked and did not work.

c. Review the examples and illustrations provided in Table 1 and Table 2 in the Appendix for additional ideas on how to implement the practices described in this paper.

ASSESSMENT

Key Recommendation

Assessment is a shared experience between families and professionals in which information and ideas are exchanged to benefit a child's growth and development. Assessment practices should be integrated and individualized in order to: (a) answer the questions posed by the assessment team (including family members); (b) integrate the child's everyday routines, interests, materials, caregivers, and play partners within the assessment process; and (c) develop a system for shared partnerships with professionals and families for the communication and collection of ongoing information valuable for teaching and learning. Therefore, assessment teams should implement a child- and family-centered, team-based, and ecologically valid assessment process. This process should be designed to address each child's unique strengths and needs through authentic, developmentally appropriate, culturally and linguistically responsive, multidimensional assessment methods. The methods should be matched to the purpose for the assessment, linked to curriculum and intervention, and supported by professional development.

Rationale

Assessment practices valid for all young children and appropriate to support learning and instruction should be used to identify children who may need additional services (Kagan, Scott-Little, & Clifford, 2003), to plan programs, and to monitor intervention progress (Nesiworth & Bagnato, 2005) by early childhood practitioners. When engaged in assessment activities, interdisciplinary team members behave in ways congruent with DEC Recommended Practices: A Comprehensive Guide for Practical Application (Sandall et al., 2005) and the recommendations and indicators of effective assessment in the position statement of NAEYC and NAECS/SDE (2003).

While practices should be appropriate for any and all children, each child and family is unique. Therefore, the tools, methods, and team selected to assist in the assessment process should be unique and individualized to ensure the best contextual match for the child and family (Meisels & Fenichel, 1996; Neisworth & Bagnato, 2004). Team members should include individuals who can best make decisions needed to address critical questions necessary to determine the appropriate services for children with disabilities and their families. For example, for children with specific sensory or developmental needs (e.g., visual and/or hearing impairments, movement problems, or learning difficulties) the team should include individuals with both the expertise essential to assess the child's unique needs and those with the skills to use assessment procedures including appropriate (i.e., within standardization procedures) modifications, adaptations, or accommodations to describe the child's needs within the context of the his/her typical routines and activities in meaningful environments. This may mean that the professional assessment team members provide consultation or coaching to the family and other team members within an integrated assessment process (Boone & Crais, 1999). It is also essential that the child and family's cultural and linguistic preferences are considered in the development of the team and the design of the assessment process to limit bias and to promote collaboration and communication (Hanson & Lynch, 2004).

Assessments should be conducted within an ecological framework or model that accounts for each participant or aspect of the assessment process: the child, the family, the environment (home, community, and school/center), the instruments and tools, and the team members. Practitioners are encouraged to participate in assessments that: (1) contribute to intervention outcomes, (2) make sense in the child's family, community, and culture to ensure cultural and ecological validity, and (3) focus on natural systems such as families, schools, communities, and the role and contributions of caregivers and peers (Barnett, Macmann, & Carey, 1992; Neisworth & Bagnato, 1992).

Key Issues in Assessment for Young Children with Disabilities

The purpose of this section is to provide an overview of key issues related to assessment in EI/ECSE, to identify important quality indicators for those involved in the assessment process, and to provide information about additional resources that might assist those interested in or charged with implementing assessments. This section will also provide specific information on how to implement assessments that are (1) family centered and team based, and (2) individualized and appropriate. This is followed by a discussion of how to select assessment tools and utility of assessment. Finally, specific recommendations related to communicating assessment results and ethical and legal practices will be presented. The section will conclude with Indicators of Effectiveness, followed by Frequently Asked Questions.

Family centered and team based process.

The role of families in assessment is addressed in the position statement of NAEYC and NAECS/SDE (2003) but is of even greater importance when considering assessment of children with disabilities. Within integrated child- and family-centered assessment teams, family members are equal and contributing partners (Boone & Crais, 1999; Woods & McCormick, 2002). Family members provide critical and functional information to describe child status and level of functioning, identify concerns, and develop specific intervention goals. Teams must solicit the knowledge of family members to increase the richness of assessment information and engage families in the assessment process to understand and validate their concerns. The assessment process must be designed to facilitate family inclusion at multiple levels in response to family preferences and with sensitivity to family values, needs, language, and culture. Additionally, in early childhood in particular, the assessment process is often a family's first experience with early intervention and the special education process. The outcome of the assessment process may have powerful significance for family members. It is therefore the responsibility of professional team members to ensure an honest and collaborative experience for family team members.

The role of the family as the child's first and most significant teacher is firmly acknowledged within the fields of early childhood, early intervention, and preschool special education. The assessment team benefits from the family's "teaching experience when they inquire about the child's preferences for activities, materials, play partners, and schedules" (Woods & McCormick, 2002. p.4).

Families contribute to the assessment process in multiple ways. Families:

- Enhance team observations by describing their child's performance in other settings;
- Suggest options, activities, and materials for interaction;
- Facilitate child engagement; and
- Interact with their child in play and care-giving routines (Bailey, 2004; McCormick & Nellis, 2004).

Families not only support their child during the assessment process but also validate the findings suggested by other team members, identify discrepancies in performance, report on typical patterns of behavior, and co-assess with team members to ensure the best performance by their child. In addition, professional-family partnership in assessment provides opportunities for family members to identify their preferences for roles and acknowledges their expertise and competence as team members (Boone & Crais, 1999).

Individualized and appropriate process.

The assessment of young children requires an individualized and appropriate multimodal assessment model to generate and confirm findings (McCormick & Nellis, 2004; Roid & Sampers, 2004). The NAEYC-NAECS/SDE position statement (2003) asserts that an effective assessment system "emphasizes repeated, systematic observation, documentation, and other forms of criterion- or performance-oriented assessment using broad, varied, and complementary methods ..." (p.11). There is an even stronger rationale for this approach for children with disabilities, who need more and perhaps different opportunities to respond. Tools used to gather information may include direct evaluation of child skills; assessment within a group; dynamic, formal, and informal observation; video recordings; interviews; and ratings of skills and behaviors. Modifications of response demand and other forms of adaptations and accommodations must also be considered. As discussed previously, this multimodal assessment process is more easily, accurately, and reliably accomplished by a team of professionals and family members who are jointly responsible for conducting and supporting data gathering.

The assessment process should be initiated through a problem-solving model that seeks to answer specific questions about the child. These specific questions should be answered in a family-friendly, linguistically, and culturally responsive manner, and in the mode that best addresses any challenges that might be present (i.e., learning concerns for a child with visual impairment). Therefore, the team begins the assessment process with conversations with staff and family members to determine measures, times for observations, and appropriate team members/participants. Multiple observations by professional and family team members may be the primary method of data gathering in tandem with a review of existing information collected by staff. Team members

should also review strategies used previously to enhance development, learning, academic, or social skills to determine child sensory, behavioral, and learning preferences.

The assessment process answers important questions related to family concerns, eligibility for services, and ongoing service provision for a child. It is individualized for the child and family and incorporates high-quality and technically sound tools and procedures based on the child's developmental, physical, sensory, and behavioral needs. A high-quality assessment is comprehensive and addresses appropriate domains of learning, levels of support necessary for success, and sufficiency of skill use in a variety of environments (i.e., generalization). The team should provide opportunities to gather information from multiple settings and sources using multiple measures so that they can support the child and family's participation in meaningful and authentic routines and activities.

Information gathered through the assessment process should be used to support the family and professional team members in the decision-making process. The formative and summative analysis of assessment information for decision making goes beyond the generation of labels or scores and the use of deficit models and descriptors to a more useful and functionally meaningful summary. The assessment process seeks to identify the child's needs and family preferences so that specific decisions can be made about screening and program eligibility; individual service development and plans (goals and objectives); placement; and intervention. The assessment tools used by the team must also be carefully reviewed and selected to meet recommended practices and standards. A discussion of three critical attributes of high-quality assessments follows.

1. *Assessment tools have utility and are used for specific purposes.*

Assessment team processes and decisions answer important questions including: (a) What do we need to know about this child? (b) What information do we already have? (c) What questions do family members want answered? (d) What are family priorities and concerns? (e) What environments are important to successful integration within the community? and (f) How can child participation within these environments be reliably assessed? The assessment process necessary to answer these questions integrates criterion-based instruments, informal assessment tools, and published or teacher-made checklists and behavior samples with traditional norm-referenced assessment tools.

The utility or usefulness of the assessment is an important consideration when choosing an assessment tool. For young children with disabilities, assessment tools are typically selected to address seven different purposes: (1) screening, (2) diagnosis (or identification) of delay or disability, (3) eligibility determination for early intervention or special education services, (4) instructional program planning/intervention assessment, (5) placement, (6) progress monitoring, and (7) program evaluation (Wolery, Strain, & Bailey, 1992). These purposes are consistent with, and elaborate on, the broader purposes of assessment as described in the NAEYC-NAECS/SDE position statement (2003) and in the work of the National Education Goals Panel on assessment (Shepard, Kagan, & Wurtz, 1998). The decisions and measurement practices within these areas are included in Table 3 in the Appendix. It cannot be overstated that one tool or procedure will not successfully fulfill all seven assessment purposes. For example, children should never qualify for special education or related services based on screening information or based on a single test score. Such a practice violates the non-discriminatory principle included in special education law (IDEA, 2004).

Finally, the assessment team must also select assessment tools that address specific questions and concerns from the family that may be outside the scope of the child's referral and/or eligibility determination. Often these questions may not be easily answered with a traditional assessment. For example, families may be concerned with important attributes such as child temperament or social development, playing with friends, or adaptive and self-help behaviors. These important family questions and concerns about their child's performance in typical and daily routines and activities can and should become part of the assessment process.

The specific assessment tools are selected based on the purpose of assessment, child need, family concern, service model, and setting. The assessment team should select tools and methods that allow family members to participate to the greatest extent possible. Potential assessment tools include: (1) record review/developmental history, (2) interviews, (3) observations, (4) checklists/rating scales, (5) portfolios, and (6) tests. Tests may be norm-referenced, criterion-referenced or curriculum-based; however, the most reliable outcomes for young children are generated when these tools are used within an authentic assessment model. Because data gathered from traditional norm-referenced assessments may not provide adequate information for developing IFSP/IEPs, monitoring child progress, evaluating the effectiveness of intervention, or planning new services, norm-referenced assessments should always be used concurrently with criterion or curriculum-based and ecological assessments.

The purpose for assessment also drives the selection of assessment tools. The issues here are similar to those discussed in the NAEYC-NAECS/SDE position statement (2003), but with additional considerations when assessing children with or at risk for disabilities and developmental delays. First and foremost, any assessment instrument selected for use must have the ability to provide necessary information to answer the referral concern and family/team questions. Second, selected instruments must have technical adequacy, or evidence of reliability (consistency) and validity (meaning). If a measure is reliable, results across examiners, children, and over time can be trusted. The validity of an assessment tool communicates whether it is measuring what it says it measures (e.g., a "language test" actually measuring language development).

Assessment team members make multiple decisions throughout the assessment process. Two critical decisions are (a) the determination of the existence of a delay or disability, and (b) the determination of the child's eligibility for services. For diagnostic and eligibility decisions to be valid, collaboration between families and professionals is essential. When a young child is assessed to determine eligibility for special education services, a team must select tests capable of providing information to help make this decision. Assessment teams must keep potential IFSP/IEP goals in mind and gather appropriate assessment information to inform the goal-writing process. Assessment information should describe a child's current state of development, as well specific skill strengths and skill weaknesses. To accomplish this, it is critical that families are included in the assessment process and that the tools used are ecologically valid and authentic.

In addition to determination of eligibility for specialized services, IEP development, and program planning, assessment teams also participate in assessment for the purpose of ongoing assessment and progress monitoring. Ongoing assessment and progress monitoring are critical and often forgotten processes in the assessment system. The primary purpose of ongoing assessment is to help teachers implement and modify curriculum and teaching practices to ensure that all children, including children with disabilities, are progressing toward identified goals. For some children this may include full participation in the classroom or center assessment with little or no adaptation or modification necessary; other children may need minimum or significant modification. (See the Curriculum section of this paper for more information on this topic.)

Ongoing assessment and progress monitoring create an integrated assessment system whereby initial assessment decisions are monitored and evaluated through an integrated loop of assessment that is continuous, ensuring that services are meeting the child's current and relevant needs. Ongoing assessment provides the mechanism for both individual programming and program evaluation. (See the Program Evaluation section of this paper for more information.) Assessment outcomes may also be used within a program evaluation plan to inform program, school, and district-wide decisions. In short, collaborative family and professional team decision making occurs at multiple points in the assessment process.

Assessment teams have two general assessment options for monitoring a child's progress: (a) a critical skills mastery approach, in which the mastery of individual skills at single points in time is examined for progress, or (b) a general outcome measurement approach, where indicators or skills (e.g., vocabulary, phonological awareness) related to a larger developmental domain (e.g., literacy) are monitored over time to determine progress (McConnell, 2000).

There are benefits and drawbacks to both options. Assessments with a focus on critical skills mastery can be helpful for both setting IFSP/IEP goals and for determining whether children are meeting IFSP/IEP goals, but they contribute little understanding of whether children are making progress toward long-term goals over time—information that children's classroom teachers and early interventionists find essential to their planning and curriculum implementation. General outcome measures address this weakness. Data generated from ongoing, standardized assessments with general outcome measures produce growth trends reflective of development in the larger domain, and growth trends can be interpreted for response to intervention (Greenwood, Luze, & Carta, 2002; McConnell, Priest, Davis, & McEvoy, 2002). All general outcome measurement models tend to follow the process in Figure 1, where use of general outcome measures generate data for interpretation and decision making to improve the overall trend of performance and to provide an ongoing measure of progress over time.

Figure 1 *General outcome measurement model process.*

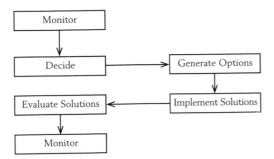

2. *Assessment tools are authentic.*

In practice, an integrated child- and family-centered model of assessment relies heavily on authentic assessments and observations of young children in interaction with objects, peers, and family members in familiar settings during typical routines (Losardo & Notari-Syverson, 2001; Neisworth & Bagnato, 2004). Criterion-referenced measures and informal, teacher-made checklists and behavior samples (administered non-intrusively through observation of the child within the context of daily routines and activities) provide valid and functional information

for understanding the child within the family and community. An accurate assessment of all environments in which the child participates is also essential in an integrated child- and family-centered model of assessment.

Assessments that are child-centered and interactive, rather than those that simply enumerate or quantify the presence or absence of isolated skills, generate a strong base of knowledge about the child and the child's ability to interact with the everyday environment (Fewell, 2000). Assessments that yield information about child behavior and preferences with people, objects, events, and settings together with information obtained from standardized developmental assessments provide a more accurate and holistic view of the child. Therefore, the goal of the assessment team is the development of an effective multi-method data collection process that is driven by family and team concerns and focused on decision making to fully reflect child status and need and to plan appropriate intervention and related services.

Using authentic, ecological, and criterion- or curriculum-based assessments has several advantages. These types of assessment tools typically include a large number of behaviors across multiple domains and therefore provide a level of specificity sufficient to accurately reflect child developmental status. Items are typically useful and relevant to family concerns. The tools also allow the child multiple opportunities to demonstrate a behavior or skill in multiple settings with preferred and multiple partners, objects, and materials, resulting in a more valid estimate of developmental status (Fewell, 2000). Because the participants or informants for most criterion- or curriculum-based assessments are teachers and care providers who know the child best, these assessments may be more efficient and may also facilitate the development of collaborative partnerships. Results also provide a direct and functional link to IFSP/IEP development, curriculum planning, and implementation. The information collected can easily be translated for use in instruction.

Evaluating the child within the context of play, social interactions, and care-giving routines requires that the assessment process focus on the demands and expectations of the environments where children live, learn, play, and work rather than merely children's relative standing in a normative group. This ecological perspective recognizes that physical, social, and psychological contexts are interwoven and affect performance; and that domain (e.g., communication, motor, cognitive), discipline (e.g., speech and language pathology, occupational therapy), and specific skills and behaviors (e.g., pincer grasp, personal pronouns, spatial relations) are inconsequential when assessed out of context (Neisworth & Bagnato, 2005).

Strategies to provide ecologically valid and community relevant information include the use of observation or data-gathering techniques such as questionnaires, document review, anecdotal records, and interviews. Within this model, the assessment process addresses functional supports in a way that is congruent with the child's natural environment and supports the relationship of the child within the ecological context. In this way, the support and interventions are part of a typical routine rather that an intervention that separates the child from the world. For example, the assessment and recommended intervention of motor activities evolve not by the child visiting the physical therapist at an office or clinic, but by the therapist watching and observing the child on the playground with a group of children as she participates in activities that demonstrate motor skills. The therapist may then use the information to consult or coach the teacher or family member in activities that would support the development of motor skills on the playground. In addition, the assessment process for children with disabilities often includes an analysis of the child's interaction with the environment (i.e., physical, social, and instructional) in order to address the concerns of teachers and families and to provide immediate and meaningful data for program planning. This model also easily incorporates the necessary adaptations, modifications, and accommodations.

3. Assessment tools have good psychometric qualities.

In early childhood, good psychometric evidence is of particular concern for three reasons. First, many early childhood measures tend to produce scores that are relatively unstable (Bailey, 2004). Very young children learn and grow at remarkable and unpredictable rates that are unmatched during other age periods. Because of this, scores from assessments administered to very young children tend to be unstable. Tests of cognitive development (e.g., IQ tests) are the most frequent culprit of this phenomenon, but it is true of assessment in other developmental domains as well (Sattler, 2001). Second, young children with disabilities introduce even more instability to results because although they experience growth spurts just like young children without disabilities, their rates of growth in general tend to be more unpredictable (McLean, 2004). Third, particularly when the interest is early academic development (e.g., literacy and reading), many measures in early childhood lack predictive validity, meaning that test results have not been determined to be related to later development (Bracken, 2000). Given that the purpose of assessment of early academic development is often to identify and improve skills to increase the likelihood of later educational and life success for a child, early educators should look for instruments with evidence of predictive validity.

The assessment process often may include the use of individually administered tools that are norm-referenced. These tools are often used to address specific questions (e.g., eligibility) regarding a child's development (Roid & Sampers, 2004). Where some tests require a contrived setting, results for these tests require additional confirmation of the child's typical behavior in other settings. Other assessment tools are applied in more authentic, realistic settings and situations

that provide a more natural measure of abilities. Methods that can be used in the natural environment can support the assessment process continuously over time by using repeated measurements, and can provide more specific evidence for service modifications (Neisworth, 1993).

The assessment tools and process must be appropriate for the age and characteristics of the child and must specifically address referral or intervention questions. The response demands of the assessment tool must be carefully analyzed during assessment planning to determine individual and developmental appropriateness. For example, some tools require verbal fluency and high levels of expressive communication; others require motor behavior for responding; most place demands on the child's sensory system (McCormick & Nellis, 2004). The assessment team must select tools that best reveal the child's skills and abilities while minimizing the impact of disability on the results.

Genuine and meaningful communication.

Because most families involved in early childhood assessment are learning about the assessment process and special education for the first time, assessment teams must be thorough, explicit, sensitive, and patient communicators. Even if family members have been active partners in the assessment process and are aware of all the assessment details, it is still critically important to communicate assessment results sensitively and thoroughly. Assessment reports must accurately and completely include the: (1) purpose for assessment, (2) titles and descriptions of all assessment tools used, (3) scores from tools including detailed explanations of what scores mean in general (e.g., a percentile rank is a comparison to other children of the same age) and for the child specifically (e.g., average range), (4) implications of assessment results, and (5) suggestions for placement, service, and intervention (Sattler, 2001). Because family members have the right to refuse intervention or special education services offered as a result of an eligibility determination, teams must be very careful not to presume what parents will decide. Teams must write assessment reports that offer suggestions rather than plans for next steps. Families need time to digest assessment results and often they need an additional meeting (or several) to talk seriously about intervention planning.

Ethical and legal practices.

Professionals completing assessments are responsible for adhering to the requirements of the state in which they practice, their professional group affiliations, and publisher qualifications for test administration. Ethics also dictate that assessors use the most appropriate and recent version or edition of the test. In the case of norm-referenced testing, this means that the assessor uses the most recent test edition because the norms are more likely to reflect the child's development (NAEYC, 2005).

In summary, the assessment process should provide opportunities for families and professionals to work as a team to make decisions about eligibility for program services, settings, and the identification of appropriate IEP/IFSP goals and instructional strategies, ongoing progress monitoring, and program evaluation. Throughout the assessment process team members must be diligent in focusing on the child and xfamily. Conversations, review of records, observations, direct assessment, and reflection provide team members the opportunity to begin to know the child and understand his or her needs. They can better answer the important questions: What are the educational and therapeutic needs of this child? Do these needs require specialized intervention or education? What is the best way to meet these needs in the community and at home? What behaviors should be targeted for change? Where, when, with whom, and how should intervention and subsequent evaluation occur? Do these decisions honor family preference and community values? In other words, the assessment "begins where the team wants to end" and keeps that goal in mind.

Indicators of Effectiveness

Effective assessment in ECSE has several hallmark features. Foremost, the assessment process is centered on the child and family. As such, open and safe communication occurs on a regular basis between families and school or program staff in response to identified priorities, goals, and concerns. At the same time, a breadth of information is collected in unique ways from multiple sources in ethical and professional practices. Finally, effective assessment is ongoing, with the goal of collecting information to make decisions that will improve the education of and services for young children with disabilities—including day-to-day decisions about what to teach and how to teach. The process, style, and measures of assessment in EI/ECSE have evolved significantly over the years. The DEC Recommended Practices: A Comprehensive Guide for Practical Application (Sandall et al., 2005) recognizes the importance of the assessment process as an entry into the system of services for young children with disabilities and their families, as well as a key source of information to inform instruction in early childhood programs.

Key features described as essential to the overall assessment process include: (a) developing partnerships with parents and families as essential stakeholders in the assessment process, and (b) using assessment methods and materials that are developmentally appropriate and culturally and linguistically responsive (Neisworth & Bagnato, 2005). These important ideas are critical to assessment from the beginning of the process. It is also critical that assessment be individualized in the identification of appropriate and functional supports for young children with disabilities and their families and that a team process be utilized. The following indicators are aligned with DEC Recommended Practices: A Comprehensive Guide for Practical Application (Sandall et al., 2005) and are closely aligned with indicators from the NAEYC-NAECS/SDE position statement.

Assessment involves family-professional partnerships.

Assessment involves shared experiences between families and professionals in which information and ideas are exchanged to benefit a child's growth and development. Family concerns, resources, and priorities are integral to the individualized process the team develops. The process must be designed to facilitate family inclusion at multiple levels in response to family-identified preference and with sensitivity to family values, needs, language, and culture. It is the responsibility of professional team members to ensure an honest and collaborative experience for family team members.

The assessment process should involve the family and professionals working together to capture the child's way of learning about the world and the child's developmental status (Meisels & Fenichel, 1996). From this team advantage, members share information that will help to identify children needing additional assessment and services, enhance the quality of the child's individual service plan and education, and influence the child's daily activities and instruction. Ultimately, the assessment process should support the family's decision making on behalf of their child (Preator & McAllister, 1995).

Communication among all team members—including families—supports planning and implementation of an assessment process that answers the questions team members pose. Families and professionals initiate communication by sharing information related to the purpose for the assessment, process, and specific information about the child. Families and staff must feel comfortable sharing information related to the assessment process as well as specific information about the child (Roid & Sampers, 2004). This process is reciprocal. Family members share information related to the families' routines and history (e.g., medical records, photographs, videos, journals). Team members share information about the logistics of the assessment process (e.g., who to contact, participating team members, locations and times, roles for team members and the family), environmental characteristics and demands, available supports, adaptations, accommodations, and program options.

The team's communication supports comfortable and confident family member participation. The team works jointly to ensure confirmation of observations and substantiate findings. Good team processing supports family understanding of why the child is being assessed, what the assessment process is, how the information from assessment will be used, and the family's rights in the process. Information generated through the assessment process results in a sensitive discussion of findings and a formal report. The report reflects complete and clear, family-friendly, culturally responsive information.

Assessments should be developmentally and individually appropriate and educationally significant.

Assessments that are developmentally and individually appropriate include the use of authentic and multiple measures and sources to assess child status, progress, and program impact and outcomes. Children are assessed within typical routines and daily activities using familiar materials, and assessment results inform decisions about curriculum and instructional practices. Assessment procedures are designed to accurately reflect child status and need, using materials and procedures that accommodate sensory, physical, and temperamental differences.

As discussed in the Curriculum section of this paper, assessment to plan intervention and curriculum for young children with disabilities must incorporate two critical elements. First, measurement tools include items sufficient for documenting incremental and small rates of growth. In other words, they must be sensitive to individual rates of growth and development and include a broad range of developmental tasks. Second, and equally important, assessments reflect socially valid goals and outcomes (e.g., language, literacy, social development) for natural and inclusive environments. Natural environments include home and community routines; therefore assessment should involve the functioning of children and families in those routines.

When assessment is for monitoring progress or measuring outcomes, the assessment must provide sufficient information to accomplish this purpose. This includes documentation of the attainment of IFSP and IEP goals and objectives, response to intervention, and fidelity of intervention implementation. The behavior of all young children tends to be greatly influenced by context. This is especially true for young children with disabilities, particularly with infants and toddlers. Therefore, the assessment process requires use of varied and multiple methods (e.g., observation, testing, interview, record interviews) and sources of information (e.g., parents, teachers, caregivers, relatives) collected over time.

Special care should be taken to ensure adherence to professional ethics and practices.

Use of assessment instruments for their intended purposes is particularly critical in the assessment of children with disabilities. An array of assessment tools is available for use in early childhood: checklists, rating scales, criterion-referenced tools, norm-referenced tools, interviews, and observations. Ethical practice requires selecting tools and interpreting results in accordance with the purpose of the assessment and the characteristics and applications of the tools as recommended by the publisher (NAEYC, 2005). It may be necessary to go beyond assessment of general functioning, using assessment tools matched to developmental concerns (e.g., challenging behaviors, pervasive developmental delays, early language development). The appropriateness of the assess-

ment process to the child's cultural, ethnic, and linguistic experiences is also important, including familiarity and comfort in group settings and taking directions from a non-familial adult. The validity of the assessment is tied to the appropriateness of the procedures and tools for the specific child being assessed.

Because the assessment of young children with disabilities may often result in critical decisions such as eligibility for early intervention and special education services or the maintenance of services, professionals must be diligent in their use of standardized procedures and adherence to the intended purpose and use as recommended by the publisher. Therefore, assessment tools with measurement or categorization properties should hold the highest level of psychometric quality and integrity.

Early childhood professionals should work collaboratively with families and with one another to design individualized and appropriate assessment activities that are aligned with specific purposes and decisions. This includes the use of authentic measures that inform instruction and intervention decisions and link to program content and goals. Professionals should share information with family members about all aspects of the assessment process including appropriate adaptations, modifications, and accommodations. When using norm-referenced tools, professionals should ensure that they are developed, validated, standardized, and normed with children similar to the child being assessed. Finally, assessment team members (including family members) participate in an ongoing review of child progress and instructional utility/effectiveness.

The first step of the intervention process for children with disabilities and their families is the knowledge of and participation in the assessment process by family and staff as members of the team. This requires a commitment to on-going professional development on the part of both staff and administrators. Staff must be supported in their professional development to gain knowledge and skills for conducting assessment in culturally and linguistically sensitive ways, and to work collaboratively with a wide range of diverse families. Additionally, staff must have regular access to training that allows them to incorporate and apply assessment results to home- or classroom-based intervention and improved out-comes for children.

Frequently Asked Questions

1. *Are there standards for how the assessment process works for children with disabilities?*

IDEA Parts C and B clearly outline legal mandates for the assessment process. Individual states work within these federal guidelines to determine acceptable assessment methods and components, as well as eligibility criteria. Readers are referred to their Department of Education and Part C lead agency's state guidelines.

2. *What should be assessed?*

First and foremost, an identified question or concern about a child's development and learning should be posed. For example, a referral concern from a parent, a question about a child's progress in relation to expectations for growth and development, or early learning standards should all drive assessment. In other words, only relevant information directly linked to the purpose of the assessment should be gathered. With that in mind, assessors should gather information from multiple sources and people close to the child.

3. *Which assessment tools should be used?*

Assessment tools should be appropriate for gathering information about the topic of interest (e.g., motor development, language development); appropriate for the person completing the evaluation (e.g., parent, trained professional); and appropriate for the purpose (e.g., screening, evaluation, program planning, and progress monitoring).

4. *For what purpose is norm-referenced testing appropriate?*

Truly, it depends on what the assessment team wants to know, what decisions must be made, or what the purpose is of conducting the assessment. Because norm-referenced tests tend to be lengthy and comprehensive, they are typically most appropriate for eligibility determination. They can have a place in program evaluation (see section on Program Evaluation) and progress monitoring; however, it should be noted that oftentimes a less time- and energy-intensive measurement can be just as informative.

5. *Which assessment tools are most appropriate for monitoring children's progress?*

The best assessment tools for progress monitoring have the following features: (1) efficient to administer (e.g., fast and inexpensive), (2) easy to administer (e.g., the administrator does not need extensive specialized training or certifications), (3) reliable and valid, (4) related to outcomes of importance (e.g., reading, social competence), (5) sensitive to skill growth over time, and (6) repeatable.

6. *How should families be included in assessment?*

Family members are equal and integral members of the assessment team. The entire assessment process should acknowledge, respect, and accommodate the family's needs, values, and priorities. Accordingly, assessment team members must understand the assessment process from the family's perspective. Families should be included in every phase of assessment. Families should be heavily involved in helping assessment team members understand the areas of concern and provide information in those areas (i.e., through interviews, testing, questionnaires). Families should be part of assessment interpretation and intervention planning, as well as goal writing and evaluation.

7. *What happens after assessment is complete?*

Assessment is an ongoing process. If after completion of the evaluation for eligibility component, the determination is that the child is not in need of intervention at the current time, the child's developmental progress should continue to be monitored. If, however, the determination is that the child is in need of specialized intervention, assessment is also ongoing in the form of progress monitoring. As a result of initial assessment, goals for improvement are developed and the child's progress toward the goals must be documented. Additionally, intervention services must be designed to meet children's needs and help them reach their individual goals. As children reach their goals, intervention services are modified accordingly. The assessment process is really never complete—the gathering of information continues to modify services according to the child's needs.

8. *How does assessment link to service and support?*

Service is in direct response to the child's needs as determined by assessment. "Service" really means "unique environment designed specifically to address a child/family's needs and assist his/her development." Service is a broad term that includes a diverse array of direct, consultative, and informational supports such as resources for the family or specific supports to an early care educator and should not be limited to mean the delivery of a service such as physical therapy. "Service" should be determined by the team, should be based on the child and family priorities, and change as a result of data-based decision making using assessment information in the form of progress monitoring. As a result, service must be flexible, ongoing, and responsive to immediate child/family needs.

9. *What is the distinction between assessment and evaluation?*

In general, the term "assessment" is used in reference to gathering information for an evaluation. Assessment includes multiple methods of measurement and as many sources of information as possible. "Evaluation" is the overall process of summarizing present concerns, collecting information, and determining what (if anything) to do next (e.g., special placement or intervention). For Part C programs these terms have very different meanings or definitions as prescribed by IDEA (2004). For more guidance about program evaluation, see the Program Evaluation section in this document.

PROGRAM EVALUATION

Key Recommendation

Program evaluations should be conducted so that they (a) focus on clearly specified program goals, (b) gather reliable and valid data, (c) assess desired outcomes and impacts, (d) consider factors that mediate outcomes, (e) involve stakeholders as partners in key aspects of the evaluation, and (f) facilitate decision-making about the program. Contemporary program evaluations should advance understandings about what kinds of services have what kinds of impacts on which children and families, under what circumstances, and at what cost (Shonkoff, 2004).

Rationale

Program evaluation has been defined as the process of "systematically collecting, synthesizing, and interpreting information about programs for the purpose of assisting with decision making" (Snyder & Sheehan, 1996, p. 359). Many EI/ECSE programs have conducted program evaluations as required by their federal, state, or local funding agencies or perhaps as required by an accrediting program such as the NAEYC. Typically, the focus of evaluation has been on "process" or "input" variables such as staff qualifications, staff-child ratios, hours of service, or quality of the environment. Program evaluation traditionally has been an administrative responsibility, and typically the focus of program evaluation has been shaped by the requirements of funding or accrediting agencies.

Key Issues in Program Evaluation for Young Children with Disabilities

The purpose of this section is to provide an overview of key issues related to program evaluation in EI/ECSE, to identify important quality indicators for those involved in program evaluation efforts, and to provide information about additional resources that might assist those interested in or charged with implementing program evaluation.

Contemporary perspectives about program evaluation: Interfaces with accountability.

Recently, the concept of accountability, which can be one focus of program evaluation, has gained increased attention in education. Accountability in public education refers to the "systematic collection, analysis, and use of information to hold schools, educators, and others responsible for the performance of students and the education system" (Education Commission of the States, 1998, p. 3). America's k-12 education system has come under increasing pressure to demonstrate results in the form of increased student achievement. The increased emphasis on results is actually government-wide, and affects all federally funded programs, including EI/ECSE. The Government Performance and Results Act (GPRA) requires that all federal programs establish and report

evaluation data related to specific program goals. In addition, the federal Office of Management and Budget (OMB) reviews and rates federal programs each year according to the Program Assessment Rating Tool (PART) as part of the budget development process.

For educators, accountability has been most evident in school-age policies like the No Child Left Behind Act. Early care and education programs also have been impacted through legislation tied to the Head Start program and recently through the Good Start, Grow Smart early childhood initiatives. IDEA (2004) also has accountability requirements that will have an increasing impact on EI/ECSE programs. In addition, many states are focusing increased attention on efforts designed to demonstrate the cost-effectiveness and value of human service programs. In fact, the multiple initiatives at federal and state levels, which have been evolving separately, frequently intersect at the program level, creating challenges for program personnel charged with addressing complex and diverse accountability or program evaluation requirements (Harbin, Rous & McLean, 2005).

In the current era of accountability, program evaluation is a complex process, particularly in relation to documenting which interventions lead to what outcomes and impacts for which children and families. Continuous improvement and continuing evaluation, or what Haskins (2004) has referred to as "continuing accountability," is having significant impacts on how program evaluations are designed and implemented in EI/ECSE. Programs are challenged to answer the simple question, "Does it work?" (Gilliam & Leiter, 2003). Complexity is introduced as efforts are directed to defining and measuring "it" (i.e., the program) and "work" (i.e., outcomes and impacts).

Unique aspects of program evaluation in early intervention/early childhood special education.

From a program evaluation perspective, defining the term "program" is essential because this definition helps determine the nature of evaluation goals and outcomes, factors that affect outcomes, and the range of stakeholders who have a significant investment in the results of the evaluation.

An ecological framework (see Figure 2 on page 20) can be used to illustrate that there might be multiple EI/ECSE programs and services delivered or managed at local, state, and federal levels and to highlight relationships that might exist across evaluations at the various levels.

At the center of the ecological framework, each child with or at risk for a disability or developmental delay who is eligible for EI or ECSE services has an individualized program— either an IFSP or IEP. These individual programs are evaluated on an ongoing basis by the teams that develop them, including the child's parent(s), to evaluate progress related to each specified outcome or goal/objective.

FIGURE 2

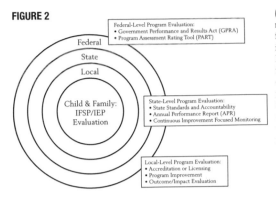

Evaluation at the individual child/family level is necessary for assessment and curriculum and/or intervention decisions that are made for individual children or their families.

At a local program level, evaluation might focus on an administrative issue (e.g., impact of program policies on child/family participation levels), an intervention-oriented strategy (e.g., impact of new routines-based intervention model implemented in the program), or general outcomes for children and families served by the program. Locally initiated program evaluation often differs from evaluations required by state, federal, or licensing agencies. Most local programs, however, contribute key information to state and federal program evaluation efforts, as required by funding agencies. For example, all local IDEA programs provide data on the number of children served through IDEA so these data can be aggregated statewide and submitted to the federal government. In addition, an early intervention program might be required to contribute child and family outcome data to the state led agency as a requirement of participation in the statewide program. These evaluation data might be useful not only for the state but for the local program.

State evaluations typically involve monitoring state-funded programs for compliance with operational standards or using evaluation information across local programs to understand trends in program processes, outcomes, or impacts (Kellegrew, O'Brien, & Groppenbacher, 2003). For operational standards, an example might be data reporting by local Part C (early intervention) programs on the percentage of children served in natural environments.

States also are held accountable to the federal government for the implementation of their early intervention and preschool special education programs. States must set targets in multiple components of the IDEA program (e.g., transition, inclusion, and natural environments) and report on annual progress for meeting these targets in an annual performance report

(APR). In this way, the APR serves as the planning and reporting tool of the federal continuous improvement and focused monitoring system, which is designed to help states improve performance and compliance with IDEA requirements. In addition to demonstrating that they are meeting all of the federal requirements under IDEA, there is also an increased emphasis on demonstrating the positive impact of IDEA programs in relation to child and family outcomes. States receiving IDEA funds to support EI/ECSE programs must report annually on the achievement of child and family outcomes through the APR. From a program evaluation perspective, this system emphasizes planning, implementing, and evaluating improvement strategies.

At the federal level, the U.S. Department of Education, Office of Special Education and Rehabilitative Services, Office of Special Education Programs uses these state evaluation data to report to Congress on IDEA goals established under the GPRA. Currently there are five Part C GPRA indicators and three Preschool GPRA indicators. Indicators that measure child outcomes include:

- "The percentage of children participating in Part C that demonstrate positive social-emotional skills (including social relationships); acquire and use knowledge and skills (including early language /communication); and demonstrate appropriate behaviors to meet their needs" (Individuals with Disabilities Education Act Amendments, 2004, 20 U.S.C. 1416 (a)(3)(A) and 1442); and

- "The percentage of preschool children with disabilities participating in the Preschool Grants Program who demonstrate positive social-emotional skills (including social relationships); acquire and use knowledge and skills (including early language/ communication and early literacy); and use appropriate behaviors to meet their needs" (Individuals with Disabilities Education Act Amendments, 2004, 20 U.S.C. 1416 (a)(3)(A)).

In addition, one of the Part C indicators measures a family outcome:

- "The percentage of families that report that early intervention services have helped them 1) know their rights; 2) effectively communicate their children's needs; and 3) help their children develop and learn" (Individuals with Disabilities Education Act Amendments, 2004, 20 U.S.C. 1416 (a)(3)(A) and 1442).

These outcomes are important to local programs because programs might be asked to collect and report data about these outcomes as part of their participation in EI/ECSE programs funded under IDEA.

Evaluation beyond accountability.

At a local level, program evaluation is often conducted for purposes other than program accountability. Results from a well-planned evaluation can inform program decision making and improvement planning. A melding of the earlier described "process" or "input" variables and "outcome/impact" data is needed to look at relationships between what the program does and what difference it makes for participants.

One of the biggest challenges in program evaluation is resisting the urge to try to be all things to all audiences. It is important, but sometimes difficult, to clarify the purpose of the evaluation and to design the evaluation to answer the most important questions. For example, is the purpose of the evaluation to respond to an external accountability demand, to make a specific decision about how to reduce costs, or to find out which intervention strategy works best for specific children?

Also challenging in evaluating programs for young children, and especially programs for young children with disabilities, is finding appropriate tools for measuring child and family outcomes. As discussed previously in the Assessment section of this paper, assessment of young children is generally more difficult than assessment of older children, and assessment of young children with disabilities is more difficult than the assessment of young children without disabilities. Difficulties include the variability in a young child's behavior from day-to-day and setting-to-setting. This variability might lead to reduced reliability in assessment scores and extreme variations in functional levels among the population of young children with disabilities. Many assessments that are used to measure growth and development of children who are typically developing might not be well suited for young children with disabilities.

Inclusion of children with disabilities or delays in program evaluations of early education and care programs.

The NAEYC-NAECS/SDE position statement on early childhood curriculum, assessment, and program evaluation (2003) suggests that a snapshot of children and families served by early childhood programs today would look very different than one taken in 1990. The snapshot of today would include more children with disabilities, as well as more children who are immigrants, more who live in poverty, and more whose home language is not English. The diversity of the children and families served by early care and education programs has greatly increased and will probably continue to increase in the future.

In recent years, there has been increased recognition of the importance of early education by those working toward educational reform in our country (Bowman, Burns, & Donovan, 2001; Shonkoff, J. & Phillips, D., 2000). Federal policies such as Good Start Grow Smart have focused on the development of state standards for pre-kindergarten children, and these standards are increasingly linked to curriculum and evaluation frameworks. The early childhood standards and curriculum frameworks being developed by states should apply to children with disabilities and other special

needs (Scott-Little, Kagan & Frelow, 2003). Similarly, evaluation efforts designed to measure progress toward standards will also include children with disabilities and special needs. According to the federal IDEA, children with disabilities must be included in any state- or district-wide assessments that are established for typically developing children.

Evaluation of progress toward state standards might be considered to be "high stakes" assessment to the extent that programs are penalized by lack of improvement over time. Programs that serve the most "vulnerable" children might be at risk of being penalized by the misuse of child outcome data (Hebbeler, 2004). To ensure the appropriate interpretation of child outcome data for all children, including children with disabilities, and in keeping with the procedures included in the position statement of NAEYC and NAECS/SDE (2003), program evaluation should be used for continuous improvement rather than to penalize programs for poor outcomes.

Indicators of Effectiveness

When considering indicators of effective program evaluation, standards developed by the Joint Committee on Standards for Educational Evaluation (1994) are a useful place to start. A brief description of these standards and related documents follow. Additional indicators of effective program evaluation that we believe are particularly relevant in EI/ECSE are also discussed. A list of the suggested indicators of effectiveness in program evaluation is included in Table 4 in the Appendix.

Evaluation efforts conform to evaluation standards including utility, propriety, feasibility, and accuracy.

The Joint Committee on Standards for Educational Evaluation (1994) suggest sound program evaluations, regardless of their emphasis or focus, should adhere to four basic standards: (a) utility, (b) propriety, (c) feasibility, and (d) accuracy.

Utility refers to ensuring that the informational needs of intended program evaluation users are met. An example of a utility standard is, "Persons involved in or affected by the evaluation should be identified, so that their needs can be addressed."

Feasibility refers to promoting realistic, prudent, diplomatic, and frugal evaluations. An example of a feasibility standard is, "The evaluation procedures should be practical to keep disruption to a minimum while needed information is obtained." Propriety means evaluations will be conducted legally, ethically, and with due regard for the welfare of those involved in the evaluation and those affected by the results. An example of a propriety standard related to complete and fair assessment is, "The evaluation should be complete and fair in its examination and recording of strengths and weaknesses of the program being evaluated, so that strengths can be built upon and problem areas addressed."

Accuracy standards focus on ensuring the evaluation provides technically adequate information about features that determine worth or merit of the program. In relation to validity or meaningfulness of findings, an example of accuracy standards is "The information-gathering procedures should be chosen or developed and then implemented so they will assure that the interpretation arrived at is valid for the intended use."

The Joint Committee also has developed explicit advice about conducting program evaluations, which are based on the standards. Among the evaluation functions addressed in these documents are (a) defining the evaluation problem, (b) designing the evaluation, (c) collecting information, (d) analyzing information, and (e) reporting information. The evaluation standards and related documents are excellent resources for those interested in program evaluation and can be found at the following Web site: http://www.wmich.edu/evalctr/jc/

Logical approaches for conceptualizing and conducting program evaluations are used.

Most decisions made about programs concern allocation of resources to improve program success and serve needs. Program evaluations should therefore (a) inform stakeholders about achievement of program goals, (b) identify the factors that are associated with program outcomes, and (c) describe unmet needs of children, families, and communities. This requires that program evaluation clearly specify the program's aspirations for children, families, community, and staff and collect data from the targeted groups. While program evaluations can focus on one or more outcome(s) or need area(s), program administrators are ultimately responsible for documenting

and evaluating the major outcomes. Data might also be collected about costs, resources, staff activities, or other factors that impact program success. Documenting child progress on the IEP/IFSP or common measures of child development might be informative but typically will not provide sufficient information to inform key program evaluation decisions.

One way to conceptualize and conduct program evaluation is to use a logic model. Although not the only type of program evaluation model available, the logic model approach to program evaluation shares several features in common with other types of goal-based evaluation approaches (Stufflebeam, 1985; Patton, 1997).

A logic model is a depiction (often graphic) of program processes and outcomes. The logic model details what the program is, what anticipated outcomes are expected for participants, and how anticipated outcomes are expected to be reached (Gilliam & Leiter, 2003). From a logic model perspective, program processes involve three components: (a) inputs, (b) activities, and (c) outputs. Outcomes include two aspects: intermediate (proximal) and end (distal).

Figure 3 shows an example of a logic model. In this example, staff from an early intervention program wants to implement a routines-based approach to delivering services and supports, and to evaluate outcomes.

Inputs include resources available to the program (e.g., funds, staffing patterns, facilities, equipment, supplies) or constraints on the program (e.g., regulations, policies, funding restrictions). Activities are what the program does with its inputs to carry out its program goals and objectives. In the example, activities include participating in professional development focused on routines-based intervention (RBI), modifying a policy and

FIGURE 3

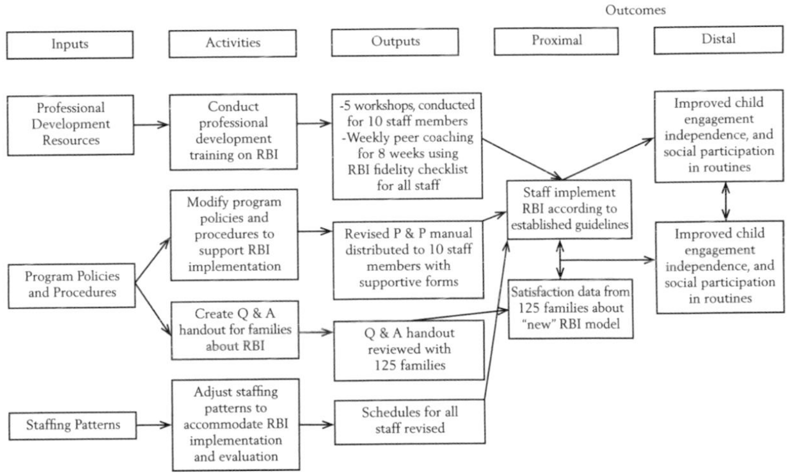

procedure manual to support implementation of RBI, and adjusting staffing patterns to implement RBI.

Outputs are direct products of program activities and typically are measured in terms of the amount of service or supports provided to participants. Using the example, this might include collecting information about the mean number of child-focused, routines-based intervention sessions conducted during a 1-year period.

Outcomes are the results for participants during and after program activities are implemented. Intermediate or proximal outcomes frequently focus on attitudes of consumers, their perspectives about the services, supports they receive, or how these services and supports are delivered to them. Intermediate or proximal outcomes might include participants' views about the timeliness, accessibility, satisfaction, or helpfulness of the services they receive. In the example, parents might be asked to complete a measure that seeks their perspectives about the RBI approach. Distal or end outcomes are associated directly with program goals and objectives. If one anticipated outcome of using an RBI approach is to improve child independence, engagement, and social participation, then measures that operationalize these three outcomes and yield valid and reliable scores might be administered to participating children. This permits evaluation of whether the program, as designed, is achieving intended outcomes for participants.

Correspondence should exist between program goals/objectives and evaluation questions and methods.

Although it seems obvious that there should be a match between program goals/objectives, measured goals/objectives, and evaluation questions and methods, as Sheehan and Gallagher (1983) noted, this frequently does not occur. All program evaluation activities should begin with specification of program goals/objectives. What is the program attempting to accomplish? For whom is the program attempting to accomplish its goals/objectives? Evaluation questions should follow logically, based on the program goals/objectives. Based on the evaluation questions posed, those involved in conducting the evaluation should determine which program evaluation design and methodologies should be used to address evaluation questions.

Evaluation efforts employ participatory models.

A key purpose of program evaluation is to promote sound decision-making regarding program performance and program improvement. To support effective decision making, it is logical that the evaluation should involve those persons who will be impacted by the decisions and those who will be accountable for implementing any proposed reforms to policies, practices, or expenditures. To the extent feasible, staff, families, and community representatives should be involved when (a) determining the goals of an evaluation, (b) designing the evaluation, (c) disseminating and interpreting results, and (d) supporting the implementation of valid and reliable decisions informed by the evaluation. Involvement of people who have a legitimate investment in the program's success encourages shared ownership of the value, conduct, and use of the program evaluation. Program evaluation is not something that is "done to" program staff and program participants. It is something that is "done with" them.

Program evaluation describes what happened to participants.

One area of program evaluation often overlooked when attempting to address questions such as "Did it work?" is defining what it means. In the context of program evaluation, this involves describing what happens to participants (e.g., what interventions are delivered) and the extent to which programs were implemented as intended. This often is accomplished by documenting "treatment fidelity." Treatment fidelity includes descriptions of the program implementation schedule (e.g., frequency and intensity of intervention). Preferably, treatment fidelity also should document the extent of implementation and descriptions of participants' involvement in the program. Treatment fidelity involves documenting what services were actually delivered to children and families.

Failure to achieve desired program evaluation outcomes might be a function of inconsistent delivery of services or failure to implement a model of intervention correctly. Similarly, program evaluations designed to evaluate the impact of staff training efforts might not show desired changes in knowledge, skills, or dispositions if the training was of poor quality, delivered inconsistently, or poorly attended or practiced by staff. Further, an intervention program is not the only thing children or families might experience that impacts their achievement of desired outcomes. Experiences of children and families outside of the intervention program might contribute just as much (or more) to outcomes as the intervention program itself.

Describing what happens to participants and measuring treatment fidelity is critical to supporting claims about program effectiveness and to improving program operations. Documenting influences outside of the program that potentially impact outcomes is also necessary to put program evaluation results into perspective.

Data collection is efficient and feasible.

Ideally, program evaluation should be an ongoing, routine, and integrated component of program delivery and management. When designing program evaluations, the simplest procedures that provide valid and reliable answers to questions and inform decisions are typically most desirable. Simple and efficient data collection procedures reduce disruptions within program delivery and facilitate clear communication to groups of stakeholders. Data collection systems that cannot be easily integrated into the ongoing routines of program staff risk compromising service delivery by taking staff away from critical roles or compromising data quality due to the lack of attention.

Measures used in program evaluation yield reliable and valid scores for young children with disabilities and their families.

Reliability refers to the consistency of scores and reflects the extent to which scores derived from measurement are free from error. The more error a score contains, the less reliable it is. Validity refers to the types of meaningful conclusions that can be drawn from scores obtained from program evaluation measures.

To draw meaningful conclusions about program evaluation outcomes, measures used in program evaluation must yield reliable and valid scores for the samples of young children with disabilities and their families with whom they are used. Reliability and validity, however, are not static features of measures and should be evaluated each time a measure is used with a sample of children or families in a specified program evaluation context. This is particularly important when characteristics of the children or families differ substantially from those involved in normative studies or in other program evaluation situations in which the measure was used. For example, a measure normed using a sample of young children without disabilities might not yield comparable reliability and validity estimates when used with young children with disabilities. Establishing reliability and validity of scores as part of program evaluation activities before using these scores to answer evaluation questions is important. Failure to consider reliability and validity of scores could result in inaccurate conclusions about program impacts. For example, suppose an intervention is designed that in reality yields extraordinarily positive impacts. However, scores on an outcome measure used as part of program evaluation have poor reliability for the sample included in the program evaluation. The program evaluator might incorrectly conclude that the intervention is worthless (Snyder, Lawson, Thompson, Stricklin, & Sexton, 1993).

Program evaluation data are used to inform decision making.

Evaluation data should be used to inform decisions about program processes and implementation as well as whether programs are achieving desired results. At the individual child level, data might be used to evaluate response to intervention and to determine whether instructional modifications are needed. At the local program level, decisions about whether a routines-based intervention approach is effective for particular children and families might be based on data related to changes in children's levels of participation in routines over time or families' perspectives about changes in caregiving demands. At the state level, data related to the percentages of children served in natural environments in the Part C program might prompt a state to create fiscal incentives for serving children in natural environments. At the federal level, data that show the percentage of children identified as eligible for early intervention (under age 1) to

be below established benchmarks might inform decisions about allocating resources to establish a national center focused on Child Find.

The most significant challenge facing local program administrators when designing evaluations is to understand why they are doing the evaluation. What decisions do they or key stakeholders want to make? How can the evaluation inform these decisions? The data that must be collected, aside from data required for compliance reporting, should be determined by the nature of decisions that the program faces. Staff, families, and community members will believe in the importance of data collection and program evaluation when they see the information being used to inform programmatic decisions. From an administrative perspective, stakeholder investment in program evaluation will increase when the staff can describe improvements to the program that have resulted from program evaluation. Without this connection, program evaluation will feel like an exercise rather than a tool to serve the needs of children and families.

Program evaluation data are used to inform continuous program improvement.

The goal of program evaluation is continuous program improvement. As a result of the program evaluation process and associated findings, program goals and objectives might be modified, new elements might be added to the program, or existing elements might be refined, and strategies used to collect program evaluation might be changed. Evaluation should be viewed as a continuous process, rather than a once-a-year review of the extent to which program goals and objectives have been met.

Program evaluation needs to be alert to unforeseen positive or negative consequences of a program.

Although intended consequences of a program are specified when the evaluation is planned by specifying important variables to be measured, unforeseen consequences might arise. These consequences should be acknowledged, particularly if they are relevant to interpretations of findings. Morell (2005) defined unforeseen consequences as those that are easily observable but not examined. In the context of program evaluation in a preschool program, an unforeseen consequence might occur when a program specifies that the literacy skills of all children enrolled in the program will be evaluated at program entry and program exit to evaluate impacts of an early literacy curriculum used in the program. An unintended positive consequence of the early literacy curriculum, which might place emphasis on shared storybook reading, could be increases in children's social-emotional skills, particularly their interactions with peers. Conversely, too much emphasis on early literacy might have negative consequences for the development of children's social competence and peer relations.

Evaluation results are presented in formats relevant to diverse stakeholders.

A variety of stakeholders might be interested in the results from a program evaluation, including program consumers, program staff, policy makers, and funding agencies. These individuals might have preferences for evaluation results to be presented in different formats based on their viewpoint related to the evaluation. For example, families might be interested in succinct and easy to understand descriptions of how a program was structured and delivered to children and the resulting outcomes for children, including whether different outcomes occurred for children with disabilities or those who are English-language learners. Policy makers might be interested in short, executive summaries. Program staff might be interested in reports that clearly describe purposes, procedures, and findings of the evaluation, including implications or recommendations for program improvement. Evaluation results should be presented in formats that are relevant and useful for diverse stakeholders.

Program evaluators distinguish between formal efficacy research and program evaluation.

Program evaluation focuses on gathering data for the purposes of documenting program delivery and assisting with decision making. Formal efficacy research seeks to make generalizable connections between features of programs and outcomes. Such research often tests treatment models and typically involves comparison between such models. Because of the commitment to reaching scientifically generalizable conclusions (i.e., results that apply to children and families beyond the program evaluated), formal efficacy research requires substantially greater technical rigor than might be required for a program evaluation. To collect and interpret data required for state or national compliance monitoring does not require a rigorous research design, but it does require rigorous data collection procedures. Collecting data for the purpose of making internal improvements to a specific program does not require the development and implementation of complex research designs. This is not to say that program evaluation does not require attention to technical issues. Rather, the point is that program evaluation is more akin to "action research" with a focus on internal program improvement rather than scientific inference. If administrators at a state or national level are interested in determining which program model works best in different conditions (e.g., varying fiscal or community resources, children of different ages or disabilities) to impose or recommend treatment policies, efficacy or effectiveness research is appropriate.

Sampling may be used in large-scale program evaluation.

As discussed in the NAEYC-NAECS/SDE position statement, sampling is a technique that can be used for large-scale program evaluation. For children with disabilities who participate in large-scale program evaluation requirements under the Individuals with Disabilities Education Act, the

Office of Special Education Programs is permitting states to use one of three approaches: 1) sampling, 2) phase-in of representative samples, or 3) including every child in the large-scale evaluation (population-based). Arguments for and against each of these approaches should be considered to increase the likelihood that data will be valid and most representative of the population. If sampling is used for a statewide evaluation of early childhood programs that include young children with disabilities, then children with disabilities must be included in the sample and potentially over-sampled in order to provide any results that are meaningful and useful for program improvement.

Frequently Asked Questions

1. *Why has the emphasis on program evaluation increased over the past five years?*

The accountability movement has resulted in increased emphasis on program evaluation. A variety of stakeholders (e.g., policy makers, consumers, administrators) are interested in learning whether program investments are resulting in meaningful and measurable results. In addition, with an emphasis on program results, increased attention also is being directed to documenting what participants experienced and examining intervention impacts in relation to interventions being delivered.

2. *What are the types of questions posed by program evaluators?*

Evaluation questions are generally divided into two types: formative and summative. Formative questions focus on the process of program implementation, looking for ways to improve service delivery at any point in the program's life cycle. Summative questions focus on determining a program's effectiveness to make decisions about its ongoing use.

Examples of formative questions include: Which aspects of the program are easy to implement and which are difficult? How do the program's "consumers" perceive the program? What can be done to make implementing the program more efficient? How much does it truly cost to implement the program? Examples of summative questions include: Did the program achieve the intended outcomes for children and families? Is it worthwhile to continue the program? If not, why?

While understanding the distinction between these two types of evaluation questions is helpful, the most important issue is asking the questions specific to your program that will allow you to know if and how your program is making a meaningful difference in the lives of the children and families you serve. In most cases, you will need to ask (and answer) formative and summative questions to achieve this goal.

3. *Can program evaluation data be "misused"?*

Yes, program evaluation data can be misused in a number of ways. Program staff might pay exclusive attention to outcome (summative) data without paying sufficient attention to procedural (formative) data, thus making it difficult to know how to improve the program to enhance outcomes, particularly if outcome data reinforce regard for problems rather than nudge evaluators to seek solutions. Program evaluation data can also be misused if outcomes are disseminated without paying sufficient attention to understanding and describing the population of children and families served by the program. Programs serving children with disabilities or children considered at risk for experiencing developmental difficulties, such as children living in poverty or children labeled as English-language learners, might be penalized if outcome data are compared to results of programs serving children without disabilities or children not considered at risk, without taking these child- and family-level differences into account. While the full range of data misuse cannot be described here, or even predicted, following the indicators of effectiveness in program evaluation explained in this paper will substantially reduce the risk of misusing data.

4. *What resources are available if I want to learn more about program evaluation across the various levels?*

Readers interested in learning more about conducting program evaluation in early intervention are encouraged to read the references cited in this paper. While it is beyond the scope of this paper to provide a comprehensive list of relevant sources, several key resources warrant comment. The Evaluation Exchange is an online journal published by the Harvard Family Research Project. Recent issues of the journal have focused on evaluation of family involvement programs (Winter 2004/2005) and evaluation of early childhood programs (Summer 2004). The archives of this journal contain other valuable articles. In addition, two online resources provide useful places to start for readers interested in finding more resources. The National Early Childhood Technical Assistance Center provides a number of references and resources related to program evaluation at http//www.nectac.org. The Early Childhood Outcomes Center provides a number of resources relating to measuring child and family outcomes as well as some discussion of program evaluation at http://www.fpg.unc.edu/~eco/index.cfm.

Appendix

References

Bailey, D. B. (2004). Tests and test development. In M. McLean, M. Wolery, & D. B.

Bailey (Eds.), Assessing infants and preschoolers with special needs (3rd ed., pp. 22–44). Upper Saddle River, NJ: Pearson.

Barnett, D. W., Macmann, G. M., & Carey, K. T. (1992). Early intervention and the assessment of developmental skills: challenges and directions. Topics in Early Childhood Special Education, 12(1), 21–43.

Blackhurst, E., Carnine, D., Cohen, L., Kame'enui, E., Langone, J., Palley, D., Pisha, B., Powers, K., & Stewart, R. (1999, Fall). Universal design: Ensuring access to the general education curriculum. Retrieved October 6, 2004, from http://eric.ed.gov/ERICWebPortal/custom/portlets/recordDetails/detailmini.jsp?_nfpb=true&_&ERICExtSearch_SearchValue_0=ED 433666&ERICExtSearch_SearchType_0=eric_accno&accno=ED433666

Bodrova, E., Leong, D., Paynter, D., & Semenov, D. (2000). A framework for early literacy instruction: Aligning standards to developmental accomplishments and student behaviors (revised ed.). Retrieved May 27, 2004, from http://www.mcrel.org/PDF/Literacy/4006CM_EL_Framework.pdf

Boone, H. A., & Crais, E. (1999). Strategies for achieving family-driven assessment and intervention planning. Young Exceptional Child. 3(1). 2–11.

Bowman, B., Burns, M., & Donovan, M. (Eds.). (2001). Eager to Learn: Educating our preschoolers. Washington, DC: National Academy Press.

Bracken, B. (2000). The clinical observation of preschool assessment behavior. In B. Bracken (Ed.), The Psychoeducational Assessment of Preschool Children (3rd ed., pp. 45–56). Boston: Allyn & Bacon.

Branscombe, N. A., Castle, K., Dorsey, A. G., Surbeck, E., & Taylor, J. B. (2003). Early childhood curriculum: A constructivist perspective. Boston: Houghton Mifflin.

Bredekamp, S., & Rosegrant, T. (1992). Reaching potentials: Appropriate curriculum and assessment for young children (Vol. 1). Washington, DC: National Association for the Education of Young Children.

Bredekamp, S., & Rosegrant, T. (1995). Reaching potentials: Transforming early childhood curriculum and assessment (Vol. 2). Washington, DC: National Association for the Education of Young Children.

Bryant, D., Maxwell, K., Taylor, K., Poe, M., Peisner-Feinberg, E., & Bernier, K. (2003). Smart start and preschool child care quality in NC: Change over time and relation to children's readiness. Chapel Hill, NC: FPG Child Development Institute.

Center for Applied Special Technology. (2004, March 12). Universal design for learning. Retrieved October 6, 2004, from http://www.cast.org/udl/

Davis, M. D., Kilgo, J. L., & Gamel-McCormick, M. (1998). Young children with special needs: A developmentally appropriate approach. Needham Heights, MA: Viacom.

Dodge, Trister D. (2000). What it takes to implement a curriculum. Retrieved February 22, 2004, from http://www.teachingstrategies.com/content/pageDocs/Whatitmeans.pdf

Dodge, Trister D., & Bickart, T. (2003). Curriculum, assessment, and outcomes: Putting them all in perspective. Children and Families, 17(1), 28–32.

Education Commission of the States. (1998). Designing and implementing standards-based accountability systems. Denver, CO: Author.

Fewell, R. (2000). Assessment of young children with special needs foundation for tomorrow. Topics in Early Childhood Special Education, 20(1), 38–42.

Gilliam, W. S., & Leiter, V. (2003). Evaluating early childhood programs: Improving quality and informing policy. Zero to Three, 23 (6), 6–13.

Goffin, S. G., & Wilson, C. (2001). Curriculum models and early childhood education: Appraising the relationship (2nd ed.). Upper Saddle River, NJ: Merrill/Prentice Hall.

Good, R., & Kaminski, R. (2003). DIBELSTM Administration and scoring guide. Longmont, CO: Sopris West.

Greenwood, C. R., Luze, G. J., & Carta, J. J. (2002). Assessment of intervention results with infants and toddlers. In A. Thomas, & J. Grimes (Eds.), Best Practices in School Psychology IV (Vol. 2) (pp. 1219–1230). Washington, DC: NASP.

Grisham-Brown, J. L., & Pretti-Frontczak, K. L. (2003). Preschool teachers' use of planning time for the purpose of individualizing instruction for young children with special needs. Journal of Early Intervention, 26(1), 31–46.

Grisham-Brown, J. L., Hemmeter, M. L., & Pretti-Frontczak, K. L. (2005). Blended practices for teaching young children in inclusive settings. Baltimore, MD: Brookes.

Hanson, M. J., & Lynch, E. W. (2004). Understanding families: Approaches to diversity, disability, and risk. Baltimore, MD: Brookes.

Harbin, G., Rous, B., & McLean, M. (2005). Issues in designing state accountability systems. Journal of Early Intervention, 27(3), 137–164.

Haskins, R. (2004). Closing the achievement gap: Head Start and beyond [Ask the expert]. In L. Klein (Ed.), The Evaluation Exchange, 10 (2), 9–12.

Hass, G. (2000). Curriculum planning: A contemporary approach (7th ed.). Boston: Allyn & Bacon.

Hebbeler, K. (2004) Uses and misuses of data on outcomes for young children with disabilities. Chapel Hill, NC: Early Childhood Outcomes Center.

Helm, J. H., Beneke, S., & Steinheimer, K. (1998). Windows on learning: Documenting young children's work. New York: Teachers College Press.

Helm, J. H., & Gronlund, G. (2000). Linking standards and engaged learning in the early years. Early Childhood Research & Practice, 2(1). Retrieved May 27, 2004, from http://ecrp.uiuc.edu/v2n1/helm.html

High/Scope Educational Research Foundation. (2003). Preschool child observation record (2nd Ed.). Ypsilanti, MI: High/Scope Press.

Hitchcock, C., Meyer, A., Rose, D., & Jackson, R. (2002). Providing new access to the general curriculum: Universal design for learning. Teaching Exceptional Children, 35(2), 8–17.

Horn, E., Lieber, J., Li, S. M., Sandall, S., & Schwartz, I. (2000). Supporting young children's IEP goals in inclusive settings through embedded learning opportunities. Topics in Early Childhood Special Education, 20, 208–223.

Individuals with Disabilities Education Act Amendments. (2004). 20 U.S.C. 1400 et seq.

Joint Committee on Standards for Educational Evaluation. (1994). The program evaluation standards. Thousand Oaks, CA: Sage.

Kagan, S. L., Scott-Little, C., & Clifford, R. M. (2003). Assessing young children: What policy makers need to know and do. In C. Scott-Little, S. L. Kagan, & R. M. Clifford (Eds). Assessing the state of state assessments; perspectives on assessing young children (pp.5–11). Greensboro, NC: SERVE.

Kaminski, R. A., & Good, R. H. (1996). Toward a technology for assessing basic early literacy skills. School Psychology Review, 25, 215–227.

Karger, J., & Hitchcock, C. (2003). Access to the general curriculum for students with disabilities: A brief legal interpretation. Wakefield, MA: National Center on Accessing the General Curriculum. Retrieved October 6, 2004, from http://www.cast.org/publications/ncac/ncac_accesslegal.html

Katz, L. (1997). A developmental approach to assessment of young children. Champaign, IL: ERIC Clearinghouse on Elementary and Early Childhood Education.

Kellegrew, D. H., O'Brien, S., & Groppenbacher, E. (2003). Evidence-based program evaluation: A guide for agencies to self-assess their practices and policies. Zero to Three, 23(6), 53–59.

Kurtenbach, K. (2000). Standards-based reform: The power of external change agents [Electronic version]. Connections, A Journal of Public Education Advocacy, 7(1), 1, 4–5.

Losardo, A., & Notari-Syverson, A. (2001). Alternative approaches to assessing young children. Baltimore, MD: Brookes.

McAfee, R., & Leong, D. (2002). Assessing and guiding young children's development and learning (3rd ed.). Boston: Allyn & Bacon.

McConnell, S. R. (2000). Assessment in early intervention and early childhood special education: Building on the past to project into our future. Topics in Early Childhood Special Education, 20(1), 43–48.

McConnell, S. R., Priest, J. S., Davis, S. D., & McEvoy, M. A., (2002). Best practices in measuring growth and development for preschool children. In A. Thomas, & J. Grimes (Eds.), Best Practices in School Psychology (4th ed.) (Vol. 2, pp. 1231–1246). Washington, DC: NASP.

McCormick, K., & Nellis, L. (2004). Assessing cognitive development. In M. McLean, M. Wolery, & D. B. Bailey (Eds.), Assessing infants and preschoolers with special needs (pp. 256–300). Upper Saddle River, NJ: Pearson.

McLaughlin, M. W., & Shepard, L. A. (1995). Improving education through standards-based reform: A report of the National Academy of Education panel on standards-based reform. Stanford, CA: The National Academy of Education.

McLean, M. (2004). Assessment and its importance in early intervention/early childhood special education. In M. McLean, M. Wolery, & D. B. Bailey (Eds.), Assessing infants and preschoolers with special needs (pp. 1–21). Upper Saddle River, NJ: Pearson.

Meisels, S. J. (2000). On the side of the child: Personal reflections on testing, teaching, and early childhood education. Young Children, 66(6), 16–19.

Meisels, S. J., & Fenichel, E. (Eds.). (1996). New visions for the developmental assessment of infants and young children. Washington, DC: Zero To Three.

Meisels, S. J., Jablon, J., Marsden, D. B., Dichtelmiller, M. L., & Dorfman, A. (1994). The work sampling system. Ann Arbor, MI: Rebus Planning Associates, Inc.

Morell, J.A. (2005). Why are there unintended consequences of program action, and what are the implications for doing evaluation? American Journal of Evaluation, 26(4), 444-463.

NAEYC (2005). Code of ethical conduct and statement of commitment. Retrieved May 15, 2006, from http://www.naeyc.org/about/positions.asp

NAEYC and NAECS/SDE (2003). Early childhood curriculum, assessment, and program evaluation: building an effective, accountable system in programs for children birth through age 8. Retrieved January 27, 2004, from http:// www.naeyc.org/about/positions.asp

Neisworth, J. (1993). Assessment: DEC recommended practices. In DEC recommended practices: Indicators of quality in programs for infants and young children (pp. 11-17). Denver, CO: DEC

Neisworth, J. T., & Bagnato, S. J. (1992). The case against intelligence testing in early childhood. Topics in Early Childhood Special Education, 12(1), 11-17.

Neisworth, J. T., & Bagnato, S. J. (2004). The mis-measure of young children: The authentic assessment alternative. Infants & Young Children, 17(3), 198–212.

Neisworth, J.T. & Bagnato, S.J. (2005). DEC recommended practices: Assessment. In S. Sandall, M. L. Hemmeter, B. Smith, & M. McLean. (Ed.).DEC recommended practices: A comprehensive guide for practical application (pp. 45-69). Missoula, MT: DEC.

Nolet, V., & McLaughlin, M. J., (2000). Accessing the general curriculum: Including students with disabilities in standards-based reform. Thousand Oaks, CA: Corwin Press Inc.

Orkwis, R. (1999). Curriculum access and universal design for learning. (Report No. EDD-EC-99-14). Reston, VA: ERIC Clearing House on Disabilities and Gifted Education. (ED437767)

Orkwis, R., & McLane, K. (1998). A curriculum every student can use: Design principles for student access. Reston, VA: ERIC Clearing House on Disabilities and Gifted Education. (ED423654)

Patton, M. Q. (1997). Utilization-focused evaluation (3rd ed.). Thousand Oaks, CA: Sage.

Preator, K., & McAllister, J. R. (1995). Assessing infants and toddlers. In A. Thomas, & J. Grimes (Eds.), Best practices in school psychology III, (pp. 775–788). Washington, DC: NASP.

Pretti-Frontczak, K., & Bricker, D. (2004). An activity-based approach to early intervention (3rd ed.). Baltimore, MD: Brookes.

Robertson, J., Green, K. Schloss, P. J., & Kohler, F. (2003). Using a peer-mediated intervention to facilitate children's participation in inclusive child care activities. Education and Treatment of Children 26(2), 182–197.

Roid, G., & Sampers, J. (2004). Merrill-Palmer-R: Scales of development manual. Chicago: Stoelting Co.

Sandall, S., Hemmeter, M. L., Smith, B. J., & McLean, M. (2005). DEC recommended practices: A comprehensive guide for practical application. Missoula, MT: DEC.

Sandall, S. R., Schwartz, I. S., Joseph, G., Chou, H., Horn, E., Lieber, J., Odom, S. L., & Wolery, R. (2002). Building blocks for successful early childhood programs: Strategies for including all children. Baltimore, MD: Brookes.

Sands, D. J., Adams, L., & Stout, D. M. (1995). A statewide exploration of the nature and use of curriculum in special education. Exceptional Children, 62(1), 68–83.

Sattler, J. M. (2001). Assessment of children: Cognitive applications (4th ed.). La Mesa, CA: Author.

Schumacher, R., Irish, K., & Lombardi, J. (2003). Meeting great expectations: Integrating early education program standards in child care. Washington, DC: Center for Law and Social Policy. (ED480607)

Scott-Little, C., Kagan, S. L., & Frelow, V. (2003). Standards for pre-school children's learning and development: Who has standards, how were they developed and how are they used? Greensboro, NC: SERVE.

Scott-Little, C., Kagan, S. L., & Frelow, V. S. (2005). Inside the content: The depth and breadth of early learning standards. Greensboro, NC: SERVE.

Sheehan, R., & Gallagher, R. J. (1983). Conducting evaluations of infant intervention programs. In S. G. Garwood, & R. R. Fewell (Eds.), Educating handicapped infants: Issues in development and intervention (pp. 495–519). Rockville, MD: Aspen.

Shepard, L., Kagan, S. L., & Wurtz, E. (1998). Principles and recommendationsfor early childhood assessments. Washington, DC: National Education Goals Panel.

Shonkoff, J., & Phillips, D., (Eds.). (2000). From neurons to neighborhoods: The science of early childhood development. Washington, DC: National Academy Press.

Shonkoff, J. (2004). Evaluating early childhood services: What's really behind the curtain? The Evaluation Exchange, 10 (2), 3–4.

Snyder, P., Lawson, S., Thompson, B., Stricklin, S., & Sexton, D. (1993). Evaluating the psychometric integrity of instruments used in early intervention research: The Battelle developmental inventory. Topics in Early Childhood Special Education, 13(2), 216–232.

Snyder, S., & Sheehan, R. (1996). Program evaluation in early childhood special education. In S. L. Odom, & M. E. McLean (Eds.), Early intervention for infants and young children with disabilities and their families: Recommended practices (pp. 359–378). Austin, TX: PRO-ED.

Stufflebeam, D. (1985). Systematic evaluation: A self-instructional guide to theory and practice. Boston, MA: Kluwer/Nijhoff.

Vaughn, S., Ae-Hwa, K., Morris-Sloan, C. V., Hughes, M. T., Batya, E., & Dheepa, S. (2003). Social skills interventions for young children with disabilities. Remedial & Special Education, 24(1), 2–16.

Widerstrom, A. H. (2005). Achieving learning goals through play: Teaching young children with special needs (2nd ed.). Baltimore: Brookes.

Wolery, M., Strain, P., & Bailey, D. (1992). Reaching potentials of children with special needs. In S. Bredekamp, & T. Rosengrant, (Eds.), Reaching potentials: Appropriate curriculum and assessment for young children (Vol.1) (pp. 92–112). Washington, DC: NAEYC.

Wolery, M., & Sainato, D. (1996). General curriculum and intervention strategies. In S. L. Odom, & M. McLean (Eds.), Early intervention/early childhood special education (pp. 125–158). Austin, TX: PRO-ED.

Wolery, M. (2004). Monitoring child progress. In M. McLean, M. Wolery, & D. B. Bailey (Eds.), Assessing infants and preschoolers with special needs, (3rd ed., pp. 545–584). Englewood Cliffs, NJ: Prentice-Hall.

Woods, J., & McCormick, K. (2002). Toward an integration of child- and family-centered practices in the assessment of preschool children: Welcoming the family. Young Exceptional Children, 5(3), 2–11.

Wrightslaw. (n.d.). Glossary of special education legal terms. Retrieved December 14, 2004, from http://www.wrightslaw.com/links/glossary.sped.legal.htm

Tables

The following tables have been designed to extend the information presented in this paper. None of the information on the tables is designed to be exhaustive in terms of how the practices described in this paper should be applied, but rather the information should serve as examples of recommended practice.

Table 1 is composed of three parts: multiple means of representation, multiple means of engagement, and multiple means of expression. Each part contains definitions and examples of how the principles of universal design for learning might appear when working with infants/toddlers, preschoolers, and students in early elementary classrooms. Readers are encouraged to examine all of the examples provided but might want to focus on those related to the population of children they serve.

Table 2 provides examples and illustrations of how each element of a comprehensive and universally designed curriculum framework goes from generic to individualized (i.e., how each panel of the umbrella can be divided into three layers). As with Table 1, the information is arranged by practices that would be applicable for working with three different age groups. Readers are again encouraged to review all examples but may want to center their efforts on the population of children they serve.

Table 3 provides a summary of the assessment decision-making practices presented by Wolery, Strain, & Bailey (1994) across seven areas: (1) screening; (2) diagnosis (or identification) of delay or disability; (3) eligibility determination for early intervention or special education services; (4) instructional program planning/intervention assessment; (5) placement; (6) progress monitoring; and (7) program evaluation.

Table 1: Curriculum in programs for infants, toddlers, preschoolers, kindergartners, and primary grade children.

KEY RECOMMENDATION: *All learners have access to and participate in the curriculum through multiple means of representation, engagement, and expression.*

Table 1A

Infants/Toddlers	Preschoolers	Kindergarten/Primary
Multiple Means of Representation		

Multiple means of representation are built into the curriculum to address the widest range of learners possible. The goals and expectations, learning opportunities and lessons, toys/materials, and resources are designed to be multi-sensory, available in different formats, flexible, and to have multiple access points and levels of complexity, allowing children to participate in ways that best meet their needs. This chart describes just a few of the numerous possibilities.

Infants/Toddlers	Preschoolers	Kindergarten/Primary
Caregivers provide toys/materials that combine **different and multiple sensory features** for children to experience. For example: • Colorful toys/materials that make sounds. • Toys/materials with interesting shapes and textures. • Toys/materials that move. • Toys/materials that can be held, shaken, and mouthed. Caregivers communicate/interact with children in many different ways including: • Talking. • Singing songs. • Reading books. • Showing pictures. • Playing music. • Dancing. • Sharing toys and materials. • Playing finger games. • Using gestures.	Teachers use **different and multiple formats** to provide important information. For example, teachers inform children about the daily schedule by: • Presenting the schedule verbally. • Discussing the schedule in groups or one-on-one. • Posting the schedule on the wall in a series of simple icons and/or photographs. • Writing the schedule with simple words. • Making the schedule available on rings of cards or with Velcro pictures to provide visual reminders of the daily routine. • Recording the schedule on a cassette tape that is available in the listening center. • Preparing the schedule for children to use on a computer. Teachers use **multiple means of support.** For example, to help children learn to share teachers might: • Role-play sharing situations. • Read stories about sharing. • Watch and discuss a video. • Depict sharing with drawings. • Discuss sharing prior to activities.	Teachers use **different and multiple formats** to provide new information and review critical concepts. For example, when teaching a new letter of the alphabet, a kindergarten teacher might provide opportunities to: • Write the letter on paper or on an overhead transparency that is projected on the wall. • Make the letter out of Play Doh. • Write the letter in sand/shaving cream. • Find the letter in alphabet noodles. • Move the children's bodies into the letter shape. • Sing silly letter songs. • Read books about the letter. More complex opportunities are simultaneously provided for children who are ready, such as a creative writing center where children work on their own stories using the new letter. New concepts are explained in many ways. For example, co-teachers might explain a new science concept using: • Graphic organizers. • Pictures and 3-dimensional models. • Charts with critical points mounted on the wall. • Individual materials for later study/review. • Models for children to manipulate and explore through touch. • Interactive computer programs.

KEY RECOMMENDATION: *All learners have access to and participate in the curriculum through multiple means of representation, engagement, and expression.*

Table 1B

Infants/Toddlers	Preschoolers	Kindergarten/Primary
Multiple Means of Engagement		
Multiple means of engagement are provided in order to appeal to, motivate, and meet the needs of a wide range of children. Children may choose for themselves from an array of options, enabling children to pursue their goals, develop preferences, build confidence, establish priorities, persist in the face of difficulty, and care about learning. These examples are just a few possibilities.		

Caregivers provide toys/materials that offer **different levels of complexity**, such as:

- Rattles that can be held with one or two hands.
- Blocks of different sizes, weights and textures.

Caregivers ensure that multiple and varied learning opportunities, daily activities, and toys/materials are available so children can select what appeals to them. For example:

- Children may choose various levels of independence by selecting activities and toys/materials that are simple, straight-forward, and foster independent play, or choose things that require adult support and organization. For example, a child may be able to explore a mirror mounted in an easily held rattle frame but may need support to explore a pop-up book.
- Children may select activities and toys/materials that are familiar and predictable, such as an easily activated light-up music box, or items that are new and surprising, such as a jack-in-the-box.
- At different times children may prefer toys/materials that are soft and cuddly, or things that invite active, boisterous play.

Teachers provide multiple and varied ways for children to direct their play and be involved in routine and planned activities. For example:

- Children may select from an inspiring array of creative materials for an art project. Rather than just copying an adult's model, children may cut or tear, color or paint, glue or tape, build a model, and create alone or work with a peer.
- Children in the dramatic play area may choose among a collection of creative, open-ended materials such as scarves, writing supplies, and containers of odds and ends that encourage them to participate in personally meaningful ways. They may choose to act out roles and scenarios that are either fantasy- or reality-based, that represent their own or other cultures, and that are simple and customary or complex and imaginative.

Teachers provide multiple and varied opportunities for children to be involved in learning. For example:

- The kindergarten teacher designs many different opportunities to engage children in practicing their mathematics skills. Children are encouraged to:
  - Distribute snacks and determine how many napkins are needed.
  - Choose among a variety of manipulatives such as cubes, links, beads and tiles, as well as equipment for measuring, counting and solving problems.
  - Play a rousing board game with dice, or quietly connect the dots.
  - Select among number books, computer software programs, and counting songs.
- Everyone in a second grade class will be reading about the same topic, and the teacher provides resources and enables children to:
  - Choose among a collection of narrative and expository books with varied levels of difficulty.
  - Explore a number of Web sites and software options, and decide for themselves which combination of resources will work best for them.

KEY RECOMMENDATION: *All learners have access to and participate in the curriculum through multiple means of representation, engagement, and expression.*

Table 1C

Infants/Toddlers	Preschoolers	Kindergarten/Primary
Multiple Means of Expression		
Multiple means of expression ensures children have a variety of formats for responding, demonstrating what they know, and for expressing ideas, feelings, and preferences. In addition, children have options in their use of resources, toys, and materials, addressing individual strengths, preferences, and abilities. This chart presents just a few examples of the many ways that children might demonstrate what they know and are able to do.		
Children are encouraged to show preferences, what they are able to do, and what they know in different and multiple ways. For example: • Children show how they prefer to play with blocks by acting upon them in different ways such as building, stacking, linking, making patterns, banging, holding, or mouthing. • Children respond to caregiver comments and questions using verbal expressions (e.g., speaking, using assistive technology with voice output) and/or non-verbal expressions (e.g., facial expression, gestures, pointing to pictures). • Children are allowed to participate during a playgroup by answering simple questions, labeling, reciting, watching, sorting, or remaining with the group.	Children are encouraged to express their understanding in **many** different ways. For example, children learning nursery rhymes may: • Recite or sing the rhymes individually or in small groups. • Act them out in the dramatic play area or with puppets. • Create a visual representation in the art area. • Review the rhymes in the listening center, and record themselves saying the rhymes or creating their own rhymes. • Use the overhead projector to create and display their work. • Use the Smart Board to visit an interactive Web site to share with their peers. **Children are encouraged to communicate with peers in a variety of ways including:** • Using words to talk. • Writing notes and letters. • Making pictures. • Creating songs or poems. • Using sign language or gestures. • Using communication boards or assistive devices.	Children have multiple opportunities to demonstrate their knowledge and skills, ideas, feelings, and preferences. For example, children in third grade are given a list from which they may select the way they want to show what they have learned in their social studies lesson. They may work alone, with a partner, or may form small groups to: • Write a report on one of several key topics. • Write a story about the time period discussed. • Create a newspaper representing stories and goods from the time period. • Put on a dramatization. • Write and/or perform a song or rap. • Create a PowerPoint slide show. • Make a model or diagram. • Create a collage or artistic representation.

Table 2: Elements of a Comprehensive and Universally Designed Curriculum Framework.

KEY RECOMMENDATION: *Implement an integrated, developmentally appropriate, universally designed curriculum framework that is flexible, comprehensive, and linked to assessment and program evaluation activities.*

Table 2A

Infants/Toddlers	Preschoolers	Kindergarten/Primary
Assessment/Progress Monitoring		
Assessment/Progress monitoring conducted on groups of children or an individual child should be done by collaborative teams using multiple valid and reliable measures. Assessment/progress monitoring procedures should vary in terms of (a) format of items/questions (e.g., presented/posed through verbal questions, written directions, gestures, tactile models, and/or pictures); (b) complexity, wherein items represent a wide range of developmental skills and abilities; and (c) expectations, wherein children can demonstrate their knowledge and skills in a variety of ways (e.g., use of speech, signs, gestures, pictures, writing, art, and assistive technology). Assessment/progress monitoring procedures do not penalize children for physical, sensory, or cultural differences. Assessments used with young children should also accommodate their individual strengths, preferences, abilities, and visual, auditory, and kinesthetic needs. Program administration provides support for collaborative data collection, analysis, interpretation, and use in decision making.		
Foundational Practices for All Children		
• Assessment/progress monitoring is ongoing and conducted in the natural environment during typical routines and interactions by those who know the child best (e.g., family members, early intervention specialists, and therapists). For example, a child's caregiver observes during bathing, dinner, car travel, at the grocery store, and during play at the child care center. • All areas of infants' and toddlers' growth and development are assessed/monitored using a common comprehensive, universally designed, authentic, curriculum-based assessment(s) that provides information regarding strengths, interests, and emerging skills (e.g., Assessment, Evaluation, and Programming System (AEPS) presented by Bricker, 2002). • Assessment/monitoring data are used to inform day-to-day practices and enhance the lives of children and families, not just to meet federal, state, or agency requirements. For example, teams should use data to make changes to the physical environment (make toys more accessible), create additional learning opportunities, and/or provide more support to enhance learning.	• Assessment/progress monitoring is ongoing and conducted during child-directed, routine, and planned activities by those who know the child best (e.g., family members, teachers, early childhood educators, therapists). For example, a child's preschool teacher and family observe during playtime, snack/lunch, and art. • All areas of preschool age children's health, growth, and development are assessed/monitored using a common comprehensive, universally designed, authentic, curriculum-based assessment(s) (e.g., The Work Sampling System presented by Meisels, Jablon, Marsden, Dichtelmiller, & Dorfman, 1994) that aligns with federal, state, and agency standards. • Assessment/monitoring data are used to inform day-to-day practices and enhance the lives of children and families, not just to meet federal, state, or agency requirements. For example, teams should use data to plan daily activities, adapt equipment, and/or guide the type and frequency of services.	• Assessment/progress monitoring is ongoing and conducted across all aspects of the curriculum by those who know the child best (e.g., family members, teachers, therapists). For example, a child's teacher observes during specific lessons and transitions, and families help observe during extracurricular activities such as after-school club meetings. • All areas of students' health, growth, and development are assessed/monitored using a common comprehensive, universally designed, authentic, and curriculum-based measure(s) that aligns with state standards (e.g., writing and spelling probes and commercially available measures such as the Dynamic Indicators of Basic Early Literacy Skills (DIBELS) presented by Good & Kaminski, 2003). • Assessment/monitoring data are used to inform day-to-day practices and enhance the lives of children and families, not just to meet federal, state, or agency requirements. For example, teams should use data to plan daily lessons, adapt equipment and learning materials, and/or guide the type and frequency of services.

KEY RECOMMENDATION: *All learners have access to and participate in the curriculum through multiple means of representation, engagement, and expression.*

Table 2A continued...

Infants/Toddlers	Preschoolers	Kindergarten/Primary
• Summaries or aggregated data are presented clearly to stakeholders including policymakers. Age equivalencies are avoided due to confusion surrounding interpretation. For example, teams describe what the child can do and is starting to do (e.g., the child can take two steps when holding onto an adult's hand and is beginning to stand unsupported), rather than using broad statements such as a child is functioning at a 12-month level.	• Summaries or aggregated data are presented clearly to stakeholders including policymakers. For example, teams compile children's work into a portfolio or electronic slide show, graph children's performance, talk about strengths and emerging skills, and write narrative summaries that are objective and positive. Age equivalencies are avoided due to confusion surrounding interpretation.	• Summaries or aggregated data are presented clearly to stakeholders including policymakers. Age and grade equivalencies are avoided due to confusion surrounding interpretation. For example, teams describe a student's reading skills (e.g., fluency, number of sight words, comprehension, oral reading abilities, vocabulary), rather than using broad statements such as the student reads at a 1st grade level. Teams can also compile students' work into a portfolio or electronic slide show, graph performance, talk about strengths and emerging skills, and write narrative summaries that are objective and positive.
Adding Accommodations As Needed		
Accommodations to assessment toys/ materials, procedures, and items are made as needed. For example: • Extended wait or performance time. • Presentation of information verbally and/or visually. • Increased size of print/pictures. • Presentation of toys/materials that are adjustable and flexible in how they are used.	Accommodations to assessment toys/ materials, procedures, and items are made as needed. For example: • Extended wait or performance time. • Presentation of information verbally and/or visually. • Increased size of print/pictures. • Presentation of toys/materials that are adjustable and flexible in how they are used.	Accommodations to assessment toys/ materials, procedures, and items are made as needed. For example: • Extended wait or performance time. • Presentation of information verbally and/or visually. • Increased size of print/pictures. • Presentation of toys/materials that are adjustable and flexible in how they are used.
Making Modifications		
Modifications to assessment practices are also made as needed. For example: • Using an alternative measure. • Changing how a child demonstrates or performs. • Assessing critical earlier or prerequisite skills. • Reducing the number of items assessed/monitored.	Modifications to assessment practices are also made as needed. For example: • Using an alternative measure. • Changing how a child demonstrates or performs. • Assessing critical earlier or prerequisite skills. • Reducing the number of items assessed/monitored.	Modifications to assessment practices are also made as needed. For example: • Using an alternative measure. • Changing how a child demonstrates or performs. • Assessing critical earlier or prerequisite skills. • Reducing the number of items assessed/monitored.

KEY RECOMMENDATION: *All learners have access to and participate in the curriculum through multiple means of representation, engagement, and expression.*

Table 2B

Infants/Toddlers	Preschoolers	Kindergarten/Primary
Scope and Sequence		
The scope and sequence of a curriculum framework is identified by the aims of all caregivers, professionals, and members of the community (e.g., medical and school personnel) involved in the lives of young children. The skills and processes specified by the curriculum framework's scope and sequence represent all areas of growth, development, and learning(e.g., fine motor, gross motor, adaptive, cognition, communication, social, literacy, mathematics, science, social studies, health and safety, creativity etc.) and are culturally and individually relevant. Expectations regarding children's performance allows for individual differences and abilities. Children are exposed and encouraged to learn at their own rate rather than based upon contrived milestones or age equivalencies.		
Foundational Practices for All Children		

• The scope of the curriculum framework for infants and toddlers is comprehensive and inclusive of all areas of development and learning. No one area is prioritized over another.
• The order in which skills are taught or expected is based upon an understanding that development is variable and cannot be predicted or dictated by information found on charts, assessments, or standards.
  • For example, if a milestone chart states that 18-month olds typically speak about 15 words it does not mean that all 18-month olds will use 15 words; some will continue to rely more on gestures and sounds while their expressive language continues to develop.
	• The scope of the curriculum framework for infants and toddlers is comprehensive and inclusive of all areas of development and learning. No one area is prioritized over another.
	• The order in which skills are taught or expected is based upon an understanding that development is variable and cannot be predicted or dictated by information found on charts, assessments, or standards.
	  • For example, if a screening instrument contains an item as to whether children can write their first name it should not be assumed that all children will be able to do so at a given age or that all children, even if they can write their first name, will demonstrate the ability during the screening.
		• The scope of the curriculum framework for infants and toddlers is comprehensive and inclusive of all areas of development and learning. No one area is prioritized over another.
		• The order in which skills are taught or expected is based upon an understanding that development is variable and cannot be predicted or dictated by information found on charts, assessments, or standards, or based upon arbitrary grade assignment. Further, the way students demonstrate their knowledge may differ across skills.
		  • For example, if a state standard indicates second graders should be able to model problem situations using objects, pictures, numbers and other symbols, teams need to allow students to use any of the methods versus allowing only one acceptable way to model problem situations.

Adding Accommodation As Needed		
The same standards apply to all children but accommodations are made as needed to ensure full access and participation in daily activities and routines. • For example, teams may alter the learning environment, provide additional supports, and/or allow children to use alternative communication devices to demonstrate knowledge and skill related to state/agency standards and developmental expectations.	The same standards apply to all children but accommodations are made as needed to ensure full access and participation in daily activities and routines. • For example, teams may alter the learning environment, provide additional supports, and/or allow children to use alternative communication devices to demonstrate knowledge and skill related to state/agency standards and developmental expectations.	The same standards apply to all children but accommodations are made as needed to ensure full access and participation in daily activities and routines. • For example, teams may alter the learning environment, provide additional supports, and/or allow children to use alternative communication devices to demonstrate knowledge and skill related to state/agency standards and developmental expectations.

KEY RECOMMENDATION: *All learners have access to and participate in the curriculum through multiple means of representation, engagement, and expression.*

Table 2B continued...

Infants/Toddlers	Preschoolers	Kindergarten/Primary
Making Modifications		
Expectations for all children, while important to be high, need to be established with consideration of individual children's developmental readiness. Modifications to what is expected or addressed are necessary to meet the needs of all learners. Teams may need to develop individualized plans or target individual skills that, while aligned with common standards for all children, represent a substantial change in terms of expectations, performance criteria, and/or form or format.	Expectations for all children, while important to be high, need to be established with consideration of individual children's developmental readiness. Modifications to what is expected or addressed are necessary to meet the needs of all learners. Teams may need to develop individualized plans or target individual skills that, while aligned with common standards for all children, represent a substantial change in terms of expectations, performance criteria, and/or form or format.	Expectations for all students, while important to be high, need to be established with consideration of individual students' developmental readiness. Modifications to what is expected or addressed are necessary to meet the needs of all learners. Teams may need to develop individualized plans or target individual skills that, while aligned with common standards for all students, represent a substantial change in terms of expectations, performance criteria, and/or form or format.
• For example, if a state standard for toddlers is to "begin to use writing tools to make marks on paper" and the child is just beginning to reach, grasp, release, and cross mid-line, teams may need to address prerequisites that are necessary for a child to perform the skills identified by the standard.	• For example, if a state standard for preschoolers is to "demonstrate an understanding of time, length, weight, capacity and temperature" and the child is just beginning to answer simple yes/no questions, sort objects based upon function, and recall events, teams may need to address prerequisites that are necessary for a child to perform the skills identified by the standard.	• For example, if a state standard for Kindergarten is to "Compare and order whole numbers up to 10" and the student is just beginning to count, teams may need to address prerequisites that are necessary for a child to perform the skills identified by the standard.

KEY RECOMMENDATION: *All learners have access to and participate in the curriculum through multiple means of representation, engagement, and expression.*

Table 2C

Infants/Toddlers	Preschoolers	Kindergarten/Primary
Activities and Intervention Strategies		
Team members work collaboratively and are given adequate time to jointly design interactions, activities, and lessons to address the needs of all children. The principles of universal design are at the heart of team planning, and learning opportunities are developmentally, culturally, and individually appropriate. The child's natural environment and daily routines are used as the context for teaching by all team members. A continuum of strategies is used to provide necessary levels of support and promote independence.		
Foundational Practices for All Children		
Learning for infants and toddlers occurs as a part of the natural routines and activities of daily life and play. For example, while: • Reading cardboard books. • Playing peak-a-boo. • Taking the bus to the park. • Swimming at the YMCA. • Getting ready for bed. Universally designed, engaging, fun, and developmentally appropriate activities and routines are the foundations of quality programs intended to promote growth and learning of young children, regardless of their background, experience, culture, prior knowledge, or developmental/physical challenges.	Learning for preschoolers occurs during child-directed, routine, and planned activities. For example, during: • Snack. • Art. • Center activities. • Play at the park. • Church/synagogue services. • A stay at their grandparents. The preschool classroom activities and routines should be universally designed to meet the needs of the widest range of learners possible, regardless of their background, experience, culture, prior knowledge, or developmental/physical challenges.	Learning for elementary age students occurs during curricular and extracurricular activities. For example, while: • Engaged in a science lesson. • Reading a book. • Completing a spelling test. • Riding the bus home from school. • Visiting a local museum. Lessons and activities should be universally designed for learning, developmentally and individually appropriate, and built upon the interests and unique learning abilities of all students, regardless of their background, experience, culture, prior knowledge, or developmental/physical challenges.
Adding Accommodation as Needed		
Caregivers provide accommodations to increase access and participation by infants and toddlers. Accommodations enable children to make progress toward age appropriate outcomes. For example, caregivers may: • Reduce the amount of noise or the number of distractions for a child who needs help maintaining attention. • Provide supported seating with wrap-around headrest for a toddler who needs physical support sitting at the table. • Illuminate and/or magnify brightly colored picture books for a child with low vision.	Teams provide accommodations to increase access and participation by all preschoolers. Accommodations do not change the instructional content or the performance expectations, and children given accommodations will be expected to achieve age-appropriate outcomes. For example, teachers and family members may: • Adapt the height, angle, and positioning of work areas for a child who uses a wheelchair. • Use a personal amplification system for a child with hearing impairment. • Provide an arm support and/or a cuff/strap for a child who has difficulty holding objects.	Teachers, other school personnel, and families provide accommodations to increase access and participation for all learners. Accommodations do not change the instructional content or the performance expectations, and children given accommodations will be expected to achieve grade-level standards. For example, teachers may: • Reduce the amount of noise or the number of distractions for a student who needs help maintaining attention. • Provide screen readers, Braille, and Braille/tactile labels for a child with vision impairment. • Equip books with page fluffers so that a child with fine motor impairment can turn pages.

KEY RECOMMENDATION: *All learners have access to and participate in the curriculum through multiple means of representation, engagement, and expression.*

Table 2C continued...

Infants/Toddlers	Preschoolers	Kindergarten/Primary
• Adapt toys/materials to allow children to use a variety of movements in different positions (e.g., add Velcro, magnets, or handles for a child who has difficulty grasping objects).	• Break down multi-step activities into single steps (e.g., break clean-up into asking a child to stop a specific activity/action, ask the child to return a single toy to desired location, and then request the child line up at the door).	• Provide a voice output device for a child who needs an augmentative alternative communication system.
Making Modifications		
Modifications can also be made by using various intervention strategies to create embedded learning opportunities to address children's individual needs during ongoing routines and activities. Modifications involve changes to the developmental levels and performance expectations. For example, caregivers encouraging an 18-month-old child with developmental delays to make eye contact can create embedded learning opportunities such as: • Playfully calling the child's name during diaper changing. • Offering preferred foods during mealtime. • Playing peek-a-boo with the washcloth during bathing. • Offering a favorite toy during playtime.	Modifications can also be made by using various intervention strategies to create embedded learning opportunities to address children's individual needs during child-directed, routine, and planned activities. Modifications involve changes to the developmental and content levels and to performance expectations. For example, to help a 4-year-old child with severe language delays learn how to label objects and events: • Her father asks her if she wants juice or eggs for breakfast. • The teacher builds on her interest in the fish tank by asking her what she sees. • The teacher asks her which color paint she wants first. • She sits with two peers who speak well as they share a picture book. • During bath her mother names her body parts and invites her to repeat them.	Modifications can also be made by using various intervention strategies to create embedded learning opportunities to address children's individual needs during curricular and extracurricular activities. Modifications involve changes to the content level and to performance expectations. For example, if a third-grade student with cognitive disabilities is working on increasing reading comprehension: • Adults and peers can ask basic or developmentally earlier types of questions about what was read (e.g., "What was the main idea of the story," or "Who was the main character?"). • Adults and peers create opportunities for the child to improve reading comprehension by giving directions that involve printed materials (e.g., "Please put each letter in the corresponding teacher's mail box" and each teacher has his/her name printed on mailbox). • Embedded learning opportunities can be created by asking the child to categorize written materials based upon a common attribute (e.g., categorizes all books about volcanoes and in the classroom or sorts magazines by type (e.g., sports, fashion, hobbies) can be created. • While same-age peers may be expected to read and then write in a journal, the student with a disability may be expected to read with a partner and then explain/share/describe to adults or peers what was read (e.g., after reading a poem, the student tells a peer what he liked about the poem, or after reading a passage from a book, tells an adult what he learned).

Table 3: Assessment for Decision Making (from Wolery, Strain, & Bailey, 1992)

Decision	Assessment Type	Relevant Questions	Measurement Practices
Determine whether to refer the child for further assessment.	Screening.	Do screening outcomes indicate potential for delay? Does hearing or vision screening indicate potential sensory problems? Does health screening and physical examination indicate need for medical services?	Use of multi-domain norm-referenced screening measures. Use of screening measures with specific criteria for referral for audiological/visual follow-up. Conducted by health professional.
Determine whether the child has a developmental delay or disability.	Diagnostic.	Does a developmental delay or disability exist? If so, what is the nature and extent of the delay or disability?	Individualized measures and procedures that frequently include standardized measures.
Determine whether the child is eligible for special services.	Eligibility.	Does the child meet state criteria to receive specialized services?	Frequently synonymous with diagnostic assessments because children are made eligible for services based on established diagnosis; however, may also include other requirements.
Determine what the child should be taught.	Intervention and/or instructional program planning assessment.	What is the child's current level of functioning? What does the child need to function independently in authentic environments (class-room, home, and community)? What are the effects of environmental or instructional modifications, adaptations and levels of assistance on child performance? What response patterns and interactions with environmental variables appear to influence child performance?	Curriculum or criterion-based assessment measures used in tandem with direct observation of children in multiple natural environments, informal testing, and interviews with other professionals and/or caregivers, including families. Frequently conducted by interventionists (i.e., teachers and therapists). Direct observation in these settings and interviews with caregivers and family members. Direct observation, informal assessment with multiple levels and types of assistance in authentic and natural settings. Direct observations, informal assessments, interviews with caregivers and family members, reinforcement preference assessment, trial use of intervention and instructional procedures, and clinical judgment.

Table 3: Assessment for Decision Making (from Wolery, Strain, & Bailey, 1992)

Decision	Assessment Type	Relevant Questions	Measurement Practices
Determine where the child should receive services and what services are needed.	Placement.	What does the child need? Which placement options within authentic, natural, and least restricted environments best meet the child's needs? Does the child need specialized services (i.e., speech/language therapy, physical therapy, occupational therapy or dietary supervision)?	Intervention and instructional program planning assessment. Direct observation, rating scales, and interviews to determine the characteristics & potential of each possible placement, with consideration of family preferences. Assessments conducted by therapists in these various disciplines; may be norm-referenced measures supplemented by observation and clinical judgment.
Determine whether the child is making adequate progress in learning important skills.	Progress monitoring of intervention or instructional programs.	What is the child's typical performance of important skills? Is the child using important skills in natural environments and routines?	Data collected from unstructured and structured observations of the child in natural environments or routines; data collected from periodic probes of the child's performance. Reports by caregivers and family members of the child's application of important skills.
Determine whether the desired outcomes were achieved.	Program evaluation.	Did the child make expected progress?	Measures and measurement procedures may vary, typically include performance on developmental assessments as well as acquisition of specified objectives.

Table 4: Indicators of Effectiveness in Program Evaluation

1. Evaluation efforts conform to evaluation standards including utility, propriety, feasibility, and accuracy.

2. Logical approaches for conceptualizing and conducting program evaluations are used.

3. Correspondence should exist between program goals/objectives and evaluation questions and methods.

4. Evaluation efforts employ participatory models.

5. Program evaluation describes what happened to participants.

6. Data collection is efficient and feasible.

7. Measures used in program evaluation yield reliable and valid scores for young children with disabilities and their families.

8. Program evaluation data are used to inform decision making.

9. Program evaluation data are used to inform continuous program improvement.

10. Program evaluation needs to be alert to unforeseen positive or negative consequences of a program.

11. Evaluation results are presented in formats relevant to diverse stakeholders.

12. Program evaluators distinguish between formal efficacy research and program evaluation.

Work Group and Section Authors

Introduction and Editors

Beth Rous
DEC Board Liaison

Marilou Hyson
NAEYC Liaison

Curriculum

Kristie Pretti-Frontczak
Chair, Kent State

Lucky McKeen
Mid-Eastern Ohio Special Education Regional Resource Center

Jennifer Grisham-Brown
University of Kentucky

Eva Horn
University of Kansas

Debbie Matthews
Marion County Schools

Joan Lieber
University of Maryland

Lynn Sullivan
Private Consultant

Assessment

Katherine McCormick
Chair, University of Kentucky

Kristen Missall
University of Kentucky

Juliann Woods
Florida State University

Jackie Sampers
University of Kentucky

Program Evaluation

Mary McLean
Co-Chair, University of Wisconsin, Milwaukee

Patricia Snyder
Co-Chair, Vanderbilt University

Jeff Priest
University of New Hampshire

Scott Snyder
University of Alabama - Birmingham

Linda Goodman
CT Birth to Three Program

Lynne Kahn
Frank Porter Graham Child Development Institute

Sharon Walsh
Walsh-Taylor Associates

Additional Contributors

Virginia Buysse
Frank Porter Graham Child Development Institute

Kathleen Hebbeler
SRI International

Diane Bricker
University of Oregon

Robin McWilliam
Vanderbilt University

Pam Winton
Frank Porter Graham Child Development Institute

C

LINK
Consumer Social
Validity Survey Form

Survey of Professional Reports on Early Childhood Assessment Measures

Part 1

Tool name

How often do you use the assessment? The term "use" indicates that you administered, scored, and interpreted results from the assessment for at least one child.

☐ At least once per week

☐ 6–12 times per year

☐ 2–5 times per year

☐ Once per year

For which children do you use the assessment? Check ALL that apply.

☐ Children who are typically developing

☐ Children who are at risk

☐ Children with disabilities

For what purpose(s) do you use the assessment? Check ALL that apply.

☐ Screening

☐ If checked—do you find it useful/appropriate/meaningful for screening?

☐ Determining eligibility for special education

☐ If checked—do you find it useful/appropriate/meaningful for eligibility?

☐ Writing or updating IFSPs/IEPs

☐ If checked—do you find it useful/appropriate/meaningful for writing or updating IFSPs/IEPs?

☐ Planning intervention/activities

☐ If checked—do you find it useful/appropriate/meaningful for planning intervention/activities?

☐ Monitoring children's progress

☐ If checked—do you find it useful/appropriate/meaningful for monitoring children's progress?

☐ Program evaluation

☐ If checked—do you find it useful/appropriate/meaningful for program evaluation?

☐ State accountability reporting (e.g., children's performance toward state standards)

☐ If checked—do you find it useful/appropriate/meaningful for state accountability?

☐ Federal accountability requirements (e.g., OSEP child outcome, Head Start Outcomes Framework)

☐ If checked—do you find it useful/appropriate/meaningful for federal accountability?

How did you learn to use the assessment? Check the PRIMARY way. Check only one.

☐ Informally, from a colleague (watching, talking to others)

☐ In my undergraduate or graduate studies

☐ Through a workshop

☐ Self-taught (read the manual)

What is your PRIMARY reason for using the assessment? Check ONLY your top reason.

☐ Allows observations of children during daily activities such as play

☐ Already in place

☐ Applicable for my children

☐ Broad scope and sequence

☐ Clear and easy to use

☐ I am comfortable with the instrument

☐ Covers a wide age range

☐ Includes the family or other professionals

☐ Is valid and reliable

☐ Matches my curriculum

☐ Promotes teaming and collaboration

☐ Provides useful information

☐ Required

☐ Saves me time

Part 2

Acceptability: Social validity; social worth or appropriateness of the scale's item content as perceived by parents and other caregivers

Do the assessment items describe skills that society values and considers important for young children's development?

☐   0) No; most items focus on competencies not considered worthwhile

☐   1) Falls between Statements 0 and 2 in meeting the standard

☐   2) Somewhat; there is a mix of items, some judged worthwhile, some not

☐   3) Falls between Statements 2 and 4 in meeting the standard

☐   4) Yes; most items identify competencies judged as worthwhile, appropriate, and important for young children's development

Do parents and other caregivers notice and agree there is a match between the child's current functioning or progress and the strengths and limitations (i.e., results) yielded by the assessment measure?

☐   0) No; assessment results are not readily detectable and/or may not match parents' and others' judgments and perceptions

☐   1) Falls between Statements 0 and 2 in meeting the standard

☐   2) To some extent; most assessment results are readily noticeable but parents and others may not agree with the results

☐   3) Falls between Statements 2 and 4 in meeting the standard

☐   4) Yes; the results of the assessment are readily noticeable by parents and other caregivers and match their judgments and perceptions

Are the assessment methods and procedures judged as appropriate and acceptable (i.e., support family/cultural preferences or practices) by parents and other important caregivers?

☐   0) No; parents and other important caregivers find the assessment methods and procedures inappropriate and unacceptable for their children

☐   1) Falls between Statements 0 and 2 in meeting the standard

☐   2) Somewhat; the methods and procedures are acceptable to many parents and caregivers, but some procedures may violate family preferences or cultural values

☐   3) Falls between Statements 2 and 4 in meeting the standard

☐   4) Yes; most parents and caregivers judge the methods and procedures as appropriate and acceptable for their child and family

Part 3

Authenticity: Extent to which the assessment content and methods sample naturally occurring behaviors in everyday situations

How functional or important are the competencies described in the assessment items for participation in everyday activities?

- ☐ 0) Neither functional nor important; item content is primarily composed of discrete behaviors that children normally would not need to demonstrate during daily routines and activities
- ☐ 1) Falls between Statements 0 and 2 in meeting the standard
- ☐ 2) Some function or importance; item content is a mix of nonfunctional discrete behaviors and more functional behaviors necessary for children's active participation during daily routines and activities
- ☐ 3) Falls between Statements 2 and 4 in meeting the standard
- ☐ 4) Functional and important; most item content is necessary for children's active participation in daily routines and activities

Who conducts the assessment and what procedures (how) do they use to collect the information?

- ☐ 0) Unfamiliar people administer a test to the child through contrived procedures
- ☐ 1) Falls between Statements 0 and 2 in meeting the standard
- ☐ 2) Either familiar or unfamiliar people use a combination of direct testing through contrived procedures and observational assessment of the child's actual behavior in natural environments
- ☐ 3) Falls between Statements 2 and 4 in meeting the standard
- ☐ 4) Familiar people conduct the assessment primarily through observation in natural environments

Where is assessment information gathered?

- ☐ 0) Mostly in contrived testing arrangements
- ☐ 1) Falls between Statements 0 and 2 in meeting the standard
- ☐ 2) Through a combination of contrived testing and observations in natural environments
- ☐ 3) Falls between Statements 2 and 4 in meeting the standard
- ☐ 4) Almost all information is gathered through observations of daily interactions within familiar classroom, home, and community routines

Part 4

Collaboration: Parent–professional and interdisciplinary teamwork

To what extent do assessment materials and procedures enable parents and professionals to work together as partners?

☐   0) Not much; the testing materials and procedures emphasize separate testing situations by one or more professionals with perfunctory parent participation

☐   1) Falls between Statements 0 and 2 in meeting the standard

☐   2) Somewhat; the assessment materials and procedures support different forms of teamwork including some parent participation

☐   3) Falls between Statements 2 and 4 in meeting the standard

☐   4) Quite a bit; the assessment materials and procedures are designed to foster collaboration by parents and professionals

Are assessment materials family friendly?

☐   0) No; the materials are filled with jargon and not developed for use by parents or family members

☐   1) Falls between Statements 0 and 2 in meeting the standard

☐   2) Somewhat; the assessment materials have been developed mostly for professional use but with supplemental materials for use by parents

☐   3) Falls between Statements 2 and 4 in meeting the standard

☐   4) Yes; the materials were designed specifically for use by parents as jargon free, easy to use, economical, and acceptable to parents

Part 5

Evidence: Has a clear evidence-base for use in early childhood intervention; materials designed, developed, and field-validated for young children, particularly those with special need

Note: To answer questions related to the evidence standard, reviewers may want to consult the manuals and/or web site for the assessment measure.

Does the assessment measure and procedures conform to recommended professional practices in early childhood?

☐   0) No; the measure and procedures are at odds with recommended professional practices

☐   1) Falls between Statements 0 and 2 in meeting the standard

☐   2) Somewhat; some content and procedures adhere to recommended professional practices, but some procedures violate best practice standards, especially for children with special needs

☐   3) Falls between Statements 2 and 4 in meeting the standard

☐   4) Yes; the assessment measure and procedure represents best professional practice because designed and developed specifically for young children, including those with special needs

Has the assessment measure been validated to accomplish specific purposes in early childhood such as screening, eligibility determination, program planning, progress monitoring, program evaluation, and/or accountability?

☐   0) No; no studies support the use of the measure to accomplish any purpose

☐   1) Falls between Statements 0 and 2 in meeting the standard

☐   2) To some extent; limited studies are available to support the use for specific purposes

☐   3) Falls between Statements 2 and 4 in meeting the standard

☐   4) Yes; the measure was designed, developed, and field-validated for specific purposes

Is there research evidence that the assessment measure included young children with delays and disabilities in either the norms or the field-validation during the measure's developmental phase?

☐   0) No evidence exists

☐   1) Falls between Statements 0 and 2 in meeting the standard

☐   2) Limited and questionable evidence is reported usually by after-the-fact studies

☐   3) Falls between Statements 2 and 4 in meeting the standard

☐   4) Yes; there is rigorous and persuasive evidence that the measure included children with special needs in either the norming or the field-validation studies

Part 6

Multifactors: Collection of data across multiple methods, sources, settings, and occasions

Does the assessment measure enable the collection of information from several settings?

- ☐ 0) No; only in a single setting
- ☐ 1) Falls between Statements 0 and 2 in meeting the standard
- ☐ 2) Somewhat; in at least two situations
- ☐ 3) Falls between Statements 2 and 4 in meeting the standard
- ☐ 4) Yes; the assessment measure converges information across multiple situations

Does the assessment measure enable the collection of information by several people?

- ☐ 0) No; only a single person, most often an unfamiliar professional
- ☐ 1) Falls between Statements 0 and 2 in meeting the standard
- ☐ 2) Somewhat; more than one person but not a parent or familiar caregiver
- ☐ 3) Falls between Statements 2 and 4 in meeting the standard
- ☐ 4) Yes; multiple people including professional team members and parents or other caregivers who are familiar to the child conduct the assessment

Do assessment procedures include multiple methods (e.g., interview, rating scales, checklists, direct probes, permanent products)?

- ☐ 0) No; uses only one method, mostly direct testing
- ☐ 1) Falls between Statements 0 and 2 in meeting the standard
- ☐ 2) Somewhat; uses at least two methods, one of which is authentic
- ☐ 3) Falls between Statements 2 and 4 in meeting the standard
- ☐ 4) Yes; uses several methods that are each authentic

Can the assessment measure be used over several time-points for progress monitoring?

- ☐ 0) No; it is designed for single session testing or observation
- ☐ 1) Falls between Statements 0 and 2 in meeting the standard
- ☐ 2) Yes; it can be used at two time-points (e.g., beginning and end of year), but not often enough for detailed progress monitoring
- ☐ 3) Falls between Statements 2 and 4 in meeting the standard
- ☐ 4) Definitely; the measure is designed for repeated assessments for detailed progress monitoring

Part 7

Sensitivity: Sequential arrangement and density of items in the skill hierarchy and the graduated scoring of children's performance on those items

How is assessment content organized?

- ☐ 0) Very little assessment content is organized in developmental sequences and/or in known instructional steps
- ☐ 1) Falls between Statements 0 and 2 in meeting the standard
- ☐ 2) Some of the assessment content is organized in developmental sequences and/or in known instructional steps
- ☐ 3) Falls between Statements 2 and 4 in meeting the standard
- ☐ 4) Most assessment content is organized in developmental sequences and/or known instructional steps

Are there enough items at low functional levels to detect change/progress?

- ☐ 0) No; contains few items at low functional levels and is not sensitive enough to detect small increments of change
- ☐ 1) Falls between Statements 0 and 2 in meeting the standard
- ☐ 2) Somewhat; contains some items at low functional levels but gaps between items make detecting small increments of change difficult
- ☐ 3) Falls between Statements 2 and 4 in meeting the standard
- ☐ 4) Yes; contains a sufficient number of items at low functional levels and enough items to detect the smallest increments of change

What type of scoring is used?

- ☐ 0) Dichotomous scoring such as "Yes the child performs the skill" or "No the child does not perform the skill"
- ☐ 1) Falls between Statements 0 and 2 in meeting the standard
- ☐ 2) Multipoint scoring but scores provide little information regarding the extent or conditions under which the child's competence can be demonstrated
- ☐ 3) Falls between Statements 2 and 4 in meeting the standard
- ☐ 4) Multipoint scoring and information regarding the extent and conditions under which the child's competence can be demonstrated

Part 8

Universality: Design and/or accommodations, which enable all children to demonstrate their underlying and often-unrealized functional capabilities (i.e., identifies both strengths and limitations)

Can all children demonstrate their capabilities on the assessment measure?

- ☐ 0) No; only children who are typically functioning can demonstrate their capabilities
- ☐ 1) Falls between Statements 0 and 2 in meeting the standard
- ☐ 2) Somewhat; many children can demonstrate their capabilities but some procedures in the measure hinder the child's response
- ☐ 3) Falls between Statements 2 and 4 in meeting the standard
- ☐ 4) Yes; all children can demonstrate their capabilities on this measure; procedures do not penalize children with special needs

Do assessment items reflect what (function) children can do rather than how (form) they do it?

- ☐ 0) No; most items emphasize form versus function
- ☐ 1) Falls between Statements 0 and 2 in meeting the standard
- ☐ 2) Some assessment items emphasize the form of the response rather than its function
- ☐ 3) Falls between Statements 2 and 4 in meeting the standard
- ☐ 4) Yes; most assessment items emphasize what children can do rather than how they do it

Does the assessment measure allow the use of alternate and multisensory materials?

- ☐ 0) No; does not allow the use of alternate or multisensory materials to facilitate the child's responsiveness
- ☐ 1) Falls between Statements 0 and 2 in meeting the standard
- ☐ 2) Somewhat; allows the use of alternate or multisensory materials for only some items
- ☐ 3) Falls between Statements 2 and 4 in meeting the standard
- ☐ 4) Yes: the assessment procedures allow the flexible use of alternate/multisensory materials to facilitate the child's responsiveness

Do assessment procedures offer multiple ways for the child to show their competencies?

- ☐ 0) No; the test allows only a prescribed mode of response for all children despite their limitations
- ☐ 1) Falls between Statements 0 and 2 in meeting the standard
- ☐ 2) Somewhat: some modifications are allowed so that the child can demonstrate skills despite their functional limitations

☐ 3) Falls between Statements 2 and 4 in meeting the standard

☐ 4) Yes; the measure allows children to express their competencies any way that they can

Part 9

Utility: Treatment validity; usefulness of the scale and its assessment to accomplish specific early intervention purposes, especially planning and evaluating interventions

Can assessment items link to goals/objectives for teaching or therapy?

☐ 0) No; the items are not teachable nor translatable as objectives

☐ 1) Falls between Statements 0 and 2 in meeting the standard

☐ 2) Some items could be translated into objectives

☐ 3) Falls between Statements 2 and 4 in meeting the standard

☐ 4) Yes; all assessment items are clearly teachable as individual goals and objectives

Do assessment results provide information on what to teach?

☐ 0) No; assessment results do not provide information on what the child needs to learn and/or where to begin instruction

☐ 1) Falls between Statements 0 and 2 in meeting the standard

☐ 2) Somewhat; assessment results provide some information on what the child needs to learn and/or some information as to where to begin instruction

☐ 3) Falls between Statements 2 and 4 in meeting the standard

☐ 4) Yes; assessment results provide clear information on what the child needs to learn and where to begin instruction

Does the assessment measure provide information on how to teach?

☐ 0) No; the measure does not guide or inform how to teach or enhance young children's growth and development

☐ 1) Falls between Statements 0 and 2 in meeting the standard

☐ 2) Somewhat; the measure provides some guidance on how to teach or instructional strategies that facilitate young children's growth and development

☐ 3) Falls between Statements 2 and 4 in meeting the standard

☐ 4) Yes; the measure provides specific guidance on how to teach and promote the child's development and learning

Does the assessment measure detect progress during and after instruction or therapy?

☐   0) No; children's progress is not detected during or after instruction

☐   1) Falls between Statements 0 and 2 in meeting the standard

☐   2) Somewhat; the measure only records gross evidence of progress after instruction or therapy

☐   3) Falls between Statements 2 and 4 in meeting the standard

☐   4) Yes; the measure detects specific evidence of progress both during and as the result of instruction and therapy

D

Where We Stand on Curriculum, Assessment, and Program Evaluation
NAEYC and NAECS/SDE

where we STAND
naeyc and naecs/sde

on curriculum, assessment, and program evaluation

What should children be taught in the years from birth through age eight? How would we know if they are developing well and learning what we want them to learn? And how could we decide whether programs for children from infancy through the primary grades are doing a good job?

Answers to these questions—questions about *early childhood curriculum, child assessment, and program evaluation*—are the foundation of a joint position statement from the National Association for the Education of Young Children (NAEYC) and the National Association of Early Childhood Specialists in State Departments of Education (NAECS/SDE).

The position statement's recommendations

Curriculum

Implement curriculum that is thoughtfully planned, challenging, engaging, developmentally appropriate, culturally and linguistically responsive, comprehensive, and likely to promote positive outcomes for all young children.

Indicators of effective curriculum

• Children are active and engaged.

• Goals are clear and shared by all.

• Curriculum is evidence-based.

• Valued content is learned through investigation and focused, intentional teaching.

• Curriculum builds on prior learning and experiences.

• Curriculum is comprehensive.

• Professional standards validate the curriculum's subject-matter content.

• The curriculum is likely to benefit children.

Assessment

Make ethical, appropriate, valid and reliable assessment a central part of all early childhood programs. To assess young children's strengths, progress, and needs, use assessment methods that are developmentally

---

Beyond Curriculum, Assessment, and Program Evaluation: What Else Matters?

Without other essential components of high-quality early childhood education, these recommendations will be of limited value. Learn more about

• early learning standards, as described in NAEYC and NAECS/SDE's 2002 position statement, online at www.naeyc.org/resources/position_statements/positions_intro.asp.

• teaching strategies and other elements of developmentally appropriate practice. See S. Bredekamp & C. Copple, eds., *Developmentally Appropriate Practice in Early Childhood Programs*, rev. ed., Washington, DC: NAEYC, 1997. Position statement online at www.naeyc.org/resources/position_statements/psdap98.pdf.

• standards for early childhood programs and accreditation performance criteria, online at www.naeyc.org/accreditation/nextera.asp.

• standards for professional preparation of early childhood educators. See M. Hyson, ed., *Early Childhood Professional Preparation: NAEYC's Standards for Programs*, Washington, DC: NAEYC, 2003. Document also online at www.naeyc.org/profdev/prep_review/preprev_2001.asp.

National Association for the Education of Young Children and National Association of Early Childhood Specialists in State Departments of Education

appropriate, culturally and linguistically responsive, tied to children's daily activities, supported by professional development, inclusive of families, and connected to specific, beneficial purposes: (1) making sound decisions about teaching and learning, (2) identifying significant concerns that may require focused intervention for individual children, and (3) helping programs improve their educational and developmental interventions.

Indicators of effective assessment practices

- Ethical principles guide assessment practices.
- Assessment instruments are used for their intended purposes.
- Assessments are appropriate for ages and other characteristics of children being assessed.
- Assessment instruments are in compliance with professional criteria for quality.
- What is assessed is developmentally and educationally significant.
- Assessment evidence is used to understand and improve learning.
- Assessment evidence is gathered from realistic settings and situations that reflect children's actual performance.
- Assessments use multiple sources of evidence gathered over time.
- Screening is always linked to follow-up.
- Use of individually administered, norm-referenced tests is limited.
- Staff and families are knowledgeable about assessment.

Program evaluation and accountability

Regularly evaluate early childhood programs in light of program goals, using varied, appropriate, conceptually and technically sound evidence to determine the extent to which programs meet the expected standards of quality and to examine intended as well as unintended results.

Indicators of effective program evaluation and accountability

- Evaluation is used for continuous improvement.
- Goals become guides for evaluation.
- Comprehensive goals are used.
- Evaluations use valid designs.
- Multiple sources of data are available.
- Sampling is used when assessing individual children as part of large-scale program evaluation.

- Safeguards are in place if standardized tests are used as part of evaluations.
- Children's gains over time are emphasized.
- Well-trained individuals conduct evaluations.
- Evaluation results are publicly shared.

Creating change through support for programs

Implementing the preceding recommendations for curriculum, child assessment, and program evaluation requires a solid foundation. Calls for better results and greater accountability from programs for children in preschool, kindergarten, and the primary grades have not been backed up by essential supports for teacher recruitment and compensation, professional preparation and ongoing professional development, and other ingredients of quality early education.

The overarching need is to create an *integrated, well-financed system of early care and education* that has the capacity to support learning and development in all children, including children living in poverty, children whose home language is not English, and children with disabilities. Unlike many other countries, the United States continues to have a fragmented system for educating children from birth through age eight, under multiple auspices, with greatly varying levels of support, and with inadequate communication and collaboration.

Many challenges face efforts to provide all young children with high-quality curriculum, assessment, and evaluation of their programs. *Public commitment,* along with *investments* in a well-financed system of early childhood education and in other components of services for young children and their families, will make it possible to implement these recommendations fully and effectively.

The full NAEYC and NAECS/SDE 2003 position statement "Early Childhood Curriculum, Assessment, and Program Evaluation—Building an Effective, Accountable System in Programs for Children Birth Through Age 8" is available online at **www.naeyc.org/resources/position_statements/pscape.pdf.**

Author Index

Subject Index

Page numbers followed by *f* indicate figures; those followed by *t* indicate tables.